ISEE: Full Study Guide and Test Strategies for the Independent School Entrance Exam

To obtain permission(s) to use the material from this work for any purpose including workshops or seminars, please submit a written request to

Smart Edition Media
36 Gorham Street
Suite 1
Cambridge, MA 02138
800-496-5994

Email: info@smarteditionmedia.com

Library of Congress Cataloging-in-Publication Data
Smart Edition Media.
ISEE: Full Study Guide and Test Strategies for the Independent School Entrance Exam
ISBN: Print: 978-1-949147-31-5, 1st edition

1. ISEE Exam
2. Study Guides
3. Independent School Entrance Exam
4. High School Entrance Exam
5. Educational Assessment

Disclaimer:

The opinions expressed in this publication are the sole works of Smart Edition Media and were created independently from any National Evaluation Systems or other testing affiliates. Between the time of publication and printing, specific standards as well as testing formats and website information may change that are not included in part or in whole within this product. Smart Edition Media develops sample test questions, and they reflect similar content as on real tests; however, they are not former tests. Smart Edition Media assembles content that aligns with exam standards but makes no claims nor guarantees candidates a passing score.

Printed in the United States of America

ISEE: Full Study Guide and Test Strategies for the Independent School Entrance Exam/Smart Edition Media.

ISBN: Print: 978-1-949147-31-5
        Ebook: 978-1-949147-37-7

Print and digital composition by Book Genesis, Inc.

ISEE PRACTICE ONLINE

Smart Edition Media's Online Learning Resources allow you the flexibility to study for your exam on your own schedule and are the perfect companion to help you reach your goals! You can access online content with an Internet connection from any computer, laptop, or mobile device.

Online Learning Resources

Designed to enable you to master the content in quick bursts of focused learning, these tools cover a complete range of subjects, including:

- English Language Arts
- Reading
- Math
- Science
- Writing

Our online resources are filled with test-taking tips and strategies, important facts, and practice problems that mirror questions on the exam.

Online Sample Tests & Flashcards

Access additional full-length practice tests online!

Use these tests as a diagnostic tool to determine areas of strength and weakness before embarking on your study program or to assess mastery of skills once you have completed your studies.

FLASHCARDS **GAMES** **QUIZZES** **TESTS**

Go to the URL: **https://smarteditionmedia.com/pages/ISEE-online-resources** and follow the password/login instructions.

TABLE OF CONTENTS

INTRODUCTION

AN OVERVIEW OF THE ISEE EXAM

The Independent School Entrance Examination (ISEE) is an exam that is used to help determine a student's admission qualifications for independent schools. The makers of this test, the Educational Records Bureau (ERB), have created four exam levels: Primary, Lower, Middle, and Upper. Each one is designed to assess students' qualifications at different grade levels.

This study guide focuses on the Upper Level Exam, which is taken by 8th graders to determine their readiness to successfully transition to high school.

The ISEE is administered at schools and testing centers within the United States. The test is offered during three testing seasons annually: Fall (August–November); Winter (December–March); and Spring/Summer (April–July). Students may take the test only once per season, or up to a maximum of 3 times in a 12-month admission cycle. See the ERB website or your local testing center or school for further details about scheduling your test.

ABOUT THIS BOOK

This book provides you with an accurate and complete representation of the ISEE test and includes instructional content on the fivee core subjects of the exam: Verbal Reasoning, Quantitative Reasoning, Reading Comprehension, Mathematics Achievement, and an Essay.

The reviews in this book are designed to provide the information and strategies you need to do well on the exam.

The full-length practice test in the book is based on the ISEE and contains questions similar to those you can expect to encounter on the official test.

A detailed answer key follows each practice quiz and test. These answer keys provide explanations designed to help you completely understand the test material. Each explanation references the book chapter to allow you to go back to that section for additional review, if necessary.

How to Use This Book

Studies show that most people begin preparing for exams approximately 8 weeks before their test date. If you are scheduled to take your test in sooner than 8 weeks, do not despair! Smart Edition Media has designed this study guide to be flexible to allow you to concentrate on areas where you need the most support.

Whether you have 8 weeks to study – or much less than that – we urge you to take one of the online practice tests to determine areas of strength and weakness, if you have not done so already. These tests can be found in your online resources.

Once you have completed a practice test, use this information to help you create a study plan that suits your individual study habits and time frame. If you are short on time, look at your diagnostic test results to determine which subject matter could use the most attention and focus the majority of your efforts on those areas. While this study guide is organized to follow the order of the actual test, you are not required to complete the book from beginning to end, in that exact order.

How This Book Is Organized

Take a look at the Table of Contents. Notice that each **Section** in the study guide corresponds to a subtest of the exam. These sections are broken into **Chapters** that identify the major content categories of the exam.

Each chapter is further divided into individual **Lessons** that address the specific content and objectives required to pass the exam. Some lessons contain embedded example questions to assess your comprehension of the content "in the moment." All lessons contain a bulleted list called "**Let's Review.**" Use this list to refresh your memory before taking a practice quiz, test, or the actual exam. A **Practice Quiz**, designed to check your progress as you move through the content, follows each chapter.

Whether you plan on working through the study guide from cover to cover, or selecting specific sections to review, each chapter of this book can be completed in one sitting. If you must end your study session before finishing a chapter, try to complete your current lesson in order to maximize comprehension and retention of the material.

Online Sample Tests

The purchase of this book grants you access to two additional full-length practice tests online. You can locate these exams on the Smart Edition Media website.

STUDY STRATEGIES AND TIPS

MAKE STUDY SESSIONS A PRIORITY.

- Use a calendar to schedule your study sessions. Set aside a dedicated amount of time each day/week for studying. While it may seem difficult to manage, given your other responsibilities, remember that in order to reach your goals, it is crucial to dedicate the time now to prepare for this test. A satisfactory score on your exam is the key to unlocking a multitude of opportunities for your future success.
- Do you work? Have children? Other obligations? Be sure to take these into account when creating your schedule. Work around them to ensure that your scheduled study sessions can be free of distractions.

TIPS FOR FINDING TIME TO STUDY.
- Wake up 1-2 hours before your family for some quiet time
- Study 1-2 hours before bedtime and after everything has quieted down
- Utilize weekends for longer study periods
- Hire a babysitter to watch children

TAKE PRACTICE TESTS

- Smart Edition Media offers practice tests, both online and in print. Take as many as you can to help be prepared. This will eliminate any surprises you may encounter during the exam.

KNOW YOUR LEARNING STYLE

- Identify your strengths and weaknesses as a student. All students are different and everyone has a different learning style. Do not compare yourself to others.
- Howard Gardner, a developmental psychologist at Harvard University, has studied the ways in which people learn new information. He has identified seven distinct intelligences. According to his theory:

  "we are all able to know the world through language, logical-mathematical analysis, spatial representation, musical thinking, the use of the body to solve problems or to make things, an understanding of other individuals, and an understanding of ourselves. Where individuals differ is in the strength of these intelligences - the so-called profile of intelligences -and in the ways in which such intelligences are invoked and combined to carry out different tasks, solve diverse problems, and progress in various domains."

- Knowing your learning style can help you to tailor your studying efforts to suit your natural strengths.
- What ways help you learn best? Videos? Reading textbooks? Find the best way for you to study and learn/review the material.

WHAT IS YOUR LEARNING STYLE?

- **Visual-Spatial** – Do you like to draw, do jigsaw puzzles, read maps, daydream? Creating drawings, graphic organizers, or watching videos might be useful for you.
- **Bodily-kinesthetic** – Do you like movement, making things, physical activity? Do you communicate well through body language, or like to be taught through physical activity? Hands-on learning, acting out, role playing are tools you might try.
- **Musical** – Do you show sensitivity to rhythm and sound? If you love music, and are also sensitive to sounds in your environments, it might be beneficial to study with music in the background. You can turn lessons into lyricsor speak rhythmically to aid in content retention.
- **Interpersonal** – Do you have many friends, empathy for others, street smarts, and interact well with others? You might learn best in a group setting. Form a study group with other students who are preparing for the same exam. Technology makes it easy to connect, if you are unable to meet in person, teleconferencing or video chats are useful tools to aid interpersonal learners in connecting with others.
- **Intrapersonal** – Do you prefer to work alone rather than in a group? Are you in tune with your inner feelings, follow your intuition and possess a strong will, confidence and opinions? Independent study and introspection will be ideal for you. Reading books, using creative materials, keeping a diary of your progress will be helpful. Intrapersonal learners are the most independent of the learners.
- **Linguistic** – Do you use words effectively, have highly developed auditory skills and often think in words? Do you like reading, playing word games, making up poetry or stories? Learning tools such as computers, games, multimedia will be beneficial to your studies.
- **Logical-Mathematical** – Do you think conceptually, abstractly, and are able to see and explore patterns and relationships? Try exploring subject matter through logic games, experiments and puzzles.

CREATE THE OPTIMAL STUDY ENVIRONMENT

- Some people enjoy listening to soft background music when they study. (Instrumental music is a good choice.) Others need to have a silent space in order to concentrate. Which do you prefer? Either way, it is best to create an environment that is free of distractions for your study sessions.
- Have study guide – Will travel! Leave your house: Daily routines and chores can be distractions. Check out your local library, a coffee shop, or other quiet space to remove yourself from distractions and daunting household tasks will compete for your attention.
- Create a Technology Free Zone. Silence the ringer on your cell phone and place it out of reach to prevent surfing the Web, social media interactions, and email/texting exchanges. Turn off the television, radio, or other devices while you study.
- Are you comfy? Find a comfortable, but not *too* comfortable, place to study. Sit at a desk or table in a straight, upright chair. Avoid sitting on the couch, a bed, or in front of the TV. Wear clothing that is not binding and restricting.
- Keep your area organized. Have all the materials you need available and ready: Smart Edition study guide, computer, notebook, pen, calculator, and pencil/eraser. Use a desk lamp or overhead light that provides ample lighting to prevent eye-strain and fatigue.

HEALTHY BODY, HEALTHY MIND

- Consider these words of wisdom from Buddha, "To keep the body in good health is a duty – otherwise we shall not be able to keep our mind strong and clear."

> **KEYS TO CREATING A HEALTHY BODY AND MIND:**
> - Drink water – Stay hydrated! Limit drinks with excessive sugar or caffeine.
> - Eat natural foods – Make smart food choices and avoid greasy, fatty, sugary foods.
> - Think positively – You can do this! Do not doubt yourself, and trust in the process.
> - Exercise daily – If you have a workout routine, stick to it! If you are more sedentary, now is a great time to begin! Try yoga or a low-impact sport. Simply walking at a brisk pace will help to get your heart rate going.
> - Sleep well – Getting a good night's sleep is important, but too few of us actually make it a priority. Aim to get eight hours of uninterrupted sleep in order to maximize your mental focus, memory, learning, and physical wellbeing.

FINAL THOUGHTS

- Remember to relax and take breaks during study sessions.
- Review the testing material. Go over topics you already know for a refresher.
- Focus more time on less familiar subjects.

EXAM PREPARATION

In addition to studying for your upcoming exam, it is important to keep in mind that you need to prepare your mind and body as well. When preparing to take an exam as a whole, not just studying, taking practice exams, and reviewing math rules, it is critical to prepare your body in order to be mentally and physically ready. Often, your success rate will be much higher when you are *fully* ready.

Here are some tips to keep in mind when preparing for your exam:

SEVERAL WEEKS/DAYS BEFORE THE EXAM

- Get a full night of sleep, approximately 8 hours
- Turn off electronics before bed
- Exercise regularly
- Eat a healthy balanced diet, include fruits and vegetable
- Drink water

THE NIGHT BEFORE

- Eat a good dinner
- Pack materials/bag, healthy snacks, and water

- Gather materials needed for test: your ID and receipt of test. You do not want to be scrambling the morning of the exam. If you are unsure of what to bring with you, check with your testing center or test administrator.
- Map the location of test center, identify how you will be getting there (driving, public transportation, uber, etc.), when you need to leave, and parking options.
- Lay your clothes out. Wear comfortable clothes and shoes, do not wear items that are too hot/cold
- Allow minimum of ~8 hours of sleep
- Avoid coffee and alcohol
- Do not take any medications or drugs to help you sleep
- Set alarm

THE DAY OF THE EXAM

- Wake up early, allow ample time to do all the things you need to do and for travel
- Eat a healthy, well-rounded breakfast
- Drink water
- Leave early and arrive early, leave time for any traffic or any other unforeseeable circumstances
- Arrive early and check in for exam. This will give you enough time to relax, take off coat, and become comfortable with your surroundings.

Take a deep breath, get ready, go! You got this!

SECTION I. READING

CHAPTER 1 KEY IDEAS AND DETAILS

MAIN IDEAS, TOPIC SENTENCES, AND SUPPORTING DETAILS

To read effectively, you need to know how to identify the most important information in a text. You must also understand how ideas within a text relate to one other.

Main Ideas

The central or most important idea in a text is the **main idea**. As a reader, you need to avoid confusing the main idea with less important details that may be interesting but not central to the author's point.

The **topic** of a text is slightly different than the main idea. The topic is a word or phrase that describes roughly what a text is about. A main idea, in contrast, is a complete sentence that states the topic and explains what an author wants to say about it.

All types of texts can contain main ideas. Read the following informational paragraph and try to identify the main idea:

> The immune system is the body's defense mechanism. It fights off harmful bacteria, viruses, and substances that attack the body. To do this, it uses cells, tissues, and organs that work together to resist invasion.

The topic of this paragraph is the immune system. The main idea can be expressed in a sentence like this: "This paragraph defines and describes the immune system." Ideas about organisms and substances that invade the body are not the central focus. The topic and main idea must always be directly related to every sentence in the text, as the immune system is here.

Read the persuasive paragraph below and consider the topic and main idea:

> Football is not a healthy activity for kids. It causes head injuries that harm the ability to learn and achieve. It causes painful bodily injuries that can linger into adulthood. It teaches aggressive behavioral habits that make life harder for players after they have left the field.

The topic of this paragraph is youth football, and the main idea is that kids should not play the game. Note that if you are asked to state the main idea of a persuasive text, it is your job to be objective. This means you should describe the author's opinion, not make an argument of your own in response.

Both of the example paragraphs above state their main idea explicitly. Some texts have an implicit, or suggested, main idea. In this case, you need to figure out the main idea using the details as clues.

FOR EXAMPLE

The following fictional paragraph has an implicit main idea:

Daisy parked her car and sat gripping the wheel, not getting out. A few steps to the door. A couple of knocks. She could give him the news in two words. She'd already decided what she was going to do, so it didn't matter what he said, not really. Still, she couldn't make her feet carry her to the door.

The main idea here is that Daisy feels reluctant to speak to someone. This point is not stated outright, but it is clear from the details of Daisy's thoughts and actions.

Topic Sentences

Many paragraphs identify the topic and main idea in a single sentence. This is called a **topic sentence,** and it often appears at the beginning of a paragraph. However, a writer may choose to place a topic sentence anywhere in the text.

Some paragraphs contain an introductory sentence to grab the reader's attention before clearly stating the topic. A paragraph may begin by asking a rhetorical question, presenting a striking idea, or showing why the topic is important. When authors use this strategy, the topic sentence usually comes second:

> Have you ever wondered how your body fights off a nasty cold? **It uses a complex defense mechanism called the immune system.** The immune system fights off harmful bacteria, viruses, and substances that attack the body. To do this, it uses cells, tissues, and organs that work together to resist invasion.

Here, the first sentence grabs the attention, and the second, **boldfaced** topic sentence states the main idea. The remaining sentences provide further information, explaining what the immune system does and identifying its basic components.

COMPARE!

The informational paragraph above contains a question that grabs the attention at the beginning. The writer could convey the same information with a little less flair by omitting this device. The version you read in Section 1 does exactly this. (The topic sentence below is **boldfaced.**)

> **The immune system is the body's defense mechanism.** It fights off harmful bacteria, viruses, and substances that attack the body. To do this, it uses cells, tissues, and organs that work together to resist invasion.

Look back at the football paragraph from Section 1. Which sentence is the topic sentence?

Sometimes writers wait until the end of a paragraph to reveal the main idea in a topic sentence. When you're reading a paragraph that is organized this way, you may feel like you're reading a bit of a puzzle. It's not fully clear what the piece is about until you get to the end:

> It causes head injuries that harm the ability to learn and achieve. It causes painful bodily injuries that can linger through the passage of years. It teaches aggressive behavioral habits that make life harder for players after they have left the field. **Football is not a healthy activity for kids.**

Note that the topic—football—is not actually named until the final, **boldfaced** topic sentence. This is a strong hint that this final sentence is the topic sentence. Other paragraphs with this structure may contain several examples or related ideas and then tie them together with a summary statement near the end.

Supporting Details

The **supporting details** of a text develop the main idea, contribute further information, or provide examples.

All of the supporting details in a text must relate back to the main idea. In a text that sets out to define and describe the immune system, the supporting details could explain how the immune system works, define parts of the immune system, and so on.

> **Main Idea:** The immune system is the body's defense mechanism.
>
> **Supporting Detail:** It fights off harmful bacteria, viruses, and substances that attack the body.
>
> **Supporting Detail:** To do this, it uses cells, tissues, and organs that work together to resist invasion.

The above text could go on to describe white blood cells, which are a vital part of the body's defense system against disease. However, the supporting details in such a text should *not* drift off into descriptions of parts of the body that make no contribution to immune response.

Supporting details may be facts or opinions. A single text can combine both facts and opinions to develop a single main idea.

> **Main Idea:** Football is not a healthy activity for kids.
>
> **Supporting Detail:** It teaches aggressive behavioral habits that make life harder for players after they have left the field.
>
> **Supporting Detail:** In a study of teenage football players by Dr. Sophia Ortega at Harvard University, 28% reported involvement in fights or other violent incidents, compared with 19% of teenage boys who were not involved in sports.

The first supporting detail above states an opinion. The second is still related to the main idea, but it provides factual information to back up the opinion. Further development of this paragraph could contain other types of facts, including information about football injuries and anecdotes about real players who got hurt playing the game.

Let's Review!

- The main idea is the most important piece of information in a text.
- The main idea is often expressed in a topic sentence.
- Supporting details develop the main idea, contribute further information, or provide examples.

SUMMARIZING TEXT AND USING TEXT FEATURES

Effective readers need to know how to identify and restate the main idea of a text through summary. They must also follow complex instructions, figure out the sequence of events in a text that is not presented in order, and understand information presented in graphics.

Summary Basics

A **summary** is a text that restates the ideas from a different text in a new way. Every summary needs to include the main idea of the original. Some summaries may include information about the supporting details as well.

The content and level of detail in a summary vary depending on the purpose. For example, a journalist may summarize a recent scientific study in a newspaper profile of its authors. A graduate student might briefly summarize the same study in a paper questioning its conclusions. The journalist's version would likely use fairly simple language and restate only the main points. The student's version would likely use specialized scientific vocabulary and include certain supporting details, especially the ones most applicable to the argument the student intends to make later.

The language of a summary must be substantially different from the original. It should not retain the structure and word choice of the source text. Rather, it should provide a completely new way of stating the ideas.

Read the passage below and the short summary that follows:

Original: There is no need for government regulations to maintain a minimum wage because free market forces naturally adjust wages on their own. Workers are in short supply in our thriving economy, and businesses must offer fair wages and working conditions to attract labor. Business owners pay employees well because common sense dictates that they cannot succeed any other way.

Effective Summary: The author argues against minimum wage laws. He claims free market forces naturally keep wages high in a healthy economy with a limited labor supply.

KEY POINT!

Many ineffective summaries attempt to imitate the structure of the original text and change only individual words. This makes the writing process difficult, and it can lead to unintentional plagiarism.

Ineffective Summary (Plagiarism): It is unnecessary for government regulations to create a minimum wage because capitalism adjusts wages without help. Good labor is rare in our excellent economy, and businesses need to offer fair wages and working conditions in order to attract workers.

The above text is an example of structural plagiarism. Summary writing does not just involve rewriting the original words one by one. An effective summary restates the main ideas of the text in a wholly original way.

The effective summary above restates the main ideas in a new but objective way. Objectivity is a key quality of an effective summary. A summary does not exaggerate, judge, or distort the author's original ideas.

> **Not a Summary:** The author makes a wild and unsupportable claim that minimum wage laws are unnecessary because market forces keep wages high without government intervention.

Although the above text might be appropriate in persuasive writing, it makes its own claims and judgments rather than simply restating the original author's ideas. It would not be an effective sentence in a summary.

In some cases, particularly dealing with creative works like fiction and poetry, summaries may mention ideas that are clearly implied but not stated outright in the original text. For example, a mobster in a thriller novel might turn to another character and say menacingly, "I wouldn't want anything to happen to your sweet little kids." A summary of this passage could objectively say the mobster had threatened the other character. But everything in the summary needs to be clearly supportable in the text. The summary could not go on to say how the other character feels about the threat unless the author describes it.

Attending to Sequence and Instructions

Events happen in a sequence. However, many written texts present events out of order to create an effect on the reader. Nonfiction writers such as journalists and history writers may use this strategy to create surprise or bring particular ideas to the forefront. Fiction writers may interrupt the flow of a plot to interweave bits of a character's history or to provide flashes of insight into future events. Readers need to know how to untangle this presentation of events and figure out what actually happened first, second, and third. Consider the following passage:

> The man in dark glasses was looking for something. He checked his pockets. He checked his backpack. He walked back to his car, unlocked the doors, and inspected the area around the seats. Shaking his head, he re-locked the doors and rubbed his forehead in frustration. When his hand bumped his sunglasses, he finally realized where he had put them.

This passage does not mention putting the sunglasses on until the end, but it is clear from context that the man put them on first, before beginning his search. You can keep track of sequence by paying attention to time words like *when* and *before,* noticing grammatical constructions *he had* that indicate when events happened, and making common sense observations like the fact that the man is wearing his dark glasses in the first sentence.

Sequence is also an important aspect of reading technical and functional documents such as recipes and other instructions. If such documents present many steps in a large text block without illustrations or visual breaks, you may need to break them down and categorize them yourself. Always read all the steps first and think about how to follow them before jumping in.

To see why, read the pancake recipe below:

Combine flour, baking powder, sugar, and salt. Break the eggs into a separate bowl. Add milk and oil to the beaten eggs. Combine dry and liquid ingredients and stir. While you are doing the above, put a small amount of oil into a pan and heat it on medium heat. When it is hot, spoon batter onto the pan.

To follow directions like these effectively, a reader must break them down into categories, perhaps even rewriting them in a numbered list and noting when to start steps like heating the pan, which may be worth doing in a different order than it appears above.

Interpreting Graphics

Information is often presented in pictures, graphs, or diagrams. These **graphic elements** may provide information to back up an argument, illustrate factual information or instructions, or present key facts and statistics.

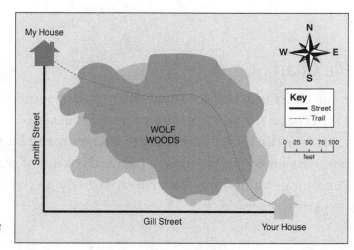

When you read charts and graphs, it is important to look carefully at all the information presented, including titles and labels, to be sure that you are interpreting the visuals correctly.

Diagram

A diagram presents a picture with labels that shows the parts of an object or functions of a mechanism. The diagram of a knee joint below shows the parts of the knee. Like many diagrams, it is placed in relation to a larger object—in this case, a leg—to clarify how the labeled parts fit into a larger context.

Flowchart

A flowchart shows a sequence of actions or decisions involved in a complex process. A flowchart usually begins with an oval-shaped box that asks a yes-no question or gives an instruction. Readers follow arrows indicating possible responses. This helps readers figure out how to solve a problem, or it illustrates how a complex system works.

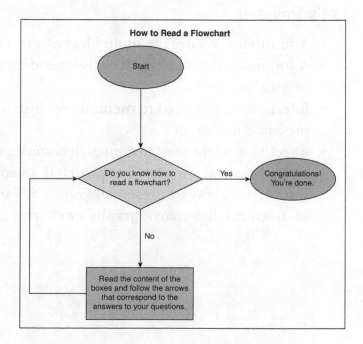

Bar Graph

A bar graph uses bars of different sizes to represent numbers. Larger bars show larger numbers to convey the magnitude of differences between two numeric values at a glance. In this case, each rectangle shows the number of candy bars of different types that a particular group of people ate.

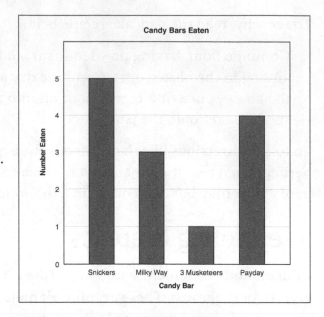

Pie Chart

A pie chart is useful for representing all of something— in this case, the whole group of people surveyed about their favorite kind of pie. Larger wedges mean larger percentages of people liked a particular kind of pie. Percentage values may be written directly on the chart or in a key to the side.

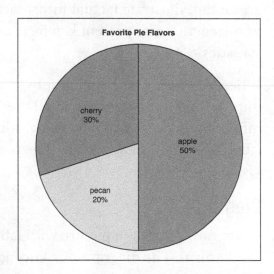

Let's Review!

- A summary restates the main ideas of a text in different words.
- A summary should objectively restate ideas in the present tense and give credit to the original author.
- Effective readers need to mentally reconstruct the basic sequence of events authors present out of order.
- Effective readers need to approach complex instructions by grouping steps into categories or considering how best to approach the steps.
- Information may be presented graphically in the form of diagrams, flowcharts, graphs, or charts.

UNDERSTANDING PRIMARY SOURCES, MAKING INFERENCES, AND DRAWING CONCLUSIONS

Effective readers must understand the difference between types of sources and choose credible sources of information to support research. Readers must also consider the content of their reading materials and draw their own conclusions.

Primary Sources

When we read and research information, we must differentiate between different types of sources. Sources are often classified depending on how close they are to the original creation or discovery of the information they present.

Primary sources include firsthand witness accounts of events, research described by the people who conducted it, and any other original information. Contemporary researchers can often access mixed media versions of primary sources such as video and audio recordings, photographs of original work, and so on. Note that original content is still considered primary even if it is reproduced online or in a book.

> **Examples:** Diaries, scientific journal articles, witness testimony, academic conference presentations, business memos, speeches, letters, interviews, and original literature and artwork.

Secondary sources respond to, analyze, summarize, or comment on primary sources. They add value to a discussion of the topic by giving readers new ways to think about the content. However, they may also introduce errors or layers of bias. Secondary sources may be very good sources of information, but readers must evaluate them carefully.

> **Examples:** Biographies, books and articles that summarize research for wider audiences, analyses of original literature and artwork, histories, political commentary.

Tertiary sources compile information in a general, highly summarized, and sometimes simplified way. Their purpose is not to add anything to the information, but rather to present the information in an accessible manner, often for audiences who are only beginning to familiarize themselves with a topic.

> **Examples:** Encyclopedias, guidebooks, literature study guides.

Source Materials in Action

Primary sources are often considered most trustworthy because they are closest to the original material and least likely to contain errors. However, readers must take a common sense approach to evaluating trustworthiness. For example, a single letter written by one biased witness of a historical event may not provide as much insight into what really happened as a secondary account by a historian who has considered the points of view of a dozen firsthand witnesses.

Tertiary sources are useful for readers attempting to gain a quick overview of understanding about a subject. They are also a good starting point for readers looking for keywords and subtopics to use for further research of a subject. However, they are not sufficiently detailed or credible to support an article, academic paper, or other document intended to add valuable analysis and commentary on a subject.

Evaluating Credibility

Not everything you read is equally trustworthy. Many sources contain mistakes, faulty reasoning, or deliberate misinformation designed to manipulate you. Effective readers seek out information from **credible**, or trustworthy, sources.

There is no single formula for determining credibility. Readers must make judgment calls based on individual texts and their purpose.

FOR EXAMPLE

Most sources should attempt to be objective. But if you're reading an article that makes an argument, you do not need to demand perfect objectivity from the source. The purpose of a persuasive article is to defend a point of view. As long as the author does this openly and defends the point of view with facts, logic, and other good argumentative techniques, you may trust the source.

Other sources may seem highly objective but not be credible. For example, some scientific studies meet all the criteria for credibility below except the one about trustworthy publishers. If a study is funded or conducted by a company that stands to profit from it, you should treat the results with skepticism no matter how good the information looks otherwise.

Sources and References

Credible texts are primary sources or secondary sources that refer to other trustworthy sources. If the author consults experts, they should be named, and their credentials should be explained. Authors should not attempt to hide where they got their information. Vague statements like "studies show" are not as trustworthy as statements that identify who completed a study.

Objectivity

Credible texts usually make an effort to be objective. They use clear, logical reasoning. They back arguments up with facts, expert opinions, or clear explanations. The assumptions behind the arguments do not contain obvious stereotypes.

Emotional arguments are acceptable in some argumentative writing, but they should not be manipulative. For example, photos of starving children may be acceptable for raising awareness of a famine, but they need to be respectful of both the victims and the audience—not just there for shock value.

Date of Publication

Information changes quickly in some fields, especially the sciences and technology. When researching a fast-changing topic, look for sources published in the last ten years.

Author Information

If an author and/or a respected organization take public credit for information, it is more likely to be reliable. Information published anonymously on the Internet may be suspicious because nobody is clearly responsible for mistakes. Authors with strong credentials such as university professors in a given field are more trustworthy than authors with no clear resume.

Publisher Information

Information published by the government, a university, a major national news organization, or another respected organization is often more credible. On the Internet, addresses ending in .edu or .gov may be more trustworthy than .com addresses. Publishers who stand to profit or otherwise benefit from the content of a text are always questionable.

BE CAREFUL!

Strong credentials only make a source more trustworthy if the credentials are related to the topic. A Columbia University Professor of Archeology is a credible source on ancient history. But if she writes a parenting article, it's not necessarily more credible than a parenting article by someone without a flashy university title.

Professionalism

Credible sources usually look professional and present information free of grammatical errors or major factual errors.

Making Inferences and Drawing Conclusions

In reading—and in life—people regularly make educated guesses based on limited information. When we use the information we have to figure out something nobody has told us directly, we are making an **inference**. People make inferences every day.

> **Example:** You hear a loud thump. Then a pained voice says, "Honey, can you bring the first aid kit?"

From the information above, it is reasonable to infer that the speaker is hurt. The thumping noise, the pain in the speaker's voice, and the request for a first aid kit all suggest this conclusion.

When you make inferences from reading, you use clues presented in the text to help you draw logical conclusions about what the author means. Before you can make an inference, you must read the text carefully and understand the explicit, or overt, meaning. Next, you must look for clues to any implied, or suggested, meanings behind the text. Finally, consider the clues in light of your prior knowledge and the author's purpose, and draw a conclusion about the meaning.

> As soon as Raizel entered the party, someone handed her a plate. She stared down at the hot dog unhappily.
>
> "What?" asked an unfamiliar woman nearby with an edge to her voice. "You don't eat dead animal?"

From the passage above, it would be reasonable to infer that the unfamiliar woman has a poor opinion of vegetarians. Several pieces of information suggest this: her combative tone, the edge in her voice, and the mocking question at the end.

When you draw inferences from a text, make sure your conclusion is truly indicated by the clues provided.

> Author Glenda Davis had high hopes for her children's book *Basketball Days.* But when the novel was released with a picture of a girl on the cover, boys refused to pick it up. The author reported this to her publisher, and the paperback edition was released with a new cover—this time featuring a dog and a basketball hoop. After that, many boys read the book. And Davis never heard anyone complain that the main character was a girl.

BE CAREFUL!

Before you make a conclusion about a text, consider it in light of your prior knowledge and the clues presented.

After reading the paragraph above, you might suspect that Raizel is a vegetarian. But the text does not fully support that conclusion. There are many reasons why Raizel might not want to eat a hot dog.

Perhaps she is keeping kosher, or she has social anxiety that makes it difficult to eat at parties, or she simply isn't hungry. The above inference about the unfamiliar woman's dislike for vegetarians is strongly supported. But you'd need further evidence before you could safely conclude that Raizel is actually a vegetarian.

The text above implies that boys are reluctant to read books with a girl on the cover. A hasty reader might stop reading early and conclude that boys are reluctant to read about girls—but this inference is not suggested by the full text.

Let's Review!

- Effective readers must consider the credibility of their sources.
- Primary sources are usually considered the most trustworthy.
- Readers must often make inferences about ideas that are implied but not explicitly stated in a text.

CHAPTER 1 KEY IDEAS AND DETAILS PRACTICE QUIZ 1

1. Which type of graphic element would be most helpful for teaching the names of the parts of a bicycle?

   A. Diagram   C. Bar graph

   B. Pie chart   D. Flowchart

Read the following sentence and answer questions 2-4.

Numerous robotic missions to Mars have revealed tantalizing evidence of a planet that may once have been capable of supporting life.

2. Imagine this sentence is a *supporting detail* in a well-developed paragraph. Which of the following sentences would best function as a *topic sentence*?

   A. Venus is an intensely hot planet surrounded by clouds full of drops of sulfuric acid.

   B. Of all the destinations within human reach, Mars is the planet most similar to Earth.

   C. Liquid water—a necessary ingredient of life—may once have flowed on the planet's surface.

   D. Space research is a costly, frivolous exercise that brings no clear benefit to people on Earth.

3. Imagine this sentence is the *topic sentence* of a well-developed paragraph. Which of the following sentences would best function as a *supporting detail*?

   A. Of all the destinations within human reach, Mars is the planet most similar to Earth.

   B. Venus is an intensely hot planet surrounded by clouds full of drops of sulfuric acid.

   C. Space research is a costly, frivolous exercise that brings no clear benefit to people on Earth.

   D. Liquid water—a necessary ingredient of life—may once have flowed on the planet's surface.

4. How could this sentence function as a *supporting detail* in a persuasive text arguing that space research is worth the expense and effort because it teaches us more about Earth and ourselves?

   A. By using statistics to back up an argument that needs support to be believed

   B. By showing how a space discovery could earn money for investors here on Earth

   C. By providing an example of a space discovery that enhances our understanding of life

   D. By developing the main idea that no space discovery can reveal information about Earth

The bar graph below provides information about book sales for a book called *The Comings*, which is the first book in a trilogy. Study the image and answer questions 5-6.

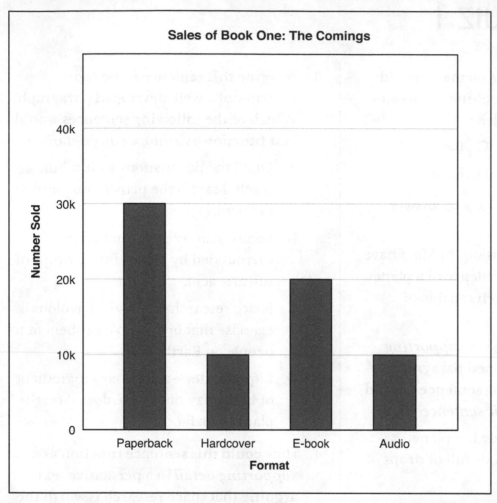

5. Which type of book has sold the most copies?

   A. E-book   C. Paperback

   B. Hardcover   D. Audio book

6. The marketing director for *The Comings* wants to use a different strategy for publishing book two in the series. Which argument does the bar graph *best* support?

   A. The first book in the trilogy has only sold 10,000 copies.

   B. The second book in the trilogy should not be released in hardcover.

   C. The second book in the trilogy should only be released as an e-book.

   D. The second and third books in the trilogy should be combined into one.

Study the infographic below and answer questions 7-9.

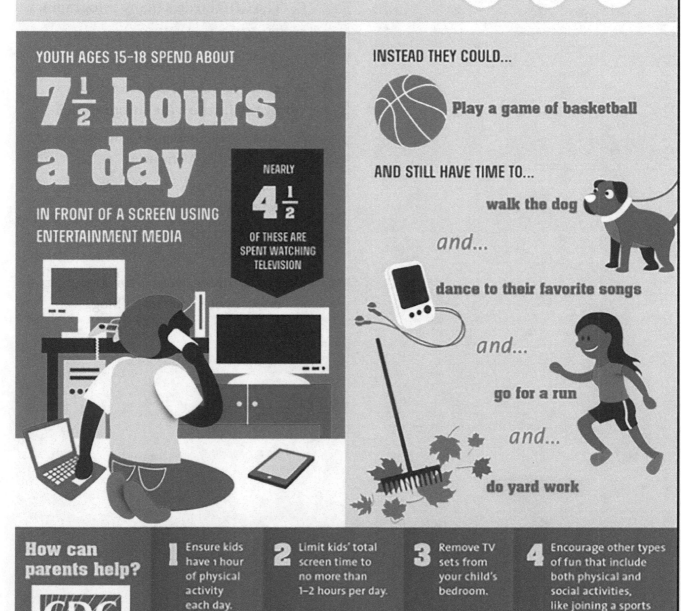

SCREEN TIME
VS LEAN TIME

Do you know how much entertainment screen time kids get? Time in front of a screen is time kids aren't active. See how much screen time kids of different ages get and tips for healthier activities.

AGE GROUP > 8-10 11-14 15-18

YOUTH AGES 15-18 SPEND ABOUT

7½ hours a day

IN FRONT OF A SCREEN USING ENTERTAINMENT MEDIA

NEARLY **4½** OF THESE ARE SPENT WATCHING TELEVISION

INSTEAD THEY COULD...

Play a game of basketball

AND STILL HAVE TIME TO...

walk the dog

and...

dance to their favorite songs

and...

go for a run

and...

do yard work

How can parents help?

1 Ensure kids have 1 hour of physical activity each day.

2 Limit kids' total screen time to no more than 1–2 hours per day.

3 Remove TV sets from your child's bedroom.

4 Encourage other types of fun that include both physical and social activities, like joining a sports team or club.

CDC

FOR MORE INFORMATION, VISIT MakingHealthEasier.org/GetMoving

Credit: Center for Disease Control and Prevention. https://www.cdc.gov/nccdphp/dnpao/multimedia/infographics/getmoving.html

7. Which of the following is not a sign that the infographic is credible?

   A. The use of verifiable facts

   B. The list of source materials

   C. The professional appearance

   D. The inclusion of an author's name

8. Zetta is unsure of the credibility of this source and has never heard of the Centers for Disease Control (CDC). Which fact could help her decide to trust it?

   A. The CDC is located in Atlanta.

   B. The CDC has a .gov web address.

   C. The CDC creates many infographics.

   D. The CDC is also listed as a source consulted.

9. What could a skeptical reader do to verify the facts on the infographic?

   A. Interview one teenager to ask about his or her screen time.

   B. Follow the links for the sources and determine their credibility.

   C. Check a tertiary source like Wikipedia to verify the information.

   D. Find different values for screen time on someone's personal blog.

Chapter 1 Key Ideas and Details
Practice Quiz 1 – Answer Key

1. A. A diagram illustrates complex visual ideas, so it could show which part of a bicycle is which and how they fit together. **See Lesson: Summarizing Text and Using Text Features.**

2. B. The sentence above conveys factual information about Mars in an excited tone that suggests a positive interest in the subject. This makes it most likely to fit into an informational paragraph sharing facts about Mars. **See Lesson: Main Ideas, Topic Sentences, and Supporting Details.**

3. D. If the above sentence were a topic sentence, its supporting details would likely share information to develop the idea that Mars may have supported life in the past. **See Lesson: Main Ideas, Topic Sentences, and Supporting Details.**

4. C. The sentence above could act as an example to show how space discoveries teach us about Earth and ourselves. **See Lesson: Main Ideas, Topic Sentences, and Supporting Details.**

5. C. Larger bars in a bar graph indicate higher numbers. This book has sold more paperback copies than any other. **See Lesson: Summarizing Text and Using Text Features.**

6. B. The bar graph shows fewer hardcover sales than any other kind. This could help support an argument that later books should only be released in electronic and paperback forms. **See Lesson: Summarizing Text and Using Text Features.**

7. D. It is usually a good sign if an author is clearly named in a source. Although this source is authored by an organization, the CDC, instead of a single author, there are many other signs it is credible. **See Lesson: Understanding Primary Sources Making Inferences and Drawing Conclusions.**

8. B. When presenting this type of information, a government organization with a .gov web address is typically considered a reputable source. **See Lesson: Understanding Primary Sources Making Inferences and Drawing Conclusions.**

9. B. One way to verify facts is to check the sources an author used. Verifying facts elsewhere may also be a good idea, but it is important to use reputable primary or secondary sources. **See Lesson: Understanding Primary Sources Making Inferences and Drawing Conclusions.**

CHAPTER 1 KEY IDEAS AND DETAILS PRACTICE QUIZ 2

Read the following paragraph and answer questions 1-3.

It is challenging to grow tomatoes in a cool, wet climate with a short growing season. In this kind of marginal area, it is rarely successful to sow seeds directly in the garden. It is better to plant seeds in pots indoors, or to buy plant starts at a nursery. If possible, select seed varieties from local seed companies. These are more likely than national brands to carry tomato varieties that fruit quickly. Plant your starts outdoors only after your warm season begins in earnest. Water the plants regularly all summer, and watch the fall forecasts and harvest as many tomatoes as possible before the cool and rain return to spoil the crop.

1. **Which phrase most accurately states the topic of this paragraph?**

    A. Growing tomatoes from seed

    B. Gardening in a cool, wet climate

    C. Gardening with local seed varieties

    D. Growing tomatoes in a cool, wet climate

2. **Which sentence best summarizes the main idea of this paragraph?**

    A. Gardeners should select tomato varieties that bear fruit quickly.

    B. Gardeners should not try to grow tomatoes in cool, wet climates.

    C. Gardeners must follow a special process to grow tomatoes in cool, wet climates.

    D. Gardeners should harvest tomatoes before the warm weather of summer is over.

3. **How does the supporting detail about local seed companies help develop the main idea?**

    A. It doesn't develop the main idea; this sentence is off-topic.

    B. It provides readers with a way to get gardening advice specific to their area.

    C. It gives gardeners a way to buy plants instead of sowing seeds directly themselves.

    D. It explains how to find plant varieties that are successful in a short growing season.

Study the flowchart below and answer questions 4-5.

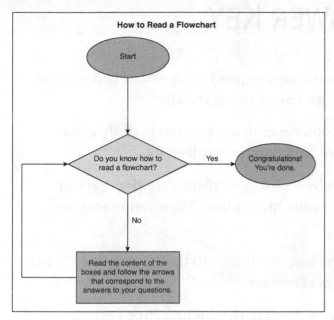

How to Read a Flowchart

Start

Do you know how to read a flowchart? — Yes → Congratulations! You're done.

No

Read the content of the boxes and follow the arrows that correspond to the answers to your questions.

4. **What is the first thing the chart asks you to do if you are hungry?**

   A. Eat.

   B. Look in the kitchen.

   C. Consider whether you can afford to eat out.

   D. Consider whether you want to eat what you have.

5. **According to the flowchart, what do you need to do if you cannot afford to eat out?**

   A. Grow a garden.

   B. Get a better job.

   C. Buy a recipe book.

   D. Find food in the kitchen.

6. **Which of the following statements accurately describes a summary?**

   A. A summary makes a judgment about the original text.

   B. A summary leaves out the main idea of the original text.

   C. A summary restates implicit ideas from the original text.

   D. A summary copies words and phrases from the original text.

7. **Which of the following is an example of a primary source?**

   A. An encyclopedia

   B. A biography

   C. A guidebook

   D. An interview

8. **Readers make inferences when they:**

   A. restate the main idea of a text in different words.

   B. differentiate between primary and secondary sources.

   C. determine that a text is not a credible source of information.

   D. use clues in the text to help them deduce implicit information.

9. **Which of the following is a secondary source?**

   A. The diary of Anne Frank

   B. A biography of Anne Frank

   C. A study guide on the diary of Anne Frank

   D. An encyclopedia article about Anne Frank

CHAPTER 1 KEY IDEAS AND DETAILS PRACTICE QUIZ 2 — ANSWER KEY

1. D. This paragraph focuses on one specific gardening topic—growing tomatoes in a cool, wet climate. **See Lesson: Main Ideas, Topic Sentences, and Supporting Details.**

2. C. This paragraph describes how gardeners in cool, wet climates can successfully grow tomatoes. **See Lesson: Main Ideas, Topic Sentences, and Supporting Details.**

3. D. The supporting detail develops the main idea by focusing on plant varieties that can be successful in a particular kind of climate. **See Lesson: Main Ideas, Topic Sentences, and Supporting Details.**

4. B. There is only one arrow leading from the start box, and it goes to the "look in the kitchen" box. **See Lesson: Summarizing Text and Using Text Features.**

5. D. The arrow that is labeled "No" directs readers to "Look in the kitchen." **See Lesson: Summarizing Text and Using Text Features.**

6. C. A summary may restate implicit ideas as long as they are clearly indicated in the original text. **See Lesson: Summarizing Text and Using Text Features.**

7. D. Primary sources are written by people who witnessed the original creation or discovery of the information they present. An interview would be an example of a primary source. **See Lesson: Understanding Primary Sources, Making Inferences and Drawing Conclusions.**

8. D. Readers make inferences when they deduce implicit information in a text. **See Lesson: Understanding Primary Sources, Making Inferences and Drawing Conclusions.**

9. B. A biography of Anne Frank would be a historical or analytical account that added insight on the topic. This makes it a secondary source. **See Lesson: Understanding Primary Sources, Making Inferences and Drawing Conclusions.**

Chapter 2 Craft and Structure

Formal and Informal Language

In English, there is formal language that is used most often in writing, and informal language that is most often used in speaking, but there are situations where one is more appropriate than the other. This lesson will cover differentiating contexts for (1) formal language and (2) informal language.

Formal Language

Formal language is often associated with writing for professional and academic purposes, but it is also used when giving a speech or a lecture. An essay written for a class will always use **formal language**. **Formal language** is used in situations where people are not extremely close and when one needs to show respect to another person. Certain qualities and contexts differentiate **formal language** from informal language.

Formal language does not use contractions.

- It doesn't have that - It does not have that.
- He's been offered a new job - He has been offered a new job.

Formal language also uses complete sentences.

- So much to tell you - I have so much to tell you.
- Left for the weekend - We left for the weekend.

Formal language includes more formal and polite vocabulary.

- The class starts at two - The class commences at two.
- I try to be the best person I can be - I endeavor to be the best person I can be.

Formal language is not personal and normally does not use the pronouns "I" and "We" as the subject of a sentence.

- I argue that the sky is blue - This essay argues that the sky is blue.
- We often associate green with grass - Green is often associated with grass.

Formal language also does not use slang.

- It's raining cats and dogs - It is raining heavily.
- Patients count on doctors to help them - Patients expect doctors to help them.

Informal Language

Informal language is associated with speaking, but is also used in text messages, emails, letters, and postcards. It is the language a person would use with their friends and family.

Informal language uses contractions.

- I can't go to the movie tomorrow.
- He doesn't have any manners.

Informal language can include sentence fragments.

- See you
- Talk to you later

Informal language uses less formal vocabulary such as slang.

- The dog drove me up the wall.
- I was so hungry I could eat a horse.
- I can always count on you.

Informal language is personal and uses pronouns such as "I" and "We" as the subject of a sentence.

- I am in high school.
- We enjoy going to the beach in the summer.

Let's Review!

- **Formal language** is used in professional and academic writing and talks. It does not have contractions, uses complete sentences, uses polite and formal vocabulary, not slang, and is not personal and generally does not use the pronouns "I" and "We" as the subject of a sentence.
- **Informal language** is used in daily life when communicating with friends and family through conversations, text messages, emails, letters, and postcards. It uses contractions, can be sentence fragments, uses less formal vocabulary and slang, and is personal and uses pronouns such as "I" and "We" as the subject of a sentence.

TONE, MOOD, AND TRANSITION WORDS

Authors use language to show their emotions and to make readers feel something too. They also use transition words to help guide the reader from one idea to the next.

Tone and Mood

The **tone** of a text is the author's or speaker's attitude toward the subject. The tone may reflect any feeling or attitude a person can express: happiness, excitement, anger, boredom, or arrogance.

Readers can identify tone primarily by analyzing word choice. The reader should be able to point to specific words and details that help to establish the tone.

> **Example:** The train rolled past miles and miles of cornfields. The fields all looked the same. They swayed the same. They produced the same dull nausea in the pit of my stomach. I'd been sent out to see the world, and so I looked, obediently. What I saw was sameness.

Here, the author is expressing boredom and dissatisfaction. This is clear from the repetition of words like "same" and "sameness." There's also a sense of unpleasantness from phrases like "dull nausea" and passivity from words like "obediently."

Sometimes an author uses an ironic tone. Ironic texts often mean the opposite of what they actually say. To identify irony, you need to rely on your prior experience and common sense to help you identify texts with words and ideas that do not quite match.

> **Example:** With that, the senator dismissed the petty little problem of mass shootings and returned to the really important issue: his approval ratings.

BE CAREFUL!

When you're asked to identify the tone of a text, be sure to keep track of *whose* tone you're supposed to identify, and which part of the text the question is referencing. The author's tone can be different from that of the characters in fiction or the people quoted in nonfiction.

Example: The reporter walked quickly, panting to catch up to the senator's entourage. "Senator Biltong," she said. "Are you going to take action on mass shootings?"

"Sure, sure. Soon," the senator said vaguely. Then he turned to greet a newcomer. "Ah ha! Here's the man who can fix my approval ratings!" And with that, he returned to the really important issue: his popularity.

*

In the example above, the author's tone is ironic and angry. But the tone of the senator's dialogue is different. The line beginning with the words "Sure, sure" has a distracted tone. The line beginning with "Ah ha!" has a pleased tone.

Here the author flips around the words most people would usually use to discuss mass murder and popularity. By calling a horrific issue "petty" and a trivial issue "important," the author highlights what she sees as a politician's backwards priorities. Except for the phrase "mass shootings," the words here are light and airy—but the tone is ironic and angry.

A concept related to tone is **mood**, or the feelings an author produces in the reader. To determine the mood of a text, a reader can consider setting and theme as well as word choice and tone. For example, a story set in a haunted house may produce an unsettled or frightened feeling in a reader.

Tone and mood are often confused. This is because they are sometimes the same. For instance, in an op-ed article that describes children starving while food aid lies rotting, the author may use an outraged tone and simultaneously arouse an outraged mood in the reader.

However, tone and mood can be different. When they are, it's useful to have different words to distinguish between the author's attitude and the reader's emotional reaction.

> **Example:** I had to fly out of town at 4 a.m. for my trip to the Bahamas, and my wife didn't even get out of bed to make me a cup of coffee. I told her to, but she refused just because she'd been up five times with our newborn. I'm only going on vacation for one week, and she's been off work for a month! She should show me a little consideration.

Here, the tone is indignant. The mood will vary depending on the reader, but it is likely to be unsympathetic.

Transitions

Authors use connecting words and phrases, or **transitions**, to link ideas and help readers follow the flow of their thoughts. The number of possible ways to transition between ideas is almost limitless.

Below are a few common transition words, categorized by the way they link ideas.

Transitions	Examples
Time and sequence transitions orient the reader within a text. They can also help show when events happened in time.	*First, second, next, now, then, at this point, after, afterward, before this, previously, formerly, thereafter, finally, in conclusion*
Addition or emphasis transitions let readers know the author is building on an established line of thought. Many place extra stress on an important idea.	*Moreover, also, likewise, furthermore, above all, indeed, in fact*
Example transitions introduce ideas that illustrate a point.	*For example, for instance, to illustrate, to demonstrate*
Causation transitions indicate a cause-and-effect relationship.	*As a result, consequently, thus*
Contrast transitions indicate a difference between ideas.	*Nevertheless, despite, in contrast, however*

Transitions may look different depending on their function within the text. Within a paragraph, writers often choose short words or expressions to provide transitions and smooth the flow. Between paragraphs or larger sections of text, transitions are usually longer. They may use some of the key words or ideas above, but the author often goes into detail restating larger concepts and explaining their relationships more thoroughly.

Between Sentences: Students who cheat do not learn what they need to know. *As a result,* they get farther behind and face greater temptation to cheat in the future.

Between Paragraphs: *As a result of the cheating behaviors described above,* students find themselves in a vicious cycle.

Longer transitions like the latter example may be useful for keeping the reader clued in to the author's focus in an extended text. But long transitions should have clear content and function. Some long transitions, such as the very wordy "due to the fact that" take up space without adding more meaning and are considered poor style.

Let's Review!

- Tone is the author's or speaker's attitude toward the subject.
- Mood is the feeling a text creates in the reader.
- Transitions are connecting words and phrases that help readers follow the flow of a writer's thoughts.

THE AUTHOR'S PURPOSE AND POINT OF VIEW

In order to understand, analyze, and evaluate a text, readers must know how to identify the author's purpose and point of view. Readers also need to attend to an author's language and rhetorical strategies.

Author's Purpose

When writers put words on paper, they do it for a reason. This reason is the author's **purpose**. Most writing exists for one of three purposes: to inform, to persuade, or to entertain.

TEST TIP

You may have learned about a fourth purpose for writing: conveying an emotional experience. Many poems as well as some works of fiction, personal essays, and memoirs are written to give the reader a sense of how an event or moment might feel. This type of text is rarely included on placement tests, and if it is, it tends to be lumped in with literature meant to entertain.

If a text is designed to share knowledge, its purpose is to **inform**. Informational texts include technical documents, cookbooks, expository essays, journalistic newspaper articles, and many nonfiction books. Informational texts are based on facts and logic, and they usually attempt an objective tone. The style may otherwise vary; some informational texts are quite dry, whereas others have an engaging style.

If a text argues a point, its purpose is to **persuade**. A persuasive text attempts to convince a reader to believe a certain point of view or take a certain action. Persuasive texts include op-ed newspaper articles, book and movie reviews, project proposals, and argumentative essays. Key signs of persuasive texts include judgments, words like *should,* and other signs that the author is sharing opinions.

If a text is primarily for fun, its purpose is to **entertain**. Entertaining texts usually tell stories or present descriptions. Entertaining texts include novels, short stories, memoirs, and some poems. Virtually all stories are lumped into this category, even if they describe unpleasant experiences.

CONNECTIONS

You may have read elsewhere that readers can break writing down into the following basic categories. These categories are often linked to the author's purpose.

Narrative writing tells a story and is usually meant to entertain.
Expository writing explains an idea and is usually meant to inform.
Technical writing explains a mechanism or process and is usually meant to inform.
Persuasive writing argues a point and, as the label suggests, is meant to persuade.

A text can have more than one purpose. For example, many traditional children's stories come with morals or lessons. These are meant both to entertain children and persuade them to behave in ways society considers appropriate. Also, commercial nonfiction texts like popular science books are often written in an engaging or humorous style. The purpose of such a text is to inform while also entertaining the reader.

Point of View

Every author has a general outlook or set of opinions about the subject. These make up the author's **point of view**.

To determine point of view, a reader must recognize implicit clues in the text and use them to develop educated guesses about the author's worldview. In persuasive texts, the biggest clue is the author's explicit argument. From considering this argument, a reader can usually make some inferences about point of view. For instance, if an author argues that parents should offer kids opportunities to exercise throughout the day, it would be reasonable to infer that the author has an overall interest in children's health, and that he or she is troubled by the idea of kids pursuing sedentary behaviors like TV watching.

It is more challenging to determine point of view in a text meant to inform. Because the writer does not present an explicit argument, readers must examine assumptions and word choice to determine the writer's point of view.

> **Example:** Models suggest that at the current rate of global warming, hurricanes in 2100 will move 9 percent slower and drop 24 percent more rain. Longer storm durations and rainfall rates will likely translate to increased economic damage and human suffering.

It is reasonable to infer that the writer of this passage has a general trust for science and scientists. This writer assumes that global warming is happening, so it is clear he or she is not a global warming denier. Although the writer does not suggest a plan to prevent future storm damage, the emphasis on negative effects and the use of negative words like "damage" and "suffering" suggest that the author is worried about global warming.

Texts meant to entertain also contain clues about the author's point of view. That point of view is usually evident from the themes and deeper meanings. For instance, a memoirist who writes an upbeat story about a troubled but loving family is likely to believe strongly in the power of love. Note, however, that in this type of work, it is not possible to determine point of view merely from one character's words or actions. For instance, if a character says, "Your mother's love doesn't matter much if she can't take care of you," the reader should *not* automatically assume the writer agrees with that statement. Narrative writers often present a wide range of characters with varying outlooks on life. A reader can only determine the author's point of view by considering the work as a whole. The attitudes that are most emphasized and the ones that win out in the end are likely to reflect the author's point of view.

Rhetorical Strategies

Rhetorical strategies are the techniques an author uses to support an argument or develop a main idea. Effective readers need to study the language of a text and determine how the author is supporting his or her points.

One strategy is to appeal to the reader's reason. This is the foundation of effective writing, and it simply means that the writer relies on factual information and the logical conclusions that follow from it. Even persuasive writing uses this strategy by presenting facts and reasons to back up the author's opinions.

> **Ineffective:** Everyone knows *Sandra and the Lumps* is the best band of the new millennium.

> **Effective:** The three most recent albums by *Sandra and the Lumps* are the first, second, and third most popular records released since the turn of the millennium.

Another strategy is to establish trust. A writer can do this by choosing credible sources and by presenting ideas in a clear and professional way. In persuasive writing, writers may show they are trustworthy by openly acknowledging that some people hold contradicting opinions and by responding fairly to those positions. Writers should never attack or misrepresent their opponents' position.

> **Ineffective:** People who refuse to recycle are too lazy to protect their children's future.

> **Effective:** According to the annual Throw It Out Questionnaire, many people dislike the onerous task of sorting garbage, and some doubt that their effort brings any real gain.

A final strategy is to appeal to the reader's emotions. For instance, a journalist reporting on the opioid epidemic could include a personal story about an addict's attempts to overcome substance abuse. Emotional content can add a human dimension to a story that would be missing if the writer only included statistics and expert opinions. But emotions are easily manipulated, so writers who use this strategy need to be careful. Emotions should never be used to distort the truth or scare readers into agreeing with the writer.

> **Ineffective:** If you don't take action on gun control, you're basically killing children.

> **Effective:** Julie was puzzling over the Pythagorean Theorem when she heard the first gunshot.

Let's Review!

- Every text has a purpose.
- Most texts are meant to inform, persuade, or entertain.
- Texts contain clues that imply an author's outlook or set of opinions about the subject.
- Authors use rhetorical strategies to appeal to reason, establish trust, or invoke emotions.

CHAPTER 2 CRAFT AND STRUCTURE PRACTICE QUIZ 1

1. Which of the following sentences uses the MOST informal language?

   A. The house creaked at night.

   B. I ate dinner with my friend.

   C. It's sort of a bad time.

   D. The water trickled slowly.

2. In which of the following situations would it be best to use informal language?

   A. In a seminar.

   B. Writing a postcard.

   C. Talking to your boss.

   D. Participating in a professional conference.

3. Which of the following sentences uses the MOST formal language?

   A. Thanks for letting me know.

   B. I want to thank you for telling me.

   C. Thank you for telling me about this issue.

   D. I appreciate you bringing this issue to my attention.

Read the passage below and answer questions 4-6.

The train was the most amazing thing ever even though it didn't go "choo choo." The toddler pounded on the railing of the bridge and supplied the sound herself. "Choo choo! Choo choooooo!" she shouted as the train cars whizzed along below.

In the excitement, she dropped her favorite binky.

Later, when she noticed the binky missing, all the joy went out of the world. The wailing could be heard three houses down. The toddler's usual favorite activities were garbage—even waving to Hank the garbage man, which she refused to do, so that Hank went away looking mildly hurt. It was clear the little girl would never, ever, ever recover from her loss.

Afterward, she played at the park.

4. Which adjectives best describe the tone of the passage?

   A. Ironic, angry

   B. Earnest, angry

   C. Ironic, humorous

   D. Earnest, humorous

5. Which sentence from the passage is clearly ironic?

   A. "Choo choo! Choo choooooo!" she shouted as the train cars whizzed along below.

   B. Later, when she noticed the binky missing, all the joy went out of the world.

   C. The wailing could be heard three houses down.

   D. Afterward, she played at the park.

6. The author of the passage first establishes the ironic tone by:

    A. describing the child's trip to play at the park.

    B. calling the train "the most amazing thing ever."

    C. pretending that the child can make the sounds "choo chooooo!"

    D. claiming inaccurately that the lost binky was the child's "favorite."

7. What is the most likely purpose of a popular science book describing recent advances in genetics?

    A. To decide   C. To persuade

    B. To inform   D. To entertain

8. Which phrase describes the set of techniques an author uses to support an argument or develop a main idea?

    A. Points of view

    B. Logical fallacies

    C. Statistical analyses

    D. Rhetorical strategies

9. What is the most likely purpose of an article that claims some genetic research is immoral?

    A. To decide   C. To persuade

    B. To inform   D. To entertain

CHAPTER 2 CRAFT AND STRUCTURE PRACTICE QUIZ 1 – ANSWER KEY

1. **C.** *It's sort of a bad time.* The sentence has contractions and uses informal and slang words. **See Lesson: Formal and Informal Language.**

2. **B.** *Writing a postcard.* It is an informal mode of communication between close friends and relatives. **See Lesson: Formal and Informal Language.**

3. **D.** *I appreciate you bringing this issue to my attention.* The sentence uses the most formal and polite vocabulary. **See Lesson: Formal and Informal Language.**

4. **C.** This passage ironically is a humorous description of a toddler's emotions, written by an adult who has enough experience to know that a toddler's huge emotions will pass. **See Lesson: Tone and Mood, Transition Words.**

5. **B.** Authors use irony when their words do not literally mean what they say. The joy does not really go out of the world when a toddler loses her binky—but it may seem that way to the child. **See Lesson: Tone and Mood, Transition Words.**

6. **B.** This passage establishes irony in the opening sentence by applying the superlative phrase "the most amazing thing ever" to an ordinary occurrence. **See Lesson: Tone and Mood, Transition Words.**

7. **B.** If a book is describing information, its purpose is to inform. **See Lesson: Understanding the Author's Purpose, Point of View, and Rhetorical Strategies.**

8. **D.** The techniques an author uses to support an argument or develop a main idea are called rhetorical strategies. **See Lesson: Understanding the Author's Purpose, Point of View, and Rhetorical Strategies.**

9. **C.** An article that takes a moral position is meant to persuade. **See Lesson: Understanding the Author's Purpose, Point of View, and Rhetorical Strategies.**

CHAPTER 2 CRAFT AND STRUCTURE PRACTICE QUIZ 2

1. Which of the following sentences uses the MOST formal language?

   A. Congrats!

   B. Congratulations!

   C. Congratulations on your recent success.

   D. Congrats to you.

2. In which of the following situations would it be best to use informal language?

   A. A charity event

   B. A football game

   C. A job interview

   D. A dentist's office

3. Which of the following sentences uses the MOST informal language?

   A. Where's the best café in these parts?

   B. Could you direct me to a nice café in the area?

   C. Would you be able to show me to a nice café?

   D. Could you tell me where a nice café is around here?

4. Which word functions as a transition in the sentence below?

   Cassandra loved reading and writing books as a child. Thus she became an English teacher in her adult life.

   A. Loved   C. Thus

   B. Child   D. Became

5. Readers can determine tone primarily by examining:

   A. setting.

   B. word choice.

   C. their feelings.

   D. connecting words.

6. Transitions tend to be longer and more detailed when they occur between:

   A. words   C. sentences

   B. clauses   D. paragraphs

7. What is the most likely purpose of a cookbook full of Mediterranean recipes?

   A. To decide   C. To persuade

   B. To inform   D. To entertain

8. An author's point of view is a(n):

   A. lack of purpose.

   B. general outlook.

   C. rhetorical strategy.

   D. appeal to the emotions.

9. The author's _____ is the reason for writing.

   A. purpose   C. main idea

   B. rhetoric   D. point of view

CHAPTER 2 CRAFT AND STRUCTURE PRACTICE QUIZ 2 — ANSWER KEY

1. **C.** Congratulations on your recent success. It is the sentence with the most formal language and no slang. **See Lesson: Formal and Informal Language.**

2. **B.** A football game. A stadium is an informal setting where formal language is not necessary. **See Lesson: Formal and Informal Language.**

3. **A.** Where's the best café in these parts? The sentence is informal because it has a contraction and uses more colloquial language. **See Lesson: Formal and Informal Language.**

4. **C.** The transition is the word that links the two ideas: *thus*. This word shows how the two sentences have a cause-and-effect relationship. **See Lesson: Tone and Mood, Transition Words.**

5. **B.** Word choice, or diction, is the reader's most important tool in determining tone. **See Lesson: Tone and Mood, Transition Words.**

6. **D.** Transitions between paragraphs or longer sections of text tend to be detailed and may include a short recap of related ideas from earlier parts of the text. **See Lesson: Tone and Mood, Transition Words.**

7. **B.** Informational texts like cookbooks are usually meant to inform. **See Lesson: Understanding Author's Purpose, Point of View, and Rhetorical Strategies.**

8. **B.** An author's point of view is a general outlook on the subject. **See Lesson: Understanding the Author's Purpose, Point of View, and Rhetorical Strategies.**

9. **A.** The main idea of a text is its key point, and the point of view is the author's outlook on the subject. The purpose is the reason for writing. **See Lesson: Understanding the Author's Purpose, Point of View, and Rhetorical Strategies.**

Chapter 3 Integration of Knowledge and Ideas

Facts, Opinions, and Evaluating an Argument

Nonfiction writing is based on facts and real events, but most nonfiction nevertheless expresses a point of view. Effective readers must evaluate the author's point of view and form their own conclusions about the points in the text.

Fact and Opinion

Many texts make an **argument**. In this context, the word *argument* has nothing to do with anger or fighting. It simply means the author is trying to convince readers of something.

Arguments are present in a wide variety of texts. Some relate to controversial issues, for instance by advocating support for a political candidate or change in laws. Others may defend a certain interpretation of facts or ideas. For example, a literature paper may argue that an author's story suggests a certain theme, or a science paper may argue for a certain interpretation of data. An argument may also present a plan of action such as a business strategy.

To evaluate an argument, readers must distinguish between **fact** and **opinion**. A fact is verifiably true. An opinion is someone's belief.

> **Fact:** Seattle gets an average of 37 inches of rain per year.

> **Opinion:** The dark, rainy, cloudy weather makes Seattle an unpleasant place to live in winter.

Meteorologists measure rainfall directly, so the above fact is verifiably true. The statement "it is unpleasant" clearly reflects a feeling, so the second sentence is an opinion.

The difference between fact and opinion is not always straightforward. For instance, a text may present a fact that contains an opinion within it:

> **Fact:** Nutritionist Fatima Antar questions the wisdom of extreme carbohydrate avoidance.

Assuming the writer can prove that this sentence genuinely reflects Fatima Antar's beliefs, it is a factual statement of her point of view. The reader may trust that Fatima Antar really holds this opinion, whether or not the reader is convinced by it.

If a text makes a judgment, it is not a fact:

Opinion: The patient's seizure drug regimen caused horrendous side effects.

This sentence uses language that different people would interpret in different ways. Because people have varying ideas about what they consider "horrendous," this sentence is an opinion as it is written, even though the actual side effects and the patient's opinion of them could both be verified.

COMPARE!

Small changes to the statement about seizure drugs could turn it into a factual statement:

Fact: The patient's seizure drug regiment caused side effects such as migraines, confusion, and dangerously high blood pressure.

The above statement can be verified because the patient and other witnesses could confirm the exact nature of her symptoms. This makes it a fact.

Fact: The patient reported that her seizure drug regimen caused horrendous side effects.

This statement can also be verified because the patient can verify that she considers the side effects horrendous. By framing the statement in this way, the writer leaves nothing up to interpretation and is clearly in the realm of fact.

The majority of all arguments contain both facts and opinions, and strong arguments may contain both fact and opinion elements. It is rare for an argument to be composed entirely of facts, but it can happen if the writer is attempting to convince readers to accept factual information that is little-known or widely questioned. Most arguments present an author's opinion and use facts, reasoning, and expert testimony to convince readers.

Evaluating an Argument

Effective readers must evaluate an argument and decide whether or not it is valid. To do this, readers must consider every claim the author presents, including both the main argument and any supporting statements. If an argument is based on poor reasoning or insufficient evidence, it is not valid—even if you agree with the main idea.

KEY POINT!

Most of us want to agree with arguments that reflect our own beliefs. But it is inadvisable to accept an argument that is not properly rooted in good reasoning. Consider the following statements about global climate change:

Poor Argument: It just snowed fifteen inches! How can anyone say the world is getting warmer?

Poor Argument: It's seventy degrees in the middle of February! How can anyone deny global warming?

Both of these arguments are based on insufficient evidence. Each relies on *one* weather event in *one* location to support an argument that the entire world's climate is or is not changing. There is not nearly enough information here to support an argument on either side.

Beware of any argument that presents opinion information as fact.

False Claim of Fact: I know vaccines cause autism because my niece began displaying autism symptoms after receiving her measles vaccine.

The statement above states a controversial idea as fact without adequate evidence to back it up. Specifically, it makes a false claim of cause and effect about an incident that has no clear causal relationship.

Any claim that is not supported by sufficient evidence is an example of **faulty reasoning**.

Type of Faulty Reasoning	Definition	Example	Explanation
Circular Reasoning	Restating the argument in different words instead of providing evidence	Baseball is the best game in the world because it is more fun than any other game.	Here, everything after the word *because* says approximately the same thing as everything before it. It looks like the author is providing a reason, but no evidence has actually been offered.
Either/Or Fallacy	Presenting an issue as if it involves only two choices when in fact it is not so simple	Women should focus on motherhood, not careers.	This statement assumes that women cannot do both. It also assumes that no woman needs a career in order to provide for her children.
Overgeneralizations	Making a broad claim based on too little evidence	All elderly people have negative stereotypes of teenagers.	This statement lumps a whole category of people into a group and claims the whole group shares the same belief—always an unlikely prospect.

Most texts about evaluating arguments focus on faulty reasoning and false statements of fact. But arguments that attempt to misrepresent facts as opinions are equally suspicious. A careful reader should be skeptical of any text that denies clear physical evidence or questions the truth of events that have been widely verified.

Assumptions and Biases

A well-reasoned argument should be supported by facts, logic, and clearly explained opinions. But most arguments are also based on **assumptions,** or unstated and unproven ideas about what is true. Consider the following argument:

Argument: To improve equality of opportunity for all children, schools in underprivileged areas should receive as much taxpayer funding as schools in wealthy districts.

This argument is based on several assumptions. First is the assumption that all children should have equal opportunities. Another is that taxpayer-funded public schools are the best way to provide these opportunities. Whether or not you disagree with either of these points, it is worth noting that the second idea in particular is not the only way to proceed. Readers who examine the assumptions behind an argument can sometimes find points of disagreement even if an author's claims and logic are otherwise sound.

Examining an author's assumptions can also reveal a writer's biases. A **bias** is a preconceived idea that makes a person more likely to show unfair favor for certain thoughts, people, or groups. Because every person has a different experience of the world, every person has a different set of biases. For example, a person who has traveled widely may feel differently about world political events than someone who has always lived in one place.

Virtually all writing is biased to some degree. However, effective writing attempts to avoid bias as much as possible. Writing that is highly biased may be based on poor assumptions that render the entire argument invalid.

Highly biased writing often includes overgeneralizations. Words like *all, always, never*, and so on may indicate that the writer is overstating a point. While these words can exist in true statements, unbiased writing is more likely to qualify ideas using words like *usually, often*, and *rarely*.

Another quality of biased writing is excessively emotional word choice. When writers insult people who disagree with them or engage the emotions in a way that feels manipulative, they are being biased.

> **Biased:** Power-hungry politicians don't care that their standardized testing requirements are producing a generation of overanxious, incurious, impractical kids.

> **Less biased:** Politicians need to recognize that current standardized testing requirements are causing severe anxiety and other negative effects in children.

Biased writing may also reflect stereotypical thinking. A **stereotype** is a particularly harmful type of bias that applies specifically to groups of people. Stereotypical thinking is behind racism, sexism, homophobia, and so on. Even people who do not consider themselves prejudiced can use language that reflects common stereotypes. For example, the negative use of the word *crazy* reflects a stereotype against people with mental illnesses.

Historically, writers in English have used male nouns and pronouns to indicate all people. Revising such language for more inclusivity is considered more effective in contemporary writing.

> **Biased:** The history of the human race proves that man is a violent creature.

> **Less biased:** The history of the human race proves that people are violent.

Let's Review!

- A text meant to convince someone of something is making an argument.
- Arguments may employ both facts and opinions.
- Effective arguments must use valid reasoning.
- Arguments are based on assumptions that may be reasonable or highly biased.
- Almost all writing is biased to some degree, but strong writing makes an effort to eliminate bias.

EVALUATING AND INTEGRATING DATA

Effective readers do more than absorb and analyze the content of sentences, paragraphs, and chapters. They recognize the importance of features that stand out in and around the text, and they understand and integrate knowledge from visual features like maps and charts.

Text Features

Elements that stand out from a text are called **text features**. Text features perform many vital functions.

- **Introducing the Topic and Organizing Information**

> **COMPARE!**
> The title on a fictional work does not always state the topic explicitly. While some titles do this, others are more concerned with hinting at a theme or setting up the tone.

  - *Titles* – The title of a nonfiction text typically introduces the topic. Titles are guiding features of organization because they give clues about what is and is not covered. The title of this section, "Text Features," covers exactly that—not, for example, implicit ideas.
  - *Headings and Subheadings* – Headings and subheadings provide subtopic information about supporting points and let readers scan to see how information is organized. The subheadings of this page organize text features according to the functions they perform.

- **Helping the Reader Find Information**

  - *Table of Contents* – The table of contents of a long work lists chapter titles and other large-scale information so readers can predict the content. This helps readers to determine whether or not a text will be useful to them and to find sections relevant to their research.
  - *Index* – In a book, the index is an alphabetical list of topics covered, complete with page numbers where the topics are discussed. Readers looking for information on one small subtopic can check the index to find out which pages to view.
  - *Footnotes and Endnotes* – When footnotes and endnotes list sources, they allow the reader to find and evaluate the information an author is citing.

- **Emphasizing Concepts**

  - *Formatting Features* – Authors may use formatting features such as *italics*, **boldfacing** or underlining to emphasize a word, phrase, or other important information in a text.
  - *Bulleting and numbering* – Bullet points and numbered lists set off information and allow readers to scan for bits of information they do not know. It also helps to break down a list of steps.

- **Presenting Information and Illustrating Ideas**

  - *Graphic Elements* – Charts, graphs, diagrams, and other graphic elements present data succinctly, illustrate complex ideas, or otherwise convey information that would be difficult to glean from text alone.

- **Providing Peripheral Information**

  - *Sidebars* – Sidebars are text boxes that contain information related to the topic but not essential to the overall point.

  - *Footnotes and Endnotes* – Some footnotes and endnotes contain information that is not essential to the development of the main point but may nevertheless interest readers and researchers.[1]

FUN FACT!

Online, a sidebar is sometimes called a *doobly doo*.

P.S. This is an example of a sidebar.

Maps and Charts

To read maps and charts, you need to understand what the labels, symbols, and pictures mean. You also need to know how to make decisions using the information they contain.

Maps

Maps are stylized pictures of places as seen from above. A map may have a box labeled "Key" or "Legend" that provides information about the meanings of colors, lines, or symbols. On the map below, the key shows that a solid line is a road and a dotted line is a trail.

There may also be a line labeled "scale" that helps you figure out how far you need to travel to get from one point on the map to another. In the example below, an inch is only 100 feet, so a trip from one end to the other is not far.

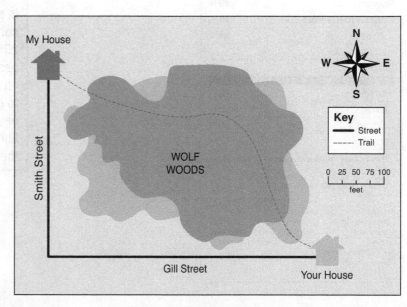

Some maps, including the example above, have compasses that show directions. If no compass is pictured, assume the top of the map is north.

---

[1] Anthony Grafton's book *The Footnote: A Curious History* is an in-depth history of the origins and development of the footnote. (Also, this is an example of a footnote.)

Charts

Nutrition Facts Labels

Nutrition facts labels are charts many people see daily, but not everyone knows how to read them. The top third of the label lists calorie counts, serving sizes, and amount of servings in a package. If a package contains more than one serving, a person who eats the entire contents of the package may be consuming many times the number of calories listed per serving.

The label below lists the content of nutrients such as fats and carbohydrates, and so on. According to the label, a person who eats one serving of the product in the package will ingest 30 mg of cholesterol, or 10% of the total cholesterol he or she should consume in a day.

KEEP IN MIND . . .

The percentages on a Nutrition Facts label do not (and are not meant to) add up to 100. Instead, they show how much of a particular nutrient is contained in a serving of the product, as a proportion of a single person's Daily Value for that nutrient. The Daily Value is the total amount of a nutrient a person is supposed to eat in a day, based on a 2000-calorie diet.

In general, a percentage of 5% or less is considered low, whereas a percentage of 20% or more is considered high. A higher percentage can be good or bad, depending on whether or not a person should be trying to get more of a particular ingredient. People need to get plenty of vitamins, minerals, and fiber. In contrast, most people need to limit their intake of fat, cholesterol, and sodium.

Tables

Tables organize information into vertical columns and horizontal rows. Below is a table that shows how much water falls on areas of various sizes when it rains one inch. It shows, for instance, that a 40' x 70' roof receives 1,743 gallons of rain during a one-inch rainfall event.

Area	Area (square miles)	Area (square kilometers)	Amount of Water (gallons)	Amount of Water (liters)
My roof 40 x 70 feet	.0001	.000257	1,743 gallons	6,601 liters
1 acre (1 square mile = 640 acres)	.00156	.004	27,154 gallons	102,789 liters
1 square mile	1	2.6	17.38 million gallons	65.78 million liters
Atlanta, Georgia	132.4	342.9	2.293 billion gallons	8.68 billion liters
United States	3,537,438	9,161,922	61,474 billion gallons	232,700 billion liters

Let's Review!

- Readers must understand how and why text features make certain information stand out from the text.
- Readers must understand and interpret the content of maps and charts.

TYPES OF PASSAGES, TEXT STRUCTURES, GENRE AND THEME

To read effectively, you must understand what kind of text you are reading and how it is structured. You must also be able to look behind the text to find its deeper meanings.

Types of Passages

There are many ways of breaking texts down into categories. To do this, you need to consider the author's **purpose**, or what the text exists to do. Most texts exist to inform, persuade, or entertain. You also need to consider what the text does—whether it tells a story, describes facts, or develops a point of view.

Type of Passage	Examples
Narrative writing tells a story. The story can be fictional, or it can describe real events. The primary purpose of narrative writing is to entertain.	<ul><li>An autobiography</li><li>A memoir</li><li>A short story</li><li>A novel</li></ul>
Expository writing provides an explanation or a description. Many academic essays and informational nonfiction books are expository writing. Stylistically, expository writing is highly varied. Although the explanations can be dry and methodical, many writers use an artful or entertaining style. Expository writing is nonfiction. Its primary purpose is to inform.	<ul><li>A book about a historical event</li><li>An essay describing the social impacts of a new technology</li><li>A description of changing gender roles in marriages</li><li>A philosophical document exploring the nature of truth.</li></ul>
Technical writing explains a complex process or mechanism. Whereas expository writing is often academic, technical writing is used in practical settings such as businesses. The style of a technical document is almost always straightforward and impersonal. Technical writing is nonfiction, and its purpose is to inform.	<ul><li>Recipes</li><li>Instructions</li><li>User manuals</li><li>Process descriptions</li></ul>
Persuasive writing makes an argument. It asks readers to believe something or do something. Texts that make judgments, such as movie reviews, are persuasive because they are attempting to convince readers to accept a point of view. Texts that suggest a plan are also persuasive because they are trying to convince readers to take an action. As the name "persuasive writing" indicates, the author's primary purpose is to persuade.	<ul><li>Op-ed newspaper articles</li><li>Book reviews</li><li>Project proposals</li><li>Advertisements</li><li>Persuasive essays</li></ul>

BE CAREFUL!

Many texts have more than one purpose.

A text that tells a story is usually meant to entertain, but it can also be meant to persuade. For example, there is a well-known story called "Never Cry Wolf" about a boy who habitually lies. At the end, when he needs help, nobody believes him. This story is meant to entertain, but it is also trying to convince readers not to tell lies.

Similarly, many explanatory texts are meant to inform readers in an entertaining way. For example, a nonfiction author may describe a scientific topic using humor and wacky examples to make it fun for popular audiences to read.

Also, expository writing can look similar to persuasive writing, especially when it touches on topics that are controversial or emotional. For example, if an essay says social media is changing society, many readers assume it means social media is changing society *in a negative way*. If the writing makes this kind of value judgment or uses words like *should,* it is persuasive writing. But if the author is merely describing changes, the text is expository.

Text Structures

Authors rarely present ideas within a text in a random order. Instead, they organize their thoughts carefully. To read effectively, you must be able to recognize the **structure** of a text. That is, you need to identify the strategies authors use to organize their ideas. The five most common text structures are listed below.

Text Structure	Examples
In a **sequence** text, an author explains what happened first, second, third, and so on. In other words, a sequence text is arranged in **chronological order**, or time order. This type of text may describe events that have already happened or events that may happen in the future.	• A story about a birthday party. • A historical paper about World War II. • A list of instructions for baking a cake. • A series of proposed steps in a plan for business expansion.
A **compare/contrast** text explains the similarities and differences between two or more subjects. Authors may compare and contrast people, places, ideas, events, cultures, and so on.	• An essay describing the similarities and differences between women's experiences in medieval Europe and Asia. • A section in an op-ed newspaper article explaining the similarities and differences between two types of gun control.
A **cause/effect** text describes an event or action and its results. The causes and effects discussed can be actual or theoretical. That is, the author can describe the results of a historical event or predict the results of a possible future event.	• An explanation of ocean acidification and the coral bleaching that results. • A paper describing a proposed new law and its likely effects on the economy.
A **problem-solution** text presents a problem and outlines a solution. Sometimes it also predicts or analyzes the results of the solution. The solution can be something that already happened or a plan the author is proposing. Note that a problem can sometimes be expressed in terms of a wish or desire that the solution fulfills.	• An explanation of the problems smallpox caused and the strategies scientists used to eradicate it. • A business plan outlining a group of potential customers and the strategy a company should use to get their business.

Text Structure	Examples
A **description** text creates a mental picture for the reader by presenting concrete details in a coherent order. Description texts are usually arranged spatially. For instance, authors may describe the subject from top to bottom, or they may describe the inside first and then the outside, etc.	• An explanation of the appearance of a character in a story. • A paragraph in a field guide detailing the features of a bird. • A section on an instruction sheet describing how the final product should look.

CONNECTIONS

Different types of texts can use the same structures.

1. A story about a birthday party is a narrative, and its purpose is to entertain.
2. A historical paper about a war is an expository text meant to inform.
3. A list of instructions for baking a cake is a technical text meant to inform.
4. A series of proposed steps in a plan for business expansion is a persuasive text meant to persuade.

If all of these texts list ideas in chronological order, explaining what happened (or what may happen in the future) first, second, third, and so on, they are all using a sequence structure.

Genre and Theme

Literature can be organized into categories called **genres**. The two major genres of literature are fiction and nonfiction.

Fiction is made up. It can be broken down into many sub-genres, or sub-categories. The following are some of the common ones:

- Short story – Short work of fiction.
- Novel – Book-length work of fiction.
- Science fiction – A story set in the future
- Romance – A love story
- Mystery – A story that answers a concrete question, often about who committed a crime
- Mythology – A traditional story that reflects cultural traditions and beliefs but does not usually teach an explicit lesson
- Legends – Traditional stories that are presented as histories, even though they often contain fantastical or magical elements
- Fables – Traditional stories meant to teach an explicit lesson

COMPARE!

The differences between myths and fables are sometimes hard to discern.

Myths are often somewhat religious in nature. For instance, stories about Ancient Greek gods and goddesses are myths. These stories reflect cultural beliefs, for example by showing characters being punished for failing to please their gods. But the lesson is implicit. These stories do not usually end with a moral lesson that says to readers, "Do not displease the gods!"

Fables are often for children, and they usually end with a sentence stating an explicit moral. For example, there's a story called "The Tortoise and the Hare," in which a tortoise and a hare agree to have a race. The hare, being a fast animal, gets cocky and takes a lot of breaks while the tortoise plods slowly toward the finish line without stopping. Because the tortoise keeps going, it eventually wins. The story usually ends with the moral, "Slow and steady win the race."

Nonfiction is true. Like fiction, it can be broken down into many sub-genres. The following are some of the common ones:

- Autobiography and memoir – The author's own life story
- Biography – Someone else's life story (not the author's)
- Histories – True stories about real events from the past
- Criticism and reviews – A response or judgment on another piece of writing or art
- Essay – A short piece describing the author's outlook or point of view.

CONNECTIONS

Everything under "Fiction" and several items under "Nonfiction" above are examples of narrative writing. We use labels like "narrative" and "persuasive" largely when we discuss writing tasks or the author's purpose. We could use these labels here too, but at the moment we're more concerned with the words that are most commonly used in discussions about literature's deeper meanings.

Literature reflects the human experience. Texts from different genres often share similar **themes**, or deeper meanings. Texts from different cultures do too. For example, a biography of a famous civil rights activist may highlight the same qualities of heroism and interconnectedness that appear in a work of mythology from Ancient India. Other common themes in literature may relate to war, love, survival, justice, suffering, growing up, and other experiences that are accessible to virtually all human beings.

Many students confuse the term *theme* with the term *moral*. A **moral** is an explicit message contained in the text, like "Don't lie" or "Crime doesn't pay." Morals are a common feature of fables and other traditional stories meant to teach lessons to children. Themes, in contrast, are implicit. Readers must consider the clues in the story and figure out themes for themselves. Because of this, themes are debatable. For testing purposes, questions focus on themes that are clearly and consistently indicated by clues within the text.

Let's Review!

- Written texts can be organized into the following categories: narrative, expository, technical, and persuasive.
- Texts of all categories may use the following organizational schemes or structures: sequence, compare/contrast, cause/effect, problem-solution, description.
- Literature can be organized into genres including fiction, nonfiction, and many sub-genres.
- Literature across genres and cultures often reflects the same deeper meanings, or themes.

KEEP IN MIND . . .

The text structures above do not always work in isolation. Authors often combine two or more structures within one text. For example, a business plan could be arranged in a problem-solution structure as the author describes what the business wants to achieve and how she proposes to achieve it. The "how" portion could also use a sequence structure as the author lists the steps to follow first, second, third, and so on.

Chapter 3 Integration of Knowledge and Ideas
Practice Quiz 1

1. Which of the following is *not* a function of text features?

   A. Introducing the topic

   B. Emphasizing a concept

   C. Making the theme explicit

   D. Providing peripheral information

2. If a map does not have a compass, north is:

   A. up.   C. right.

   B. down.   D. left.

3. The purpose of an index is to tell readers:

   A. how to find sources that back up key ideas in the text.

   B. who wrote the text and what his or her credentials are.

   C. where to find information on a given subject within a book.

   D. why the author believes the main idea of a text is important.

Read the following passage and answer questions 4-5.

Overworked public school teachers are required by law to spend extra time implementing

Individual Educational Plans for students with learning and attention challenges. This shortchanges children who are actually engaged in their education by depriving them of an equal amount of individualized attention.

4. What assumption behind this passage reflects negative stereotypical thinking?

   A. Public school teachers are generally overworked and underpaid.

   B. Students with learning disabilities are not engaged in their education.

   C. Laws require teachers to provide accommodations to certain students.

   D. Teachers have a finite amount of attention to divide between students.

5. The above argument is invalid because the author:

   A. suggests that some students do not need as much attention because they learn the material more quickly.

   B. uses derogatory and disrespectful word choice to describe people who think, learn, and process information differently.

   C. describes public school teachers in a negative way that makes it seem as though they have no interest in helping students.

   D. professes an interest in equality for all students while simultaneously suggesting some students are more worthy than others.

6. Which statement, if true, is a fact?

    A. The 1918 flu pandemic killed more people than World War I.

    B. The 1918 flu pandemic was more devastating than World War I.

    C. The 1918 flu pandemic was a terrifying display of nature's power.

    D. The 1918 flu pandemic caused greater social instability than the plague.

Read the following passage and answer questions 7-9.

There is inherent risk associated with the use of Rip Gym facilities. Although all Rip Gym customers sign a Risk Acknowledgment and Consent Form before gaining access to our grounds and equipment, litigation remains a possibility if customers suffer injuries due to negligence. Negligence complaints may include either staff mistakes or avoidable problems with equipment and facilities. It is therefore imperative that all Rip Gym employees follow the Safety Protocol in the event of a customer complaint.

Reports of Unsafe Equipment and Environs

Rip Gym employees must always respond promptly and seriously to any customer report of a hazard in our equipment or facilities, even if the employee judges the complaint frivolous. **Customers may not use rooms or equipment that have been reported unsafe until the following steps** have been taken, in order, to confirm and/or resolve the problem.

1. Place "Warning," "Out of Order," or "Off Limits" signs in the affected area or on the affected equipment, as appropriate. **Always follow this step first, before handling paperwork or attempting to resolve the reported problem.**

2. Fill out a Hazard Complaint Form. Include the name of the customer making the complaint and the exact wording of the problems being reported.

3. Visually check the area or equipment in question to verify the problem.

    a) If the report appears to be **accurate** and a resolution is necessary, proceed to step 4.

    b) If the report appears to be **inaccurate**, consult the manager on duty.

4. Determine whether you are qualified to correct the problem. Problems **all** employees are qualified to correct are listed on page 12 of the Employee Handbook.

    a) Employees who have **not** undergone training for equipment repair and maintenance must....

7. This passage is best described as a(n):

    A. narrative text.

    B. technical text.

    C. expository text.

    D. persuasive text.

8. Which term best describes the structure of the opening paragraph?

    A. Sequence

    B. Description

    C. Problem-solution

    D. Compare/Contrast

9. Which term best describes the structure of the section under the subheading "Reports of Unsafe Equipment and Environs"?

    A. Sequence

    B. Description

    C. Cause/effect

    D. Compare/contrast

CHAPTER 3 INTEGRATION OF KNOWLEDGE AND IDEAS
PRACTICE QUIZ 1 – ANSWER KEY

1. **C.** Although the title of a fictional work may hint at a theme, a theme is a message that is, by definition, not stated explicitly. **See Lesson: Evaluating and Integrating Data.**

2. **A.** By convention, north on a map is up. Mapmakers include a compass if they break this convention for some reason. **See Lesson: Evaluating and Integrating Data.**

3. **C.** An index lists subtopics of a book along with page numbers where those topics will be covered. **See Lesson: Evaluating and Integrating Data.**

4. **B.** The writer of this passage suggests implicitly that only students without learning and attention challenges are engaged in their education. This assumption reflects a negative stereotype that renders the entire argument faulty. **See Lesson: Facts, Opinions, and Evaluating an Argument.**

5. **B.** The author of the passage uses the phrase "students with learning and attention challenges" to refer to students who think and learn differently. This is not derogatory, but even so, the passage implies that people who experience these differences are less engaged in their education. **See Lesson: Facts, Opinions, and Evaluating an Argument.**

6. **A.** All of these statements contain beliefs or feelings that are subject to interpretation except the statement about the number of people killed in the 1918 flu pandemic compared to World War I. This is a verifiable piece of information, or a fact. **See Lesson: Facts, Opinions, and Evaluating an Argument.**

7. **B.** This is a technical text written to inform the reader about a complex process. **See Lesson: Types of Passages, Text Structures, Genre and Theme.**

8. **C.** The opening paragraph has a problem-solution structure. The problem it describes involves risks of injury and litigation, and the solution is that employees follow a process designed to minimize those risks. **See Lesson: Types of Passages, Text Structures, Genre and Theme.**

9. **A.** The step-by-step instructions under the subheading follow a sequential structure. Note key words and phrases such as "first" and "in order." **See Lesson: Types of Passages, Text Structures, Genre and Theme.**

Chapter 3 Integration of Knowledge and Ideas
Practice Quiz 2

1. **What is a bias?**

    A. A preconceived and sometimes unfair belief

    B. A person or group that often faces prejudice

    C. An unstated idea that underlies an argument

    D. A sweeping statement that may not always be true

2. **Which statement is an opinion?**

    A. Freshman Anita Jones states that excessive homework requirements cause her undue stress.

    B. Students reported symptoms such as headaches, anxiety attacks, and difficulty sleeping.

    C. Excessive homework requirements causes students undue stress and harm their quality of life.

    D. Students who do homework more than three hours per day show elevated cortisol levels compared to students who do no homework.

3. **Which statement, if true, is a fact?**

    A. The 2018 London New Year's Day Parade had more spectators than the 2018 NFL Super Bowl.

    B. The 2018 London New Year's Day Parade was more exciting than the 2018 NFL Super Bowl.

    C. The 2018 London New Year's Day Parade was a fantastic display of award-winning marching bands, creatively designed parade floats, and international celebrities.

    D. The 2018 London New Year's Day Parade caused greater joy and entertainment than the 2018 NFL Super Bowl.

4. **On a chart, horizontal lines are called _____, whereas vertical lines are called _____.**

    A. keys, rows

    B. legends, keys

    C. rows, columns

    D. columns, legends

5. **Which of the following is not a formatting feature?**

    A. Italics   C. Boldfacing

    B. Charts   D. Underlining

6. **What do footnotes do?**

    A. Show the reader how ideas are organized

    B. Illustrate ideas that cannot clearly be stated in words

    C. Provide source information and peripheral information

    D. Provide nutrition facts about the contents of a package

Read the following text and answer questions 7-9.

When my mother was a teenager, most kids didn't have cell phones. If she wanted to talk to her friends after school, she had to call their landline. Sometimes a friend's mom or dad answered, and she had to ask to talk to their kid. She says that was awkward. Also, if she and a friend talked on the phone for a long time, the whole family's phone line was busy, so nobody else could get calls. Parents got mad at kids for tying up the phone too long.

Today, every kid I know has a smartphone. We talk and text whenever we want, and none of us ever have awkward conversations with our friends' parents. But in some ways, parents today have more control. A lot of parents check kids' phone records and read their texts, so they can tell if their kids are up to no good. Families don't all rely on one phone line, so when kids talk for a long time, we don't prevent anyone else in the family from communicating with their friends. But parents today still get mad—

mainly because kids' phone habits cost too much money.

7. **What category of writing is this?**

    A. Narrative   C. Expository

    B. Technical   D. Persuasive

8. **The structure of the passage is:**

    A. description.

    B. cause/effect.

    C. problem-solution.

    D. compare/contrast.

9. **What is the genre of the passage?**

    A. Essay

    B. Criticism

    C. Biography

    D. Autobiography

CHAPTER 3 INTEGRATION OF KNOWLEDGE AND IDEAS
PRACTICE QUIZ 2 – ANSWER KEY

1. A. Biases may be stated or unstated, and they are not necessarily sweeping. They are preconceived and sometimes unfair ideas about the world. **See Lesson: Facts, Opinions, and Evaluating an Argument.**

2. C. Words like "excessive" and "undue" are subject to interpretation and reflect beliefs rather than verifiable facts. However, words like these may appear in factual statements about what people said they felt or believed. **See Lesson: Facts, Opinions, and Evaluating an Argument.**

3. A. All of these statements contain beliefs or feelings that are subject to interpretation except the statement about the number of people attending the 2018 London New Year's Day Parade compared to the 2018 NFL Super Bowl. This is a verifiable piece of information, or a fact. **See Lesson: Facts, Opinions, and Evaluating an Argument.**

4. C. Horizontal lines on a chart are called rows, and vertical lines are called legends. Using this terminology, it is possible to describe the spaces on the chart (e.g. "What is the value in the fourth column of the second row?") **See Lesson: Evaluating and Integrating Data.**

5. B. Formatting features make text stand out in a title or within a paragraph. Charts are graphic elements that present data or illustrate information. **See Lesson: Evaluating and Integrating Data.**

6. C. Footnotes may provide information about source materials or give the reader interesting information that is not essential to the main point. **See Lesson: Evaluating and Integrating Data.**

7. C. This passage is an explanation of phone habits in two eras. Although it uses a few time words, it does not describe narrative scenes. It is an expository piece. **See Lesson: Types of Passages, Text Structures, Genre and Theme.**

8. D. The passage describes phone use in two eras, highlighting similarities and differences. This makes it a compare/contrast piece. **See Lesson: Types of Passages, Text Structures, Genre and Theme.**

9. A. This piece describes parts of both the author's life and another person's life, but it is not an autobiography or biography because it is not telling a story of either one. Rather, it is an essay— short description of a subject from the author's point of view. **See Lesson: Types of Passages, Text Structures, Genre and Theme.**

SECTION II. WRITING AND LANGUAGE

CHAPTER 4 CONVENTIONS OF STANDARD ENGLISH

SPELLING

Spelling correctly is important to accurately convey thoughts to an audience. This lesson will cover (1) vowels and consonants, (2) suffixes and plurals, (3) homophones and homographs.

Vowels and Consonants

Vowels and **consonants** are different speech sounds in English.

The letters A, E, I, O, U and sometimes Y are **vowels** and can create a variety of sounds. The most common are short sounds and long sounds. Long **vowel** sounds sound like the name of the letter such as the *a* in late. Short **vowel** sounds have a unique sound such as the *a* in cat. A rule for **vowels** is that when two vowels are walking, the first does the talking as in pain and meat.

Consonants include the other twenty-one letters in the alphabet. **Consonants** are weak letters and only make sounds when paired with **vowels**. That is why words always must have a **vowel**. This also means that **consonants** need to be doubled to make a stronger sound like sitting, grabbed, progress. Understanding general trends and patterns for **vowels** and **consonants** will help with spelling. The table below represents the difference between short and long **vowels** and gives examples for each.

	Symbol	Example Words
Short a	a	Cat, mat, hat, pat
Long a	ā	Late, pain, pay, they, weight, straight
Short e	e	Met, said, bread
Long e	ē	Breeze, cheap, dean, equal
Short i	i	Bit, myth, kiss, rip
Long i	ī	Cry, pie, high
Short o	o	Dog, hot, pop
Long o	ō	Snow, nose, elbow
Short u	u	Run, cut, club, gum
Long u	ū	Duty, rule, new, food
Short oo	oo	Book, foot, cookie
Long oo	ōō	Mood, bloom, shoot

Suffixes and Plurals

A **suffix** is a word part that is added to the ending of a root word. A **suffix** changes the meaning and spelling of words. There are some general patterns to follow with **suffixes**.

- Adding -er, -ist, or -or changes the root to mean *doer* or *performer*

  - Paint → Painter
  - Abolition → Abolitionist
  - Act → Actor

- Adding -ation or -ment changes the root to mean *an action* or *a process*

  - Ador(e) → Adoration
  - Develop → Development

- Adding -ism changes the root to mean *a theory or ideology*

  - Real → Realism

- Adding -ity, -ness, -ship, or -tude changes the root to mean *a condition, quality, or state*

  - Real → Reality
  - Sad → Sadness
  - Relation → Relationship
  - Soli(tary) → Solitude

Plurals are similar to suffixes as letters are added to the end of the word to signify more than one person, place, thing, or idea. There are also general patterns to follow when creating **plurals**.

- If a word ends in -s,-ss,-z,-zz,-ch, or -sh, add -es.

  - Bus → Buses

- If a word ends in a -y, drop the -y and add -ies.

  - Pony → Ponies

- If a word ends in an -f, change the f to a v and add -es.

  - Knife → Knives

- For all other words, add an -s.

  - Dog → Dogs

Homophones and Homographs

A **homophone** is a word that has the same sound as another word, but does not have the same meaning or spelling.

- To, too, and two
- There, their, and they're
- See and sea

A **homograph** is a word that has the same spelling as another word, but does not have the same sound or meaning.

- Lead (to go in front of) and lead (a metal)
- Bass (deep sound) and bass (a fish)

Let's Review!

- Vowels include the letters A, E, I, O, U and sometimes Y and have both short and long sounds.
- Consonants are the other twenty-one letters and have weak sounds. They are often doubled to make stronger sounds.
- Suffixes are word parts added to the root of a word and change the meaning and spelling.
- To make a word plural, add -es, -ies, -ves, or -s to the end of a word.
- Homophones are words that have the same sound, but not the same meaning or spelling.
- Homographs are words that have the same spelling, but not the same meaning or sound.

CAPITALIZATION

Correct capitalization helps readers understand when a new sentence begins and the importance of specific words. This lesson will cover the capitalization rules of (1) geographic locations and event names, (2) organizations and publication titles, (3) individual names and professional titles, and (4) months, days, and holidays.

Geographic Locations and Event Names

North, east, south, and west are not capitalized unless they relate to a **definite region**.

- Go north on I-5 for 200 miles.
- The West Coast has nice weather.

Words like northern, southern, eastern, and western are also not capitalized unless they describe **people or the cultural and political activities of people**.

- There is nothing interesting to see in eastern Colorado.
- Midwesterners are known for being extremely nice.
- The Western states almost always vote Democratic.

These words are not capitalized when placed before a name or region unless it is part of the **official name**.

- She lives in southern California.
- I loved visiting Northern Ireland.

Continents, countries, states, cities, and **towns** need to be capitalized.

- Australia has a lot of scary animals.
- Not many people live in Antarctica.
- Albany is the capital of New York.

Historical events should be capitalized to separate the specific from the general.

- The bubonic plague in the Middle Ages killed a large portion of the population in Europe.
- The Great Depression took place in the early 1930s.
- We are living in the twenty-first century.

Organizations and Publication Titles

The **names of national organizations** need to be capitalized. Short prepositions, articles, and conjunctions within the title are not capitalized unless they are the first word.

- The National American Woman Suffrage Association was essential in passing the Nineteenth Amendment.
- The House of Representatives is one part of Congress.

- Most kids' favorite holiday is Christmas.
- The new school year usually starts after Labor Day.
- It is nice to go to the beach over Memorial Day weekend.

The **seasons** are not capitalized.

- It gets too hot in the summer and too cold in the winter.
- The flowers and trees bloom so beautifully in the spring.

Let's Review!

- Only capitalize directional words like north, south, east, and, west when they describe a definite region, people, and their political and cultural activities, or when it is part of the official name.
- Historical periods and events are capitalized to represent their importance and specificity.
- Every word except short prepositions, conjunctions, and articles in the names of national organizations are capitalized.
- The titles of publications follow the same rules as organizations.
- The names of individual people need to be capitalized.
- Professional titles are capitalized if they precede a name or are used as a direct address.
- All months of the year, days of the week, and holidays are capitalized.
- Seasons are not capitalized.

- The National Football League consists of thirty-two teams.

The **titles of books, chapters, articles, poems, newspapers, and other publications** should be capitalized.

- Her favorite book is *A Wrinkle in Time*.
- I do the crossword in *The New York Times* every Sunday.
- *The Jabberwocky* by Lewis Carroll has many silly sounding words.

Individual Names and Professional Titles

People's names as well as their **familial relationship title** need to be capitalized.

- Barack Obama was our first African American president.
- Uncle Joe brought the steaks for our Memorial Day grill.
- Aunt Sarah lives in California, but my other aunt lives in Florida.

Professional titles need to be capitalized when they precede a name, or as a direct address. If it is after a name or is used generally, titles do not need to be capitalized.

- Governor Cuomo is trying to modernize the subway system in New York.
- Andrew Cuomo is the governor of New York.
- A governor runs the state. A president runs the country.
- Thank you for the recommendation, Mr. President.
- I need to see Doctor Smith.
- I need to see a doctor.

Capitalize the **title of high-ranking government officials** when an individual is referred to.

- The Secretary of State travels all over the world.
- The Vice President joined the meeting.

With **compound titles**, the prefixes or suffixes do not need to be capitalized.

- George W. Bush is the ex-President of the United States.

Months, Days, and Holidays

Capitalize **all months of the year** (January, February, March, April, May, June, July, August, September, October, November, December) and **days of the week** (Sunday, Monday, Tuesday, Wednesday, Thursday, Friday, Saturday).

- Her birthday is in November.
- People graduate from college in May or June.
- Saturdays and Sundays are supposed to be fun and relaxing.

Holidays are also capitalized.

PUNCTUATION

Punctuation is important in writing to accurately represent ideas. Without correct punctuation, the meaning of a sentence is difficult to understand. This lesson will cover (1) periods, question marks, and exclamation points, (2) commas, semicolons, and colons, and (3) apostrophes, hyphens, and quotation marks.

Terminal Punctuation Marks: Periods, Question Marks, and Exclamation Points

Terminal punctuation is used at the end of a sentence. Periods, question marks, and exclamation points are the three types of terminal punctuation.

Periods (.) mark the end of a declarative sentence, one that states a fact, or an imperative sentence, one that states a command or request). Periods can also be used in abbreviations.

- Doctors save lives.
- She has a B.A. in Psychology.

Question Marks (?) signify the end of a sentence that is a question. Where, when, who, whom, what, why, and how are common words that begin question sentences.

- Who is he?
- Why is the sky blue?
- Where is the restaurant?

Exclamation Points (!) indicate strong feelings, shouting, or emphasize a feeling.

- Watch out!
- I hate you!
- That is incredible!

Internal Punctuation: Commas, Semicolons, and Colons

Internal punctuation is used within a sentence to help keep words, phrases, and clauses in order. These punctuation marks can be used to indicate elements such as direct quotations and definitions in a sentence.

A **comma (,)** signifies a small break within a sentence and separates words, clauses, or ideas.

Commas are used before conjunctions that connect two independent clauses.

- I ate some cookies, and I drank some milk.

Commas are also used to set off an introductory phrase.

- After the test, she grabbed dinner with a friend.

Short phrases that emphasis thoughts or emotions are enclosed by **commas**.

- The school year, thankfully, ends in a week.

Commas set off the words yes and no.

- Yes, I am available this weekend.
- No, she has not finished her homework.

Commas set off a question tag.

- It is beautiful outside, isn't it?

Commas are used to indicate direct address.

- Are you ready, Jack?
- Mom, what is for dinner?

Commas separate items in a series.

- We ate eggs, potatoes, and toast for breakfast.
- I need to grab coffee, go to the store, and put gas in my car.

Semicolons (;) are used to connect two independent clauses without a coordinating conjunction like *and* or *but*. A **semicolon** creates a bond between two sentences that are related. Do not capitalize the first word after the **semicolon** unless it is a word that is normally capitalized.

- The ice cream man drove down my street; I bought a popsicle.
- My mom cooked dinner; the chicken was delicious.
- It is cloudy today; it will probably rain.

Colons (:) introduce a list.

- She teaches three subjects: English, history, and geography.

Within a sentence, **colons** can create emphasis of a word or phrase.

- She had one goal: pay the bills.

More Internal Punctuation: Apostrophes, Hyphens, and Quotation Marks

Apostrophes (') are used to indicate possession or to create a contraction.

- Bob has a car - Bob's car is blue.
- Steve's cat is beautiful.

For plurals that are also possessive, put the **apostrophe** after the s.

- Soldiers' uniforms are impressive.

Make contractions by combining two words.

- I do not have a dog - I don't have a dog
- I can't swim.

Its and it's do not follow the normal possessive rules. Its is possessive while it's means "it is."

- It's a beautiful day to be at the park.
- The dog has many toys, but its favorite is the rope.

Hyphens (-) are mainly used to create compound words.

- The documentary was a real eye-opener for me.
- We have to check-in to the hotel before midnight.
- The graduate is a twenty-two-year-old woman.

Quotation Marks (") are used when directly using another person's words in your own writing. Commas and periods, sometimes question marks and exclamation points, are placed within **quotation marks**. Colons and semicolons are placed outside of the **quotation marks**, unless they are part of the quoted material. If quoting an entire sentence, capitalize the first word. If it is a fragment, do not capitalize the first word.

- Ernest Hemingway once claimed, "There is nothing noble in being superior to your fellow man; true nobility is being superior to your former self."
- Steve said, "I will be there at noon."

An indirect quote which paraphrases what someone else said does not need **quotation marks**.

- Steve said he would be there at noon.

Quotation marks are also used for the titles of short works such as poems, articles, and chapters. They are not italicized.

- Robert Frost wrote "The Road Not Taken."

Let's Review!

- **Periods (.)** signify the end of a sentence or are used in abbreviations.
- **Question Marks (?)** are also used at the end of a sentence and distinguish the sentence as a question.
- **Exclamation Points (!)** indicate strong feelings, shouting, or emphasis and are usually at the end of the sentence.
- **Commas (,)** are small breaks within a sentence that separate clauses, ideas, or words. They are used to set off introductory phrases, the words yes and no, question tags, indicate direct address, and separate items in a series.
- **Semicolons (;)** connect two similar sentences without a coordinating conjunctions such as and or but.
- **Colons (:)** are used to introduce a list or emphasize a word or phrase.
- **Apostrophes (')** indicate possession or a contraction of two words.
- **Hyphens (-)** are used to create compound words.
- **Quotation Marks (")** are used when directly quoting someone else's words and to indicate the title of poems, chapters, and articles.

CHAPTER 4 CONVENTIONS OF STANDARD ENGLISH
PRACTICE QUIZ 1

1. Which word(s) in the following sentence should NOT be capitalized?

   Can You Speak German?

   A. You and Speak

   B. Can and German

   C. Can, You, and Speak

   D. You, Speak, and German

2. Fill in the blank with the correctly capitalized form.

   Every week, they get together to watch _____.

   A. the bachelor   C. The bachelor

   B. The Bachelor   D. the Bachelor

3. Choose the correct sentence.

   A. They used to live in the pacific northwest.

   B. They used to live in the Pacific northwest.

   C. They used to live in the pacific Northwest.

   D. They used to live in the Pacific Northwest.

4. What is the sentence with the correct use of punctuation?

   A. Offcampus apartments are nicer.

   B. Off campus apartments are nicer.

   C. Off-campus apartments are nicer.

   D. Off-campus-apartments are nicer.

5. Which of the following sentences is correct?

   A. I asked Scott, How was your day?

   B. Scott said, it was awesome.

   C. He claimed, "My history presentation was great!"

   D. I said, That's wonderful!

6. What is the mistake in the following sentence?

   The highestranking officer can choose his own work, including his own hours.

   A. *Highestranking* needs a hyphen.

   B. There should be a comma after *officer*.

   C. There should be no comma after *work*.

   D. There should be a semicolon after *work*.

7. Which of the following spellings is correct?

   A. Busines   C. Buseness

   B. Business   D. Bussiness

8. What is the correct plural of morning?

   A. Morning   C. Morninges

   B. Mornings   D. Morningies

9. On Earth, _____ are seven continents.

   A. their   C. theer

   B. there   D. they're

CHAPTER 4 CONVENTIONS OF STANDARD ENGLISH
PRACTICE QUIZ 1 – ANSWER KEY

1. **A.** *You and Speak.* Can is the first word in the sentence and needs to be capitalized. German is a nationality and needs to be capitalized. The other two words do not need to be capitalized. **See Lesson: Capitalization.**

2. **B.** *The Bachelor.* The names of TV shows are capitalized. *The* is capitalized here because it is the first word in the name. **See Lesson: Capitalization.**

3. **D.** *They used to live in the Pacific Northwest.* Specific geographic regions are capitalized. **See Lesson: Capitalization.**

4. **C.** *Off-campus apartments are nicer.* Hyphens are often used for compound words that are placed before the noun to help with understanding. **See Lesson: Punctuation.**

5. **C.** *He claimed, "My history presentation was great!"* Quotation marks enclose direct statements. **See Lesson: Punctuation.**

6. **A.** *Highestranking needs a hyphen.* Hyphens are used for compound words that describe a person or object. **See Lesson: Punctuation.**

7. **B.** *Business* is the only correct spelling. **See Lesson: Spelling.**

8. **B.** For most words ending in consonants, just add -s. **See Lesson: Spelling.**

9. **B.** *There* describes a place or position and is correctly spelled. **See Lesson: Spelling.**

CHAPTER 4 CONVENTIONS OF STANDARD ENGLISH
PRACTICE QUIZ 2

1. **What is the correct plural of bush?**

    A. Bush   C. Bushes

    B. Bushs   D. Bushies

2. **Subjects ____ to their king to show respect.**

    A. bow   C. baw

    B. bou   D. beau

3. **We saw a _____ in the woods while hiking.**

    A. bair   C. bare

    B. baer   D. bear

4. **Which of the following is correct?**

    A. May   C. easter

    B. Spring   D. sunday

5. **Fill in the blank with the correctly capitalized form.**

    My favorite book in the Harry Potter series is _____.

    A. *harry potter and the prisoner of azkaban*

    B. *Harry Potter and the prisoner of azkaban*

    C. *Harry Potter And The Prisoner Of Azkaban*

    D. *Harry Potter and the Prisoner of Azkaban*

6. **Which of the following is correct?**

    A. Rome, Italy   C. rome, italy

    B. rome, Italy   D. Rome, italy

7. **What is the sentence with the correct use of punctuation?**

    A. Who is he.   C. Who is he?

    B. Who is he: D. Who is he!

8. **What is the correct use of a period in the following sentence?**

    A. She had a bad day

    B. She had a bad day.

    C. She had. a bad day.

    D. She. Had. A. bad. Day.

9. **What is missing from the following sentence?**

    He asked, When is the assignment due?

    A. There should be quotation marks.

    B. There needs to be a semicolon after asked.

    C. There should be a comma after assignment.

    D. Nothing is missing.

Chapter 4 Conventions of Standard English
Practice Quiz 2 – Answer Key

1. C. With a word ending in -sh, add -es. **See Lesson: Spelling.**

2. A. People *bow*, or bend down, to show respect. **See Lesson: Spelling.**

3. D. *Bear* is the correctly spelled form of the animal. **See Lesson: Spelling.**

4. A. May. Months, days, and holidays need to be capitalized, and seasons do not need to be. **See Lesson: Capitalization.**

5. D. Harry Potter and the Prisoner of Azkaban. Short prepositions, conjunctions, and articles are not capitalized in publication titles. **See Lesson: Capitalization.**

6. A. Rome, Italy. Cities and countries are capitalized. **See Lesson: Capitalization.**

7. C. *Who is he?* Who is a common word that begins a question, and the question mark is placed at the end of a question. **See Lesson: Punctuation.**

8. B. *She had a bad day.* A period is only used at the end of a sentence, and not anywhere in between. **See Lesson: Punctuation.**

9. A. *There should be quotation marks.* Direct quotes from someone else should be enclosed in quotation marks. **See Lesson: Punctuation.**

CHAPTER 5 PARTS OF SPEECH

NOUNS

In this lesson, you will learn about nouns. A noun is a word that names a person, place, thing, or idea. This lesson will cover (1) the role of nouns in sentences and (2) different types of nouns.

Nouns and Their Role in Sentences

A **noun** names a person, place, thing, or idea.

Some examples of nouns are:

- Gandhi
- New Hampshire
- garden
- happiness

A noun's role in a sentence is as **subject** or **object**. A subject is the part of the sentence that does something, whereas the object is the thing that something is done to. In simple terms, the subject acts, and the object is acted upon.

Look for the nouns in these sentences.

1. The Louvre is stunning. (subject noun: The Louvre)
2. Marco ate dinner with Sara and Petra. (subject noun: Marco; object nouns: dinner, Sara, Petra)
3. Honesty is the best policy. (subject noun: honesty; object noun: policy)
4. After the election, we celebrated our new governor. (object nouns: governor, election)
5. I slept. (0 nouns)

KEEP IN MIND . . .
The subjects *I* and *we* in the two sentences to the left are pronouns, not nouns.

Look for the nouns in these sentences.

1. Mrs. Garcia makes a great pumpkin pie. (subject noun: Mrs. Garcia; object noun: pie)
2. We really need to water the garden. (object noun: garden)
3. Love is sweet. (subject noun: love)
4. Sam loves New York in the springtime. (subject noun: Sam; object nouns: New York, springtime)
5. Lin and her mother and father ate soup, fish, potatoes, and fruit for dinner. (subject nouns: Lin, mother, father; object nouns: soup, fish, potatoes, fruit, dinner)

Why isn't the word *pumpkin* a noun in the first sentence? *Pumpkin* is often a noun, but here it is used as an adjective that describes what kind of *pie*.

Why isn't the word *water* a noun in the second sentence? Here, *water* is an **action verb**. To *water the garden* is something we do.

How is the word *love* a noun in the third sentence and not in the fourth sentence? *Love* is a noun (thing) in sentence 3 and a verb (action) in the sentence 4.

> **BE CAREFUL!**
> Words can change to serve different roles in different sentences. A word that is usually a noun can sometimes be used as an adjective or a verb. Determine a word's function in a sentence to be sure of its part of speech.

How many nouns can a sentence contain? As long as the sentence remains grammatically correct, it can contain an unlimited number of nouns.

Types of Nouns

Singular and Plural Nouns

Nouns can be **singular** or **plural**. A noun is singular when there is only one. A noun is plural when there are two or more.

- The book has 650 pages.

Book is a singular noun. *Pages* is a plural noun.

Often, to make a noun plural, we add *-s* at the end of the word: *cat/cats*. This is a **regular** plural noun. Sometimes we make a word plural in another way: *child/children*. This is an **irregular** plural noun. Some plurals follow rules, while others do not. The most common rules are listed here:

> **KEEP IN MIND . . .**
> **Some nouns are countable,** and others are not. For example, we eat *three blueberries*, but we **do not** drink *three milks*. Instead, we drink *three glasses of milk* or *some milk*.

Singular noun	Plural noun	Rule for making plural
star	stars	for most words, add *-s*
box	boxes	for words that end in *-j*, *-s*, *-x*, *-z*, *-ch* or *-sh*, add *-es*
baby	babies	for words that end in *-y*, change *-y* to *-i* and add *-es*
woman	women	irregular
foot	feet	irregular

Common and Proper Nouns

Common nouns are general words, and they are written in lowercase. **Proper nouns** are specific names, and they begin with an uppercase letter.

Examples:

Common noun	Proper noun
ocean	Baltic Sea
dentist	Dr. Marx
company	Honda
park	Yosemite National Park

Concrete and Abstract Nouns

Concrete nouns are people, places, or things that physically exist. We can use our senses to see or hear them. *Turtle*, *spreadsheet*, and *Australia* are concrete nouns.

Abstract nouns are ideas, qualities, or feelings that we cannot see and that might be harder to describe. *Beauty, childhood, energy, envy, generosity, happiness, patience, pride, trust, truth*, and *victory* are abstract nouns.

Some words can be either concrete or abstract nouns. For example, the concept of *art* is abstract, but *art* that we see and touch is concrete.

- We talked about *art*. (abstract)
- She showed me the *art* she had created in class. (concrete)

Let's Review!

- A noun is a person, place, thing, or idea.
- A noun's function in a sentence is as subject or object.
- Common nouns are general words, while proper nouns are specific names.
- Nouns can be concrete or abstract.

PRONOUNS

A pronoun is a word that takes the place of or refers to a specific noun. This lesson will cover (1) the role of pronouns in sentences and (2) the purpose of pronouns.

Pronouns and Their Role in Sentences

A **pronoun** takes the place of a noun or refers to a specific noun.

Subject, Object, and Possessive Pronouns

A pronoun's role in a sentence is as **subject, object,** or **possessive**.

Subject Pronouns	Object Pronouns	Possessive Pronouns
I	me	my, mine
you	you	your, yours
he	her	his
she	him	her, hers
it	it	its
we	us	ours
they	them	their, theirs

In simple sentences, subject pronouns come before the verb, object pronouns come after the verb, and possessive pronouns show ownership.

Look at the pronouns in these examples:

BE CAREFUL!

It is easy to make a mistake when you have multiple words in the role of subject or object.

- <u>She</u> forgot <u>her</u> coat. (subject: she; possessive: her)
- <u>I</u> lent <u>her</u> <u>mine</u>. (subject: I; object: her; possessive: mine)
- <u>She</u> left <u>it</u> at school. (subject: she; object: it)
- <u>I</u> had to go and get <u>it</u> the next day. (subject: I; object: it)
- <u>I</u> will never lend <u>her</u> something of <u>mine</u> again! (subject: I; object: her; possessive: mine)

Correct	Incorrect	Why?
John and I went out.	*John and me* went out.	*John and I* is a subject. *I* is a subject pronoun; *me* is not.
Johan took *Sam and me* to the show.	Johan took *Sam and I* to the show.	*Sam and me* is an object. *Me* is an object pronoun; *I* is not.

Relative Pronouns

Relative pronouns connect a clause to a noun or pronoun.

These are some relative pronouns:

who, whom, whoever, whose, that, which

- Steve Jobs, _who founded Apple_, changed the way people use technology.

The pronoun _who_ introduces a clause that gives more information about Steve Jobs.

- This is the movie _that Emily told us to see_.

The pronoun _that_ introduces a clause that gives more information about the movie.

Other Pronouns

Some other pronouns are:

this, that, what, anyone, everything, something

> **DID YOU KNOW?**
> Pronouns can sometimes refer to general or unspecified things.

Look for the pronouns in these sentences.

- What is that?
- There is something over there!
- Does anyone have a pen?

Pronouns and Their Purpose

The purpose of a pronoun is to replace a noun. Note the use of the pronoun _their_ in the heading of this section. If we did not have pronouns, we would have to call this section _Pronouns and Pronouns' Purpose._

What Is an Antecedent?

A pronoun in a sentence refers to a specific noun, and this noun called the **antecedent**.

- John Hancock signed the Declaration of Independence. He signed it in 1776.

The antecedent for _he_ is John Hancock. The antecedent for _it_ is the Declaration of Independence.

> **BE CAREFUL!**
> Look out for unclear antecedents, such as in this sentence:
>
> - Take the furniture out of the room and paint _it_.
>
> What needs to be painted, the furniture or the room?

Find the pronouns in the following sentence. Then identify the antecedent for each pronoun.

Erin had an idea *that she* suggested to Antonio: "*I'll* help *you* with *your* math homework if *you* help *me* with *my* writing assignment."

Pronoun	Antecedent
that	idea
she	Erin
I	Erin
you	Antonio
your	Antonio's
you	Antonio
me	Erin
my	Erin's

What Is Antecedent Agreement?

A pronoun must agree in **gender** and **number** with the antecedent it refers to. For example:

- Singular pronouns *I, you, he, she*, and *it* replace singular nouns.
- Plural pronouns *you, we*, and *they* replace plural nouns.
- Pronouns *he, she*, and *it* replace masculine, feminine, or neutral nouns.

Correct	Incorrect	Why?
Students should do their homework every night.	A student should do their homework every night.	The pronoun *their* is plural, so it must refer to a plural noun such as *students*.
When an employee is sick, he or she should call the office.	When an employee is sick, they should call the office.	The pronoun *they* is plural, so it must refer to a plural noun. *Employee* is not a plural noun.

Let's Review!

- A pronoun takes the place of or refers to a noun.
- The role of pronouns in sentences is as subject, object, or possessive.
- A pronoun must agree in number and gender with the noun it refers to.

ADJECTIVES AND ADVERBS

An **adjective** is a word that describes a noun or a pronoun. An **adverb** is a word that describes a verb, an adjective, or another adverb.

Adjectives

An **adjective** describes, modifies, or tells us more about a **noun** or a **pronoun**. Colors, numbers, and descriptive words such as *healthy*, *good*, and *sharp* are adjectives.

> **KEEP IN MIND . . .**
>
> Adjectives typically come **before the noun** in English. However, with **linking verbs** (non-action verbs such as *be, seem, look*), the adjective may come **after the verb** instead. Think of it like this: a linking verb **links** the adjective to the noun or pronoun.

Look for the adjectives in the following sentences:

	Adjective	Noun or pronoun it describes
I rode the blue bike.	blue	bike
It was a long trip.	long	trip
Bring two pencils for the exam.	two	pencils
The box is brown.	brown	box
She looked beautiful.	beautiful	she
That's great!	great	that

Multiple adjectives can be used in a sentence, as can multiple nouns. Look at these examples:

	Adjectives	Noun or pronoun it describes
The six girls were happy, healthy, and rested after their long beach vacation.	six, happy, healthy, rested; long, beach	girls; vacation
Leo has a good job, but he is applying for a better one.	good; better	job; one

> **KEEP IN MIND . . .**
>
> Note comparative and superlative forms of adjectives, such as:
>
> fast, faster, fastest
>
> far, farther, farthest
>
> good, better, best
>
> bad, worse, worst

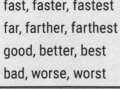

Articles: *A, An, The*

Articles are a unique part of speech, but they work like adjectives. An article tells more about a noun. *A* and *an* are **indefinite** articles. Use *a* before a singular **general** noun. Use *an* before a singular general noun that begins with a vowel.

The is a **definite** article. Use *the* before a singular or plural **specific** noun.

Look at how articles are used in the following sentences:

- I need *a* pencil to take *the* exam. (any pencil; specific exam)
- Is there *a* zoo in town? (any zoo)
- Let's go to *the* zoo today. (specific zoo)
- Can you get me *a* glass of milk? (any glass)
- Would you bring me *the* glass that's over there? (specific glass)

Adverbs

An **adverb** describes, modifies, or tells us more about a **verb**, an **adjective**, or another **adverb**. Many adverbs end in *-ly*. Often, adverbs tell when, where, or how something happened. Words such as *slowly, very*, and *yesterday* are adverbs.

Adverbs that Describe Verbs

Adverbs that describe verbs tell something more about the action.

Look for the adverbs in these sentences:

	Adverb	Verb it describes
They walked quickly.	quickly	walked
She disapproved somewhat of his actions, but she completely understood them.	somewhat; completely	disapproved; understood
The boys will go inside if it rains heavily.	inside; heavily	go; rains

Adverbs that Describe Adjectives

Adverbs that describe adjectives often add intensity to the adjective. Words like *quite, more*, and *always* are adverbs.

Look for the adverbs in these sentences:

	Adverb	Adjective it describes
The giraffe is very tall.	very	tall
Do you think that you are more intelligent than them?	more	intelligent
If it's really loud, we can make the volume slightly lower.	really; slightly	loud; lower

79

Adverbs that Describe Other Adverbs

Adverbs that describe adverbs often add intensity to the adverb.

Look for the adverbs in these sentences:

	Adverb	Adverb it describes
The mouse moved too quickly for us to catch it.	too	quickly
This store is almost never open.	almost	never
Those women are quite fashionably dressed.	quite	fashionably

Adjectives vs. Adverbs

Not sure whether a word is an adjective or an adverb? Look at these examples.

	Adjective	Adverb	Explanation
fast	You're a *fast* driver.	You drove *fast*.	The adjective *fast* describes *driver* (noun); the adverb *fast* describes *drove* (verb).
early	I don't like *early* mornings!	Try to arrive *early*.	The adjective *early* describes *mornings* (noun); the adverb *early* describes *arrive* (verb).
good/well	They did *good* work together.	They worked *well* together.	The adjective *good* describes *work* (noun); the adverb *well* describes *worked* (verb).
bad/badly	The dog is *bad*.	The dog behaves *badly*.	The adjective *bad* describes *dog* (noun); the adverb *badly* describes *behaves* (verb).

Let's Review!

- An **adjective** describes, modifies, or tells us more about a **noun** or a **pronoun**.
- An **adverb** describes, modifies, or tells us more about a **verb**, an **adjective**, or another **adverb**.

BE CAREFUL!

When an adverb ends in *-ly*, add *more* or *most* to make comparisons.

Correct: The car moved *more slowly*.

Incorrect: The car moved *slower*.

CONJUNCTIONS AND PREPOSITIONS

A **conjunction** is a connector word; it connects words, phrases, or clauses in a sentence. A **preposition** is a relationship word; it shows the relationship between two nearby words.

Conjunctions

A **conjunction** connects words, phrases, or clauses.

And, so, and *or* are conjunctions.

Types of Conjunctions

- **Coordinating** conjunctions connect two words, phrases, or independent clauses. The full list of coordinating conjunctions is: *and, or, but, so, for, nor, yet.*
- **Subordinating** conjunctions connect a main (independent) clause and a dependent clause. The conjunction may show a relationship or time order for the two clauses. Some subordinating conjunctions are: *after, as soon as, once, if, even though, unless.*
- **Correlative** conjunctions are pairs of conjunctions that work together to connect two words or phrases. Some correlative conjunctions are: *either/or, neither/nor, as/as.*

> **KEEP IN MIND . . .**
>
> A clause is a phrase that has a subject and a verb.
>
> Some clauses are **independent**. An independent clause can stand alone.
>
> Some clauses are **dependent**. A dependent clause relies on another clause in order to make sense.

Example	Conjunction	What it is connecting
Verdi, Mozart, **and** *Wagner* are famous opera composers.	and	three nouns
Would you like *angel food cake, chocolate lava cake,* **or** *banana cream pie* for dessert?	or	three noun phrases
I took the bus to work, **but** *I walked home.*	but	two independent clauses
It was noisy at home, **so** *we went to the library.*	so	two independent clauses
They have to clean the house **before** *the realtor shows it.*	before	a main clause and a dependent clause
Use **either** *hers* **or** *mine.*	either/or	two pronouns
After *everyone leaves*, make sure you lock up.	after	a main clause and a dependent clause
I'd **rather** *fly* **than** *take the train.*	rather/than	two verb phrases
As soon as *they announced the winning number*, she looked at her ticket and shouted, "Whoopee!"	as soon as	a main clause and a dependent clause

> **DID YOU KNOW?**
>
> In the last example above, *"Whoopee!"* is an interjection. An **interjection** is a short phrase or clause that communicates emotion.
>
> Some other interjections are:
>
> - *Way to go!*
> - *Yuck.*
> - *Hooray!*
> - *Holy cow!*
> - *Oops!*

Prepositions

A **preposition** shows the relationship between two nearby words. Prepositions help to tell information such as direction, location, and time. *To, for,* and *with* are prepositions.

> **KEEP IN MIND . . .**
>
> Some prepositions are more than one word. *On top of* and *instead of* are prepositions.

Example	Preposition	What it tells us
The desk is in the classroom.	in	location
We'll meet you at 6:00.	at	time
We'll meet you at the museum.	at	place
The book is on top of the desk.	on top of	location

Prepositional Phrases

A preposition must be followed by an **object of the preposition**. This can be a noun or something that serves as a noun, such as a pronoun or a gerund.

> **DID YOU KNOW?**
>
> A gerund is the *-ing* form a verb that serves as a noun. *Hiking* is a gerund in this sentence:
>
> I wear these shoes for *hiking*.

A **prepositional phrase** is a preposition plus the object that follows it.

Look for the prepositional phrases in the following examples. Note that a sentence can have more than one prepositional phrase.

Example	Preposition	Object of the preposition
The tiny country won the war *against all odds*.	against	all odds
Look *at us*!	at	us
Why don't we go swimming *instead of sweating in this heat*?	instead of; in	sweating; this heat
Aunt Tea kept the trophy *on a shelf of the cabinet between the sofas in the living room*.	on; of; between; in	a shelf; the cabinet; the sofas; the living room

BE CAREFUL!

Sometimes a word looks like a preposition but is actually part of the verb. In this case, the verb is called a phrasal verb, and the preposition-like word is called a particle. Here is an example:

- *Turn on* the light. (*Turn on* has a meaning of its own; it is a phrasal verb. *On* is a particle here, rather than a preposition.)
- Turn *on that street*. (*On that street* shows location; it is a prepositional phrase. *On* is a preposition here.)

Let's Review!

- A **conjunction** connects words, phrases, or clauses. *And, so,* and *or* are conjunctions.
- A **preposition** shows the relationship between two nearby words. *To, for,* and *with* are prepositions.
- A **prepositional phrase** includes a preposition plus the object of the preposition.

VERBS AND VERB TENSES

A **verb** is a word that describes a **physical or mental action** or a **state of being**. This lesson will cover the role of verbs in sentences, verb forms and tenses, and helping verbs.

The Role of Verbs in Sentences

A verb describes an action or a state of being. A complete sentence must have at least one verb.

Verbs have different tenses, which show time.

Verb Forms

Each verb has three primary forms. The **base form** is used for simple present tense, and the **past form** is used for simple past tense. The **participle form** is used for more complicated time situations. Participle form verbs are accompanied by a helping verb.

Base Form	Past Form	Participle Form
end	ended	ended
jump	jumped	jumped
explain	explained	explained
eat	ate	eaten
take	took	taken
go	went	gone
come	came	come

Some verbs are **regular**. To make the **past** or **participle** form of a regular verb, we just add *-ed*. However, many verbs that we commonly use are **irregular**. We need to memorize the forms for these verbs.

In the chart above, *end, jump,* and *explain* are regular verbs. *Eat, take, go,* and *come* are irregular.

Using Verbs

A simple sentence has a **subject** and a **verb**. The subject tells us who or what, and the verb tells us the action or state.

Example	Subject	Verb	*Explanation/Time*
They ate breakfast together yesterday.	They	ate	*happened yesterday*
I walk to school.	I	walk	*happens regularly*
We went to California last year.	We	went	*happened last year*
She seems really tired.	She	seems	*how she seems right now*
The teacher is sad.	teacher	is	*her state right now*

You can see from the examples in this chart that **past tense verbs** are used for a time in the past, and **present tense verbs** are used for something that happens regularly or for a state or condition right now.

Often a sentence has more than one verb. If it has a connector word or more than one subject, it can have more than one verb.

- The two cousins <u>live</u>, <u>work</u>, and <u>vacation</u> together. (3 verbs)
- The girls <u>planned</u> by phone, and then they <u>met</u> at the movies. (2 verbs)

> **BE CAREFUL!**
> When you have more than one verb in a sentence, make sure both verb tenses are correct.

Helping Verbs and Progressive and Perfect Tenses

Helping Verbs

A **helping verb** is a supporting verb that accompanies a main verb.

Questions, negative sentences, and certain time situations require helping verbs.

forms of helping verb "to be"	forms of helping verb "to have"	forms of helping verb "to do"	some modals (used like helping verbs)
am, are, is, was, were, be, being, been	have, has, had, having	do, does, did, doing	will, would, can, could, must, might, should

Here are examples of helping verbs in questions and negatives.

- Where *is* he *going*?
- *Did* they *win*?
- I *don't want* that.
- The boys *can't* go.

Progressive and Perfect Tenses

Helping verbs accompany main verbs in certain time situations, such as when an action is or was ongoing, or when two actions overlap in time. To form these tenses, we use a **helping verb** with the **base form plus -*ing*** or with the **participle form** of the main verb.

The **progressive tense** is used for an action that is or was ongoing. It takes base form of the main verb plus -*ing*.

Example sentence	Tense	*Explanation/Time*
I <u>am taking</u> French this semester.	Present progressive	*happening now, over a continuous period of time*
I <u>was working</u> when you stopped by.	Past progressive	*happened over a continuous period of time in the past*

85

The **perfect tense** is used to cover two time periods. It takes the *participle* form of the main verb.

Example sentence	Tense	*Explanation/Time*
I have lived here for three years.	Present perfect	*started in the past and continues to present*
I had finished half of my homework when my computer stopped working.	Past perfect	*started and finished in the past, overlapping in time with another action*

Sometimes we use both the **progressive** and **perfect** tenses together.

Example sentence	Tense	*Explanation/Time*
I have been walking for hours!	Present perfect progressive	*started in the past, took place for a period of time, and continues to present*
She had been asking for a raise for months before she finally received one.	Past perfect progressive	*started in the past, took place for a period of time, and ended*

Let's Review!

- A verb describes an action or state of being.
- Each verb has three primary forms: base form, past form, and participle form.
- Verbs have different tenses, which are used to show time.
- Helping verbs are used in questions, negative sentences, and to form progressive and perfect tenses.

Chapter 5 Parts of Speech Practice Quiz 1

1. Select the part of speech of the underlined word in the following sentence.

   She did <u>quite</u> well on the exam.

   A. Noun   C. Adjective

   B. Adverb   D. Preposition

2. Select the noun that the underlined adjectives describe.

   Two weeks after his surgery, Henry felt <u>strong</u> and <u>healthy</u>.

   A. weeks   C. surgery

   B. his   D. Henry

3. Which word is an adverb that describes the underlined verb?

   The man <u>spoke</u> to us wisely.

   A. man   C. us

   B. to   D. wisely

4. Identify the conjunction in the following sentence.

   He is sick, yet he came to work.

   A. is   C. came

   B. yet   D. to

5. Which is <u>not</u> a prepositional phrase?

   Keep me informed about the status of the problem throughout the day.

   A. Keep me informed

   B. about the status

   C. of the problem

   D. throughout the day

6. How many prepositions are in the following sentence?

   The athletes traveled from Boston to Dallas for the competition.

   A. 0   C. 2

   B. 1   D. 3

7. Which words in the following sentence are proper nouns?

   Matthew had a meeting with his supervisor on Tuesday.

   A. Matthew, meeting

   B. Matthew, Tuesday

   C. meeting, supervisor

   D. supervisor, Tuesday

8. How many plural nouns are in the following sentence?

   Marie's father's appendix was taken out.

   A. 0   C. 2

   B. 1   D. 3

9. Which of the following words is an abstract noun?

   A. Car   C. Ruler

   B. Tent   D. Health

10. Which word in the following sentence is a pronoun?

    To whom should the applicant address the letter?

    A. To   C. whom

    B. the   D. should

11. **Which pronoun correctly completes the following sentence?**

    Nigel introduced Van and ____ to the new administrator.

    A. I

    B. me

    C. she

    D. they

12. **Select the noun to which the underlined pronoun refers.**

    Greta Garbo, <u>who</u> performed in both silent and talking pictures, is my favorite actress.

    A. actress

    B. pictures

    C. performed

    D. Greta Garbo

13. **How many verbs are in the following sentence?**

    They toured the art museum and saw the conservatory.

    A. 0

    B. 1

    C. 2

    D. 3

14. **Which word in the following sentence is a helping verb?**

    They did not ask for our help.

    A. did

    B. ask

    C. for

    D. our

15. **Select the correct verb form to complete the following sentence.**

    William didn't think he would enjoy the musical, but he ____.

    A. do

    B. did

    C. liked

    D. would

CHAPTER 5 PARTS OF SPEECH
PRACTICE QUIZ 1 – ANSWER KEY

1. B. *Quite* is an adverb that describes the adverb *well*. **See Lesson: Adjectives and Adverbs.**

2. D. These adjectives describe *Henry*. **See Lesson: Adjectives and Adverbs.**

3. D. *Wisely* is an adverb that describes the verb *spoke*. **See Lesson: Adjectives and Adverbs.**

4. B. *Yet* is a conjunction. **See Lesson: Conjunctions and Prepositions.**

5. A. *Keep me informed* does not contain a preposition. *About, of,* and *throughout* are prepositions. **See Lesson: Conjunctions and Prepositions.**

6. D. *From, to,* and *for* are prepositions. **See Lesson: Conjunctions and Prepositions.**

7. B. *Matthew* and *Tuesday* are proper nouns. **See Lesson: Nouns.**

8. A. *Marie's* and *father's* are possessive; neither is plural. *Appendix* is a singular noun. **See Lesson: Nouns.**

9. D. *Health* is an abstract noun; it does not physically exist. **See Lesson: Nouns.**

10. C. *Whom* is a pronoun. **See Lesson: Pronouns.**

11. B. An object pronoun must be used here. **See Lesson: Pronouns.**

12. D. *Who* is a relative pronoun that refers to the subject *Greta Garbo*. **See Lesson: Pronouns.**

13. C. *Toured* and *saw* are verbs. **See Lesson: Verbs and Verb Tenses.**

14. A. *Did* is a helping verb; *ask* is the main verb. **See Lesson: Verbs and Verb Tenses.**

15. B. *Did* can be used here, for a shortened form of *did enjoy it*. **See Lesson: Verbs and Verb Tenses.**

CHAPTER 5 PARTS OF SPEECH PRACTICE QUIZ 2

1. Which of the following nouns can be made plural by simply adding -s?
    A. Fox
    B. Frog
    C. Cherry
    D. Potato

2. How many nouns in the following sentence have incorrect capitalization?

    The Patel Family moved to the United States, and now they live in the Boston Area.
    A. 0
    B. 1
    C. 2
    D. 3

3. Select the correct nouns for the blanks in the following sentence.

    We can use these _____ to cut these fillets of _____.
    A. knives, salmon
    B. knifes, salmon
    C. knifes, salmons
    D. knives, salmons

4. Which word in the following sentence is a pronoun?

    The driver checked her side mirror.
    A. The
    B. her
    C. side
    D. driver

5. Select the pronoun that could be used in the following sentence.

    Mrs. Sato, _____ lives down the street, is 99 years old.
    A. she
    B. who
    C. which
    D. whom

6. How many pronouns are in the following sentence?

    Suri and Marc asked about you.
    A. 0
    B. 1
    C. 2
    D. 3

7. Which word in the following sentence is an adjective?

    After they signed the mortgage on their first house, they went out to celebrate.
    A. they
    B. signed
    C. mortgage
    D. first

8. How many adjectives are in the following sentence?

    The new building is tall and modern.
    A. 1
    B. 2
    C. 3
    D. 4

9. Select the correct word to complete the following sentence.

    I don't think I did very _____ at the tryouts.
    A. best
    B. well
    C. good
    D. better

10. Which word in the following sentence is a conjunction?

    Margot can speak English, Russian, and Polish fluently.
    A. can
    B. speak
    C. and
    D. fluently

11. **Identify the preposition in the following sentence.**

    It's really hot in that room.

    A. It   C. in

    B. hot   D. that

12. **Which word in the following sentence is a preposition?**

    Our flight will leave at 10:20 a.m.

    A. Our   C. at

    B. will   D. a.m.

13. **Which word <u>cannot</u> be used to complete the following sentence?**

    ____ Stephanie and her brother take classes at the university?

    A. Do   C. Can

    B. Will   D. Are

14. **What is the main verb in the following sentence?**

    Can I ask you another question?

    A. Can   C. another

    B. ask   D. question

15. **How many verbs are in the following sentence?**

    Emile and Olga traveled up the coast from San Diego to San Francisco.

    A. 0   C. 2

    B. 1   D. 3

CHAPTER 5 PARTS OF SPEECH
PRACTICE QUIZ 2 – ANSWER KEY

1. **B.** To make the word *frog* plural, simply add *-s.* **See Lesson: Nouns.**

2. **C.** *Family* and *area* are common nouns and should not be capitalized. **See Lesson: Nouns.**

3. **A.** *Knives* is the plural form of knife. *Salmon* is a non-count noun, so it does not have a plural form. **See Lesson: Nouns.**

4. **B.** *Her* is a possessive pronoun. **See Lesson: Pronouns.**

5. **B.** The relative pronoun *who* introduces a clause that gives more information about the noun *Mrs. Sato.* **See Lesson: Pronouns.**

6. **B.** *You* is the only pronoun listed. **See Lesson: Pronouns.**

7. **D.** *First* is an adjective that describes the noun *house.* **See Lesson: Adjectives and Adverbs.**

8. **C.** The adjectives *new, tall,* and *modern* describe the noun *building.* **See Lesson: Adjectives and Adverbs.**

9. **B.** The adverb *well* describes the verb *did.* **See Lesson: Adjectives and Adverbs.**

10. **C.** *And* is a conjunction. **See Lesson: Conjunctions and Prepositions.**

11. **C.** *In* is a preposition. **See Lesson: Conjunctions and Prepositions.**

12. **C.** *At* is a preposition. **See Lesson: Conjunctions and Prepositions**

13. **D.** *Are* is not the correct helping verb to form a question with *take. Do* is the correct helping verb, and *will* and *can*can also be used because they are modals. **See Lesson: Verbs and Verb Tenses.**

14. **B.** *Ask* is the main verb. **See Lesson: Verbs and Verb Tenses.**

15. **B.** *Traveled* is the only verb in the sentence. **See Lesson: Verbs and Verb Tenses.**

CHAPTER 6 KNOWLEDGE OF LANGUAGE

TYPES OF SENTENCES

Sentences are a combination of words that communicate a complete thought. Sentences can be written in many ways to signal different relationships among ideas. This lesson will cover (1) simple sentences (2) compound sentences (3) complex sentences (4) parallel structure.

Simple Sentences

A **simple sentence** is a group of words that make up a **complete thought**. To be a complete thought, simple sentences must have one **independent clause.** An independent clause contains a single **subject** (who or what the sentence is about) and a **predicate** (a **verb** and something about the subject.)

Let's take a look at some simple sentences:

Simple Sentence	Subject	Predicate	Complete Thought?
The car was fast.	car	was fast (verb = was)	Yes
Sally waited for the bus.	Sally	waited for the bus (verb = waited)	Yes
The pizza smells delicious.	pizza	smells delicious (verb = smells)	Yes
Anton loves cycling.	Anton	loves cycling (verb = loves)	Yes

It is important to be able to recognize what a simple sentence is in order to avoid **run-ons** and **fragments**, two common grammatical errors.

A **run-on** is when two or more independent clauses are combined without proper punctuation:

FOR EXAMPLE

Gregory is a very talented actor he was the lead in the school play.

If you take a look at this sentence, you can see that it is made up of 2 independent clauses or simple sentences:

1. *Gregory is a very talented actor*
2. *he was the lead in the school play*

You <u>cannot</u> have two independent clauses running into each other without proper punctuation.

You can fix this run-on in the following way:

Gregory is a very talented actor. He was the lead in the school play.

A **fragment** is a group of words that looks like a sentence. It starts with a capital letter and has end punctuation, but when you examine it closely you will see it is not a complete thought.

Let's put this information all together to determine whether a group of words is a simple sentence, a run-on, or a fragment:

Group of Words	Category
Mondays are the worst they are a drag.	Run-On: These are two independent clauses running into one another without proper punctuation. FIX: *Mondays are the worst. They are a drag.*
Because I wanted soda.	Fragment: This is a dependent clause and needs more information to make it a complete thought. FIX: *I went to the store because I wanted soda.*
Ereni is from Greece.	Simple Sentence: YES! This is a simple sentence with a subject (*Ereni*) and a predicate (*is from Greece*), so it is a complete thought.
While I was apple picking.	Fragment: This is a dependent clause and needs more information to make it a complete thought. FIX: *While I was apple picking, I spotted a bunny.*
New York City is magical it is my favorite place.	Run-On: These are two independent clauses running into one another without proper punctuation. FIX: *New York City is magical. It is my favorite place.*

Compound Sentences

A **compound sentence** is a sentence made up of two independent clauses connected with a **coordinating conjunction**.

Let's take a look at the following sentence:

> *Joe waited for the bus, but it never arrived.*

If you take a close look at this compound sentence, you will see that it is made up of two independent clauses:

1. *Joe waited for the bus*
2. *it never arrived*

The word *but* is the coordinating conjunction that connects these two sentences. Notice that the coordinating conjunction has a comma right before it. This is the proper way to punctuate compound sentences.

Here are other examples of compound sentences:

> **FOR EXAMPLE**
>
> *I want to try out for the baseball team, and I also want to try out for track.*
>
> *Sally can play the clarinet in the band, **or** she can play the violin in the orchestra.*
>
> *Mr. Henry is going to run the half marathon, **so** he has a lot of training to do.*
>
> All these sentences are compound sentences since they each have two independent clauses joined by a comma and a coordinating conjunction.

The following is a list of **coordinating conjunctions** that can be used in compound sentences. You can use the mnemonic device "FANBOYS" to help you remember them:

For

And

Nor

But

Or

Yet

So

Think back to Section 1: Simple Sentences. You learned about run-ons. Another way to fix run-ons is by turning the group of words into a compound sentence:

RUN-ON: *Gregory is a very talented actor he was the lead in the school play.*

FIX: *Gregory is a very talented actor, **so** he was the lead in the school play.*

Complex Sentences

A **complex** sentence is a sentence that is made up of an independent clause and one or more dependent clauses connected to it.

Think back to Section 1 when you learned about fragments. You learned about a **dependent clause**, the part of a sentence that cannot stand by itself. These clauses need other information to make them complete.

You can recognize a dependent clause because they always begin with a **subordinating conjunction**. These words are a key ingredient in complex sentences.

Here is a list of **subordinating conjunctions:**

after	although	as	because	before
despite	even if	even though	if	in order to
that	once	provided that	rather than	since
so that	than	that	though	unless
until	when	whenever	where	whereas
wherever	while	why		

Let's take a look at a few complex sentences:

FOR EXAMPLE

Since the alarm clock didn't go off, I was late for class.

This is an example of a complex sentence because it contains:

A dependent clause:	*Since the alarm clock didn't go off*
An independent clause:	*I was late for class*
A subordinating conjunction:	*since*

Sarah studied all night for the exam even though she did not receive an A.

This is an example of a complex sentence because it contains:

A dependent clause:	*even though she did not receive an A*
An independent clause:	*Sarah studied all night*
A subordinating conjunction:	*even though*

*NOTE: *To make a complex sentence, you can either start with the dependent clause or the independent clause. When beginning with the dependent clause, you need a comma after it. When beginning with an independent clause, you do not need a comma after it.*

Parallel Structure

Parallel structure is the repetition of a grammatical form within a sentence to make the sentence sound more harmonious. Parallel structure comes into play when you are making a list of items. Stylistically, you want all the items in the list to line up with each other to make them sound better.

Let's take a look at when to use parallel structure:

1. Use parallel structure with verb forms:

   In a sentence listing different verbs, you want all the verbs to use the same form:

   Manuel likes hiking, biking, and mountain climbing.

   In this example, the words *hiking, biking* and *climbing* are all gerunds (having an -ing ending), so the sentence is balanced since the words are all using the gerund form of the verb.

   Manuel likes to hike, bike, and mountain climb.

In this example, the words *hike, bike* and *climb* are all infinitives (using the basic form of the verb), so the sentence is balanced.

You do not want to mix them up:

Manuel likes hiking, biking, and to mountain climb.

This sentence **does not** use parallel structure since *hiking* and *biking* use the gerund form of the verb and *to mountain climb* uses the infinitive form.

2. Use parallel structure with active and passive voice:

   In a sentence written in the **active voice**, the subject performs the action:

   Sally kicked the ball.

   Sally, the subject, is the one doing the action, kicking the ball.

   In a sentence written in the **passive voice**, the subject is acted on by the verb.

   The ball was kicked by Sally.

   When using parallel structure, you want to make sure your items in a list are either all in **active voice**:

   Raymond baked, frosted, and decorated the cake.

   Or all in **passive voice**:

   The cake was baked, frosted, and decorated by Raymond.

   You do not want to mix them up:

   The cake was baked, frosted, and Raymond decorated it.

   This sentence **does not** use parallel structure because it starts off with passive voice and then switches to active voice.

3. Use parallel structure with the length of terms within a list:

   When making a list, you should either have all short individual terms or all long phrases.

   Keep these consistent by either choosing short, individual terms:

   Cassandra is bold, courageous, and strong.

   Or longer phrases:

   Cassandra is brave in the face of danger, willing to take risks, and a force to be reckoned with.

   You do not want to mix them up:

   Cassandra is bold, courageous, and a force to be reckoned with.

This sentence **does not** use parallel structure because the first two terms are short, and the last one is a longer phrase.

Let's Review!

- A simple sentence consists of a clause, which has a single subject and a predicate.
- A compound sentence is made up of two independent clauses connected by a coordinating conjunction.
- A complex sentence is made up of a subordinating conjunction, an independent clause and one or more dependent clauses connected to it.
- Parallel structure is the repetition of a grammatical form within a sentence to make the sentence sound more harmonious.

Types of Clauses

There are four types of clauses that are used to create sentences. Sentences with several clauses, and different types of clauses, are considered complex. This lesson will cover (1) independent clauses, (2) dependent clauses and subordinate clauses, and (3) coordinate clauses.

Independent Clause

An **independent clause** is a simple sentence. It has a subject, a verb, and expresses a complete thought.

- Steve went to the store.
- She will cook dinner tonight.
- The class was very boring.
- The author argues that listening to music helps productivity.

Two **independent clauses** can be connected by a semicolon. There are some common words that indicate the beginning of an **independent clause** such as: moreover, also, nevertheless, however, furthermore, consequently.

- I wanted to go to dinner; however, I had to work late tonight.
- She had a job interview; therefore, she dressed nicely.

Dependent and Subordinate Clauses

A **dependent clause** is not a complete sentence. It has a subject and a verb but does not express a complete thought. **Dependent clauses** are also called **subordinate clauses**, because they depend on the **independent or main clause** to complete the thought. A sentence that has both at least one **independent clause** and one **subordinate clause** are considered complex.

Subordinate clauses can be placed before or after the **independent clause**. When the **subordinate clause** begins the sentence, there should be a comma before the **main clause**. If the **subordinate clause** ends the sentence, there is no need for a comma.

Dependent clauses also have common indicator words. These are often called **subordinating conjunctions** because they connect a **dependent clause** to an **independent clause**. Some of these include: although, after, as, because, before, if, once, since, unless, until, when, whether, and while. Relative pronouns also signify the beginning of a **subordinate clause**. These include: that, which, who, whom, whichever, whoever, whomever, and whose.

- When I went to school...
- Since she joined the team...
- After we saw the play...
- *Because she studied hard*, she received an A on her exam.
- *Although the professor was late*, the class was very informative.
- I can't join you *unless I finish my homework*.

Coordinate Clause

A **coordinate clause** is a sentence or phrase that combines clauses of equal grammatical rank (verbs, nouns, adjectives, phrases, or independent clauses) by using a coordinating conjunction (and, but, for, nor, or so, yet). **Coordinating conjunctions** cannot connect a **dependent or subordinate clause** and an **independent clause.**

- She woke up, and he went to bed.
- We did not have cheese, so I went to the store to get some.
- Ice cream and candy taste great, but they are not good for you.
- Do you want to study, or do you want to go to Disneyland?

Let's Review!

- An **independent clause** is a simple sentence that has a noun, a verb, and a complete thought. Two **independent clauses** can be connected by a semicolon.
- A **dependent or subordinate clause** depends on the main clause to complete a thought. A **dependent or subordinate clause** can go before or after the **independent clause** and there are indicator words that signify the beginning of the **dependent or subordinate clause**.
- A **coordinate clause** connects two verbs, nouns, adjectives, phrases, or **independent clauses** using a **coordinating conjunction** (and, but, for, nor, or, so, yet).

SUBJECT AND VERB AGREEMENT

Every sentence must include a **subject** and a **verb**. The subject tells **who or what**, and the verb describes an **action or condition**. Subject and verb agree in number and person.

Roles of Subject and Verb

A complete sentence includes a **subject** and a **verb**. The verb is in the part of the sentence called the **predicate**. A predicate can be thought of as a verb phrase.

Simple Sentences

A sentence can be very simple, with just one or two words as the **subject** and one or two words as the **predicate**.

Sometimes, in a command, a subject is "understood," rather than written or spoken.

BE CAREFUL!
It's is a contraction of *it is*.
Its (without an apostrophe) is the possessive of the pronoun *it*.

Look at these examples of short sentences:

Sentence	Subject	Predicate, with main verb(s) underlined
I ate.	I	<u>ate</u>
They ran away.	They	<u>ran</u> away
It's OK.	It	<u>is</u> OK
Go and find the cat!	(You)	<u>go</u> and <u>find</u> the cat

Complex Sentences

Sometimes a subject or predicate is a long phrase or clause.

Some sentences have more than one subject or predicate, or even a predicate within a predicate.

Sentence	Subject(s)	Predicate(s), with main verb(s) underlined
My friend from work had a bad car accident.	My friend from work	<u>had</u> a bad car accident
John, his sister, and I plan to ride our bikes across the country this summer.	John, his sister, and I	<u>plan</u> to ride our bikes across the country this summer
I did so much for them, and they didn't even thank me.*	I; they	<u>did</u> so much for them; didn't even <u>thank</u> me
She wrote a letter that explained the problem.**	She	<u>wrote</u> a letter that explained the problem

*This sentence consists of two clauses, and each clause has its own subject and its own predicate.

**In this sentence, *that explained the problem* is part of the predicate, and it is also a relative clause with own subject and predicate.

Subject and Verb Agreement

Subjects and verbs must agree in **number** and **person**. This means that different subjects take different forms of a verb.

With **regular** verbs, simply add *-s* to the singular third person verb, as shown below:

	Singular		Plural	
	Subject	Verb	Subject	Verb
(first person)	I	play	we	play
(second person)	you	play	you	play
(third person)	he/she/it	plays	they	play

Some verbs are **irregular**, so simply adding *-s* doesn't work. For example:

Verb	Form for Third Person Singular Subject
have	has
do	does
fix	fixes

Look for subject-verb agreement in the following sentences:

- *I* usually <u>eat</u> a banana for breakfast.
- *Marcy* <u>does</u> well in school.
- The *cat* <u>licks</u> its fur.

Subject-Verb Agreement for the Verb *Be*

Present		Past	
I am	we are	I was	we were
you are	you are	you were	you were
he/she/it is	they are	they were	they were

Things to Look Out For

Subject-verb agreement can be tricky. Be careful of these situations:

- **Sentences with more than one subject:** If two subjects are connected by *and*, the subject is **plural**. When two singular subjects are connected by *neither/nor*, the subject is **singular**.

Sandra and Luiz <u>shop</u>. (plural)
Neither Sandra nor Luiz <u>has</u> money. (singular)

- **Collective nouns:** Sometimes a noun stands for a group of people or things. If the subject is **one group**, it is considered **singular**.

Those students are still on chapter three. (plural)
That class <u>is</u> still on chapter three. (singular)

- ***There is*** and ***there are***: With pronouns such as *there, what,* and *where,* the verb agrees with the noun or pronoun that follows it.

There<u>'s</u> a rabbit! (singular)
Where <u>are</u> my shoes? (plural)

- **Indefinite pronouns:** Subjects such as *everybody, someone,* and *nobody* are **singular**. Subjects such as *all, none,* and *any* can be either **singular or plural**.

Everyone in the band <u>plays</u> well. (singular)
All of the students <u>are</u> there. (plural)
All <u>is</u> well. (singular)

Let's Review!

- Every sentence has a subject and a verb.
- The predicate is the part of the sentence that contains the verb.
- The subject and verb must agree in number and person.
- The third person singular subject takes a different verb form.

MODIFIERS

A modifier is a word, phrase, or clause that adds detail or changes (modifies) another word in the sentence. Descriptive words such as adjectives and adverbs are examples of modifiers.

The Role of Modifiers in a Sentence

Modifiers make a sentence more descriptive and interesting.

Look at these simple sentences. Notice how much more interesting they are with modifiers added.

Simple sentence	With Modifiers Added
I drove.	I drove my family along snowy roads to my grandmother's house.
They ate.	They ate a fruit salad of blueberries, strawberries, peaches, and apples.
The boy looked.	The boy in pajamas looked out the window at the birds eating from the feeder.
He climbed.	He climbed the ladder to fix the roof.

Look at the modifiers in bold type in the following sentences. Notice how these words add description to the basic idea in the sentence.

	Modifier	Word It Modifies	Type
The hungry man ate **quickly.**	1. the; 2. hungry; 3. quickly	1. man 2. man; 3. ate	1. article 2. adjective; 3. adverb
The small child, **who had scraped his knee,** cried **quietly.**	1. the; 2. small; 3. who had scraped his knee; 4. quietly	1. child; 2. child; 3. child; 4. cried	1. article; 2. adjective; 3. adjective clause; 4. adverb
The horse **standing near the fence** is **beautiful.**	1. the; 2. standing near the fence; 3. beautiful	1. horse; 2. horse; 3. horse	1. article; 2. participle phrase; 3. adjective
Hana and Mario stood **by the lake** and watched **a gorgeous** sunset.	1. by the lake; 2. a; 3. gorgeous	1. stood; 2. sunset; 3. sunset	1. prepositional phrase; 2. article; 3. adjective
They tried **to duck out of the way as the large spider dangled from the ceiling.**	1. to duck out of the way; 2. as the large spider dangled; 3. from the ceiling	1. tried; 2. duck; 3. dangled	1. infinitive phrase; 2. adverb clause; 3. prepositional phrase

DID YOU KNOW?

Adjectives and adverbs are not the only modifiers. With a participle phrase, *an -ing verb* can act as a modifier. For example, *eating from the feeder* modifies *the birds*. With an infinitive, *to plus the main form of a verb* can act as a modifier. For example, *to fix the roof* modifies *climbed*.

Misplaced and Dangling Modifiers

A **misplaced modifier** is a modifier that is placed incorrectly in a sentence, so that it modifies the wrong word.

A **dangling modifier** is a modifier that modifies a word that should be included in the sentence but is not.

Look at these examples.

- First, notice the modifier, in bold.
- Next, look for the word it modifies.

> **BE CAREFUL!**
>
> Sometimes there is a modifier within a modifier. For example, in the clause *as the large spider dangled, the* and *large* are words that modify *spider*.

Incorrect	Problem	How to Fix It	Correct
Sam wore his new shirt to school, **which was too big for him.**	Misplaced modifier. Notice the placement of the modifier ***which was too big for him***. It is placed after the word *school*, which makes it seem like *school* is the word it describes. However, this was not the writer's intention. The writer intended for ***which was too big for him*** to describe the word *shirt*.	The modifier needs to be placed after the word *shirt*, rather than after the word *school*.	Sam wore his new shirt, **which was too big for him**, to school.
Running down the hallway, Maria's bag of groceries fell.	Dangling modifier. The modifier ***running down the hallway*** is placed before the phrase *Maria's bag of groceries*, which makes it seem this is what it describes. However, this was not the writer's intention; the *bag of groceries* cannot run! The correct reference would be the noun *Maria*, which was omitted from the sentence completely.	The modifier must reference *Maria*, rather than *Maria's bag of groceries*. This can be fixed by adding the noun *Maria* as a subject.	**Running down the hallway,** Maria dropped her bag of groceries.
With a leash on, my sister walked the dog.	Misplaced modifier. The modifier ***with a leash on*** is placed before *my sister*, which makes it seem like she is wearing a leash.	Move the modifier so that it is next to *the dog*, rather than *my sister*.	My sister walked the dog, **who had a leash on**.

Let's Review!

- A modifier is a word, phrase, or clause that adds detail by describing or modifying another word in the sentence.
- Adverbs, adjectives, articles, and prepositional phrases are some examples of modifiers.
- Misplaced and dangling modifiers have unclear references, leading to confusion about the meaning of a sentence.

> **BE CAREFUL!**
>
> A modifier should be placed next to the word it modifies. Misplaced and dangling modifiers lead to confusion about the meaning of a sentence.

DIRECT OBJECTS AND INDIRECT OBJECTS

A direct or indirect object has a relationship with the action verb that precedes it. A direct object directly receives the action of the verb. An indirect object indirectly receives the action.

Direct and Indirect Objects in a Sentence

An **object** in grammar is something that is acted on. The **subject** does the action; the **object** receives it.

An object is usually a noun or a pronoun.

There are three types of objects:

- direct object
- indirect object
- object of the preposition

KEEP IN MIND . . .

When there is an **indirect object**, it will be placed between the verb and the direct object.

Many sentences have a direct object. Some sentences also have an indirect object.

Look at these examples:

- Kim threw *the ball. The ball* is the direct object. *Ask yourself:* What did she throw?
- Kim threw *Tommy* the ball. *Tommy* is the indirect object. *Ask yourself:* Who did she throw it to?

Look for the objects in the sentences below.

Sentence	Direct Object	Indirect Object	Be Careful!
Her mom poured her a glass of milk.	a glass of milk (*ask:* what did she pour?)	her (*ask:* who did she pour it for?)	The indirect object, when there is one, can be found between the verb and the direct object.
They work hard.			Not all sentences have objects. Here, *hard* is not an object. It is not the recipient of *work*. Instead, it is a modifier; it describes the work.
Kazu bought Katrina a present.	a present (*ask:* what did he buy?)	Katrina (*ask:* whom did he buy it for?)	
Kazu bought a present for Katrina.	a present (*ask:* what did he buy?)		Don't confuse indirect objects with prepositional phrases. *For* is a preposition, so *Katrina* is the object of the preposition; it is not an indirect object.

BE CAREFUL!

Some verbs can never take **direct objects**. These are:

- **Linking verbs** such as *is* and *seem*.
- **Intransitive verbs** such as *snore, go, sit,* and *die*.
- *Ask yourself:* Can you *snore* something? No. Therefore, this verb cannot take a direct object.

Let's Review!

- A direct object directly receives the action of the verb.
- An indirect object indirectly receives the action of the verb.
- An indirect object comes between the verb and the direct object.

KEEP IN MIND . . .

If there is a preposition, the object is the **object of the preposition** rather than an **indirect object**.

Compare these two sentences:

- She made *me* dinner. (*Me* is an indirect object.)
- She made dinner *for me*. (*For me* is a prepositional phrase.)

CHAPTER 6 KNOWLEDGE OF LANGUAGE PRACTICE QUIZ 1

1. Identify the direct object in the following sentence.

   Paulo accidentally locked his keys in his car.

   A. Paulo   C. his keys

   B. accidentally   D. his car

2. Select the word that is an object of the underlined verb.

   The graduates <u>held</u> lit candles.

   A. The   C. lit

   B. graduates   D. candles

3. Select the verb that acts on the underlined direct object in the following sentence.

   We have no choice but to sit here and wait for these cows to cross <u>the road</u>!

   A. have   C. wait

   B. sit   D. cross

4. Which modifier, if any, modifies the underlined word in the following sentence?

   We always visit the <u>bakery</u> on the corner when we are in town.

   A. always

   B. on the corner

   C. when we are in town

   D. No modifier describes it.

5. Identify the dangling or misplaced modifier, if there is one.

   Having been repaired, we can drive the car again.

   A. Having been repaired

   B. we can drive

   C. the car again

   D. There is no dangling or misplaced modifier.

6. Which ending does <u>not</u> create a sentence with a dangling modifier?

   Trying to earn some extra money, _____.

   A. the new position paid more.

   B. he got a second job.

   C. the job was difficult.

   D. it was an extra shift.

7. Select the "understood" subject with which the underlined verb must agree.

   <u>Watch</u> out!

   A. You   C. I

   B. He   D. Out

8. How many verbs must agree with the underlined subject in the following sentence?

   <u>Kareem Abdul-Jabbar</u>, my favorite basketball player, dribbles, shoots, and scores to win the game!

   A. 0   C. 2

   B. 1   D. 3

9. **Select the correct verb to complete the following sentence.**

    Our family ____ staying home for the holidays this year.

    A. is
    B. be
    C. am
    D. are

10. **Fill in the blank with the correct subordinating conjunction.**

    You cannot go to the movies with your friends _____ you finish your homework.

    A. If
    B. Once
    C. Since
    D. Unless

11. **Identify the dependent clause in the following sentence.**

    We decided to take our dog to the park although it was hot outside.

    A. We decided to take our dog
    B. to the park
    C. although it was hot outside
    D. to take our dog

12. **Identify the independent clause in the following sentence.**

    After eating dinner, the couple went on a stroll through the park.

    A. After eating dinner
    B. The couple went on a stroll through the park
    C. Through the park
    D. Went on a stroll

13. **Which of the following is an example of a simple sentence?**

    A. Tamara's sporting goods store.
    B. Tamara has a sporting goods store in town.
    C. Tamara has a sporting goods store it is in town.
    D. Tamara's sporting goods store is in town, and she is the owner.

14. **Which of the following uses a conjunction to combine the sentences below so the focus is on puppies requiring a lot of work?**

    Puppies are fun-loving animals. They do require a lot of work.

    A. are fun-loving animals; they do require a lot of work.
    B. Puppies are fun-loving animals, so they do require a lot of work.
    C. Since puppies are fun-loving animals they do require a lot of work.
    D. Although puppies are fun-loving animals, they do require a lot of work.

15. **Which of the following options would complete the above sentence to make it a compound sentence?**

    The class of middle school students _____.

    A. served food at.
    B. served food at a soup kitchen.
    C. served food at a soup kitchen, and they enjoyed the experience.
    D. served food at a soup kitchen even though they weren't required to.

CHAPTER 6 KNOWLEDGE OF LANGUAGE PRACTICE QUIZ 1 – ANSWER KEY

1. C. *His keys* is the direct object of the verb *locked*. **See Lesson: Direct Objects and Indirect Objects.**

2. D. *Candles* is the direct object of the verb *held*. **See Lesson: Direct Objects and Indirect Objects.**

3. D. *The road* is a direct object of the verb *cross*. **See Lesson: Direct Objects and Indirect Objects.**

4. B. *On the corner* modifies *bakery*. **See Lesson: Modifiers, misplaced modifiers, dangling modifiers.**

5. A. *Having been repaired* is placed where it references *we*, but it should reference *the car*. **See Lesson: Modifiers, misplaced modifiers, dangling modifiers**

6. B. Of these choices, *trying to earn some extra money* can only reference *he*. **See Lesson: Modifiers, misplaced modifiers, dangling modifiers.**

7. A. In a command like this one, the "understood" subject is *you*. **See Lesson: Subject and Verb Agreement.**

8. D. The verbs *dribbles, shoots*, and *scores* must agree with the subject *Kareem Abdul-Jabbar*. **See Lesson: Subject and Verb Agreement.**

9. A. The subject *family* is singular and takes the verb *is*. **See Lesson: Subject and Verb Agreement.**

10. D. Unless. The word "unless" signifies the beginning of a dependent clause and is the only conjunction that makes sense in the sentence. **See Lesson: Types of Clauses.**

11. C. Although it was hot outside. It is dependent because it does not express a complete thought and relies on the independent clause. The word "although" also signifies the beginning of a dependent clause. **See Lesson: Types of Clauses.**

12. B. The couple went on a stroll through the park. It is independent because it has a subject, verb, and expresses a complete thought. **See Lesson: Types of Clauses.**

13. B. This is a simple sentence since it contains one independent clause consisting of a simple subject and a predicate. **See Lesson: Types of Sentences.**

14. D. The subordinate conjunction "although" combines the sentences and puts the focus on puppies requiring a lot of work. **See Lesson: Types of Sentences.**

15. C. This option would make the sentence a compound sentence. **See Lesson: Types of Sentences.**

CHAPTER 6 KNOWLEDGE OF LANGUAGE PRACTICE QUIZ 2

1. **Which of the following is an example of a simple sentence?**

   A. Although termites are insects.

   B. Termites are very industrious insects.

   C. Termites are insects, and they are very industrious.

   D. Because termites are insects, they are very industrious.

2. **Which of the following is an example of a compound sentence?**

   A. The Jankowskis typically go out for Italian food, tonight they tried Thai.

   B. The Jankowskis typically go out for Italian food and tonight they tried Thai.

   C. The Jankowskis typically go out for Italian food, but tonight they tried Thai.

   D. The Jankowskis typically go out for Italian food even though tonight they tried Thai.

3. **Fill in the blank with the correct coordinating conjunction.**

   My daughter is in the school play, _____ I want to go to every performance.

   A. So   C. But

   B. Or   D. And

4. **Which sentence combines all of the information below using a parallel structure?**

   I like reading books. I also like to draw. I write stories too.

   A. I like reading books, to draw, and writing stories.

   B. I like reading books, drawing, and writing stories.

   C. I like reading books, to draw, and to write stories.

   D. I like reading books, drawing, and to write stories.

5. **Identify the dependent clause in the following sentence.**

   Joe always did his homework before he went to bed.

   A. Went to bed

   B. Before he went to bed

   C. Joe always did his homework

   D. Did his homework

6. **Select the subject that would be incorrect in the following sentence.**

   ____ are excited about the upcoming election.

   A. He   C. You

   B. We   D. They

7. How would you connect the following clauses?

She gave her dog a long walk.

He slept well that night.

A. She gave her a dog a long walk and he slept well that night.

B. She gave her dog a long walk but he slept well that night.

C. She gave her dog a long walk or he slept well that night.

D. She gave her dog a long walk yet he slept well that night.

8. Select the correct verbs to complete the following sentence.

My dentist, who I _____ visited for years, _____ suddenly disappeared.

A. has, has   C. has, have

B. have, has   D. have, have

9. What is the verb in the following sentence?

It's time for lunch.

A. It   C. time

B. is   D. lunch

10. Which word is a modifier in the following sentence?

I am following the news story closely.

A. I   C. following

B. am   D. closely

11. How many modifiers describe the underlined word in the following sentence?

Pass that large silver <u>bowl</u>.

A. 1   C. 3

B. 2   D. 4

12. Identify the likely misplaced modifier in the following sentence.

Earlier this week, the young fishermen caught twenty fish, who were out all day.

A. Earlier this week

B. young

C. twenty

D. who were out all day

13. Select the direct object of the underlined verb.

Andrei was happy to help his daughter and her fiancé <u>plan</u> their wedding.

A. was happy

B. to help

C. his daughter and her fiancé

D. their wedding

14. Identify the indirect object in the following sentence, if there is one.

Snowflakes fell softly to the ground.

A. Snowflakes

B. softly

C. ground

D. There is no indirect object.

15. What part of speech correctly describes the underlined word in the following sentence?

I don't think you should give <u>her</u> that.

A. Direct object   C. Verb

B. Indirect object   D. Preposition

CHAPTER 6 KNOWLEDGE OF LANGUAGE PRACTICE QUIZ 2 – ANSWER KEY

1. B. This is a simple sentence since it contains one independent clause consisting of a simple subject and a predicate. **See Lesson: Types of Sentences.**

2. C. This is a compound sentence joining two independent clauses with a comma and the conjunction *but*. **See Lesson: Types of Sentences.**

3. A. So. It is the only conjunction that fits within the context of the sentence. **See Lesson: Types of Clauses.**

4. B. This sentence combines the information using parallel structure. **See Lesson: Types of Sentences.**

5. B. Before he went to bed. It is dependent because it does not express a complete thought and relies on the independent clause. The word "before" also signifies the beginning of a dependent clause. **See Lesson: Types of Clauses.**

6. A. The subject *he* takes the verb form *is*, not *are*. **See Lesson: Subject and Verb Agreement.**

7. A. She gave her dog a long walk and he slept well that night. These two clauses are of equal grammatical rank and can be connected with a coordinating conjunction. "And" is the conjunction that makes the most sense. **See Lesson: Types of Clauses.**

8. B. This sentence has a predicate within a predicate. The "inside" predicate is *who I have visited for years*, and the "outside" predicate is *my dentist has suddenly disappeared*. **See Lesson: Subject and Verb Agreement.**

9. B. *It's* is a contraction of *it is*. The verb is *is*. **See Lesson: Subject and Verb Agreement.**

10. D. *Closely* is a modifier; it is an adverb that describes *following*. **See Lesson: Modifiers, misplaced modifiers, dangling modifiers.**

11. C. *That, large,* and *silver* describe *bowl*. **See Lesson: Modifiers, misplaced modifiers, dangling modifiers.**

12. D. *Who were out all day* most likely refers to *fishermen*, so it should be placed after that word, not after *fish*. **See Lesson: Modifiers, misplaced modifiers, dangling modifiers.**

13. D. *Their wedding* is a direct object of the verb *plan*. **See Lesson: Direct Objects and Indirect Objects.**

14. D. There is no indirect object. **See Lesson: Direct Objects and Indirect Objects.**

15. B. *Her* is an indirect object in this sentence. **See Lesson: Direct Objects and Indirect Objects.**

CHAPTER 7 VOCABULARY ACQUISITION

ROOT WORDS, PREFIXES, AND SUFFIXES

A root word is the most basic part of a word. You can create new words by: adding a prefix, a group of letters placed before the root word; or a suffix, a group of letters placed at the end of a root word. In this lesson you will learn about root words, prefixes, suffixes, and how to determine the meaning of a word by analyzing these word parts.

Root Words

Root words are found in everyday language. They are the most basic parts of words. Root words in the English language are mostly derived from Latin or Greek. You can add beginnings (prefixes) and endings (suffixes) to root words to change their meanings. To discover what a root word is, simply remove its prefix and/or suffix. What you are left with is the root word, or the core or basis of the word.

At times, root words can be stand-alone words.

Here are some examples of stand-alone root words:

Stand-Alone Root Word	Meaning
dress	*clothing*
form	*shape*
normal	*typical*
phobia	*fear of*
port	*carry*

Most root words, however, are **not** stand-alone words. They are not full words on their own, but they still form the basis of other words when you remove their prefixes and suffixes.

Here are some common root words in the English language:

Root Word	Meaning	Example
ami, amic	*love*	amicable
anni	*year*	anniversary
aud	*to hear*	auditory
bene	*good*	beneficial
biblio	*book*	bibliography
cap	*take, seize*	capture
cent	*one hundred*	century
chrom	*color*	chromatic

Root Word	Meaning	Example
chron	*time*	chronological
circum	*around*	circumvent
cred	*believe*	credible
corp	*body*	corpse
dict	*to say*	dictate
equi	*equal*	equality
fract; rupt	*to break*	fracture
ject	*throw*	eject
mal	*bad*	malignant
min	*small*	miniature
mort	*death*	mortal
multi	*many*	multiply
ped	*foot*	pedestrian
rupt	*break*	rupture
sect	*cut*	dissect
script	*write*	manuscript
sol	*sun*	solar
struct	*build*	construct
terr	*earth*	terrain
therm	*heat*	thermometer
vid, vis	*to see*	visual
voc	*voice; to call*	vocal

Prefixes

Prefixes are the letters added to the **beginning** of a root word to make a new word with a different meaning.

Prefixes on their own have meanings, too. If you add a prefix to a root word, it can change its meaning entirely.

Here are some of the most common prefixes, their meanings, and some examples:

Prefix	Meaning	Example
auto	*self*	autograph
con	*with*	conclude
hydro	*water*	hydrate
im, in, non, un	*not*	unimportant
inter	*between*	international
mis	*incorrect, badly*	mislead

Prefix	Meaning	Example
over	*too much*	over-stimulate
post	*after*	postpone
pre	*before*	preview
re	*again*	rewrite
sub	*under, below*	submarine
trans	*across*	transcribe

Let's look back at some of the root words from Section 1. By adding prefixes to these root words, you can create a completely new word with a new meaning:

Root Word	Prefix	New Word	Meaning
dress (*clothing*)	un (*remove*)	**un**dress	*remove clothing*
sect (*cut*)	inter (*between*)	**inter**sect	*cut across or through*
phobia (*fear*)	hydro (*water*)	**hydro**phobia	*fear of water*
script (*write*)	post (*after*)	**post**script	*additional remark at the end of a letter*

Suffixes

Suffixes are the letters added to the **end** of a root word to make a new word with a different meaning.

Suffixes on their own have meanings, too. If you add a suffix to a root word, it can change its meaning entirely.

Here are some of the most common suffixes, their meanings, and some examples:

Suffix	Meanings	Example
able, ible	*can be done*	agreeable
an, ean, ian	*belonging or relating to*	European
ed	*happened in the past*	jogged
en	*made of*	wooden
er	*comparative (more than)*	stricter
est	*comparative (most)*	largest
ful	*full of*	meaningful
ic	*having characteristics of*	psychotic
ion, tion, ation, ition	*act, process*	hospitalization
ist	*person who practices*	linguist
less	*without*	artless
logy	*study of*	biology

Let's look back at some of the root words from Section 1. By adding suffixes to these root words, you can create a completely new word with a new meaning:

Root Word	Suffix	New Word	Meaning
aud (*to hear*)	logy (*study of*)	audio**logy**	*the study of hearing*
form (*shape*)	less (*without*)	form**less**	*without a clear shape*
port (*carry*)	able (*can be done*)	port**able**	*able to be carried*
normal (*typical*)	ity (*state of*)	normal**ity**	*condition of being normal*

Determining Meaning

Knowing the meanings of common root words, prefixes, and suffixes can help you determine the meaning of unknown words. By looking at a word's individual parts, you can get a good sense of its definition.

If you look at the word *transportation*, you can study the different parts of the word to figure out what it means.

If you were to break up the word you would see the following:

PREFIX: *trans = across*	ROOT: *port = carry*	SUFFIX: *tion = act or process*

If you put all these word parts together, you can define transportation as: *the act or process of carrying something across.*

Let's define some other words by looking at their roots, prefixes and suffixes:

Word	Prefix	Root	Suffix	Working Definition
indestructible	in (*not*)	struct (*build*)	able (*can be done*)	Not able to be "un" built (torn down)
nonconformist	non (*not*) con (*with*)	form (*shape*)	ist (*person who practices*)	A person who can not be shaped (someone who doesn't go along with the norm)
subterranean	sub (*under, below*)	terr (*earth*)	ean (*belonging or relating to*)	Relating or belonging to something under the earth

Let's Review!

- A root word is the most basic part of a word.
- A prefix is the letters added to beginning of a root word to change the word and its meaning.
- A suffix is the letters added to the end of a root word to change the word and its meaning.
- You can figure out a word's meaning by looking closely at its different word parts (root, prefixes, and suffixes).

CONTEXT CLUES AND MULTIPLE MEANING WORDS

Sometimes when you read a text, you come across an unfamiliar word. Instead of skipping the word and reading on, it is important to figure out what that word means so you can better understand the text. There are different strategies you can use to determine the meaning of unfamiliar words. This lesson will cover (1) how to determine unfamiliar words by reading context clues, (2) multiple meaning words, and (3) using multiple meaning words properly in context.

Using Context Clues to Determine Meaning

When reading a text, it is common to come across unfamiliar words. One way to determine the meaning of unfamiliar words is by studying other context clues to help you better understand what the word means.

Context means the other words in the sentences around the unfamiliar word.

You can look at these other words to find **clues** or **hints** to help you figure out what the word means.

FOR EXAMPLE

Look at the following sentence:

Some of the kids in the cafeteria _ostracized_ Janice because she dressed differently; they never allowed her to sit at their lunch table, and they whispered behind her back.

If you did not know what the word _ostracized_ meant, you could look at the **other words** for **clues** to help you.

Here is what we know based on the clues in the sentence:

- Janice dressed differently
- Some kids did not allow her to sit at their table
- They whispered behind her back

We know that the kids **never allowed her to sit at their lunch** table and that they **whispered behind her back**. If you put all these clues together, you can conclude that the other students were **mistreating** Janice by **excluding** her.

Therefore, based on these context clues, _ostracized_ means "excluded from the group."

Here's another example:

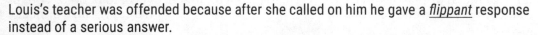

EXAMPLE 2

Look at this next sentence:

Louis's teacher was offended because after she called on him he gave a *flippant* response instead of a serious answer.

If you did not know what the word *flippant* meant, you could look at the **other words** for **clues** to help you.

Here is what we know based on the clues in the sentence:

- Louis's teacher was offended
- He gave a flippant response instead of a serious answer

We know that Louis said something that **offended** his teacher. Another keyword in this sentence is the word **instead**. This means that **instead of a serious answer** Louis gave the **opposite** of a serious answer.

Therefore, based on these context clues, *flippant* means "lacking respect or seriousness."

Multiple Meaning Words

Sometimes when we read words in a text, we encounter words that have **multiple meanings**.

Multiple meaning words are words that have **more than one definition** or meaning.

FOR EXAMPLE

The word **current** is a multiple meaning word. Here are the different definitions of *current*:

CURRENT:

1. adj: happening or existing in the present time

    Example: *It is important to keep up with current events so you know what's happening in the world.*

2. noun: the continuous movement of a body of water or air in a certain direction

    Example: *The river's current was strong as we paddled down the rapids.*

3. noun: a flow of electricity

    Example: *The electrical current was very weak in the house.*

Here are some other examples of words with multiple meanings:

Multiple Meaning Word	Definition #1	Definition #2	Definition #3
Buckle	noun: a metal or plastic device that connects one end of a belt to another	verb: to fasten or attach	verb: to bend or collapse from pressure or heat
Cabinet	noun: a piece of furniture used for storing things	noun: a group of people who give advice to a government leader	-
Channel	noun: a radio or television station	noun: a system used for sending something	noun: a long, narrow place where water flows
Doctor	noun: a person skilled in the science of medicine, dentistry, or one holding a PhD	verb: to change something in a way to trick or deceive	verb: to give medical treatment
Grave	noun: a hole in the ground for burying a dead body	adj: very serious	-
Hamper	noun: a large basket used for holding dirty clothes	verb: to slow the movement, action, or progress of	-
Plane	noun: a mode of transportation that has wings and an engine and can carry people and things in the air	noun: a flat or level surface that extends outward	noun: a level of though, development, or existence
Reservation	noun: an agreement to have something (such as a table, room, or seat) held for use at a later time	noun: a feeling of uncertainty or doubt	noun: an area of land kept separate for Native Americans to live an area of land set aside for animals to live for protection
Season	noun: one of the four periods in which a year is divided (winter, spring, summer, and fall)	noun: a particular period of time during the year	verb: to add spices to something to give it more flavor
Sentence	noun: a group words that expresses a statement, question, command, or wish	noun: the punishment given to someone by a court of law	verb: to officially state the punishment given by a court of law

From this chart you will notice that words with multiple meanings may have different **parts of speech**. A part of speech is a category of words that have the same grammatical properties. Some of the main parts of speech for words in the English language are: nouns, adjectives, verbs, and adverbs.

Part of Speech	Definition	Example
Noun	a person, place, thing, or idea	*Linda, New York City, toaster, happiness*
Adjective	a word that describes a noun or pronoun	*adventurous, young, red, intelligent*
Verb	an action or state of being	*run, is, sleep, become*
Adverb	a word that describes a verb, adjective, or other adverb	*quietly, extremely, carefully, well*

For example, in the chart above, *season* can be a **noun** or a **verb**.

Using Multiple Meaning Words Properly in Context

When you come across a **multiple meaning word** in a text, it is important to discern which meaning of the word is being used so you do not get confused.

You can once again turn to the **context clues** to clarify which meaning of the word is being used.

Let's take a look at the word *coach*. This word has several definitions:

COACH:
1. noun: a person who teaches and trains an athlete or performer
2. noun: a large bus with comfortable seating used for long trips
3. noun: the section on an airplane with the least expensive seats
4. verb: to teach or train someone in a specific area
5. verb: to give someone instructions on what to do or say in a certain situation

Since *coach* has so many definitions, you need to look at the **context clues** to figure out which definition of the word is being used:

The man was not happy that he had to sit in coach on the 24-hour flight to Australia.

In this sentence, the context clues **sit in** and **24-hour flight** help you see that *coach* means the least expensive seat on an airplane.

Let's look at another sentence using the word *coach*:

The lawyer needed to coach her witness so he would answer all the questions properly.

In this sentence, the context clues **so he would answer all the questions properly** help you see that the lawyer was giving the witness instructions on what to say.

Let's Review!

- When you come across an unfamiliar word in a text you can use context clues to help you define it.
- Context clues can also help you determine which definition of a multiple meaning word to use.

SYNONYMS, ANTONYMS, AND ANALOGIES

In order to utilize language to the best of your ability while reading, writing, or speaking, you must know how to interpret and use new vocabulary words, and also understand how these words relate to one another. Sometimes words have the same meaning. Sometimes words are complete opposites of each other. Understanding how the words you read, write, and speak with relate to each other will deepen your understanding of how language works. This lesson will cover (1) synonyms, (2) antonyms, and (3) analogies.

Synonyms

A **synonym** is a word that has the same meaning or close to the same meaning as another word. For example, if you look up the words *irritated* and *annoyed* in a dictionary, you will discover that they both mean "showing or feeling slight anger." Similarly, if you were to look up *blissful* and *joyful*, you will see that they both mean "extremely happy." The dictionary definition of a word is called its **denotation**. This is a word's literal or direct meaning.

When you understand that there are multiple words that have the same **denotation**, it will broaden your vocabulary.

It is also important to know that words with similar meanings have **nuances**, or subtle differences.

One way that words have nuances is in their **shades of meanings**. This means that although they have a similar definition, if you look closely, you will see that they have slight differences.

FOR EXAMPLE

If you quickly glance at the following words, you will see that they all have a similar meaning. However, if you look closely, you will see that their meanings have subtle differences. You can see their differences by looking at their various **levels** or **degrees**:

LEAST ⟶ MOST

---

nibble	bite	eat	devour
upset	angry	furious	irate
wet	soggy	soaked	drenched
good	great	amazing	phenomenal

Another way that words have nuance are in their **connotations.** A word's connotation is its **positive** or **negative** association. This can be the case even when two words have the same **denotations**, or dictionary definitions.

For example, the words *aroma* and *stench* both have a similar dictionary definition or **denotation**: "a smell." However, their **connotations** are quite different. *Aroma* has a **positive connotation** because it describes a *pleasant* smell. But *stench* has a **negative connotation** because it describes an unpleasant smell.

FOR EXAMPLE

Look at the following words. Although they have the same denotation, their connotations are very different:

Denotation	Positive Connotation	Negative Connotation
CLIQUE and *CLUB* both mean "a group of people."	*CLUB* has a positive connotation because it describes a group of people coming together to accomplish something.	*CLIQUE* has a negative connotation because it describes a group of people who exclude others.
INTERESTED and *NOSY* both mean "showing curiosity."	*INTERESTED* has a positive connotation because it means having a genuine curiosity about someone or something.	*NOSY* has a negative connotation because it describes who tries to pry information out of someone else to gossip or judge.
EMPLOY and *EXPLOIT* both mean "to use someone."	*EMPLOY* has a positive connotation because it means to use someone for a job.	*EXPLOIT* has a negative connotation because it means to use someone for one's own advantage.

Seeing that synonymous words have different **shades of meaning** and **connotations** will allow you to more precisely interpret and understand the nuances of language.

Antonyms

An **antonym** is a word that means the opposite or close to the opposite of another word. Think of an antonym as the direct opposite of a **synonym**. For example, *caring* and *apathetic* are antonyms because *caring* means "displaying concern and kindness for others" whereas *apathetic* means "showing no interest or concern."

Antonyms can fall under three categories:

Graded Antonyms:	Word pairs whose meanings are opposite and lie on a spectrum or continuum; there are many other words that fall between the two words. If you look at *hot* and *cold*, there are other words on this spectrum: *scalding*, **hot**, *warm, tepid, cool*, **cold**
Relational Antonyms:	Word pairs whose opposites make sense only in the context of the relationship between the two meanings. These two words could not exist without the other: **open - close**
Complementary Antonyms:	Word pairs that have no degree of meaning at all; there are only two possibilities, one or the other: **dead - alive**

Here are some more examples of the three types of antonyms:

Graded Antonyms	Relational Antonyms	Complementary Antonyms
hard - soft	front - back	day - night
fast - slow	predator - prey	sink - float
bad - good	top - bottom	input - output
wet - dry	capture - release	interior - exterior
big - small	on - off	occupied - vacant

There are also common **prefixes** that help make antonyms. The most common prefixes for antonyms of words are: **UN**, **NON**, and **IN**. All these prefixes mean "not" or "without."

FOR EXAMPLE

UN:

likely – **un**likely

fortunate – **un**fortunate

IN:

tolerant – **in**tolerant

excusable – **in**excusable

NON:

conformist – **non**conformist

payment – **non**payment

Analogies

An **analogy** is a simple comparison between two things. Analogies help us understand the world around us by seeing how different things relate to one another.

In looking closely at words, analogies help us understand how they are connected.

In word analogies, they are usually set up using colons in the following way:

Pleasure: Smile :: Pain: _____

This can be read as: Pleasure **IS TO** Smile **AS** Pain **IS TO** _____

The answer: "grimace"

Sometimes you see analogies written out like this:

Pleasure is to Smile as Pain is to _____

These are the common types of word analogies that illustrate how different words relate to one another:

Type of Analogy	Relationship	Example
Synonyms	Two words with the same meaning	Beginner : Novice:: Expert : Pro
Antonyms	Two words with the opposite meaning	Hot : Cold :: Up : Down
Part/Whole	One word is a part of another word	Stars : Galaxy :: Pages : Book
Cause/Effect	One word describes a condition or action, and the other describes an outcome	Tornado : Damage :: Joke : Laughter
Object/Function	One word describes something, and the other word describes what it's used for	Needle : Sew :: Saw : Cut

Category/Type	One word is a general category, and the other is something that falls in that category	Music : Folk :: Dance : Ballet
Performer/Related Action	One word is a person or object, and the other words is the action he/she/it commonly performs	Thief : Steal :: Surgeon : Operate
Degree of Intensity	These words have similar meanings, but one word is stronger or more intense than the other	Glad : Elated :: Angry : Furious

By recognizing the type of analogy two words have, you then can explore how they are connected.

Let's Review!

- Synonyms are words that have the same meaning. Synonyms also have nuances.
- Analogies are words that have an opposite meaning. There are three types of antonyms.
- Analogies show how words relate to each other. There are different types of analogy relationships to look for.
- Understanding how words relate to each other will help you better understand language, pull meaning from texts, and write and speak with a wider vocabulary.

CHAPTER 7 VOCABULARY ACQUISITION PRACTICE QUIZ 1

1. Select the word from the following sentence that has more than one meaning.

   Cassandra's voice has a much different pitch than her brother's, so they sound great when they sing together.

   A. Voice   C. Pitch

   B. Different   D. Sing

2. Select the correct definition of the underlined word that has multiple meanings in the sentence.

   When the young boy saw his angry mother coming toward him, he made a <u>bolt</u> for the door.

   A. A large roll of cloth

   B. A quick movement in a particular direction

   C. A sliding bar that is used to lock a window or door

   D. A bright line of light appearing in the sky during a storm

3. Select the meaning of the underlined word in the sentence based on the context clues.

   When visiting the desert, the temperature tends to <u>fluctuate</u>, so you need to bring a variety of clothing.

   A. Rise   C. Change

   B. Drop   D. Stabilize

4. The use of the suffix *ous* in the word parsimonious indicates what about a person?

   A. He/she is full of stinginess

   B. He/she is against stinginess

   C. He/she is supportive of stinginess

   D. He/she is a person who studies stinginess

5. Which of the following prefixes means <u>incorrect</u>?

   A. un-   C. mis-

   B. non-   D. over-

6. What is the best definition of the word <u>pugnacious</u>?

   A. Rude   C. Deceiving

   B. Harmful   D. Combative

7. The following words have the same denotation. Which word has a negative connotation?

   A. Poised   C. Arrogant

   B. Assured   D. Confident

8. Whisk : Mix :: Flashlight: _____

   A. Hike   C. Camp

   B. Light   D. Travel

9. Which word in the list of synonyms shows the strongest degree of the word?

   A. Amusing   C. Uproarious

   B. Comical   D. Entertaining

CHAPTER 7 VOCABULARY ACQUISITION PRACTICE QUIZ 1 – ANSWER KEY

1. **C**. The word "pitch" has more than one meaning. **See Lesson: Context Clues and Multiple Meaning Words.**

2. **B**. The meaning of <u>bolt</u> in the context of this sentence is "a quick movement in a particular direction. **See Lesson: Context Clues and Multiple Meaning Words.**

3. **C**. The meaning of <u>fluctuate</u> in the context of this sentence is "change." **See Lesson: Context Clues and Multiple Meaning Words.**

4. **A**. The suffix *ous* means "full of or possessing" so a parsimonious person is one who is full of stinginess. See **Lesson: Root Words, Prefixes, and Suffixes.**

5. **C**. The prefix that means "incorrect" is *mis*. **See Lesson: Root Words, Prefixes, and Suffixes.**

6. **D**. The root *pug* means "war," or "fight," so pugnacious means combative. **See Lesson: Root Words, Prefixes, and Suffixes.**

7. **C**. Arrogant has a negative connotation. **See Lesson: Synonyms, Antonyms, and Analogies.**

8. **B**. A whisk is a tool used to mix in the same way that a flashlight is a tool used to light. **See Lesson: Synonyms, Antonyms, and Analogies.**

9. **C**. Uproarious is the word that shows the strongest degree in the list of synonyms. **See Lesson: Synonyms, Antonyms, and Analogies.**

CHAPTER 7 VOCABULARY ACQUISITION PRACTICE QUIZ 2

1. **Which of the following prefixes means <u>too much</u>?**

   A. sub-

   B. non-

   C. mis-

   D. over-

2. **Which of the following prefixes means <u>after</u>?**

   A. post-

   B. auto-

   C. trans-

   D. inter-

3. **Which of the following root words means <u>people</u>?**

   A. ject

   B. fasc

   C. dem

   D. cycl

4. **Select the word from the following sentence that has more than one meaning.**

   It was a grave situation, and many people had given up hope.

   A. Hope

   B. Grave

   C. People

   D. Situation

5. **Select the context clue from the following sentence that helps you define the multiple meaning word <u>hatch</u>.**

   The group met each month to <u>hatch</u> a plan to overthrow the government.

   A. "group"

   B. "met"

   C. "plan"

   D. "overthrow"

6. **Select the meaning of the underlined word in the sentence based on the context clues.**

   Sheila has such an <u>exuberant</u> personality; she always has a smile on her face.

   A. Sincere

   B. Cheerful

   C. Appealing

   D. Interesting

7. **The following words have the same denotation. Which word has a positive connotation?**

   A. Assertive

   B. Dictatorial

   C. Domineering

   D. Overbearing

8. **Doctor : Pediatrician :: Instrument : _____**

   A. Harp

   B. Harmony

   C. Musician

   D. Orchestra

9. **Adding which prefix to <u>intentional</u> would make the antonym of the word?**

   A. De-

   B. Un-

   C. Dis-

   D. Mis-

CHAPTER 7 VOCABULARY ACQUISITION PRACTICE QUIZ 2 – ANSWER KEY

1. **D.** The prefix that means "too much" is *over*. **See Lesson: Root Words, Prefixes, and Suffixes.**

2. **A.** The prefix that means "after" is *post*. **See Lesson: Root Words, Prefixes, and Suffixes.**

3. **C.** The root that means "people" is *dem as in the word democracy*. **See Lesson: Root Words, Prefixes, and Suffixes.**

4. **B.** The word "grave" has more than one meaning. **See Lesson: Context Clues and Multiple Meaning Words.**

5. **C.** The meaning of <u>hatch</u> in this context is "to create or produce an idea in a secret way." The word "plan" helps you figure out which meaning of <u>hatch</u> is being used. **See Lesson: Context Clues and Multiple Meaning Words.**

6. **B.** The meaning of <u>exuberant</u> in the context of this sentence is "cheerful." **See Lesson: Context Clues and Multiple Meaning Words.**

7. **A.** Assertive has a positive connotation. **See Lesson: Synonyms, Antonyms, and Analogies.**

8. **A.** A pediatrician is an example of a doctor in the same way that a harp is an example of an instrument. **See Lesson: Synonyms, Antonyms, and Analogies.**

9. **B.** Adding the prefix "un" would make the word unintentional, which is an antonym for intentional. **See Lesson: Synonyms, Antonyms, and Analogies.**

SECTION III. MATHEMATICS

CHAPTER 8 NUMBER AND QUANTITY

BASIC ADDITION AND SUBTRACTION

This lesson introduces the concept of numbers and their symbolic and graphical representations. It also describes how to add and subtract whole numbers.

Numbers

A **number** is a way to quantify a set of entities that share some characteristic. For example, a fruit basket might contain nine pieces of fruit. More specifically, it might contain three apples, two oranges, and four bananas. Note that a number is a quantity, but a **numeral** is the symbol that represents the number: 8 means the number eight, for instance.

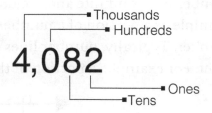

Although number representations vary, the most common is **base 10**. In base-10 format, each **digit** (or individual numeral) in a number is a quantity based on a multiple of 10. The base-10 system designates 0 through 9 as the numerals for zero through nine, respectively, and combines them to represent larger numbers. Thus, after counting from 1 to 9, the next number uses an additional digit: 10. That number means 1 group of 10 ones plus 0 additional ones. After 99, another digit is necessary, this time representing a hundred (10 sets of 10). This process of adding digits can go on indefinitely to express increasingly large numbers. For whole numbers, the rightmost digit is the ones place, the next digit to its left is the tens place, the next is the hundreds place, then the thousands place, and so on.

Classifying numbers can be convenient. The chart below lists a few common number sets.

Sets of Numbers	Members	Remarks
Natural numbers	1, 2, 3, 4, 5,...	The "counting" numbers
Whole numbers	0, 1, 2, 3, 4,...	The natural numbers plus 0
Integers	..., –3, –2, –1, 0, 1, 2, 3,...	The whole numbers plus all negative whole numbers
Real numbers	All numbers	The integers plus all fraction/decimal numbers in between
Rational numbers	All real numbers that can be expressed as p/q, where p and q are integers and q is nonzero	The natural numbers, whole numbers, and integers are all rational numbers
Irrational numbers	All real numbers that are not rational	The rational and irrational numbers together constitute the entire set of real numbers

Example

Jane has 4 pennies, 3 dimes, and 7 dollars. How many cents does she have?

A. 347 B. 437 C. 734 D. 743

The correct answer is **C**. The correct solution is 734. A penny is 1 cent. A dime (10 pennies) is 10 cents, and a dollar (100 pennies) is 100 cents. Place the digits in base-10 format: 7 hundreds, 3 tens, 4 ones, or 734.

The Number Line

The **number line** is a model that illustrates the relationships among numbers. The complete number line is infinite and includes every real number—both positive and negative. A ruler, for example, is a portion of a number line that assigns a **unit** (such as inches or centimeters) to each number. Typically, number lines depict smaller numbers to the left and larger numbers to the right. For example, a portion of the number line centered on 0 might look like the following:

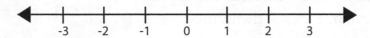

Because people learn about numbers in part through counting, they have a basic sense of how to order them. The number line builds on this sense by placing all the numbers (at least conceptually) from least to greatest. Whether a particular number is greater than or less than another is determined by comparing their relative positions. One number is greater than another if it is farther right on the number line. Likewise, a number is less than another if it is farther left on the number line. Symbolically, < means "is less than" and > means "is greater than." For example, $5 > 1$ and $9 < 25$.

Example

Place the following numbers in order from greatest to least: 5, –12, 0.

A. 0, 5, –12   C. 5, 0, –12

B. –12, 5, 0   D. –12, 0, 5

> **BE CAREFUL!**
>
> When ordering negative numbers, think of the number line. Although $-10 > -2$ may seem correct, it is incorrect. Because -10 is to the left of -2 on the number line, $-10 < -2$.

The correct answer is **C**. The correct solution is 5, 0, –12. Use the number line to order the numbers. Note that the question says *from greatest to least*.

Addition

Addition is the process of combining two or more numbers. For example, one set has 4 members and another set has 5 members. To combine the sets and find out how many members are in the new set, add 4 and 5 to get the **sum**. Symbolically, the expression is $4 + 5$, where + is the **plus sign**. Pictorially, it might look like the following:

$$\underset{\circ\circ}{\circ\circ} \quad + \quad \underset{\circ\circ\circ}{\circ\circ} \quad = \quad \underset{\circ\circ\circ\circ\circ}{\circ\circ\circ\circ}$$

To get the sum, combine the two sets of circles and then count them. The result is 9.

> **KEY POINT**
> The order of the numbers is irrelevant when adding.

Another way to look at addition involves the number line. When adding 4 + 5, for example, start at 4 on the number line and take 5 steps to the right. The stopping point will be 9, which is the sum.

Counting little pictures or using the number line works for small numbers, but it becomes unwieldy for large ones—even numbers such as 24 and 37 would be difficult to add quickly and accurately. A simple algorithm enables much faster addition of large numbers. It works with two or more numbers.

STEP BY STEP

Step 1. Stack the numbers, vertically aligning the digits for each place.

Step 2. Draw a plus sign (+) to the left of the bottom number and draw a horizontal line below the last number.

Step 3. Add the digits in the ones place.

Step 4. If the sum from Step 3 is less than 10, write it in the same column below the horizontal line. Otherwise, write the first (ones) digit below the line, then **carry** the second (tens) digit to the top of the next column.

Step 5. Going from right to left, repeat Steps 3–4 for the other places.

Step 6. If applicable, write the remaining carry digit as the leftmost digit in the sum.

Example

Evaluate the expression 154 + 98.

A. 250   B. 252   C. 352   D. 15,498

The correct answer is **B**. The correct solution is 252. Carefully follow the addition algorithm (see below). The process involves carrying a digit twice.

$$
\begin{array}{r} 154 \\ +\ 98 \\ \hline \end{array}
\longrightarrow
\begin{array}{r} ^{1} \\ 154 \\ +\ 98 \\ \hline 2 \end{array}
\longrightarrow
\begin{array}{r} ^{11} \\ 154 \\ +\ 98 \\ \hline 52 \end{array}
\longrightarrow
\begin{array}{r} ^{11} \\ 154 \\ +\ 98 \\ \hline 252 \end{array}
$$

Subtraction

Subtraction is the inverse (opposite) of addition. Instead of representing the sum of numbers, it represents the difference between them. For example, given a set containing 15 members, subtracting 3 of those members yields a **difference** of 12. Using the **minus sign**, the expression for this operation is 15 − 3 = 12. As with addition, two approaches are counting pictures and using the number line. The first case might involve drawing 15 circles and then crossing off 3 of them; the difference is the number of remaining circles (12). To use the number line, begin at 15 and move left 3 steps to reach 12.

Again, these approaches are unwieldy for large numbers, but the subtraction algorithm eases evaluation by hand. This algorithm is only practical for two numbers at a time.

STEP BY STEP

Step 1. Stack the numbers, vertically aligning the digits in each place. Put the number you are subtracting *from* on top.

Step 2. Draw a minus sign (−) to the left of the bottom number and draw a horizontal line below the stack of numbers.

Step 3. Start at the ones place. If the digit at the top is larger than the digit below it, write the difference under the line. Otherwise, **borrow** from the top digit in the next-higher place by crossing it off, subtracting 1 from it, and writing the difference above it. Then add 10 to the digit in the ones place and perform the subtraction as normal.

Step 4. Going from right to left, repeat Step 3 for the rest of the places. If borrowing was necessary, make sure to use the new digit in each place, not the original one.

When adding or subtracting with negative numbers, the following rules are helpful. Note that x and y are used as placeholders for any real number.

$x + (-y) = x-y$

$-x-y = -(x + y)$

$(-x) + (-y) = -(x + y)$

$x-y = -(y-x)$

BE CAREFUL!

When dealing with numbers that have units (such as weights, currencies, or volumes), addition and subtraction are only possible when the numbers have the same unit. If necessary, convert one or more of them to equivalent numbers with the same unit.

Example

Kevin has 120 minutes to complete an exam. If he has already used 43, how many minutes does he have left?

A. 43   B. 77   C. 87   D. 163

The correct answer is **B**. The correct solution is 77. The first step is to convert this problem to a math expression. The goal is to find the difference between how many minutes Kevin has for the exam and how many he has left after 43 minutes have elapsed. The expression would be 120 – 43. Carefully follow the subtraction algorithm (see below). The process will involve borrowing a digit twice.

$$
\begin{array}{r} 120 \\ -\ 43 \\ \hline \end{array}
\rightarrow
\begin{array}{r} {\scriptstyle 1\,10} \\ 12\!\!\!/0 \\ -\ 43 \\ \hline 7 \end{array}
\rightarrow
\begin{array}{r} {\scriptstyle 0\ 11\,10} \\ \not{1}\not{2}0 \\ -\ 43 \\ \hline 77 \end{array}
$$

Let's Review!

- Numbers are positive and negative quantities and often appear in base-10 format.
- The number line illustrates the ordering of numbers.
- Addition is the combination of numbers. It can be performed by counting objects or pictures, moving on the number line, or using the addition algorithm.
- Subtraction is finding the difference between numbers. Like addition, it can be performed by counting, moving on the number line, or using the subtraction algorithm.

BASIC MULTIPLICATION AND DIVISION

This lesson describes the process of multiplying and dividing numbers and introduces the order of operations, which governs how to evaluate expressions containing multiple arithmetic operations.

Multiplication

Addition can be tedious if it involves multiple instances of the same numbers. For example, evaluating 29 + 29 is easy, but evaluating 29 + 29 + 29 + 29 + 29 is laborious. Note that this example contains five instances—or multiples—of 29. **Multiplication** replaces the repeated addition of the same number with a single, more concise operation. Using the **multiplication (or times) symbol** ($\times$), the expression is

$$29 + 29 + 29 + 29 + 29 = 5 \times 29$$

The expression contains 5 multiples of 29. These numbers are the **factors** of multiplication. The result is called the **product.** In this case, addition shows that the product is 145. As with the other arithmetic operations, multiplication is easy for small numbers. Below is the multiplication table for whole numbers up to 12.

	1	2	3	4	5	6	7	8	9	10	11	12
1	1	2	3	4	5	6	7	8	9	10	11	12
2	2	4	6	8	10	12	14	16	18	20	22	24
3	3	6	9	12	15	18	21	24	27	30	33	36
4	4	8	12	16	20	24	28	32	36	40	44	48
5	5	10	15	20	25	30	35	40	45	50	55	60
6	6	12	18	24	30	36	42	48	54	60	66	72
7	7	14	21	28	35	42	49	56	63	70	77	84
8	8	16	24	32	40	48	56	64	72	80	88	96
9	9	18	27	36	45	54	63	72	81	90	99	108
10	10	20	30	40	50	60	70	80	90	100	110	120
11	11	22	33	44	55	66	77	88	99	110	121	132
12	12	24	36	48	60	72	84	96	108	120	132	144

When dealing with large numbers, the multiplication algorithm is more practical than memorization. The ability to quickly recall the products in the multiplication table is nevertheless crucial to using this algorithm.

STEP BY STEP

Step 1. Stack the two factors, vertically aligning the digits in each place.

Step 2. Draw a multiplication symbol (×) to the left of the bottom number and draw a horizontal line below the stack.

Step 3. Begin with the ones digit in the lower factor. Multiply it with the ones digit from the top factor.

Step 4. If the product from Step 3 is less than 10, write it in the same column below the horizontal line. Otherwise, write the first (ones) digit below the line and carry the second (tens) digit to the top of the next column.

Step 5. Perform Step 4 for each digit in the top factor, adding any carry digit to the result. If an extra carry digit appears at the end, write it as the leftmost digit in the product.

Step 6. Going right to left, repeat Steps 3–4 for the other places in the bottom factor, starting a new line in each case.

Step 7. Add the numbers below the line to get the product.

Example

A certain type of screw comes in packs of 35. If a contractor orders 52 packs, how many screws does he receive?

A. 2 B. *57* C. 245 D. 1,820

The correct answer is **D**. The first step is to convert this problem to a math expression. The goal is to find how many screws the contractor receives if he orders 52 packs of 35 each. The expression would be 52×35 (or 35×52). Carefully follow the multiplication algorithm (see below).

$$
\begin{array}{r} 52 \\ \times\ 35 \\ \hline \end{array}
\rightarrow
\begin{array}{r} {}^{1}52 \\ \times\ 35 \\ \hline 0 \end{array}
\rightarrow
\begin{array}{r} {}^{1}52 \\ \times\ 35 \\ \hline 260 \end{array}
\rightarrow
\begin{array}{r} {}^{1}52 \\ \times\ 35 \\ \hline 260 \\ 6 \end{array}
\rightarrow
\begin{array}{r} {}^{1}{}^{1}52 \\ \times\ 35 \\ \hline 260 \\ 56 \end{array}
\rightarrow
\begin{array}{r} {}^{1}{}^{1}52 \\ \times\ 35 \\ \hline 260 \\ 156 \end{array}
\rightarrow
\begin{array}{r} {}^{1}{}^{1}52 \\ \times\ 35 \\ \hline 260 \\ +\ 156 \\ \hline 1,820 \end{array}
$$

KEY POINT

As with addition, the order of numbers in a multiplication expression is irrelevant to the product. For example, $6 \times 9 = 9 \times 6$.

Division

Division is the inverse of multiplication, like subtraction is the inverse of addition. Whereas multiplication asks how many individuals are in 8 groups of 9 (8 × 9 = 72), for example, division asks how many groups of 8 (or 9) are in 72. Division expressions use either the / or ÷ symbol. Therefore, 72 ÷ 9 means: How many groups of 9 are in 72, or how many times does 9 go into 72? Thinking about the meaning of multiplication shows that 72 ÷ 9 = 8 and 72 ÷ 8 = 9. In the expression 72 ÷ 8 = 9, 72 is the **dividend**, 8 is the **divisor**, and 9 is the **quotient**.

When the dividend is unevenly divisible by the divisor (e.g., 5 ÷ 2), calculating the quotient with a **remainder** can be convenient. The quotient in this case is the maximum number of times the divisor goes into the dividend plus how much of the dividend is left over. To express the remainder, use an R. For example, the quotient of 5 ÷ 2 is 2R1 because 2 goes into 5 twice with 1 left over.

Knowing the multiplication table allows quick evaluation of simple whole-number division. For larger numbers, the division algorithm enables evaluation by hand.

Unlike multiplication—but like subtraction—the order of the numbers in a division expression is important. Generally, changing the order changes the quotient.

STEP BY STEP

Step 1. Write the divisor and then the dividend on a single line.

Step 2. Draw a vertical line between them, connecting to a horizontal line over the dividend.

Step 3. If the divisor is smaller than the leftmost digit of the dividend, perform the remainder division and write the quotient (without the remainder) above that digit. If the divisor is larger than the leftmost digit, use the first two digits (or however many are necessary) until the number is greater than the divisor. Write the quotient over the rightmost digit in that number.

Step 4. Multiply the quotient digit by the divisor and write it under the dividend, vertically aligning the ones digit of the product with the quotient digit.

Step 5. Subtract the product from the digits above it.

Step 6. Bring down the next digit from the quotient.

Step 7. Perform Steps 3–6, using the most recent difference as the quotient.

Step 8. Write the remainder next to the quotient.

Example

Evaluate the expression 468 ÷ 26.

A. 18   B. 18R2   C. 494   D. 12,168

The correct answer is **A.** Carefully follow the division algorithm. In this case, the answer has no remainder.

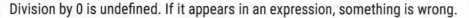

> **KEY POINT**
> Division by 0 is undefined. If it appears in an expression, something is wrong.

Signed Multiplication and Division

Multiplying and dividing signed numbers is simpler than adding and subtracting them because it only requires remembering two simple rules. First, if the two numbers have the same sign, their product or quotient is positive. Second, if they have different signs, their product or quotient is negative.

As a result, negative numbers can be multiplied or divided as if they are positive. Just keep track of the sign separately for the product or quotient. Note that negative numbers are sometimes written in parentheses to avoid the appearance of subtraction.

For Example:

$5 \times (-3) = -15$

$(-8) \times (-8) = 64$

$(-12) \div 3 = -4$

$(-100) \div (-25) = 4$

Example

Evaluate the expression (–7) × (–9).

A. −63   B. −16   C. 16   D. 63

The correct answer is **D.** Because both factors are negative, the product will be positive. Because the product of 7 and 9 is 63, the product of −7 and −9 is also 63.

Order of Operations

By default, math expressions work like most Western languages: they should be read and evaluated from left to right. However, some operations take precedence over others, which can change this default evaluation. Following this **order of operations** is critical. The mnemonic **PEMDAS** (Please Excuse My Dear Aunt Sally) helps in remembering how to evaluate an expression with multiple operations.

> **STEP BY STEP**
>
> **P.** Evaluate operations in parentheses (or braces/brackets). If the expression has parentheses within parentheses, begin with the innermost ones.
>
> **E.** Evaluate exponential operations. (For expressions without exponents, ignore this step.)
>
> **MD.** Perform all multiplication and division operations, going through the expression from left to right.
>
> **AS.** Perform all addition and subtraction operations, going through the expression from left to right.

Because the order of numbers in multiplication and addition does not affect the result, the PEMDAS procedure only requires going from left to right when dividing or subtracting. At those points, going in the correct direction is critical to getting the right answer.

Calculators that can handle a series of numbers at once automatically evaluate an expression according to the order of operations. When available, calculators are a good way to check the results.

> **BE CAREFUL!**
>
> When evaluating an expression like $4 - 3 + 2 \times 5$, remember to go from left to right when adding and subtracting or when multiplying and dividing. The first step in this case (MD) yields $4 - 3 + 10$. Avoid the temptation to add first in the next step; instead, go from left to right. The result is $1 + 10 = 11$, *not* $4 - 13 = -9$.

Example

Evaluate the expression 8 × (3 + 6) ÷ 3–2 + 5.

A. 13   B. 17   C. 27   D. 77

The correct answer is **C.** Use the PEMDAS mnemonic. Start with parentheses. Then, do multiplication/division from left to right. Finally, do addition/subtraction from left to right.

$8 \times (3 + 6) \div 3{-}2 + 5$

$8 \times 9 \div 3{-}2 + 5$

$72 \div 3{-}2 + 5$

$24{-}2 + 5$

$22 + 5$

27

Let's Review!

- The multiplication table is important to memorize for both multiplying and dividing small whole numbers (up to about 12).
- Multiplication and division of large numbers by hand typically requires the multiplication and division algorithms.
- Multiplying and dividing signed numbers follows two simple rules: If the numbers have the same sign, the product or quotient is positive. If they have different signs, the product or quotient is negative.
- When evaluating expressions with several operations, carefully follow the order of operations; PEMDAS is a helpful mnemonic.

FACTORS AND MULTIPLES

This lesson shows the relationship between factors and multiples of a number. In addition, it introduces prime and composite numbers and demonstrates how to use prime factorization to determine all the factors of a number.

Factors of a Number

Multiplication converts two or more factors into a product. A given number, however, may be the product of more than one combination of factors; for example, 12 is the product of 3 and 4 and the product of 2 and 6. Limiting consideration to the set of whole numbers, a **factor of a number** (call it x) is a whole number whose product with any other whole number is equal to x. For instance, 2 is a factor of 12 because $12 \div 2$ is a whole number (6). Another way of expressing it is that 2 is a factor of 12 because 12 is **divisible** by 2.

> **BE CAREFUL!**
>
> The term *factor* can mean any number being multiplied by another number, or it can mean a number by which another number is divisible. The two uses are related but slightly different. The context will generally clarify which meaning applies.

A whole number always has at least two factors: 1 and itself. That is, for any whole number y, $1 \times y = y$. To test whether one number is a factor of a second number, divide the second by the first. If the quotient is whole, it is a factor. If the quotient is not whole (or it has a remainder), it is not a factor.

Example

Which number is not a factor of 54?

A. 1   B. 2   C. 4   D. 6

The correct answer is **C**. A number is a factor of another number if the latter is divisible by the former. The number 54 is divisible by 1 because $54 \times 1 = 54$, and it is divisible by 2 because $27 \times 2 = 54$. Also, $6 \times 9 = 54$. But $54 \div 4 = 13.5$ (or 13R2). Therefore, 4 is not a factor.

Multiples of a Number

Multiples of a number are related to factors of a number. A **multiple of a number** is that number's product with some integer. For example, if a hardware store sells a type of screw that only comes in packs of 20, customers must buy these screws in *multiples* of 20: that is, 20, 40, 60, 80, and so on. (Technically, 0 is also a multiple.) These numbers are equal to 20×1, 20×2, 20×3, 20×4, and so on. Similarly, measurements in feet represent multiples of 12 inches. A (whole-number) measurement in feet would be equivalent to 12 inches, 24 inches, 36 inches, and so on.

When counting by twos or threes, multiples are used. But because the multiples of a number are the product of that number with the integers, multiples can also be negative. For the number 2, the multiples are the set {..., −6, −4, −2, 0, 2, 4, 6,...}, where the ellipsis dots indicate that the set continues the pattern indefinitely in both directions. Also, the number can be any real number: the multiples of π (approximately 3.14) are {..., −3π, −2π, −1π, 0, 1π, 2π, 3π,...}. Note that the notation 2π, for example, means $2 \times \pi$.

The positive multiples (along with 0) of a whole number are all numbers for which that whole number is a factor. For instance, the positive multiples of 5 are 0, 5, 10, 15, 20, 25, 30, and so on. That full set contains all (whole) numbers for which 5 is a factor. Thus, one number is a multiple of a second number if the second number is a factor of the first.

Example

If a landowner subdivides a parcel of property into multiples of 7 acres, how many acres can a buyer purchase?

A. 1   B. 15   C. 29   D. 42

The correct answer is **D**. Because the landowner subdivides the property into multiples of 7 acres, a buyer must choose an acreage from the list 7 acres, 14 acres, 21 acres, and so on. That list includes 42 acres. Another way to solve the problem is to find which answer is divisible by 7 (that is, which number has 7 as a factor).

Prime and Composite Numbers

For some real-world applications, such as cryptography, factors and multiples play an important role. One important way to classify whole numbers is by whether they are prime or composite. A **prime** number is any whole (or natural) number greater than 1 that has only itself and 1 as factors. The smallest example is 2: because 2 only has 1 and 2 as factors, it is prime. **Composite** numbers have at least one factor other than 1 and themselves. The smallest composite number is 4: in addition to 1 and 4, it has 2 as a factor.

Determining whether a number is prime can be extremely difficult—hence its value in cryptography. One simple test that works for some numbers is to check whether the number is even or odd. An **even number** is divisible by 2; an **odd number** is not. To determine whether a number is even or odd, look at the last (rightmost) digit.

> **BE CAREFUL!**
> Avoid the temptation to call 1 a prime number. Although it only has itself and 1 as factors, those factors are the same number. Hence, 1 is fundamentally different from the prime numbers, which start at 2.

If that digit is even (0, 2, 4, 6, or 8), the number is even. Otherwise, it is odd. Another simple test works for multiples of 3. Add all the digits in the number. If the sum is divisible by 3, the original number is also divisible by 3. This rule can be successively applied multiple times until the sum of digits is manageable. That number is then composite.

Example

Which number is prime?

A. 6   B. 16   C. 61   D. 116

The correct answer is **C**. When applicable, the easiest way to identify a number greater than 2 as composite rather than prime is to check whether it is even. All even numbers greater than 2 are composite. By elimination, 61 is prime.

Prime Factorization

Determining whether a number is prime, even for relatively small numbers (less than 100), can be difficult. One tool that can help both solve this problem and identify all factors of a number is **prime factorization**. One way to do prime factorization is to make a **factor tree**.

The procedure below demonstrates the process.

STEP BY STEP

Step 1. Write the number you want to factor.

Step 2. If the number is prime, stop. Otherwise, go to Step 3.

Step 3. Find any two factors of the number and write them on the line below the number.

Step 4. "Connect" the factors and the number using line segments. The result will look somewhat like an inverted tree, particularly as the process continues.

Step 5. Repeat Steps 2–4 for all composite factors in the tree.

The numbers in the factor tree are either "branches" (if they are connected downward to other numbers) or "leaves" (if they have no further downward connections). The leaves constitute all the prime factors of the original number: when multiplied together, their product is that number. Moreover, any product of two or more of the leaves is a factor of the original number. Thus, using prime factorization helps find any and all factors of a number, although the process can be tedious when performed by hand (particularly for large numbers). Below is a factor tree for the number 96. All the leaves are circled for emphasis.

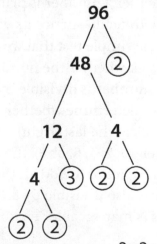

$2 \times 2 \times 3 \times 2 \times 2 \times 2 = 96$

Example

Which list includes all the unique prime factors of 84?

    A. 2, 3, 7   B. 3, 4, 7   C. 3, 5, 7   D. 1, 2, 3, 7

The correct answer is **A**. One approach is to find the prime factorization of 84. The factor tree shows that $84 = 2 \times 2 \times 3 \times 7$. Alternatively, note that answer D includes 1, which is not prime. Answer B includes 4, which is a composite number. Since answer C includes 5, which is not a factor of 84, the only possible answer is A.

Let's Review!

- A whole number is divisible by all of its factors, which are also whole numbers by definition.
- Multiples of a number are all possible products of that number and the integers.
- A prime number is a whole number greater than 1 that has no factors other than itself and 1.
- A composite number is a whole number greater than 1 that is not prime (that is, it has factors other than itself and 1).
- Even numbers are divisible by 2; odd numbers are not.
- Prime factorization yields all the prime factors of a number. The factor-tree method is one way to determine prime factorization.

STANDARDS OF MEASURE

This lesson discusses the conversion within and between the standard system and the metric system and between 12-hour clock time and military time.

Length Conversions

The basic units of measure of length in the standard measurement system are inches, feet, yards, and miles. There are 12 inches (in.) in 1 foot (ft.), 3 feet (ft.) in 1 yard (yd.), and 5,280 feet (ft.) in 1 mile (mi.).

The basic unit of measure of metric length is meters. There are 1,000 millimeters (mm), 100 centimeters (cm), and 10 decimeters (dm) in 1 meter (m). There are 10 meters (m) in 1 dekameter (dam), 100 meters (m) in 1 hectometer (hm), and 1,000 meters (m) in 1 kilometer (km).

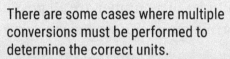

BE CAREFUL!

There are some cases where multiple conversions must be performed to determine the correct units.

To convert from one unit to the other, multiply by the appropriate factor.

Examples

1. **Convert 27 inches to feet.**

   A. 2 feet
   B. 2.25 feet
   C. 3 feet
   D. 3.25 feet

   The correct answer is **B**. The correct solution is 2.25 feet. $27 \text{ in} \times \frac{1 \text{ ft}}{12 \text{ in}} = \frac{27}{12} = 2.25$ ft.

2. **Convert 67 millimeters to centimeters.**

   A. 0.0067 centimeters
   C. 0.67 centimeters
   B. 0.067 centimeters
   D. 6.7 centimeters

   The correct answer is **D**. The correct solution is 6.7 centimeters. $67 \text{ mm} \times \frac{1 \text{ cm}}{10 \text{ mm}} = \frac{67}{10} = 6.7$ cm.

Volume and Weight Conversions

There are volume conversion factors for standard and metric volumes.

The volume conversions for standard volume are shown in the table.

Measurement	Conversion
Pints (pt.) and fluid ounces (fl. oz.)	1 pint equals 16 fluid ounces
Quarts (qt.) and pints (pt.)	1 quart equals 2 pints
Quarts (qt.) and gallons (gal.)	1 gallon equals 4 quarts

The basic unit of volume for the metric system is liters. There are 1,000 milliliters (mL) in 1 liter (L) and 1,000 liters (L) in 1 kiloliter (kL).

There are weight conversion factors for standard and metric weights.

The basic unit of weight for the standard measurement system is pounds. There are

16 ounces (oz.) in 1 pound (lb.) and

2,000 pounds (lb.) in 1 ton (T).

The basic unit of weight for the metric system is grams.

KEEP IN MIND

The conversions within the metric system are multiples of 10.

Measurement	Conversion
Milligrams (mg) and grams (g)	1,000 milligrams equals 1 gram
Centigrams (cg) and grams (g)	100 centigrams equals 1 gram
Kilograms (kg) and grams (g)	1 kilogram equals 1,000 grams
Metric tons (t) and kilograms (kg)	1 metric ton equals 1,000 kilograms

Examples

1. **Convert 8 gallons to pints.**

   A. 1 pint   B. 4 pints   C. 16 pints   D. 64 pints

   The correct answer is **D**. The correct solution is 64 pints. $8 \text{ gal} \times \frac{4 \text{ qt}}{1 \text{ gal}} \times \frac{2 \text{ pt}}{1 \text{ qt}} = 64 \text{ pt}$.

2. **Convert 7.5 liters to milliliters.**

   A. 75 milliliters   B. 750 milliliters   C. 7,500 milliliters   D. 75,000 milliliters

   The correct answer is **C**. The correct solution is 7,500 milliliters. $7.5 \text{ L} \times \frac{1,000 \text{ mL}}{1 \text{ L}} = 7,500 \text{ mL}$.

3. **Convert 12.5 pounds to ounces.**

   A. 142 ounces   B. 150 ounces   C. 192 ounces   D. 200 ounces

   The correct answer is **D**. The correct solution is 200 ounces. $12.5 \text{ lb} \times \frac{16 \text{ oz}}{1 \text{ lb}} = 200 \text{ oz}$.

4. **Convert 84 grams to centigrams.**

   A. 0.84 centigrams   B. 8.4 centigrams   C. 840 centigrams   D. 8,400 centigrams

   The correct answer is **D**. The correct solution is 8,400 centigrams. $84 \text{ g} \times \frac{100 \text{ cg}}{1 \text{ g}} = 8,400 \text{ cg}$.

Conversions between Standard and Metric Systems

The table shows the common conversions of length, volume, and weight between the standard and metric systems.

Measurement	Conversion
Centimeters (cm) and inches (in.)	2.54 centimeters equals 1 inch
Meters (m) and feet (ft.)	1 meter equals 3.28 feet
Kilometers (km) and miles (mi.)	1.61 kilometers equals 1 mile
Quarts (qt.) and liters (L)	1.06 quarts equals 1 liter
Liters (L) and gallons (gal.)	3.79 liters equals 1 gallon
Grams (g) and ounces (oz.)	28.3 grams equals 1 ounce
Kilograms (kg) and pounds (lb.)	1 kilogram equals 2.2 pounds

There are many additional conversion factors, but this lesson uses only the common ones. Most factors have been rounded to the nearest hundredth for accuracy.

STEP BY STEP

Step 1. Choose the appropriate conversion factor within each system, if necessary.

Step 2. Choose the appropriate conversion factor from the standard and metric conversion.

Step 3. Multiply and simplify to the nearest hundredth.

Examples

1. **Convert 12 inches to centimeters.**

   A. 4.72 centimeters
   B. 14.54 centimeters
   C. 28.36 centimeters
   D. 30.48 centimeters

   The correct answer is **D**. The correct solution is 30.48 centimeters. $12 \text{ in} \times \frac{2.54 \text{ cm}}{1 \text{ in}} = 30.48 \text{ cm}$.

2. **Convert 8 kilometers to feet.**

   A. 13,118.01 feet
   B. 26,236.02 feet
   C. 34,003.20 feet
   D. 68,006.40 feet

   The correct answer is **B**. The correct solution is 26,236.02 feet. $8 \text{ km} \times \frac{1 \text{ mi}}{1.61 \text{ km}} \times \frac{5,280 \text{ ft}}{1 \text{ mi}} = \frac{42,240}{1.61} = 26,236.02 \text{ ft}$.

3. **Convert 2 gallons to milliliters.**

   A. 527 milliliters
   B. 758 milliliters
   C. 5,270 milliliters
   D. 7,580 milliliters

   The correct answer is **D**. The correct solution is 7,580 milliliters.
   $2 \text{ gal} \times \frac{3.79 \text{ L}}{1 \text{ gal}} \times \frac{1,000 \text{ mL}}{1 \text{ L}} = 7,580 \text{ mL}$.

4. **Convert 16 kilograms to pounds.**

    A. 7.27 pounds   B. 18.2 pounds   C. 19.27 pounds   D. 35.2 pounds

    The correct answer is **D**. The correct solution is 35.2 pounds. $16 \text{ kg} \times \frac{2.2 \text{ lb}}{1 \text{ kg}} = 35.2 \text{ lb}$.

Time Conversions

Two ways to keep time are 12-hour clock time using a.m. and p.m. and military time based on a 24-hour clock. Keep these three key points in mind:

> **KEEP IN MIND**
> Midnight (12:00 a.m.) is 2400 or 0000 in military time.

- The hours from 1:00 a.m. to 12:59 p.m. are the same in both methods. For example, 9:15 a.m. in 12-hour clock time is 0915 in military time.
- From 1:00 p.m. to 11:59 p.m., add 12 hours to obtain military time. For example, 4:07 p.m. in 12-hour clock time is 1607 in military time.
- From 12:01 a.m. to 12:59 a.m. in 12-hour clock time, military time is from 0001 to 0059.

Example

Identify 9:27 p.m. in military time.

A. 0927   B. 1927   C. 2127   D. 2427

The correct answer is **C**. The correct solution is 2127. Add 1200 to the time, 1200 + 927 = 2127.

Let's Review!

- To convert from one unit to another, choose the appropriate conversion factors.
- In many cases, it is necessary to use multiple conversion factors.

CHAPTER 8 NUMBER AND QUANTITY PRACTICE QUIZ 1

1. Evaluate the expression 8 − 27.

   A. −35

   B. −19

   C. 0

   D. 19

2. Evaluate the expression 102 + 3 + 84 + 27.

   A. 105

   B. 216

   C. 250

   D. 513

3. How much change should a customer expect if she is buying a $53 item and hands the cashier two $50 bills?

   A. $3

   B. $47

   C. $57

   D. $100

4. When dealing with a series of multiplication and division operations, which is the correct approach to evaluating them?

   A. Evaluate all division operations first.

   B. Evaluate the expression from left to right.

   C. Evaluate all multiplication operations first.

   D. None of the above.

5. Evaluate the expression 28 × 43.

   A. 71

   B. 196

   C. 1,204

   D. 1,960

6. Evaluate the expression 3 + 1 − 5 + 2 − 6.

   A. −9

   B. −5

   C. 0

   D. 17

7. Which number is a factor of 128?

   A. 3

   B. 6

   C. 12

   D. 16

8. How many prime factors does 42 have?

   A. 1

   B. 2

   C. 3

   D. 4

9. If a factor tree for a prime factorization has four leaves—3, 2, 5, and 7—what is the number being factored?

   A. 7

   B. 5

   C. 210

   D. Not enough information

10. Convert 16,000 ounces to tons.

    A. 0.5 ton

    B. 1 ton

    C. 1.5 tons

    D. 2 tons

11. Convert 99 meters to kilometers.

    A. 0.0099 kilometers

    B. 0.099 kilometers

    C. 0.9 centimeters

    D. 9.9 centimeters

12. Identify 12:45 a.m. in military time.

    A. 0045

    B. 0145

    C. 1245

    D. 1345

Chapter 8 Number and Quantity
Practice Quiz 1 – Answer Key

1. B. The correct solution is –19. Because the subtraction algorithm does not apply directly in this case (the first number is smaller than the second), first use the rule that $x - y = -(y - x)$. So, $8 - 27 = -(27 - 8)$. Applying the algorithm to $27 - 8$ yields 19, then $-(27 - 8) = -19$. **See Lesson: Basic Addition and Subtraction.**

2. B. The correct solution is 216. Use the addition algorithm. Add the numbers two at a time or all at once. The latter approach will involve two carry digits. **See Lesson: Basic Addition and Subtraction.**

3. B. The correct solution is $47. The customer gives the cashier $100, which is the sum of $50 and $50. To find out how much change she receives, calculate the difference between $100 and $53, which is $47. **See Lesson: Basic Addition and Subtraction.**

4. B. Multiplication and division have equivalent priority in the order of operations. In this case, the expression must be evaluated from left to right. **See Lesson: Basic Multiplication and Division.**

5. C. Use the multiplication algorithm. It involves adding 84 and 1,120 to get the product of 1,204. **See Lesson: Basic Multiplication and Division.**

6. B. This expression only involves addition and subtraction, but its evaluation must go from left to right. **See Lesson: Basic Multiplication and Division.**

$3 + 1 - 5 + 2 - 6$

$4 - 5 + 2 - 6$

$(-1) + 2 - 6$

$1 - 6$

-5

7. D. To determine whether a number is a factor of another number, divide the second number by the first number. If the quotient is whole, the first number is a factor. In this case, 128 is only divisible by 16. **See Lesson: Factors and Multiples.**

8. C. The prime factorization—for example, using a factor tree—shows that 42 has the prime factors 2, 3, and 7 because $2 \times 3 \times 7 = 42$. **See Lesson: Factors and Multiples.**

9. C. The number being factored in a prime factorization is the product of all its prime factors. The leaves in a factor tree are these prime factors. Therefore, the number is their product. In this case, it is $3 \times 2 \times 5 \times 7 = 210$. **See Lesson: Factors and Multiples.**

10. A. The correct solution is 0.5 ton. $16{,}000 \; oz \times \frac{1 \, lb}{16 \, oz} \times \frac{1T}{2{,}000 \, lb} = \frac{16{,}000}{32{,}000} = 0.5 \; T$. **See Lesson: Standards of Measure.**

11. B. The correct solution is 0.099 kilometers. $99 \; m \times \frac{1 \, km}{1{,}000 \, m} = \frac{99}{1{,}000} = 0.099 \; km$. **See Lesson: Standards of Measure.**

12. A. The correct solution is 0045. Subtract 1200 from the time, $1245 - 1200 = 0045$. **See Lesson: Standards of Measure.**

CHAPTER 8 NUMBER AND QUANTITY PRACTICE QUIZ 2

1. What is 604 – 561?
   A. 34
   B. 43
   C. 53
   D. 143

2. Evaluate the expression 2,904 – 1,867.
   A. 1,037
   B. 1,867
   C. 4,771
   D. 5,000

3. Which number will appear farthest right on a standard number line?
   A. −1,024
   B. −256
   C. 32
   D. 512

4. What is 96 ÷ 12?
   A. 8
   B. 84
   C. 960
   D. 1,152

5. Evaluate the expression 8 × 15.
   A. 85
   B. 105
   C. 115
   D. 120

6. How many times can 5 go into −255?
   A. 51
   B. −5
   C. 0
   D. −51

7. Which number is *not* a factor of 1,155?
   A. 22
   B. 33
   C. 55
   D. 77

8. Which best describes the number of multiples of 10?
   A. 1
   B. 10
   C. 100
   D. An unlimited number

9. Which number is prime?
   A. 34
   B. 106
   C. 191
   D. 208

10. Convert 0.75 kilograms to grams.
    A. 0.0075 grams
    B. 0.075 grams
    C. 75 grams
    D. 750 grams

11. Convert 9 meters to yards.
    A. 4.09 yards
    B. 8.23 yards
    C. 9.84 yards
    D. 12.28 yards

12. Convert 1,000 fluid ounces to gallons.
    A. 7.8125 gallons
    B. 15.625 gallons
    C. 31.25 gallons
    D. 62.5 gallons

CHAPTER 8 NUMBER AND QUANTITY PRACTICE QUIZ 2 – ANSWER KEY

1. B. The correct solution is 43. Use the subtraction algorithm, which will require borrowing once. **See Lesson: Basic Addition and Subtraction.**

2. A. The correct solution is 1,037. Use the subtraction algorithm. It will involve borrowing twice to get a number big enough to subtract in the ones place. **See Lesson: Basic Addition and Subtraction.**

3. D. The correct solution is 512. A standard number line orders numbers from lesser (on the left) to greater (on the right). Remember that negatives are to the left of 0 and positives are to the right. Since 512 > 32, 512 is the greatest number in this list and will appear farthest right on the number line. **See Lesson: Basic Addition and Subtraction.**

4. A. Use the division algorithm. Knowing the multiplication table well helps you recognize these numbers. **See Lesson: Basic Multiplication and Division.**

5. D. Use the multiplication algorithm. It involves adding 40 and 80 to get the product of 120. **See Lesson: Basic Multiplication and Division.**

6. D. This question involves another way to express division. In this case, it is $-255 \div 5$. When dividing signed numbers, remember that if the dividend and divisor have different signs, the quotient is negative. Otherwise, the process is the same as dividing whole numbers. The division algorithm yields -51. **See Lesson: Basic Multiplication and Division.**

7. A. To determine whether a number is a factor of another number, divide the second number by the first number. If the quotient is whole, the first number is a factor. In this case, 1,155 is not divisible by 22. **See Lesson: Factors and Multiples.**

8. D. The multiples of 10 are the set {…, −30, −20, −10, 0, 10, 20, 30,…}. Therefore, the number of multiples is unlimited. **See Lesson: Factors and Multiples.**

9. C. A prime number has only 1 and itself as factors. All even numbers (except 2) are composite because they have 2 as a factor. By elimination, only answer C is a prime number. **See Lesson: Factors and Multiples.**

10. D. The correct solution is 750 grams. $0.75 \ kg \times \frac{1,000 \ g}{1 \ kg} = 750 \ g$. **See Lesson: Standards of Measure.**

11. C. The correct solution is 9.84 yards. $9 \ m \times \frac{3.28 \ ft}{1 \ m} \times \frac{1 \ yd}{3 \ ft} = \frac{29.52}{3} = 9.84 \ yd$. **See Lesson: Standards of Measure.**

12. A. The correct solution is 7.8125 gallons. $1,000 \ fl \ oz \times \frac{1 \ pt}{16 \ fl \ oz} \times \frac{1 \ qt}{2 \ pt} \times \frac{1 \ gal}{4 \ qt} = \frac{1,000}{128} = 7.8125 \ gal$. **See Lesson: Standards of Measure.**

Chapter 9 Algebra

Decimals and Fractions

This lesson introduces the basics of decimals and fractions. It also demonstrates changing decimals to fractions, changing fractions to decimals, and converting between fractions, decimals, and percentages.

Introduction to Fractions

A fraction represents part of a whole number. The top number of a fraction is the **numerator**, and the bottom number of a fraction is the **denominator**. The numerator is smaller than the denominator for a **proper fraction**. The numerator is larger than the denominator for an **improper fraction**.

Proper Fractions	Improper Fractions
$\frac{2}{5}$	$\frac{5}{2}$
$\frac{7}{12}$	$\frac{12}{7}$
$\frac{19}{20}$	$\frac{20}{19}$

An improper fraction can be changed to a **mixed number**. A mixed number is a whole number and a proper fraction. To write an improper fraction as a mixed number, divide the denominator into the numerator. The result is the whole number.

> **KEEP IN MIND**
>
> When comparing fractions, the denominators of the fractions must be the same.

The remainder is the numerator of the proper fraction, and the value of the denominator does not change. For example, $\frac{5}{2}$ is $2\frac{1}{2}$ because 2 goes into 5 twice with a remainder of 1. To write an improper fraction as a mixed number, multiply the whole number by the denominator and add the result to the numerator. The results become the new numerator. For example, $2\frac{1}{2}$ is $\frac{5}{2}$ because 2 times 2 plus 1 is 5 for the new numerator.

When comparing fractions, the denominators must be the same. Then, look at the numerator to determine which fraction is larger. If the fractions have different denominators, then a **least common denominator** must be found. This number is the smallest number that can be divided evenly into the denominators of all fractions being compared.

To determine the largest fraction from the group $\frac{1}{3}, \frac{3}{5}, \frac{2}{3}, \frac{2}{5}$, the first step is to find a common denominator. In this case, the least common denominator is 15 because 3 times 5 and 5 times 3 is 15. The second step is to convert the fractions to a denominator of 15.

The fractions with a denominator of 3 have the numerator and denominator multiplied by 5, and the fractions with a denominator of 5 have the numerator and denominator multiplied by 3, as shown below:

$$\frac{1}{3} \times \frac{5}{5} = \frac{5}{15}, \ \frac{3}{5} \times \frac{3}{3} = \frac{9}{15}, \ \frac{2}{3} \times \frac{5}{5} = \frac{10}{15}, \ \frac{2}{5} \times \frac{3}{3} = \frac{6}{15}$$

Now, the numerators can be compared. The largest fraction is $\frac{2}{3}$ because it has a numerator of 10 after finding the common denominator.

Examples

1. **Which fraction is the least?**

    A. $\frac{3}{5}$ B. $\frac{3}{4}$ C. $\frac{1}{5}$ D. $\frac{1}{4}$

    The correct answer is **C**. The correct solution is $\frac{1}{5}$ because it has the smallest numerator compared to the other fractions with the same denominator. The fractions with a common denominator of 20 are $\frac{3}{5} = \frac{12}{20}, \frac{3}{4} = \frac{15}{20}, \frac{1}{5} = \frac{4}{20}, \frac{1}{4} = \frac{5}{20}$.

2. **Which fraction is the greatest?**

    A. $\frac{5}{6}$ B. $\frac{1}{2}$ C. $\frac{2}{3}$ D. $\frac{1}{6}$

    The correct answer is **A**. The correct solution is $\frac{5}{6}$ because it has the largest numerator compared to the other fractions with the same denominator. The fractions with a common denominator of 6 are $\frac{5}{6} = \frac{5}{6}, \frac{1}{2} = \frac{3}{6}, \frac{2}{3} = \frac{4}{6}, \frac{1}{6} = \frac{1}{6}$.

Introduction to Decimals

A **decimal** is a number that expresses part of a whole. Decimals show a portion of a number after a decimal point. Each number to the left and right of the decimal point has a specific place value. Identify the place values for 645.3207.

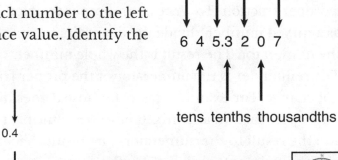

6 4 5.3 2 0 7

tens tenths thousandths

When comparing decimals, compare the numbers in the same place value. For example, determine the greatest decimal from the group 0.4, 0.41, 0.39, and 0.37. In these numbers, there is a value to the right of the decimal point. Comparing the tenths places, the numbers with 4 tenths (0.4 and 0.41) are greater than the numbers with three tenths (0.39 and 0.37).

0.4

0.41

0.39

0.37

KEEP IN MIND

When comparing decimals, compare the place value where the numbers are different.

Then, compare the hundredths in the 4 tenths numbers. The value of 0.41 is greater because there is a 1 in the hundredths place versus a 0 in the hundredths place.

Here is another example: determine the least decimal of the group 5.23, 5.32, 5.13, and 5.31. In this group, the ones value is 5 for all numbers. Then, comparing the tenths values, 5.13 is the smallest number because it is the only value with 1 tenth.

0.4

0.41

5.23

5.32

5.13

5.31

Examples

1. **Which decimal is the greatest?**

    A. 0.07 B. 0.007 C. 0.7 D. 0.0007

    The correct answer is **C**. The solution is 0.7 because it has the largest place value in the tenths.

2. **Which decimal is the least?**

    A. 0.0413 B. 0.0713 C. 0.0513 D. 0.0613

    The correct answer is **A**. The correct solution is 0.0413 because it has the smallest place value in the hundredths place.

Changing Decimals and Fractions

Three steps change a decimal to a fraction.

> **STEP BY STEP**
>
> **Step 1.** Write the decimal divided by 1 with the decimal as the numerator and 1 as the denominator.
>
> **Step 2.** Multiply the numerator and denominator by 10 for every number after the decimal point. (For example, if there is 1 decimal place, multiply by 10. If there are 2 decimal places, multiply by 100).
>
> **Step 3.** Reduce the fraction completely.

To change the decimal 0.37 to a fraction, start by writing the decimal as a fraction with a denominator of one, $\frac{0.37}{1}$. Because there are two decimal places, multiply the numerator and denominator by 100, $\frac{0.37 \times 100}{1 \times 100} = \frac{37}{100}$. The fraction does not reduce, so $\frac{37}{100}$ is 0.37 in fraction form.

Similarly, to change the decimal 2.4 to a fraction start by writing the decimal as a fraction with a denominator of one, $\frac{0.4}{1}$, and ignore the whole number. Because there is one decimal place, multiply the numerator and denominator by 10, $\frac{0.4 \times 10}{1 \times 10} = \frac{4}{10}$. The fraction does reduce: $2\frac{4}{10} = 2\frac{2}{5}$ is 2.4 in fraction form.

The decimal $0.\overline{3}$ as a fraction is $\frac{0.\overline{3}}{1}$. In the case of a repeating decimal, let $n = 0.\overline{3}$ and $10n = 3.\overline{3}$. Then, $10n - n = 3.\overline{3} - 0.\overline{3}$, resulting in $9n = 3$ and solution of $n = \frac{3}{9} = \frac{1}{3}$. The decimal $0.\overline{3}$ is $\frac{1}{3}$ as a fraction.

Examples

1. **Change 0.38 to a fraction. Simplify completely.**

   A. $\frac{3}{10}$ B. $\frac{9}{25}$ C. $\frac{19}{50}$ D. $\frac{2}{5}$

   The correct answer is **C**. The correct solution is $\frac{19}{50}$ because $\frac{0.38}{1} = \frac{38}{100} = \frac{19}{50}$.

2. **Change $1.\overline{1}$ to a fraction. Simplify completely.**

   A. $1\frac{1}{11}$ B. $1\frac{1}{9}$ C. $1\frac{1}{6}$ D. $1\frac{1}{3}$

   The correct answer is **B**. The correct solution is $1\frac{1}{9}$. Let $n = 1.\overline{1}$ and $10n = 11.\overline{1}$. Then, $10n - n = 11.\overline{1} - 1.\overline{1}$, resulting in $9n = 10$ and solution of $n = \frac{10}{9} = 1\frac{1}{9}$.

Two steps change a fraction to a decimal.

> **STEP BY STEP**
>
> **Step 1.** Divide the denominator by the numerator. Add zeros after the decimal point as needed.
>
> **Step 2.** Complete the process when there is no remainder or the decimal is repeating.

To convert $\frac{1}{5}$ to a decimal, rewrite $\frac{1}{5}$ as a long division problem and add zeros after the decimal point, $1.0 \div 5$. Complete the long division and $\frac{1}{5}$ as a decimal is 0.2. The division is complete because there is no remainder.

To convert $\frac{8}{9}$ to a decimal, rewrite $\frac{8}{9}$ as a long division problem and add zeros after the decimal point, $8.00 \div 9$. Complete the long division, and $\frac{8}{9}$ as a decimal is $0.\overline{8}$. The process is complete because the decimal is complete.

To rewrite the mixed number $2\frac{3}{4}$ as a decimal, the fraction needs changed to a decimal. Rewrite $\frac{3}{4}$ as a long division problem and add zeros after the decimal point, $3.00 \div 4$. The whole number is needed for the answer and is not included in the long division. Complete the long division, and $2\frac{3}{4}$ as a decimal is 2.75.

Examples

1. **Change $\frac{9}{10}$ to a decimal. Simplify completely.**

    A. 0.75   B. 0.8   C. 0.85   D. 0.9

    The correct answer is **D**. The correct answer is 0.9 because $\frac{9}{10} = 9.0 \div 10 = 0.9$.

2. **Change $\frac{5}{6}$ to a decimal. Simplify completely.**

    A. 0.73   B. $0.7\overline{6}$ C. $0.8\overline{3}$ D. 0.86

    The correct answer is **C**. The correct answer is $0.8\overline{3}$ because $\frac{5}{6} = 5.000 \div 6 = 0.8\overline{3}$.

Convert among Fractions, Decimals, and Percentages

Fractions, decimals, and percentages can change forms, but they are equivalent values.

There are two ways to change a decimal to a percent. One way is to multiply the decimal by 100 and add a percent sign. 0.24 as a percent is 24%.

Another way is to move the decimal point two places to the right. The decimal 0.635 is 63.5% as a percent when moving the decimal point two places to the right.

Any decimal, including repeating decimals, can change to a percent. $0.\overline{3}$ as a percent is $0.\overline{3} \times 100 = 33.\overline{3}\%$.

Example

Write 0.345 as a percent.

    A. 3.45%   B. 34.5%   C. 345%   D. 3450%

    The correct answer is **B**. The correct answer is 34.5% because 0.345 as a percent is 34.5%.

There are two ways to change a percent to a decimal. One way is to remove the percent sign and divide the decimal by 100. For example, 73% as a decimal is 0.73.

Another way is to move the decimal point two places to the left. For example, 27.8% is 0.278 as a decimal when moving the decimal point two places to the left.

Any percent, including repeating percents, can change to a decimal. For example, $44.\overline{4}\%$ as a decimal is $44.\overline{4} \div 100 = 0.\overline{4}$.

Example

Write 131% as a decimal.

    A. 0.131   B. 1.31   C. 13.1   D. 131

    The correct answer is **B**. The correct answer is 1.31 because 131% as a decimal is $131 \div 100 = 1.31$.

Two steps change a fraction to a percent.

> **STEP BY STEP**
> **Step 1.** Divide the numerator and denominator.
> **Step 2.** Multiply by 100 and add a percent sign.

To change the fraction $\frac{3}{5}$ to a decimal, perform long division to get 0.6. Then, multiply 0.6 by 100 and $\frac{3}{5}$ is the same as 60%.

To change the fraction $\frac{7}{8}$ to a decimal, perform long division to get 0.875. Then, multiply 0.875 by 100 and $\frac{7}{8}$ is the same as 87.5%.

Fractions that are repeating decimals can also be converted to a percent. To change the fraction $\frac{2}{3}$ to a decimal, perform long division to get $0.\overline{6}$. Then, multiply $0.\overline{6}$ by 100 and the percent is $66.\overline{6}\%$.

Example

Write $2\frac{1}{8}$ as a percent.

    A. 21.2%   B. 21.25%   C. 212%   D. 212.5%

    The correct answer is **D**. The correct answer is 212.5% because $2\frac{1}{8}$ as a percent is $2.125 \times 100 = 212.5\%$.

Two steps change a percent to a fraction.

> **STEP BY STEP**
>
> **Step 1.**   Remove the percent sign and write the value as the numerator with a denominator of 100.
>
> **Step 2.**   Simplify the fraction.

Remove the percent sign from 45% and write as a fraction with a denominator of 100, $\frac{45}{100}$. The fraction reduces to $\frac{9}{20}$.

Remove the percent sign from 22.8% and write as a fraction with a denominator of 100, $\frac{22.8}{100}$. The fraction reduces to $\frac{228}{1000} = \frac{57}{250}$.

Repeating percentages can change to a fraction. Remove the percent sign from $16.\overline{6}\%$ and write as a fraction with a denominator of 100, $\frac{16.\overline{6}}{100}$. The fraction simplifies to $\frac{0.1\overline{6}}{1} = \frac{1}{6}$.

Example

Write 72% as a fraction.

A. $\frac{27}{50}$ B. $\frac{7}{10}$ C. $\frac{18}{25}$ D. $\frac{3}{4}$

The correct answer is **C**. The correct answer is $\frac{18}{25}$ because 72% as a fraction is $\frac{72}{100} = \frac{18}{25}$.

Let's Review!

- A fraction is a number with a numerator and a denominator. A fraction can be written as a proper fraction, an improper fraction, or a mixed number. Changing fractions to a common denominator enables you to determine the least or greatest fraction in a group of fractions.
- A decimal is a number that expresses part of a whole. By comparing the same place values, you can find the least or greatest decimal in a group of decimals.
- A number can be written as a fraction, a decimal, and a percent. These are equivalent values. Numbers can be converted between fractions, decimals, and percents by following a series of steps.

MULTIPLICATION AND DIVISION OF FRACTIONS

This lesson introduces how to multiply and divide fractions.

Multiplying a Fraction by a Fraction

The multiplication of fractions does not require changing any denominators like adding and subtracting fractions do. To multiply a fraction by a fraction, multiply the numerators together and multiply the denominators together. For example, $\frac{2}{3} \times \frac{4}{5}$ is $\frac{2 \times 4}{3 \times 5}$, which is $\frac{8}{15}$.

Sometimes, the final solution reduces. For example, $\frac{3}{5} \times \frac{1}{9} = \frac{3 \times 1}{5 \times 9} = \frac{3}{45}$. The fraction $\frac{3}{45}$ reduces to $\frac{1}{15}$.

Simplifying fractions can occur before completing the multiplication. In the previous problem, the numerator of 3 can be simplified with the denominator of 9: $\frac{\cancel{3}^{1}}{5} \times \frac{1}{\cancel{9}^{3}} = \frac{1}{15}$. This method of simplifying only occurs with the multiplication of fractions.

> **KEEP IN MIND**
> The product of multiplying a fraction by a fraction is always less than 1.

Examples

1. **Multiply $\frac{1}{2} \times \frac{3}{4}$.**

    A. $\frac{1}{4}$ B. $\frac{1}{2}$ C. $\frac{3}{8}$ D. $\frac{2}{3}$

    The correct answer is **C**. The correct solution is $\frac{3}{8}$ because $\frac{1}{2} \times \frac{3}{4} = \frac{3}{8}$.

2. **Multiply $\frac{2}{3} \times \frac{5}{6}$.**

    A. $\frac{1}{9}$ B. $\frac{5}{18}$ C. $\frac{5}{9}$ D. $\frac{7}{18}$

    The correct answer is **C**. The correct solution is $\frac{5}{9}$ because $\frac{2}{3} \times \frac{5}{6} = \frac{10}{18} = \frac{5}{9}$.

Multiply a Fraction by a Whole or Mixed Number

Multiplying a fraction by a whole or mixed number is similar to multiplying two fractions. When multiplying by a whole number, change the whole number to a fraction with a denominator of 1. Next, multiply the numerators together and the denominators together. Rewrite the final answer as a mixed number. For example: $\frac{9}{10} \times 3 = \frac{9}{10} \times \frac{3}{1} = \frac{27}{10} = 2\frac{7}{10}$.

When multiplying a fraction by a mixed number or multiplying two mixed numbers, the process is similar.

> **KEEP IN MIND**
> Always change a mixed number to an improper fraction when multiplying by a mixed number.

For example, multiply $\frac{10}{11} \times 3\frac{1}{2}$. Change the mixed number to an improper fraction, $\frac{10}{11} \times \frac{7}{2}$. Multiply the numerators together and multiply the denominators together, $\frac{70}{22}$. Write the improper fraction as a mixed number, $3\frac{4}{22}$. Reduce if necessary, $3\frac{2}{11}$.

This process can also be used when multiplying a whole number by a mixed number or multiplying two mixed numbers.

Examples

1. **Multiply $4 \times \frac{5}{6}$.**

    A. $\frac{5}{24}$ 　　　　　B. $2\frac{3}{4}$ 　　　　　C. $3\frac{1}{3}$ 　　　　　D. $4\frac{5}{6}$

    The correct answer is **C**. The correct solution is $3\frac{1}{3}$ because $\frac{4}{1} \times \frac{5}{6} = \frac{20}{6} = 3\frac{2}{6} = 3\frac{1}{3}$.

2. **Multiply $1\frac{1}{2} \times 1\frac{1}{6}$.**

    A. $1\frac{1}{12}$ 　　　　　B. $1\frac{1}{4}$ 　　　　　C. $1\frac{3}{8}$ 　　　　　D. $1\frac{3}{4}$

    The correct answer is **D**. The correct solution is $1\frac{3}{4}$ because $\frac{3}{2} \times \frac{7}{6} = \frac{21}{12} = 1\frac{9}{12} = 1\frac{3}{4}$.

Dividing a Fraction by a Fraction

Some basic steps apply when dividing a fraction by a fraction. The information from the previous two sections is applicable to dividing fractions.

STEP BY STEP

Step 1. Leave the first fraction alone.

Step 2. Find the reciprocal of the second fraction.

Step 3. Multiply the first fraction by the reciprocal of the second fraction.

Step 4. Rewrite the fraction as a mixed number and reduce the fraction completely.

Divide, $\frac{3}{10} \div \frac{1}{2}$. Find the reciprocal of the second fraction, which is $\frac{2}{1}$.

Now, multiply the fractions, $\frac{3}{10} \times \frac{2}{1} = \frac{6}{10}$. Reduce $\frac{6}{10}$ to $\frac{3}{5}$.

Divide, $\frac{4}{5} \div \frac{3}{8}$. Find the reciprocal of the second fraction, which is $\frac{8}{3}$.

Now, multiply the fractions, $\frac{4}{5} \times \frac{8}{3} = \frac{32}{15}$. Rewrite the fraction as a mixed number, $\frac{32}{15} = 2\frac{2}{15}$.

Examples

1. **Divide $\frac{1}{2} \div \frac{5}{6}$.**

    A. $\frac{5}{12}$ 　　　　　B. $\frac{3}{5}$ 　　　　　C. $\frac{5}{6}$ 　　　　　D. $1\frac{2}{3}$

    The correct answer is **B**. The correct solution is $\frac{3}{5}$ because $\frac{1}{2} \times \frac{6}{5} = \frac{6}{10} = \frac{3}{5}$.

2. **Divide $\frac{2}{3} \div \frac{3}{5}$.**

A. $\frac{2}{15}$ B. $\frac{2}{5}$ C. $1\frac{1}{15}$ D. $1\frac{1}{9}$

The correct answer is **D**. The correct solution is $1\frac{1}{9}$ because $\frac{2}{3} \times \frac{5}{3} = \frac{10}{9} = 1\frac{1}{9}$.

Dividing a Fraction and a Whole or Mixed Number

Some basic steps apply when dividing a fraction by a whole number or a mixed number.

> **STEP BY STEP**
> **Step 1.** Write any whole number as a fraction with a denominator of 1. Write any mixed numbers as improper fractions.
> **Step 2.** Leave the first fraction (improper fraction) alone.
> **Step 3.** Find the reciprocal of the second fraction.
> **Step 4.** Multiply the first fraction by the reciprocal of the second fraction.
> **Step 5.** Rewrite the fraction as a mixed number and reduce the fraction completely.

Divide, $\frac{3}{10} \div 3$. Rewrite the expression as $\frac{3}{10} \div \frac{3}{1}$. Find the reciprocal of the second fraction, which is $\frac{1}{3}$. Multiply the fractions, $\frac{3}{10} \times \frac{1}{3} = \frac{3}{30} = \frac{1}{10}$. Reduce $\frac{3}{30}$ to $\frac{1}{10}$.

Divide, $2\frac{4}{5} \div 1\frac{3}{8}$. Rewrite the expression as $\frac{14}{5} \div \frac{11}{8}$. Find the reciprocal of the second fraction, which is $\frac{8}{11}$.

Multiply the fractions, $\frac{14}{5} \times \frac{8}{11} = \frac{112}{55} = 2\frac{2}{55}$. Reduce $\frac{112}{55}$ to $2\frac{2}{55}$.

Examples

1. **Divide $\frac{2}{3} \div 4$.**

A. $\frac{1}{12}$ B. $\frac{1}{10}$ C. $\frac{1}{8}$ D. $\frac{1}{6}$

The correct answer is **D**. The correct answer is $\frac{1}{6}$ because $\frac{2}{3} \times \frac{1}{4} = \frac{2}{12} = \frac{1}{6}$.

2. **Divide $1\frac{5}{12} \div 1\frac{1}{2}$.**

A. $\frac{17}{18}$ B. $1\frac{5}{24}$ C. $1\frac{5}{6}$ D. $2\frac{1}{8}$

The correct answer is **A**. The correct answer is $\frac{17}{18}$ because $\frac{17}{12} \div \frac{3}{2} = \frac{17}{12} \times \frac{2}{3} = \frac{34}{36} = \frac{17}{18}$.

Let's Review!

- The process to multiply fractions is to multiply the numerators together and multiply the denominators together. When there is a mixed number, change the mixed number to an improper fraction before multiplying.
- The process to divide fractions is to find the reciprocal of the second fraction and multiply the fractions. As with multiplying, change any mixed numbers to improper fractions before dividing.

EQUATIONS WITH ONE VARIABLE

This lesson introduces how to solve linear equations and linear inequalities.

One-Step Linear Equations

A **linear equation** is an equation where two expressions are set equal to each other. The equation is in the form $ax + b = c$, where a is a non-zero constant and b and c are constants. The exponent on a linear equation is always 1, and there is no more than one solution to a linear equation.

There are four properties to help solve a linear equation.

Property	Definition	Example with Numbers	Example with Variables
Addition Property of Equality	Add the same number to both sides of the equation.	$x-3 = 9$ $x-3+3 = 9+3$ $x = 12$	$x-a = b$ $x-a+a = b+a$ $x = a+b$
Subtraction Property of Equality	Subtract the same number from both sides of the equation.	$x+3 = 9$ $x+3-3 = 9-3$ $x = 6$	$x+a = b$ $x+a-a = b-a$ $x = b-a$
Multiplication Property of Equality	Multiply both sides of the equation by the same number.	$\frac{x}{3} = 9$ $\frac{x}{3} \times 3 = 9 \times 3$ $x = 27$	$\frac{x}{a} = b$ $\frac{x}{a} \times a = b \times a$ $x = ab$
Division Property of Equality	Divide both sides of the equation by the same number.	$3x = 9$ $\frac{3x}{3} = \frac{9}{3}$ $x = 3$	$ax = b$ $\frac{ax}{a} = \frac{b}{a}$ $x = \frac{b}{a}$

Example

Solve the equation for the unknown, $\frac{w}{2} = -6$.

A. -12 B. -8 C. -4 D. -3

The correct answer is **A**. The correct solution is -12 because both sides of the equation are multiplied by 2.

Two-Step Linear Equations

A two-step linear equation is in the form $ax + b = c$, where a is a non-zero constant and b and c are constants. There are two basic steps in solving this equation.

> **STEP BY STEP**
>
> **Step 1.** Use addition and subtraction properties of an equation to move the variable to one side of the equation and all number terms to the other side of the equation.
>
> **Step 2.** Use multiplication and division properties of an equation to remove the value in front of the variable.

Examples

1. **Solve the equation for the unknown, $\frac{x}{-2} - 3 = 5$.**

   A. −16 B. −8 C. 8 D. 16

   The correct answer is **A**. The correct solution is −16.

   $\frac{x}{-2} = 8$ Add 3 to both sides of the equation.

   $x = -16$ Multiply both sides of the equation by −2.

2. **Solve the equation for the unknown, $4x + 3 = 8$.**

   A. −2 B. $-\frac{5}{4}$ C. $\frac{5}{4}$ D. 2

   The correct answer is **C**. The correct solution is $\frac{5}{4}$.

   $4x = 5$ Subtract 3 from both sides of the equation.

   $x = \frac{5}{4}$ Divide both sides of the equation by 4.

3. **Solve the equation for the unknown w, $P = 2l + 2w$.**

   A. $2P - 2l = w$ B. $\frac{P-2l}{2} = w$ C. $2P + 2l = w$ D. $\frac{P+2l}{2} = w$

   The correct answer is **B**. The correct solution is $\frac{P-2l}{2} = w$.

   $P - 2l = 2w$ Subtract 2l from both sides of the equation.

   $\frac{P-2l}{2} = w$ Divide both sides of the equation by 2.

Multi-Step Linear Equations

In these basic examples of linear equations, the solution may be evident, but these properties demonstrate how to use an opposite operation to solve for a variable. Using these properties, there are three steps in solving a complex linear equation.

> **STEP BY STEP**
>
> **Step 1.** Simplify each side of the equation. This includes removing parentheses, removing fractions, and adding like terms.
>
> **Step 2.** Use addition and subtraction properties of an equation to move the variable to one side of the equation and all number terms to the other side of the equation.
>
> **Step 3.** Use multiplication and division properties of an equation to remove the value in front of the variable.

In Step 2, all of the variables may be placed on the left side or the right side of the equation. The examples in this lesson will place all of the variables on the left side of the equation.

When solving for a variable, apply the same steps as above. In this case, the equation is not being solved for a value, but for a specific variable.

Examples

1. **Solve the equation for the unknown, $2(4x + 1)-5 = 3-(4x-3)$.**

    A. $\frac{1}{4}$ B. $\frac{3}{4}$ C. $\frac{4}{3}$ D. 4

    The correct answer is **B**. The correct solution is $\frac{3}{4}$.

$8x + 2-5 = 3-4x + 3$	Apply the distributive property.
$8x-3 = -4x + 6$	Combine like terms on both sides of the equation.
$12x-3 = 6$	Add $4x$ to both sides of the equation.
$12x = 9$	Add 3 to both sides of the equation.
$x = \frac{3}{4}$	Divide both sides of the equation by 12.

2. **Solve the equation for the unknown, $\frac{2}{3}x + 2 = -\frac{1}{2}x + 2(x + 1)$.**

    A. 0 B. 1 C. 2 D. 3

    The correct answer is **A**. The correct solution is 0.

$\frac{2}{3}x + 2 = -\frac{1}{2}x + 2x + 2$	Apply the distributive property.
$4x + 12 = -3x + 12x + 12$	Multiply all terms by the least common denominator of 6 to eliminate the fractions.
$4x + 12 = 9x + 12$	Combine like terms on the right side of the equation.
$-5x = 12$	Subtract $9x$ from both sides of the equation.
$-5x = 0$	Subtract 12 from both sides of the equation.
$x = 0$	Divide both sides of the equation by -5.

3. Solve the equation for the unknown for x, $y - y_1 = m(x - x_1)$.

A. $y - y_1 + mx_1$ B. $my - my_1 + mx_1$ C. $\frac{y - y_1 + x_1}{m}$ D. $\frac{y - y_1 + mx_1}{m}$

The correct answer is **D**. The correct solution is $\frac{y - y_1 + mx_1}{m}$

$y - y_1 = mx - mx_1$ Apply the distributive property.

$y - y_1 + mx_1 = mx$ Add mx_1 to both sides of the equation.

$\frac{y - y_1 + mx_1}{m} = x$ Divide both sides of the equation by m.

Solving Linear Inequalities

A **linear inequality** is similar to a linear equation, but it contains an inequality sign ($<$, $>$, $\leq$, $\geq$). Many of the steps for solving linear inequalities are the same as for solving linear equations. The major difference is that the solution is an infinite number of values. There are four properties to help solve a linear inequality.

Property	Definition	Example
Addition Property of Inequality	Add the same number to both sides of the inequality.	$x - 3 < 9$ $x - 3 + 3 < 9 + 3$ $x < 12$
Subtraction Property of Inequality	Subtract the same number from both sides of the inequality.	$x + 3 > 9$ $x + 3 - 3 > 9 - 3$ $x > 6$
Multiplication Property of Inequality (when multiplying by a positive number)	Multiply both sides of the inequality by the same number.	$\frac{x}{3} \geq 9$ $\frac{x}{3} \times 3 \geq 9 \times 3$ $x \geq 27$
Division Property of Inequality (when multiplying by a positive number)	Divide both sides of the inequality by the same number.	$3x \leq 9$ $\frac{3x}{3} \leq \frac{9}{3}$ $x \leq 3$
Multiplication Property of Inequality (when multiplying by a negative number)	Multiply both sides of the inequality by the same number.	$\frac{x}{-3} \geq 9$ $\frac{x}{-3} \times -3 \geq 9 \times -3$ $x \leq -27$
Division Property of Inequality (when multiplying by a negative number)	Divide both sides of the inequality by the same number.	$-3x \leq 9$ $\frac{-3x}{-3} \leq \frac{9}{-3}$ $x \geq -3$

Multiplying or dividing both sides of the inequality by a negative number reverses the sign of the inequality.

In these basic examples, the solution may be evident, but these properties demonstrate how to use an opposite operation to solve for a variable. Using these properties, there are three steps in solving a complex linear inequality.

In Step 2, all of the variables may be placed on the left side or the right side of the inequality. The examples in this lesson will place all of the variables on the left side of the inequality.

Examples

1. **Solve the inequality for the unknown, $3(2 + x) < 2(3x-1)$.**

   A. $x < -\frac{8}{3}$ B. $x > -\frac{8}{3}$ C. $x < \frac{8}{3}$ D. $x > \frac{8}{3}$

   The correct answer is **D**. The correct solution is $x > \frac{8}{3}$.

$6 + 3x < 6x-2$	Apply the distributive property.
$6-3x < -2$	Subtract $6x$ from both sides of the inequality.
$-3x < -8$	Subtract 6 from both sides of the inequality.
$x > \frac{8}{3}$	Divide both sides of the inequality by -3.

2. **Solve the inequality for the unknown, $\frac{1}{2}(2x-3) \geq \frac{1}{4}(2x + 1)-2$.**

   A. $x > -7$ B. $x > -3$ C. $x \geq -\frac{3}{2}$ D. $x \geq -\frac{1}{2}$

   The correct answer is **D**. The correct solution is $x \geq -\frac{1}{2}$.

$2(2x-3) \geq 2x + 1-8$	Multiply all terms by the least common denominator of 4 to eliminate the fractions.
$4x-6 \geq 2x + 1-8$	Apply the distributive property.
$4x-6 \geq 2x-7$	Combine like terms on the right side of the inequality.
$2x-6 \geq -7$	Subtract $2x$ from both sides of the inequality.
$2x \geq -1$	Add 6 to both sides of the inequality.
$x \geq -\frac{1}{2}$	Divide both sides of the inequality by 2.

Let's Review!

- A linear equation is an equation with one solution. Using opposite operations solves a linear equation.
- The process to solve a linear equation or inequality is to eliminate fractions and parentheses and combine like terms on the same side of the sign. Then, solve the equation or inequality by using inverse operations.

EQUATIONS WITH TWO VARIABLES

This lesson discusses solving a system of linear equations by substitution, elimination, and graphing, as well as solving a simple system of a linear and a quadratic equation.

Solving a System of Equations by Substitution

A **system of linear equations** is a set of two or more linear equations in the same variables. A solution to the system is an ordered pair that is a solution in all the equations in the system. The ordered pair (1, -2) is a solution for the system of equations $\begin{matrix} 2x + y = 0 \\ -x + 2y = -5 \end{matrix}$ because $\begin{matrix} 2(1) + (-2) = 0 \\ -1 + 2(-2) = -5 \end{matrix}$ makes both equations true.

One way to solve a system of linear equations is by substitution.

> **STEP BY STEP**
>
> **Step 1.** Solve one equation for one of the variables.
>
> **Step 2.** Substitute the expression from Step 1 into the other equation and solve for the other variable.
>
> **Step 3.** Substitute the value from Step 2 into one of the original equations and solve.

All systems of equations can be solved by substitution for any one of the four variables in the problem. The most efficient way of solving is locating the $1x$ or $1y$ in the equations because this eliminates the possibility of having fractions in the equations.

Examples

1. **Solve the system of equations,** $\begin{matrix} x = y + 6 \\ 4x + 5y = 60 \end{matrix}$.

    A. (10, 12)   B. (6, 12)   C. (6, 4)   D. (10, 4)

    The correct answer is **D.** The correct solution is (10, 4).

    The first equation is already solved for x.

$4(y + 6) + 5y = 60$	Substitute $y + 6$ in for x in the first equation.
$4y + 24 + 5y = 60$	Apply the distributive property.
$9y + 24 = 60$	Combine like terms on the left side of the equation.
$9y = 36$	Subtract 24 from both sides of the equation.
$y = 4$	Divide both sides of the equation by 9.
$x = 4 + 6$	Substitute 4 in the first equation for y.
$x = 10$	Simplify using order of operations.

2. **Solve the system of equations,** $\begin{array}{l} 3x + 2y = 41 \\ -4x + y = -18 \end{array}$.

    A. (5, 13)   B. (6, 6)   C. (7, 10)   D. (10, 7)

The correct answer is **C**. The correct solution is (7, 10).

$y = 4x - 18$	Solve the second equation for y by adding $4x$ to both sides of the equation.
$3x + 2(4x - 18) = 41$	Substitute $4x - 18$ in for y in the first equation.
$3x + 8x - 36 = 41$	Apply the distributive property.
$11x - 36 = 41$	Combine like terms on the left side of the equation.
$11x = 77$	Add 36 to both sides of the equation.
$x = 7$	Divide both sides of the equation by 11.
$-4(7) + y = -18$	Substitute 7 in the second equation for x.
$-28 + y = -18$	Simplify using order of operations.
$y = 10$	Add 28 to both sides of the equation.

Solving a System of Equations by Elimination

Another way to solve a system of linear equations is by elimination.

STEP BY STEP

Step 1. Multiply, if necessary, one or both equations by a constant so at least one pair of like terms has opposite coefficients.

Step 2. Add the equations to eliminate one of the variables.

Step 3. Solve the resulting equation.

Step 4. Substitute the value from Step 3 into one of the original equations and solve for the other variable.

All system of equations can be solved by the elimination method for any one of the four variables in the problem. One way of solving is locating the variables with opposite coefficients and adding the equations. Another approach is multiplying one equation to obtain opposite coefficients for the variables.

Examples

1. Solve the system of equations, $\begin{matrix} 3x + 5y = 28 \\ -4x - 5y = -34 \end{matrix}$.

   A. $(12, 6)$ B. $(6, 12)$ C. $(6, 2)$ D. $(2, 6)$

   The correct answer is **C**. The correct solution is $(6, 2)$.

$-x = -6$	Add the equations.
$x = 6$	Divide both sides of the equation by -1.
$3(6) + 5y = 28$	Substitute 6 in the first equation for x.
$18 + 5y = 28$	Simplify using order of operations.
$5y = 10$	Subtract 18 from both sides of the equation.
$y = 2$	Divide both sides of the equation by 5.

2. Solve the system of equations, $\begin{matrix} -5x + 5y = 0 \\ 2x - 3y = -3 \end{matrix}$.

   A. $(2, 2)$ B. $(3, 3)$ C. $(6, 6)$ D. $(9, 9)$

   The correct answer is **B**. The correct solution is $(3, 3)$.

$-10x + 10y = 0$	Multiply all terms in the first equation by 2.
$10x - 15y = -15$	Multiply all terms in the second equation by 5.
$-5y = -15$	Add the equations.
$y = 3$	Divide both sides of the equation by -5.
$2x - 3(3) = -3$	Substitute 3 in the second equation for y.
$2x - 9 = -3$	Simplify using order of operations.
$2x = 6$	Add 9 to both sides of the equation.
$x = 3$	Divide both sides of the equation by 2.

Solving a System of Equations by Graphing

Graphing is a third method of a solving system of equations. The point of intersection is the solution for the graph. This method is a great way to visualize each graph on a coordinate plane.

STEP BY STEP

Step 1. Graph each equation in the coordinate plane.

Step 2. Estimate the point of intersection.

Step 3. Check the point by substituting for x and y in each equation of the original system.

The best approach to graphing is to obtain each line in slope-intercept form. Then, graph the y-intercept and use the slope to find additional points on the line.

Example

Solve the system of equations by graphing, $\begin{array}{l} y = 3x-2 \\ y = x-4 \end{array}$.

A.

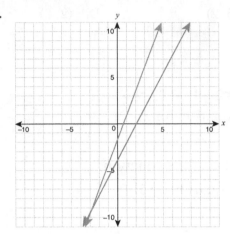

C.

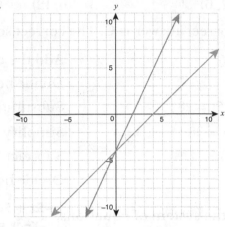

B.

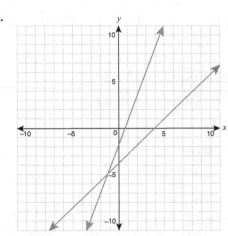

D.

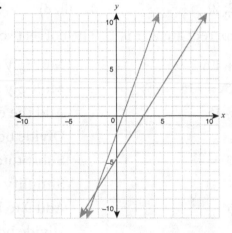

The correct answer is **B**. The correct graph has the two lines intersect at (-1, -5).

Solving a System of a Linear Equation and an Equation of a Circle

There are many other types of systems of equations. One example is the equation of a line $y = mx$ and the equation of a circle $x^2 + y^2 = r^2$ where r is the radius. With this system of equations, there can be two ordered pairs that intersect between the line and the circle. If there is one ordered pair, the line is tangent to the circle.

This system of equations is solved by substituting the expression mx in for y in the equation of a circle. Then, solve the equation for x. The values for x are substituted into the linear equation to find the value for y.

KEEP IN MIND

There will be two solutions in many cases with the system of a linear equation and an equation of a circle.

Example

Solve the system of equations, $\begin{array}{l} y = -3x \\ x^2 + y^2 = 10 \end{array}$.

A. (1, 3) and (–1, –3)

B. (1, –3) and (–1, 3)

C. (–3, 10) and (3, –10)

D. (3, 10) and (–3, –10)

The correct answer is **B.** The correct solutions are (1, –3) and (–1, 3).

$x^2 + (-3x)^2 = 10$	Substitute $-3x$ in for y in the second equation.
$x^2 + 9x^2 = 10$	Apply the exponent.
$10x^2 = 10$	Combine like terms on the left side of the equation.
$x^2 = 1$	Divide both sides of the equation by 10.
$x = \pm 1$	Apply the square root to both sides of the equation.
$y = -3(1) = -3$	Substitute 1 in the first equation and multiply.
$y = -3(-1) = 3$	Substitute -1 in the first equation and multiply.

Let's Review!

- There are three ways to solve a system of equations: graphing, substitution, and elimination. Using any method will result in the same solution for the system of equations.
- Solving a system of a linear equation and an equation of a circle uses substitution and usually results in two solutions.

SOLVING REAL-WORLD MATHEMATICAL PROBLEMS

This lesson introduces solving real-world mathematical problems by using estimation and mental computation. This lesson also includes real-world applications involving integers, fractions, and decimals.

Estimating

Estimations are rough calculations of a solution to a problem. The most common use for estimation is completing calculations without a calculator or other tool. There are many estimation techniques, but this lesson focuses on integers, decimals, and fractions.

KEEP IN MIND

An estimation is an educated guess at the solution to a problem.

To round a whole number, round the value to the nearest ten or hundred. The number 142 rounds to 140 for the nearest ten and to 100 for the nearest hundred. The context of the problem determines the place value to which to round.

In most problems with fractions and decimals, the context of the problem requires rounding to the nearest whole number. Rounding these values makes calculation easier and provides an accurate estimation to the solution of the problem.

Other estimation strategies include the following:

- Using friendly or compatible numbers
- Using numbers that are easy to compute
- Adjusting numbers after rounding

Example

There are 168 hours in a week. Carson does the following:

- Sleeps 7.5 hours each day of the week
- Goes to school 6.75 hours five days a week
- Practices martial arts and basketball 1.5 hours each three times a week
- Reads and studies 1.75 hours every day
- Eats 1.5 hours every day

Estimate the remaining number of hours.

A. 30   B. 35   C. 40   D. 45

The correct answer is **C**. The correct solution is 40. He sleeps about 56 hours, goes to school for 35 hours, practices for 9 hours, reads and studies for about 14 hours, and eats for about 14 hours. This is 128 hours. Therefore, Carson has about 40 hours remaining.

Real-World Integer Problems

The following five steps can make solving word problems easier:

1. Read the problem for understanding.
2. Visualize the problem by drawing a picture or diagram.
3. Make a plan by writing an expression to represent the problem.
4. Solve the problem by applying mathematical techniques.
5. Check the answer to make sure it answers the question asked.

BE CAREFUL!

Make sure that you read the problem fully before visualizing and making a plan.

In basic problems, the solution may be evident, but make sure to demonstrate knowledge of writing the expression. In multi-step problems, first make a plan with the correct expression. Then, apply the correct calculation.

Examples

1. **The temperature on Monday was –9°F, and on Tuesday it was 8°F. What is the difference in temperature, in °F?**

   A. –17°   B. –1°   C. 1°   D. 17°

   The correct answer is **D**. The correct solution is 17° because 8–(–9) = 17°F.

2. **A golfer's last 12 rounds were –2, +4, –3, –1, +5, +3, –4, –5, –2, –6, –1, and 0. What is the average of these rounds?**

   A. –12   B. –1   C. 1   D. 12

   The correct answer is **B**. The correct solution is –1. The total of the scores is –12. The average is –12 divided by 12, which is –1.

Real-World Fraction and Decimal Problems

The five steps in the previous section are applicable to solving real-world fraction and decimal problems. The expressions with one step require only one calculation: addition, subtraction, multiplication, or division. The problems with

KEEP IN MIND

Estimating the solution first can help determine if a calculation is completed correctly.

multiple steps require writing out the expressions and performing the correct calculations.

Examples

1. The length of a room is $7\frac{2}{3}$ feet. When the length of the room is doubled, what is the new length in feet?

   A. $14\frac{2}{3}$ B. $15\frac{1}{3}$ C. $15\frac{2}{3}$ D. $16\frac{1}{3}$

   The correct answer is **B**. The correct solution is $15\frac{1}{3}$. The length is multiplied by 2, $7\frac{2}{3} \times 2 = \frac{23}{3} \times \frac{2}{1} = \frac{46}{3} = 15\frac{1}{3}$ feet.

2. A fruit salad is a mixture of $1\frac{3}{4}$ pounds of apples, $2\frac{1}{4}$ pounds of grapes, and $1\frac{1}{4}$ pounds of bananas. After the fruit is mixed, $1\frac{1}{2}$ pounds are set aside, and the rest is divided into three containers. What is the weight in pounds of one container?

   A. $1\frac{1}{5}$ B. $1\frac{1}{4}$ C. $1\frac{1}{3}$ D. $1\frac{1}{2}$

   The correct answer is **B**. The correct solution is $1\frac{1}{4}$. The amount available for the containers is $1\frac{3}{4} + 2\frac{1}{4} + 1\frac{1}{4} - 1\frac{1}{2} = 5\frac{1}{4} - 1\frac{1}{2} = 5\frac{1}{4} - 1\frac{2}{4} = 4\frac{5}{4} - 1\frac{2}{4} = 3\frac{3}{4}$. This amount is divided into three containers, $3\frac{3}{4} \div 3 = \frac{15}{4} \times \frac{15}{12} = 1\frac{3}{12} = 1\frac{1}{4}$ pounds.

3. In 2016, a town had 17.4 inches of snowfall. In 2017, it had 45.2 inches of snowfall. What is the difference in inches?

   A. 27.2   B. 27.8   C. 28.2   D. 28.8

   The correct answer is **B**. The correct solution is 27.8 because 45.2–17.4 = 27.8 inches.

4. Mike bought items that cost $4.78, $3.49, $6.79, $9.78, and $14.05. He had a coupon worth $5.00. If he paid with a $50.00 bill, then how much change does he receive?

   A. $16.11   B. $18.11   C. $21.11   D. $23.11

   The correct answer is **A**. The correct solution is $16.11. The total bill is $38.89, less the coupon is $33.89. The amount of change is $50.00–$33.89 = $16.11.

Let's Review!

- Using estimation is beneficial to determine an approximate solution to the problem when the numbers are complex.
- When solving a word problem with integers, fractions, or decimals, first read and visualize the problem. Then, make a plan, solve, and check the answer.

Chapter 9 Algebra Practice Quiz 1

1. Which decimal is the greatest?

    A. 1.7805

    C. 1.7085

    B. 1.5807

    D. 1.8057

2. Change $0.\overline{63}$ to a fraction. Simplify completely.

    A. $\frac{5}{9}$

    C. $\frac{2}{3}$

    B. $\frac{7}{11}$

    D. $\frac{5}{6}$

3. Write $0.\overline{1}$ as a percent.

    A. $0.\overline{1}\%$

    C. $11.\overline{1}\%$

    B. $1.\overline{1}\%$

    D. $111.\overline{1}\%$

4. Solve the equation for the unknown, $4x + 3 = 8$.

    A. -2

    C. $\frac{5}{4}$

    B. $-\frac{5}{4}$

    D. 2

5. Solve the inequality for the unknown, $3x + 5 - 2(x + 3) > 4(1-x) + 5$.

    A. $x > 2$

    C. $x > 10$

    B. $x > 9$

    D. $x > 17$

6. Solve the equation for h, $SA = 2\pi rh + 2\pi r^2$.

    A. $2\pi rSA - 2\pi r^2 = h$

    B. $2\pi rSA + 2\pi r^2 = h$

    C. $\frac{SA - 2\pi r^2}{2\pi r} = h$

    D. $\frac{SA + 2\pi r^2}{2\pi r} = h$

7. Solve the system of equations, $y = -2x + 3$ $y + x = 5$.

    A. $(-2, 7)$

    C. $(2, -7)$

    B. $(-2, -7)$

    D. $(2, 7)$

8. Solve the system of equations, $2x - 3y = -1$ $x + 2y = 24$.

    A. $(7, 10)$

    C. $(6, 8)$

    B. $(10, 7)$

    D. $(8, 6)$

9. Divide $1\frac{5}{6} \div 1\frac{1}{3}$.

    A. $1\frac{5}{18}$

    C. $2\frac{4}{9}$

    B. $1\frac{3}{8}$

    D. $3\frac{1}{6}$

10. Multiply $1\frac{1}{4} \times 1\frac{1}{2}$.

    A. $1\frac{1}{8}$

    C. $1\frac{2}{3}$

    B. $1\frac{1}{3}$

    D. $1\frac{7}{8}$

11. Divide $\frac{1}{10} \div \frac{2}{3}$.

    A. $\frac{1}{15}$

    C. $\frac{3}{20}$

    B. $\frac{1}{10}$

    D. $\frac{3}{5}$

12. A store has 75 pounds of bananas. Eight customers buy 3.3 pounds, five customers buy 4.25 pounds, and one customer buys 6.8 pounds. How many pounds are left in stock?

    A. 19.45

    C. 20.45

    B. 19.55

    D. 20.55

13. A rectangular garden needs a border. The length is $15\frac{3}{5}$ feet, and the width is $3\frac{2}{3}$ feet. What is the perimeter in feet?

    A. $18\frac{5}{8}$

    C. $37\frac{1}{4}$

    B. $19\frac{4}{15}$

    D. $38\frac{8}{15}$

14. Solve the system of equations by graphing, $\begin{array}{l}3x + y = -1\\2x - y = -4\end{array}$.

A.

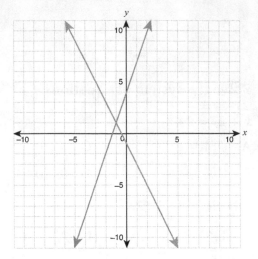

C.

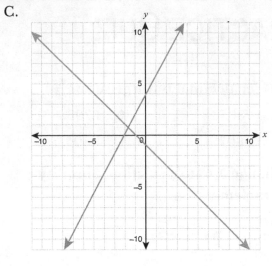

B.

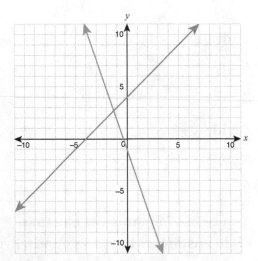

D.

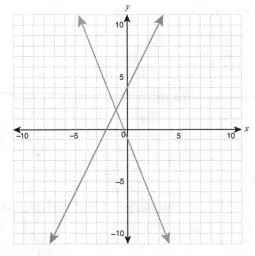

15. A historical society has 8 tours daily 5 days a week, with 32 people on each tour. Estimate the number of people who can be on the tour in 50 weeks.

A. 25,000   C. 75,000

B. 50,000   D. 100,000

CHAPTER 9 ALGEBRA
PRACTICE QUIZ 1 – ANSWER KEY

1. **D.** The correct solution is 1.8057 because 1.8075 contains the largest value in the tenths place. **See Lesson: Decimals and Fractions.**

2. **B.** The correct solution is $\frac{7}{11}$. Let $n = 0.\overline{63}$ and $100n = 63.\overline{63}$ Then, $100n - n = 63.\overline{63} - 0.\overline{63}$ resulting in $99n = 63$ and solution of $n = \frac{63}{99} = \frac{7}{11}$. **See Lesson: Decimals and Fractions.**

3. **C.** The correct answer is $11.\overline{1}\%$ because $0.\overline{1}$ as a percent is $0.\overline{1} \times 100 = 11.\overline{1}\%$. **See Lesson: Decimals and Fractions.**

4. **C.** The correct solution is $\frac{5}{4}$.

$4x = 5$	Subtract 3 from both sides of the equation.
$x = \frac{5}{4}$	Divide both sides of the equation by 4.

See Lesson: Equations with One Variable.

5. **A.** The correct solution is $x > 2$.

$3x + 5 - 2x - 6 > 4 - 4x + 5$	Apply the distributive property.
$x - 1 > -4x + 9$	Combine like terms on both sides of the inequality.
$5x - 1 > 9$	Add $4x$ to both sides of the inequality.
$5x > 10$	Add 1 to both sides of the inequality.
$x > 2$	Divide both sides of the inequality by 5.

See Lesson: Equations with One Variable.

6. **C.** The correct solution is $\frac{SA - 2\pi r^2}{2\pi r} = h$.

$SA - 2\pi r^2 = 2\pi rh$	Subtract $2\pi r^2$ from both sides of the equation.
$\frac{SA - 2\pi r^2}{2\pi r} = h$	Divide both sides of the equation by $2\pi r$.

See Lesson: Equations with One Variable.

7. A. The correct solution is (-2, 7).

	The first equation is already solved for y.
$-2x + 3 + x = 5$	Substitute $-2x + 3$ in for y in the second equation.
$-x + 3 = 5$	Combine like terms on the left side of the equation.
$-x = 2$	Subtract 3 from both sides of the equation.
$x = -2$	Divide both sides of the equation by -1.
$y = -2(-2) + 3$	Substitute -2 in the first equation for x.
$y = 4 + 3 = 7$	Simplify using order of operations.

See Lesson: Equations with Two Variables.

8. B. The correct solution is (10, 7).

$-2x-4y = -48$	Multiply all terms in the second equation by -2.
$-7y = -49$	Add the equations.
$y = 7$	Divide both sides of the equation by -7.
$x + 2(7) = 24$	Substitute 7 in the second equation for y.
$x + 14 = 24$	Simplify using order of operations.
$x = 10$	Subtract 14 from both sides of the equation.

See Lesson: Equations with Two Variables.

9. B. The correct answer is $1\frac{3}{8}$ because $\frac{11}{6} \div \frac{4}{3} = \frac{11}{6} \times \frac{3}{4} = \frac{33}{24} = 1\frac{9}{24} = 1\frac{3}{8}$. **See Lesson: Multiplication and Division of Fractions.**

10. D. The correct solution is $1\frac{7}{8}$ because $\frac{5}{4} \times \frac{3}{2} = \frac{15}{8} = 1\frac{7}{8}$. **See Lesson: Multiplication and Division of Fractions.**

11. C. The correct solution is $\frac{3}{20}$ because $\frac{1}{10} \times \frac{3}{2} = \frac{3}{20}$. **See Lesson: Multiplication and Division of Fractions.**

12. D. The correct solution is 20.55 because the number of pounds purchased is $8(3.3) + 5(4.25) + 6.8 = 26.4 + 21.25 + 6.8 = 54.55$ pounds. The number of pounds remaining is $75-54.45 = 20.55$ pounds. **See Lesson: Solving Real World Mathematical Problems.**

13. D. The correct solution is $38\frac{8}{15}$ because $15\frac{3}{5} + 3\frac{2}{3} = 15\frac{9}{15} + 3\frac{10}{15} = 18\frac{19}{15}(2) = \frac{289}{15} \times \frac{2}{1} = \frac{578}{15} = 38\frac{8}{15}$ feet. **See Lesson: Solving Real World Mathematical Problems.**

14. D. The correct graph has the two lines intersect at (-1, 2). **See Lesson: Equations with Two Variables.**

15. C. The correct solution is 75,000 because by estimation $10(5)(30)(50) = 75,000$ people can be on the tour in 50 weeks. **See Lesson: Solving Real World Mathematical Problems.**

CHAPTER 9 ALGEBRA PRACTICE QUIZ 2

1. Which decimal is the least?

    A. 2.22

    B. 2.02

    C. 2.002

    D. 2.2

2. Write 12.5% as a fraction.

    A. $\frac{1}{12}$

    B. $\frac{1}{9}$

    C. $\frac{1}{8}$

    D. $\frac{1}{7}$

3. Write 0.21 as a percent.

    A. 2.1%

    B. 20%

    C. 20.1%

    D. 21%

4. Multiply $\frac{6}{7} \times \frac{7}{10}$.

    A. $\frac{1}{17}$

    B. $\frac{1}{3}$

    C. $\frac{3}{5}$

    D. $\frac{13}{17}$

5. Divide $1\frac{2}{3} \div 3\frac{7}{12}$.

    A. $\frac{20}{43}$

    B. $3\frac{7}{18}$

    C. $3\frac{3}{4}$

    D. $5\frac{35}{36}$

6. Multiply $3\frac{1}{5} \times \frac{5}{8}$.

    A. 1

    B. 2

    C. 3

    D. 4

7. Solve the equation for the unknown, $a-10 = -20$.

    A. -30

    B. -10

    C. 2

    D. 200

8. Solve the equation for the unknown, $\frac{c}{-4} = -12$.

    A. -16

    B. -8

    C. 3

    D. 48

9. Solve the inequality for the unknown, $3(x + 1) + 2(x + 1) \geq 5(3-x) + 4(x + 2)$.

    A. $x \geq 0$

    B. $x \geq 1$

    C. $x \geq 2$

    D. $x \geq 3$

10. Solve the system of equations, $\begin{array}{l} x + 2y = 5 \\ -5x + 3y = -25 \end{array}$.

    A. (5, 0)

    B. (0, -5)

    C. (-5, 0)

    D. (0, 5)

11. Solve the system of equations, $\begin{array}{l} x = -3y + 10 \\ x = 3y-8 \end{array}$.

    A. (-1, 3)

    B. (-3, 1)

    C. (1, 3)

    D. (3, 1)

12. Solve the system of equations by graphing, $\begin{matrix} y = 4x-3 \\ y = x \end{matrix}$.

A.

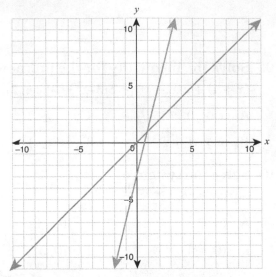

B.

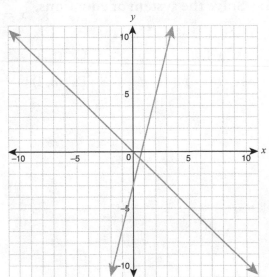

C.

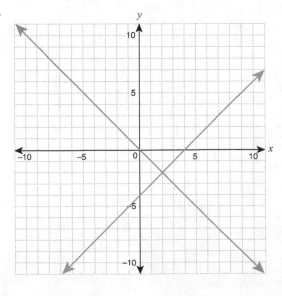

D.

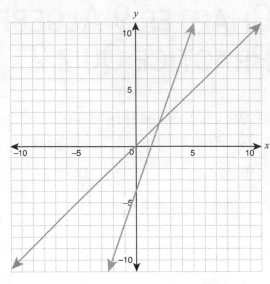

13. The temperature on Monday was –7°F, and it increased 18°F by Tuesday afternoon. What is the temperature in °F on Tuesday afternoon?

   A. –25

   B. –11

   C. 11

   D. 25

14. A diver was at 125 feet below sea level. The diver dove down another 350 feet. Where was the diver located?

   A. 475 feet below sea level

   B. 225 feet below sea level

   C. 225 feet above sea level

   D. 475 feet above sea level

15. A pair of jeans with tax costs $39.97, and a shirt with tax costs $18.49. What is the amount of change for a pair of jeans and two shirts if playing with a $100 bill?

   A. $23.05

   B. $36.98

   C. $41.54

   D. $60.03

CHAPTER 9 ALGEBRA
PRACTICE QUIZ 2 – ANSWER KEY

1. **C.** The correct solution is 2.002 because 2.002 contains the smallest values in the tenths and hundredths places. **See Lesson: Decimals and Fractions.**

2. **C.** The correct answer is $\frac{1}{8}$ because 12.5% as a fraction is $\frac{12.5}{100} = \frac{125}{1000} = \frac{1}{8}$. **See Lesson: Decimals and Fractions.**

3. **D.** The correct answer is 21% because 0.21 as a percent is $0.21 \times 100 = 21\%$. **See Lesson: Decimals and Fractions.**

4. **C.** The correct solution is $\frac{3}{5}$ because $\frac{6}{7} \times \frac{7}{10} = \frac{42}{70} = \frac{3}{5}$. **See Lesson: Multiplication and Division of Fractions.**

5. **A.** The correct answer is $\frac{20}{43}$ because $\frac{5}{3} \div \frac{43}{12} = \frac{5}{3} \times \frac{12}{43} = \frac{60}{129} = \frac{20}{43}$. **See Lesson: Multiplication and Division of Fractions.**

6. **B.** The correct solution is 2 because $\frac{16}{5} \times \frac{5}{8} = \frac{80}{40} = 2$. **See Lesson: Multiplication and Division of Fractions.**

7. **B.** The correct solution is –10 because 10 is added to both sides of the equation. **See Lesson: Equations with One Variable.**

8. **D.** The correct solution is 48 because both sides of the equation are multiplied by –4. **See Lesson: Equations with One Variable.**

9. **D.** The correct solution is $x \geq 3$.

$3x + 3 + 2x + 2 \geq 15 - 5x + 4x + 8$	Apply the distributive property.
$5x + 5 \geq -x + 23$	Combine like terms on both sides of the inequality.
$6x + 5 \geq 23$	Add x to both sides of the inequality.
$6x \geq 18$	Subtract 5 from both sides of the inequality.
$x \geq 3$	Divide both sides of the inequality by 6.

See Lesson: Equations with One Variable.

10. **A.** The correct solution is (5, 0).

$x = -2y + 5$	Solve the first equation for x by subtracting $2y$ from both sides of the equation.
$-5(-2y + 5) + 3y = -25$	Substitute $-2y + 5$ in for x in the first equation.
$10y - 25 + 3y = -25$	Apply the distributive property.
$13y - 25 = -25$	Combine like terms on the left side of the equation.

$13y = 0$	Add 25 to both sides of the equation.
$y = 0$	Divide both sides of the equation by 13.
$x + 2(0) = 5$	Substitute 0 in the second equation for y.
$x = 5$	Simplify using order of operations.

See Lesson: Equations with Two Variables.

11. **C.** The correct solution is (1, 3).

	The first equation is already solved for x.
$-3y + 10 = 3y-8$	Substitute $-3y + 10$ in for x in the second equation.
$-6y + 10 = -8$	Subtract $3y$ from both sides of the equation.
$-6y = -18$	Subtract 10 from both sides of the equation.
$y = 3$	Divide both sides of the equation by -6.
$x = -3(3) + 10$	Substitute 3 in the first equation for y.
$x = -9 + 10 = 1$	Simplify using order of operations.

See Lesson: Equations with Two Variables.

12. **A.** The correct graph has the two lines intersect at (1, 1). **See Lesson: Equations with Two Variables.**

13. **C.** The correct solution is 11 because $-7 + 18 = 11\,°F$. **See Lesson: Solving Real World Mathematical Problems.**

14. **A.** The correct solution is 475 feet below sea level because $-125-350 = -475$ feet. **See Lesson: Solving Real World Mathematical Problems.**

15. **A.** The correct solution is $23.05 because the total cost is $18.49(2) + 39.97 = 36.98 + 39.97 = 76.95$. The amount of change is $100-76.95 = 23.05. **See Lesson: Solving Real World Mathematical Problems.**

CHAPTER 10 FUNCTIONS

SOLVING QUADRATIC EQUATIONS

This lesson introduces solving quadratic equations by the square root method, completing the square, factoring, and using the quadratic formula.

Solving Quadratic Equations by the Square Root Method

A **quadratic equation** is an equation where the highest variable is squared. The equation is in the form $ax^2 + bx + c = 0$, where a is a non-zero constant and b and c are constants. There are at most two solutions to the equation because the highest variable is squared. There are many methods to solve a quadratic equation.

This section will explore solving a quadratic equation by the square root method. The equation must be in the form of $ax^2 = c$, or there is no x term.

> **STEP BY STEP**
>
> **Step 1.** Use multiplication and division properties of an equation to remove the value in front of the variable.
>
> **Step 2.** Apply the square root to both sides of the equation.

Note: The positive and negative square root make the solution true. For the equation $x^2 = 9$, the solutions are –3 and 3 because $3^2 = 9$ and $(-3)^2 = 9$.

Example

Solve the equation by the square root method, $4x^2 = 64$.

A. 4 B. 8 C. ±4 D. ±8

The correct answer is **C**. The correct solution is ±4.

$x^2 = 16$	Divide both sides of the equation by 4.
$x = \pm 4$	Apply the square root to both sides of the equation.

Solving Quadratic Equations by Completing the Square

A quadratic equation in the form $x^2 + bx$ can be solved by a process known as completing the square. The best time to solve by completing the square is when the b term is even.

STEP BY STEP

Step 1. Divide all terms by the coefficient of x^2.

Step 2. Move the number term to the right side of the equation.

Step 3. Complete the square $\left(\frac{b}{2}\right)^2$ and add this value to both sides of the equation.

Step 4. Factor the left side of the equation.

Step 5. Apply the square root to both sides of the equation.

Step 6. Use addition and subtraction properties to move all number terms to the right side of the equation.

Examples

1. **Solve the equation by completing the square, $x^2 - 8x + 12 = 0$.**

    A. –2 and –6   B. 2 and –6   C. –2 and 6   D. 2 and 6

    The correct answer is **D**. The correct solutions are 2 and 6.

$x^2 - 8x = -12$	Subtract 12 from both sides of the equation.
$x^2 - 8x + 16 = -12 + 16$	Complete the square, $\left(-\frac{8}{2}\right)^2 = (-4)^2 = 16$.
	Add 16 to both sides of the equation.
$x^2 - 8x + 16 = 4$	Simplify the right side of the equation.
$(x-4)^2 = 4$	Factor the left side of the equation.
$x - 4 = \pm 2$	Apply the square root to both sides of the equation.
$x = 4 \pm 2$	Add 4 to both sides of the equation.
$x = 4 - 2 = 2,\ x = 4 + 2 = 6$	Simplify the right side of the equation.

2. **Solve the equation by completing the square, $x^2 + 6x - 8 = 0$.**

    A. $-3 \pm \sqrt{17}$ B. $3 \pm \sqrt{17}$ C. $-3 \pm \sqrt{8}$ D. $3 \pm \sqrt{8}$

    The correct answer is **A**. The correct solutions are $-3 \pm \sqrt{17}$.

$x^2 + 6x = 8$	Add 8 to both sides of the equation.
$x^2 + 6x + 9 = 8 + 9$	Complete the square, $\left(\frac{6}{2}\right)^2 = 3^2 = 9$. Add 9 to both sides of the equation.
$x^2 + 6x + 9 = 17$	Simplify the right side of the equation.
$(x + 3)^2 = 17$	Factor the left side of the equation.
$x + 3 = \pm\sqrt{17}$	Apply the square root to both sides of the equation.
$x = -3 \pm \sqrt{17}$	Subtract 3 from both sides of the equation.

Solving Quadratic Equations by Factoring

Factoring can only be used when a quadratic equation is factorable; other methods are needed to solve quadratic equations that are not factorable.

> **STEP BY STEP**
>
> **Step 1.** Simplify if needed by clearing any fractions and parentheses.
>
> **Step 2.** Write the equation in standard form, $ax^2 + bx + c = 0$.
>
> **Step 3.** Factor the quadratic equation.
>
> **Step 4.** Set each factor equal to zero.
>
> **Step 5.** Solve the linear equations using inverse operations.

The quadratic equation will have two solutions if the factors are different or one solution if the factors are the same.

Examples

1. **Solve the equation by factoring, $x^2 - 13x + 42 = 0$.**

   A. $-6, -7$ B. $-6, 7$ C. $6, -7$ D. $6, 7$

   The correct answer is **D**. The correct solutions are 6 and 7.

$(x-6)(x-7) = 0$	Factor the equation.
$(x-6) = 0$ or $(x-7) = 0$	Set each factor equal to 0.
$x-6 = 0$	Add 6 to both sides of the equation to solve for the first factor.
$x = 6$	
$x-7 = 0$	Add 7 to both sides of the equation to solve for the second factor.
$x = 7$	

2. **Solve the equation by factoring, $9x^2 + 30x + 25 = 0$.**

   A. $-\frac{5}{3}$ B. $-\frac{3}{5}$ C. $\frac{3}{5}$ D. $\frac{5}{3}$

   The correct answer is **A**. The correct solution is $-\frac{5}{3}$.

$(3x + 5)(3x + 5) = 0$	Factor the equation.
$(3x + 5) = 0$ or $(3x + 5) = 0$	Set each factor equal to 0.
$(3x + 5) = 0$	Set one factor equal to zero since both factors are the same.
$3x + 5 = 0$	Subtract 5 from both sides of the equation and divide both sides of the equation by 3 to solve.
$3x = -5$	
$x = -\frac{5}{3}$	

Solving Quadratic Equations by the Quadratic Formula

Many quadratic equations are not factorable. Another method of solving a quadratic equation is by using the quadratic formula. This method can be used to solve any quadratic equation in the form . Using the coefficients a, b, and c, the quadratic formula is $x = \frac{-b \pm \sqrt{b^2-4ac}}{2a}$. The values are substituted into the formula, and applying the order of operations finds the solution(s) to the equation.

The solution of the quadratic formula in these examples will be exact or estimated to three decimal places. There may be cases where the exact solutions to the quadratic formula are used.

KEEP IN MIND

Watch the negative sign in the formula. Remember that a number squared is always positive.

Examples

1. **Solve the equation by the quadratic formula, $x^2-5x-6 = 0$.**

    A. –6 and –1   B. 6 and –1   C. –6 and 1   D. 6 and 1

    The correct answer is **B**. The correct solutions are 6 and –1.

$x = \dfrac{-(-5) \pm \sqrt{(-5)^2-4(1)(-6)}}{2(1)}$	Substitute 1 for a, –5 for b, and –6 for c.
$x = \dfrac{5 \pm \sqrt{25-(-24)}}{2}$	Apply the exponent and perform the multiplication.
$x = \dfrac{5 \pm \sqrt{49}}{2}$	Perform the subtraction.
$x = \dfrac{5 \pm 7}{2}$	Apply the square root.
$x = \dfrac{5 + 7}{2}$, $x = \dfrac{5-7}{2}$	Separate the problem into two expressions.
$x = \dfrac{12}{2} = 6$, $x = \dfrac{-2}{2} = -1$	Simplify the numerator and divide.

2. **Solve the equation by the quadratic formula, $2x^2 + 4x-5 = 0$.**

    A. –0.87 and –2.87   B. 0.87 and –2.87   C. –0.87 and 2.87   D. 0.87 and 2.87

    The correct answer is **B**. The correct solutions are –0.87 and –2.87.

$x = \dfrac{-4 \pm \sqrt{4^2-4(2)(-5)}}{2(2)}$	Substitute 2 for a, 4 for b, and –5 for c.
$x = \dfrac{-4 \pm \sqrt{16-(-40)}}{4}$	Apply the exponent and perform the multiplication.
$x = \dfrac{-4 \pm \sqrt{56}}{4}$	Perform the subtraction.
$x = \dfrac{-4 \pm 7.48}{4}$	Apply the square root.
$x = \dfrac{-4 + 7.48}{4}$, $x = \dfrac{-4-7.48}{4}$	Separate the problem into two expressions.
$x = \dfrac{3.48}{4} = 0.87$, $x = \dfrac{-11.48}{4} = -2.87$	Simplify the numerator and divide.

Let's Review!

There are four methods to solve a quadratic equation algebraically:

- The square root method is used when there is a squared variable term and a constant term.
- Completing the square is used when there is a squared variable term and an even variable term.
- Factoring is used when the equation can be factored.
- The quadratic formula can be used for any quadratic equation.

POLYNOMIALS

This lesson introduces adding, subtracting, and multiplying polynomials. It also explains polynomial identities that describe numerical expressions.

Adding and Subtracting Polynomials

A **polynomial** is an expression that contains exponents, variables, constants, and operations. The exponents of the variables are only whole numbers, and there is no division by a variable. The operations are addition, subtraction, multiplication, and division. Constants are terms without a variable. A polynomial of one term is a **monomial**; a polynomial of two terms is a **binomial**; and a polynomial of three terms is a **trinomial**.

KEEP IN MIND

The solution is an expression, and a value is not calculated for the variable.

To add polynomials, combine like terms and write the solution from the term with the highest exponent to the term with the lowest exponent. To simplify, first rearrange and group like terms. Next, combine like terms.

$$(3x^2 + 5x-6) + (4x^3-3x + 4) = 4x^3 + 3x^2 + (5x-3x) + (-6 + 4) = 4x^3 + 3x^2 + 2x-2$$

To subtract polynomials, rewrite the second polynomial using an additive inverse. Change the minus sign to a plus sign, and change the sign of every term inside the parentheses. Then, add the polynomials.

$$(3x^2 + 5x-6)-(4x^3-3x + 4) = (3x^2 + 5x-6) + (-4x^3 + 3x-4) = -4x^3 + 3x^2 + (5x + 3x) + (-6-4)$$
$$= -4x^3 + 3x^2 + 8x-10$$

Examples

1. **Perform the operation, $(2y^2-5y + 1) + (-3y^2 + 6y + 2)$.**

   A. $y^2 + y + 3$ B. $-y^2-y + 3$ C. $y^2-y + 3$ D. $-y^2 + y + 3$

   The correct answer is **D**. The correct solution is $-y^2 + y + 3$.

   $$(2y^2-5y + 1) + (-3y^2 + 6y + 2) = (2y^2-3y^2) + (-5y + 6y) + (1 + 2) = -y^2 + y + 3$$

2. **Perform the operation, $(3x^2y + 4xy-5xy^2)-(x^2y-3xy-2xy^2)$.**

   A. $2x^2y-7xy + 3xy^2$ C. $2x^2y + 7xy-3xy^2$

   B. $2x^2y + 7xy + 3xy^2$ D. $2x^2y-7xy-3xy^2$

   The correct answer is **C**. The correct solution is $2x^2y + 7xy-3xy^2$.

   $$(3x^2y + 4xy-5xy^2)-(x^2y-3xy-2xy^2) = (3x^2y + 4xy-5xy^2) + (-x^2y + 3xy + 2xy^2)$$
   $$= (3x^2y-x^2y) + (4xy + 3xy) + (-5xy^2 + 2xy^2) = 2x^2y + 7xy-3xy^2$$

Multiplying Polynomials

Multiplying polynomials comes in many forms. When multiplying a monomial by a monomial, multiply the coefficients and apply the multiplication rule for the power of an exponent.

BE CAREFUL!

Make sure that you apply the distributive property to all terms in the polynomials.

$$4xy(3x^2y) = 12x^3y^2.$$

When multiplying a monomial by a polynomial, multiply each term of the polynomial by the monomial.

$$4xy(3x^2y-2xy^2) = 4xy(3x^2y) + 4xy(-2xy^2) = 12x^3y^2-8x^2y^3.$$

When multiplying a binomial by a binomial, apply the distributive property and combine like terms.

$$(3x-4)(2x + 5) = 3x(2x + 5)-4(2x + 5) = 6x^2 + 15x-8x-20 = 6x^2 + 7x-20$$

When multiplying a binomial by a trinomial, apply the distributive property and combine like terms.

$$(x + 2)(3x^2-2x + 3) = (x + 2)(3x^2) + (x + 2)(-2x) + (x + 2)(3) = 3x^3 + 6x^2-2x^2-4x + 3x + 6 = 3x^3 + 4x^2-x + 6$$

Examples

1. **Multiply, $3xy^2(2x^2y)$.**

   A. $6x^2y^2$ B. $6x^3y^2$ C. $6x^3y^3$ D. $6x^2y^3$

   The correct answer is **C**. The correct solution is $6x^3y^3$. $3xy^2(2x^2y) = 6x^3y^3$.

2. **Multiply, $-2xy(3xy-4x^2y^2)$.**

   A. $-6x^2y^2 + 8x^3y^3$ B. $-6x^2y^2-8x^3y^3$ C. $-6xy + 8x^3y^3$ D. $-6xy-8x^3y^3$

   The correct answer is **A**. The correct solution is $-6x^2y^2 + 8x^3y^3$.

   $$-2xy(3xy-4x^2y^2) = -2xy(3xy)-2xy(-4x^2y^2) = -6x^2y^2 + 8x^3y^3$$

Polynomial Identities

BE CAREFUL!

Pay attention to the details of each polynomial identity and apply them appropriately.

There are many polynomial identities that show relationships between expressions.

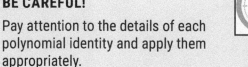

- Difference of two squares: $a^2-b^2 = (a-b)(a + b)$
- Square of a binomial: $(a + b)^2 = a^2 + 2ab + b^2$
- Square of a binomial: $(a-b)^2 = a^2-2ab + b^2$
- Sum of cubes: $a^3 + b^3 = (a + b)(a^2-ab + b^2)$
- Difference of two cubes: $a^3-b^3 = (a-b)(a^2 + ab + b^2)$

Examples

1. **Apply the polynomial identity to rewrite $x^2 + 6x + 9$.**

   A. $x^2 + 9$ B. $(x^2 + 3)^2$ C. $(x + 3)^2$ D. $(3x)^2$

   The correct answer is **C.** The correct solution is $(x + 3)^2$. The expression $x^2 + 6x + 9$ is rewritten as $(x + 3)^2$ because the value of *a* is *x* and the value of *b* is 3.

2. **Apply the polynomial identity to rewrite $8x^3 - 1$.**

   A. $(2x + 1)(4x^2 + 2x - 1)$ C. $(2x + 1)(4x^2 - 2x + 1)$

   B. $(2x - 1)(4x^2 - 2x - 1)$ D. $(2x - 1)(4x^2 + 2x + 1)$

   The correct answer is **D.** The correct solution is $(2x - 1)(4x^2 + 2x + 1)$. The expression $8x^3 - 1$ is rewritten as $(2x - 1)(4x^2 + 2x + 1)$ because the value of *a* is $2x$ and the value of *b* is 1.

Let's Review!

- Adding, subtracting, and multiplying are commonly applied to polynomials. The key step in applying these operations is combining like terms.
- Polynomial identities require rewriting polynomials into different forms.

RATIOS, PROPORTIONS, AND PERCENTAGES

This lesson reviews percentages and ratios and their application to real-world problems. It also examines proportions and rates of change.

Percentages

A **percent** or **percentage** represents a fraction of some quantity. It is an integer or decimal number followed by the symbol %. The word *percent* means "per hundred." For example, 50% means 50 per 100. This is equivalent to half, or 1 out of 2.

Converting between numbers and percents is easy. Given a number, multiply by 100 and add the % symbol to get the equivalent percent. For instance, 0.67 is equal to $0.67 \times 100 = 67\%$, meaning 67 out of 100. Given a percent, eliminate the % symbol and divide by 100. For instance, 23.5% is equal to $23.5 \div 100 = 0.235$.

Although percentages between 0% and 100% are the most obvious, a percent can be any real number, including a negative number. For example, 1.35 = 135% and −0.872 = −87.2%. An example is a gasoline tank that is one-quarter full: one-quarter is $\frac{1}{4}$ or 0.25, so the tank is 25% full. Another example is a medical diagnostic test that has a certain maximum normal result. If a patient's test exceeds that value, its representation can be a percent greater than 100%. For instance, a reading that is 1.22 times the maximum normal value is 122% of the maximum normal value. Likewise, when measuring increases in a company's profits as a percent from one year to the next, a negative percent can represent a decline. That is, if the company's profits fell by one-tenth, the change was −10%.

Example

If 15 out of every 250 contest entries are winners, what percentage of entries are winners?

A. 0.06%   B. 6%   C. 15%   D. 17%

The correct answer is **B**. First, convert the fraction $\frac{15}{250}$ to a decimal: 0.06. To get the percent, multiply by 100% (that is, multiply by 100 and add the % symbol). Of all entries, 6% are winners.

Ratios

A **ratio** expresses the relationship between two numbers and is expressed using a colon or fraction notation. For instance, if 135 runners finish a marathon but 22 drop out, the ratio of finishers to non-finishers is 135:22 or $\frac{135}{22}$. These expressions are equal.

> **BE CAREFUL!**
>
> Avoid confusing standard ratios with odds (such as "3:1 odds"). Both may use a colon, but their meanings differ. In general, a ratio is the same as a fraction containing the same numbers.

Ratios also follow the rules of fractions. Performing arithmetic operations on ratios follows the same procedures as on fractions. Ratios should also generally appear in lowest terms. Therefore, the constituent numbers in a ratio represent the relative quantities of each side, not absolute quantities. For example, because the ratio 1:2 is equal to 2:4, 5:10, and 600:1,200, ratios are insufficient to determine the absolute number of entities in a problem.

Example

If the ratio of women to men in a certain industry is 5:4, how many people are in that industry?

A. 9   B. 20   C. 900   D. Not enough information

The correct answer is **D**. The ratio 5:4 is the industry's relative number of women to men. But the industry could have 10 women and 8 men, 100 women and 80 men, or any other breakdown whose ratio is 5:4. Therefore, the question provides too little information to answer. Had it provided the total number of people in the industry, it would have been possible to determine how many women and how many men are in the industry.

KEY POINT

Mathematically, ratios act just like fractions. For example, the ratio 8:13 is mathematically the same as the fraction $\frac{8}{13}$.

Proportions

A **proportion** is an equation of two ratios. An illustrative case is two equivalent fractions:

$$\frac{21}{28} = \frac{3}{4}$$

This example of a proportion should be familiar: going left to right, it is the conversion of one fraction to an equivalent fraction in lowest terms by dividing the numerator and denominator by the same number (7, in this case).

Equating fractions in this way is correct, but it provides little information. Proportions are more informative when one of the numbers is unknown. Using a question mark (?) to represent an unknown number, setting up a proportion can aid in solving problems involving different scales. For instance, if the ratio of maple saplings to oak saplings in an acre of young forest is 7:5 and that acre contains 65 oaks, the number of maples in that acre can be determined using a proportion: $\frac{7}{5} = \frac{?}{65}$

Note that to equate two ratios in this manner, the numerators must contain numbers that represent the same entity or type, and so must the denominators. In this example, the numerators represent maples and the denominators represent oaks.

$$\frac{7 \text{ maples}}{5 \text{ oaks}} = \frac{? \text{ maples}}{65 \text{ oaks}}$$

Recall from the properties of fractions that if you multiply the numerator and denominator by the same number, the result is an equivalent fraction. Therefore, to find the unknown in this proportion, first divide the denominator on the right by the denominator on the left. Then, multiply the quotient by the numerator on the left.

$$65 \div 5 = 13$$

$$\frac{7 \times 13}{5 \times 13} = \frac{?}{65}$$

The unknown (?) is $7 \times 13 = 91$. In the example, the acre of forest has 91 maple saplings.

DID YOU KNOW?

When taking the reciprocal of both sides of a proportion, the proportion still holds. When setting up a proportion, ensure that the numerators represent the same type and the denominators represent the same type.

Example

If a recipe calls for 3 parts flour to 2 parts sugar, how much sugar does a baker need if she uses 12 cups of flour?

A. 2 cups   B. 3 cups   C. 6 cups   D. 8 cups

The correct answer is **D**. The baker needs 8 cups of sugar. First, note that "3 parts flour to 2 parts sugar" is the ratio 3:2. Set up the proportion using the given amount of flour (12 cups), putting the flour numbers in either the denominators or the numerators (either will yield the same answer): $\frac{3}{2} = \frac{12}{?}$

Since $12 \div 3 = 4$, multiply 2×4 to get 8 cups of sugar.

Rates of Change

Numbers that describe current quantities can be informative, but how they change over time can provide even greater insight into a problem. The rate of change for some quantity is the ratio of the quantity's difference over a specific time period to the length of that period. For example, if an automobile increases its speed from 50 mph to 100 mph in 10 seconds, the rate of change of its speed (its acceleration) is

$$\frac{100 \text{ mph} - 50 \text{ mph}}{10 \text{ s}} = \frac{50 \text{ mph}}{10 \text{ s}} = 5 \text{ mph per second} = 5 \text{ mph/s}$$

The basic formula for the rate of change of some quantity is $\frac{x_f - x_i}{t_f - t_i}$, where t_f is the "final" (or ending) time and t_i is the "initial" (or starting) time. Also, x_f is the (final) quantity at (final) time t_f, and x_i is the (initial) quantity at (initial) time t_i. In the example above, the final time is 10 seconds and the initial time is 0 seconds—hence the omission of the initial time from the calculation.

According to the rules of fractions, multiplying the numerator and denominator by the same number yields an equivalent fraction, so you can reverse the order of the terms in the formula:

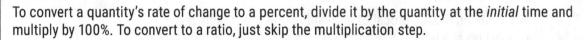

$$\frac{x_f - x_i}{t_f - t_i} = \frac{-1}{-1} \times \frac{x_f - x_i}{t_f - t_i} = \frac{x_i - x_f}{t_i - t_f}$$

The key to getting the correct rate of change is to ensure that the first number in the numerator and the first number in the denominator correspond to each other (that is, the quantity from the numerator corresponds to the time from the denominator). This must also be true for the second number.

TEST TIP

To convert a quantity's rate of change to a percent, divide it by the quantity at the *initial* time and multiply by 100%. To convert to a ratio, just skip the multiplication step.

Example

If the population of an endangered frog species fell from 2,250 individuals to 2,115 individuals in a year, what is that population's annual rate of increase?

    A. −135%   B. −6%   C. 6%   D. 135%

The correct answer is **B**. The population's rate of increase was −6%. The solution in this case involves two steps. First, calculate the population's annual rate of change using the formula. It will yield the change in the number of individuals.

$$\frac{2{,}115 - 2{,}250}{1 \text{ year} - 0 \text{ year}} = -135 \text{ per year}$$

Second, divide the result by the initial population. Finally, convert to a percent.

$$\frac{-135 \text{ per year}}{2{,}250} = -0.06 \text{ per year}$$

$$(-0.06 \text{ per year}) \times 100\% = -6\% \text{ per year}$$

Since the question asks for the *annual* rate of increase, the "per year" can be dropped. Also, note that the answer must be negative to represent the decreasing population.

Let's Review!

- A percent—meaning "per hundred"—represents a relative quantity as a fraction or decimal. It is the absolute number multiplied by 100 and followed by the % symbol.
- A ratio is a relationship between two numbers expressed using fraction or colon notation (for example, $\frac{3}{2}$ or 3:2). Ratios behave mathematically just like fractions.
- An equation of two ratios is called a proportion. Proportions are used to solve problems involving scale
- Rates of change are the speeds at which quantities increase or decrease. The formula $\frac{x_f - x_i}{t_f - t_i}$ provides the rate of change of quantity x over the period between some initial (i) time and final (f) time.

POWERS, EXPONENTS, ROOTS, AND RADICALS

This lesson introduces how to apply the properties of exponents and examines square roots and cube roots. It also discusses how to estimate quantities using integer powers of 10.

Properties of Exponents

An expression that is a repeated multiplication of the same factor is a **power**. The **exponent** is the number of times the **base** is multiplied. For example, 6^2 is the same as 6 times 6, or 36. There are many rules associated with exponents.

Property	Definition	Examples
Product Rule (Same Base)	$a^m \times a^n = a^{m+n}$	$4^1 \times 4^4 = 4^{1+4} = 4^5 = 1024$
		$x^1 \times x^4 = x^{1+4} = x^5$
Product Rule (Different Base)	$a^m \times b^m = (a \times b)^m$	$2^2 \times 3^2 = (2 \times 3)^2 = 6^2 = 36$
		$3^3 \times x^3 = (3 \times x)^3 = (3x)^3 = 27x^3$
Quotient Rule (Same Base)	$\frac{a^m}{a^n} = a^{m-n}$	$\frac{4^4}{4^2} = 4^{4-2} = 4^2 = 16$
		$\frac{x^6}{x^3} = x^{6-3} = x^3$
Quotient Rule (Different Base)	$\frac{a^m}{b^m} = \left(\frac{a}{b}\right)^m$	$\frac{4^4}{3^4} = \left(\frac{4}{3}\right)^4$
		$\frac{x^6}{y^6} = \left(\frac{x}{y}\right)^6$
Power of a Power Rule	$(a^m)^n = a^{mn}$	$(2^2)^3 = 2^{2\times3} = 2^6 = 64$
		$(x^5)^8 = x^{5\times8} = x^{40}$
Zero Exponent Rule	$a^0 = 1$	$64^0 = 1$
		$y^0 = 1$
Negative Exponent Rule	$a^{-m} = \frac{1}{a^m}$	$3^{-3} = \frac{1}{3^3} = \frac{1}{27}$
		$\frac{1}{x^{-3}} = x^3$

For many exponent expressions, it is necessary to use multiplication rules to simplify the expression completely.

Examples

1. **Simplify $(3^2)^3$.**

   A. 18   C. 243

   B. 216   D. 729

   The correct answer is **D**. The correct solution is 729 because $(3^2)^3 = 3^{2\times3} = 3^6 = 729$.

> **KEEP IN MIND**
>
> The expressions
> $(-2)^2 = (-2) \times (-2) = 4$ and
> $-2^2 = -(2 \times 2) = -4$ have different results because of the location of the negative signs and parentheses. For each problem, focus on each detail to simplify completely and correctly.

2. Simplify $(2x^2)^4$.

   A. $2x^8$ B. $4x^4$ C. $8x^6$ D. $16x^8$

   The correct answer is **D**. The correct solution is $16x^8$ because $(2x^2)^4 = 2^4(x^2)^4 = 2^4 x^{2\times4} = 16x^8$.

3. Simplify $\left(\frac{x^{-2}}{y^2}\right)^3$.

   A. $\frac{1}{x^6 y^6}$ B. $\frac{x^6}{y^6}$ C. $\frac{y^6}{x^6}$ D. $x^6 y^6$

   The correct answer is **A**. The correct solution is $\frac{1}{x^6 y^6}$ because $\left(\frac{x^{-2}}{y^2}\right)^3 = \left(\frac{1}{x^2 y^2}\right)^3 = \frac{1}{x^{2\times3} y^{2\times3}} = \frac{1}{x^6 y^6}$.

Square Root and Cube Roots

The **square** of a number is the number raised to the power of 2. The **square root** of a number, when the number is squared, gives that number. $10^2 = 100$, so the square of 100 is 10, or $\sqrt{100} = 10$. **Perfect squares** are numbers with whole number square roots, such as 1, 4, 9, 16, and 25.

Squaring a number and taking a square root are opposite operations, meaning that the operations undo each other. This means that $\sqrt{x^2} = x$ and $(\sqrt{x})^2 = x$. When solving the equation $x^2 = p$, the solutions are $x = \pm\sqrt{p}$ because a negative value squared is a positive solution.

The **cube** of a number is the number raised to the power of 3. The **cube root** of a number, when the number is cubed, gives that number. $10^3 = 1000$, so the cube of 1,000 is 10, or $\sqrt[3]{1000} = 10$. **Perfect cubes** are numbers with whole number cube roots, such as 1, 8, 27, 64, and 125.

KEEP IN MIND

Most square roots and cube roots are not perfect roots.

Cubing a number and taking a cube root are opposite operations, meaning that the operations undo each other. This means that $\sqrt[3]{x^3} = x$ and $\left(\sqrt[3]{x}\right)^3 = x$. When solving the equation $x^3 = p$, the solution is $x = \sqrt[3]{p}$.

If a number is not a perfect square root or cube root, the solution is an approximation. When this occurs, the solution is an irrational number. For example, $\sqrt{2}$ is the irrational solution to $x^2 = 2$.

Examples

1. Solve $x^2 = 121$.

   A. $-10, 10$ B. $-11, 11$ C. $-12, 12$ D. $-13, 13$

   The correct answer is **B**. The correct solution is $-11, 11$ because the square root of 121 is 11. The values of -11 and 11 make the equation true.

2. Solve $x^3 = 125$.

   A. 1   B. 5   C. 10   D. 25

   The correct answer is **B**. The correct solution is 5 because the cube root of 125 is 5.

Express Large or Small Quantities as Multiples of 10

Scientific notation is a large or small number written in two parts. The first part is a number between 1 and 10. In these problems, the first digit will be a single digit. The number is followed by a multiple to a power of 10. A positive integer exponent means the number is greater than 1, while a negative integer exponent means the number is smaller than 1.

The number 3×10^4 is the same as $3 \times 10{,}000 = 30{,}000$.

The number 3×10^{-4} is the same as $3 \times 0.0001 = 0.0003$.

For example, the population of the United States is about 3×10^8, and the population of the world is about 7×10^9. The population of the United States is $300{,}000{,}000$, and the population of the world is $7{,}000{,}000{,}000$. The world population is about 20 times larger than the population of the United States.

Examples

1. The population of China is about 1×10^9, and the population of the United States is about 3×10^8. How many times larger is the population of China than the population of the United States?

    A. 2 B. 3 C. 4 D. 5

    The correct answer is **B**. The correct solution is 3 because the population of China is about $1{,}000{,}000{,}000$ and the population of the United States is about $300{,}000{,}000$. So the population is about 3 times larger.

2. A red blood cell has a length of 8×10^{-6} meter, and a skin cell has a length of 3×10^{-5} meter. How many times larger is the skin cell?

    A. 1 B. 2 C. 3 D. 4

    The correct answer is **D**. The correct solution is 4 because 3×10^{-5} is 0.00003 and 8×10^{-6} is 0.000008. So, the skin cell is about 4 times larger.

Let's Review!

- The properties and rules of exponents are applicable to generate equivalent expressions.
- Only a few whole numbers out of the set of whole numbers are perfect squares. Perfect cubes can be positive or negative.
- Numbers expressed in scientific notation are useful to compare large or small numbers.

CHAPTER 10 FUNCTIONS
PRACTICE QUIZ 1

1. Multiply, $(x-1)(x^2 + 2x + 3)$.

    A. $x^3 + x^2 + x-3$

    C. $x^3 + x^2-x-3$

    B. x^3-x^2-x-3

    D. $x^3-x^2 + x-3$

2. Apply the polynomial identity to rewrite $9x^2-30x + 25$.

    A. $(3x + 5)(3x-5)$

    C. $(3x-5)(3x-1)$

    B. $(3x-5)^2$

    D. $(3x-5)(3x + 1)$

3. Perform the operation, $(3y^2 + 4y)-(5y^3-2y^2 + 3)$.

    A. $-5y^3 + y^2 + 4y-3$

    B. $-5y^3 + 5y^2 + 4y + 3$

    C. $-5y^3 + y^2 + 4y + 3$

    D. $-5y^3 + 5y^2 + 4y-3$

4. Solve $x^3 = 343$.

    A. 6

    C. 8

    B. 7

    D. 9

5. One online seller has about 6×10^8 online orders, and another online seller has about 5×10^7 online orders. How many times more orders does the first company have?

    A. 12

    C. 20

    B. 15

    D. 32

6. Simplify $\frac{x^2y^{-2}}{x^{-3}y^3}$.

    A. $\frac{x^5}{y^5}$

    C. $\frac{1}{x^5y^5}$

    B. $\frac{y^5}{x^5}$

    D. x^5y^5

7. What is 15% of 64?

    A. 5:48

    C. 48:5

    B. 15:64

    D. 64:15

8. Which number satisfies the proportion $\frac{378}{?} = \frac{18}{7}$?

    A. 18

    C. 972

    B. 147

    D. 2,646

9. If a tree grows an average of 4.2 inches in a day, what is the rate of change in its height per month? Assume a month is 30 days.

    A. 0.14 inches per month

    B. 4.2 inches per month

    C. 34.2 inches per month

    D. 126 inches per month

10. Solve the equation by the quadratic formula, $11x^2-14x + 4 = 0$.

    A. -0.84 and -0.43

    B. 0.84 and -0.43

    C. -0.84 and 0.43

    D. 0.84 and 0.43

11. Solve the equation by any method, $3x^2-5 = 22$.

    A. 0

    C. ±2

    B. ±1

    D. ±3

12. Solve the equation by the square root method, $5x^2 + 10 = 10$.

    A. 0

    C. 2

    B. 1

    D. 3

CHAPTER 10 FUNCTIONS
PRACTICE QUIZ 1 – ANSWER KEY

1. A. The correct solution is $x^3 + x^2 + x - 3$.

$(x-1)(x^2 + 2x + 3) = (x-1)(x^2) + (x-1)(2x) + (x-1)(3)$
$= x^3 - x^2 + 2x^2 - 2x + 3x - 3 = x^3 + x^2 + x - 3$

See Lesson: Polynomials.

2. B. The correct solution is $(3x-5)^2$. The expression $9x^2 - 30x + 25$ is rewritten as $(3x-5)^2$ because the value of a is $3x$ and the value of b is 5. **See Lesson: Polynomials.**

3. D. The correct solution is $-5y^3 + 5y^2 + 4y - 3$.

$(3y^2 + 4y) - (5y^3 - 2y^2 + 3) = (3y^2 + 4y) + (-5y^3 + 2y^2 - 3)$
$= -5y^3 + (3y^2 + 2y^2) + 4y - 3 = -5y^3 + 5y^2 + 4y - 3$

See Lesson: Polynomials.

4. B. The correct solution is 7 because the cube root of 343 is 7. **See Lesson: Powers, Exponents, Roots, and Radicals.**

5. A. The correct solution is 12 because the first company has about 600,000,000 orders and the second company has about 50,000,000 orders. So, the first company is about 12 times larger. **See Lesson: Powers, Exponents, Roots, and Radicals.**

6. A. The correct solution is $\frac{x^5}{y^5}$ because $\frac{x^2 y^2}{x^{-3} y^3} = x^{2-(-3)} y^{-2-3} = x^5 y^{-5} = \frac{x^5}{y^5}$. **See Lesson: Powers, Exponents, Roots, and Radicals.**

7. C. Either set up a proportion or just note that this question is asking for a fraction of a specific number: 15% (or $\frac{3}{20}$) of 64. Multiply $\frac{3}{20}$ by 64 to get $\frac{48}{5}$, or 48:5. **See Lesson: Ratios, Proportions, and Percentages.**

8. B. The number 147 satisfies the proportion. First, divide 378 by 18 to get 21. Then, multiply 21 by 7 to get 147. Check your answer by dividing 147 by 7: the quotient is also 21, so 147 satisfies the proportion. **See Lesson: Ratios, Proportions, and Percentages.**

9. D. The rate of change is 126 inches per month. One approach is to set up a proportion.

$$\frac{1\ day}{4.2\ inches} = \frac{30\ days}{?}$$

Since 1 month is equivalent to 30 days, multiply the rate of change per day by 30 to get the rate of change per month. 4.2 inches multiplied by 30 is 126 inches. Thus, the growth rate is 126 inches per month. **See Lesson: Ratios, Proportions, and Percentages.**

10. D. The correct solutions are 0.84 and 0.43.

$$x = \frac{-(-14) \pm \sqrt{(-14)^2 - 4(11)(4)}}{2(11)}$$ Substitute 11 for a, –14 for b, and 4 for c.

$$x = \frac{14 \pm \sqrt{196 - 176}}{22}$$ Apply the exponent and perform the multiplication.

$$x = \frac{14 \pm \sqrt{20}}{22}$$ Perform the subtraction.

$$x = \frac{14 \pm 4.47}{22}$$ Apply the square root.

$$x = \frac{14 + 4.47}{22}, x = \frac{14 - 4.47}{22}$$ Separate the problem into two expressions.

$$x = \frac{18.47}{22} = 0.84, x = \frac{9.53}{22} = 0.43$$ Simplify the numerator and divide.

See Lesson: Solving Quadratic Equations.

11. D. The correct solutions are ±3. Solve this equation by the square root method.

$3x^2 = 27$ Add 5 to both sides of the equation.

$x^2 = \pm 9$ Divide both sides of the equation by 3.

$x = \pm 3$ Apply the square root to both sides of the equation.

See Lesson: Solving Quadratic Equations.

12. A. The correct solution is 0.

$5x^2 = 0$ Subtract 10 from both sides of the equation.

$x^2 = 0$ Divide both sides of the equation by 5.

$x = 0$ Apply the square root to both sides of the equation.

See Lesson: Solving Quadratic Equations.

CHAPTER 10 FUNCTIONS
PRACTICE QUIZ 2

1. Solve the equation by factoring, $x^2-5x-50 = 0$.

   A. $-10, -5$ C. $10, -5$

   B. $-10, 5$ D. $10, 5$

2. Solve the equation by the square root method, $x^2 + 10 = 110$.

   A. ± 8 C. ± 10

   B. ± 9 D. ± 11

3. Solve the equation by the quadratic formula, $6x^2 + 11x + 1 = 0$.

   A. -1.74 and -0.10 C. 1.74 and -0.10

   B. -1.74 and 0.10 D. 1.74 and 0.10

4. Perform the operation, $(-2x^2 + 8x) + (3x^3-4x^2 + 1)$.

   A. $3x^3-6x^2 + 8x + 1$

   B. $3x^3-2x^2 + 8x + 1$

   C. $3x^3 + 6x^2 + 8x + 1$

   D. $3x^3 + 2x^2 + 8x + 1$

5. Multiply, $(5x-3)(5x + 3)$.

   A. $25x^2-9$ C. $25x^2 + 30x-9$

   B. $25x^2 + 9$ D. $25x^2 + 30x + 9$

6. Apply the polynomial identity to rewrite $x^3 + 125$.

   A. $(x + 5)(x^2-5x + 25)$

   B. $(x-5)(x^2-10x + 25)$

   C. $(x + 5)(x^2 + 5x + 25)$

   D. $(x-5)(x^2 + 10x + 25)$

7. Which is different from the others?

   A. 6.4%

   B. $\frac{8}{125}$

   C. $128:2000$

   D. All of the above are equal.

8. What is 36% as a ratio?

   A. $9:25$ C. $18:40$

   B. $36:100$ D. $25:9$

9. The number 22 is what percent of 54?

   A. 22% C. 41%

   B. 29% D. 76%

10. Solve $x^2 = 225$.

    A. $-5, 5$ C. $-15, 15$

    B. $-10, 10$ D. $-20, 20$

11. Simplify $\left(\frac{x^5}{5}\right)^4$.

    A. $\frac{x^9}{20}$ C. $\frac{x^{20}}{20}$

    B. $\frac{x^{20}}{625}$ D. $\frac{x^9}{625}$

12. The landmass of the United States is about 4×10^6 square miles, and the landmass of Alaska is about 7×10^5 square miles. How many times larger is the landmass of the United States than the landmass of Alaska?

    A. 1   C. 4

    B. 3   D. 6

Chapter 10 Functions
Practice Quiz 2 – Answer Key

1. **B.** The correct solutions are –10 and 5. **See Lesson: Solving Quadratic Equations.**

$(x + 10)(x-5) = 0$	Factor the equation.
$(x + 10) = 0 \ or \ (x-5) = 0$	Set each factor equal to 0.
$x + 10 = 0$	Subtract 10 from both sides of the equation to solve for the first factor.
$x = -10$	
$x-5 = 0$	Add 5 to both sides of the equation to solve for the second factor.
$x = 5$	

2. **C.** The correct solution is ± 10. **See Lesson: Solving Quadratic Equations.**

$x^2 = 100$	Subtract 10 from both sides of the equation.
$x \pm 10$	Apply the square root to both sides of the equation.

3. **A.** The correct solutions are –1.74 and –0.10.

$x = \dfrac{-11 \pm \sqrt{11^2-4(6)(1)}}{2(6)}$	Substitute 6 for a, 11 for b, and 1 for c.
$x = \dfrac{-11 \pm \sqrt{121-24}}{2(6)}$	Apply the exponent and perform the multiplication.
$x = \dfrac{-11 \pm \sqrt{97}}{12}$	Perform the subtraction.
$x = \dfrac{-11 \pm 9.85}{12}$	Apply the square root.
$x = \dfrac{-11 + 9.85}{12}, x = \dfrac{-11-9.85}{12}$	Separate the problem into two expressions.
$x = \dfrac{-1.15}{12} = -0.10, x = \dfrac{-20.85}{12} = -1.74$	Simplify the numerator and divide.

See Lesson: Solving Quadratic Equations.

4. **A.** The correct solution is $3x^3-6x^2 + 8x + 1$.

$$(-2x^2 + 8x) + (3x^3-4x^2 + 1) = 3x^3 + (-2x^2-4x^2) + 8x + 1 = 3x^3-6x^2 + 8x + 1$$

See Lesson: Polynomials.

5. **A.** The correct solution is $25x^2-9$.

$$(5x-3)(5x + 3) = 5x(5x + 3)-3(5x + 3) = 25x^2 + 15x-15x-9 = 25x^2-9$$

See Lesson: Polynomials.

6. A. The correct solution is $(x + 5)(x^2 - 5x + 25)$. The expression $x^3 + 125$ is rewritten as $(x + 5)(x^2 - 5x + 25)$ because the value of a is x and the value of b is 5. **See Lesson: Polynomials.**

7. D. All of the answer choices are equal. Although answer C is not in lowest terms, it is equal to $\frac{8}{125}$, which is equal to 0.064 or 6.4%. **See Lesson: Ratios, Proportions, and Percentages.**

8. A. As a ratio, 36% is 9:25. The most direct route is to convert 36% to a fraction, $\frac{36}{100}$, then reduce to lowest terms: $\frac{9}{25}$. The equivalent ratio in colon notation is 9:25. **See Lesson: Ratios, Proportions, and Percentages.**

9. C. The fraction $\frac{22}{54}$ is 41%, meaning 22 is 41% of 54. **See Lesson: Ratios, Proportions, and Percentages.**

10. C. The correct solution is –15, 15 because the square root of 225 is 15. The values of –15 and 15 make the equation true. **See Lesson: Powers, Exponents, Roots, and Radicals.**

11. B. The correct solution is $\frac{x^{20}}{625}$ because $\left(\frac{x^5}{5}\right)^4 = \frac{x^{5 \times 4}}{5^4} = \frac{x^{20}}{625}$. **See Lesson: Powers, Exponents, Roots, and Radicals.**

12. D. The correct solution is 6 because the landmass of the United States is about 4,000,000 square miles and the landmass of Alaska is about 700,000 square miles. So, the United States is about 6 times larger. **See Lesson: Powers, Exponents, Roots, and Radicals.**

CHAPTER 11 GEOMETRY

CONGRUENCE

This lesson discusses basic terms for geometry. Many polygons have the property of lines of symmetry, or rotational symmetry. Rotations, reflections, and translations are ways to create congruent polygons.

Geometry Terms

The terms *point*, *line*, and *plane* help define other terms in geometry. A point is an exact location in space with no size and has a label with a capital letter. A line has location and direction, is always straight, and has infinitely many points that extend in both directions. A plane has infinitely many intersecting lines that extend forever in all directions.

The diagram shows point W, point X, point Y, and point Z. The line is labeled as $\overleftrightarrow{WX}$, and the plane is Plane A or Plane WYZ (or any three points in the plane).

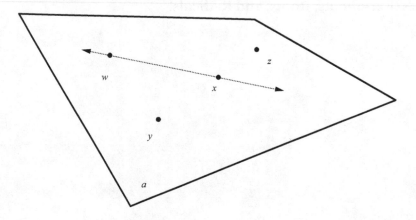

With these definitions, many other geometry terms can be defined. *Collinear* is a term for points that lie on the same line, and *coplanar* is a term for points and/or lines within the same plane. A line segment is a part of a line with two endpoints. For example, $\overline{WX}$ has endpoints W and X. A ray has an endpoint and extends forever in one direction. For example, $\longrightarrow AB$ has an endpoint of A, and $\longrightarrow BA$ has an endpoint of B. The intersection of lines, planes, segment, or rays is a point or a set of points.

Some key statements that are evident in geometry are

- There is exactly one straight line through any two points.
- There is exactly one plane that contains any three non-collinear points.
- A line with points in the plane lies in the plane.
- Two lines intersect at a point.
- Two planes intersect at a line.

Two rays that share an endpoint form an angle. The vertex is the common endpoint of the two rays that form an angle. When naming an angle, the vertex is the center point. The angle below is named $\angle ABC$ or $\angle CBA$.

An acute angle has a measure between 0° and 90°, and a 90° angle is a right angle. An obtuse angle has a measure between 90° and 180°, and a 180° angle is a straight angle.

There are two special sets of lines. Parallel lines are at least two lines that never intersect within the same plane. Perpendicular lines intersect at one point and form four angles.

Example

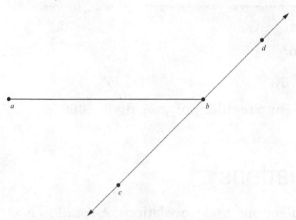

Describe the diagram.

A. Points A, B, C, and D are collinear.

B. Points A, C, and D are collinear.

C. $\overline{CD}$ intersects $\overleftrightarrow{AB}$ at point B.

D. $\overline{AB}$ intersects $\overleftrightarrow{CD}$ at point B.

The correct answer is **D**. The correct solution is $\overline{AB}$ intersects $\overleftrightarrow{CD}$ at point B. The segment intersects the line at point B.

Line and Rotational Symmetry

Symmetry is a reflection or rotation of a shape that allows that shape to be carried onto itself. Line symmetry, or reflection symmetry, is when two halves of a shape are reflected onto each other across a line. A shape may have none, one, or several lines of symmetry. A kite has one line of symmetry, and a scalene triangle has no lines of symmetry.

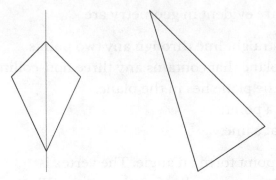

Rotational symmetry is when a figure can be mapped onto itself by a rotation about a point through any angle between 0° and 360°. The order of rotational symmetry is the number of times the object can be rotated. If there is no rotational symmetry, the order is 1 because the object can only be rotated 360° to map the figure onto itself. A square has 90° rotational symmetry and is order 4 because it can be rotated 90°, 180°, 270°, and 360°. A trapezoid has no rotational symmetry and is order 1 because it can only be rotated 360° to map onto itself.

> **KEEP IN MIND**
>
> A polygon can have both, neither, or either reflection and rotational symmetry.

Example

What is the rotational symmetry for a regular octagon?

A. 30°   B. 45°   C. 60°   D. 75°

The correct answer is **B**. The correct solution is 45°. For a regular polygon, divide 360° by the eight sides of the octagon to obtain 45°.

Rotations, Reflections, and Translations

There are three types of transformations: rotations, reflections, and translations. A rotation is a turn of a figure about a point in a given direction. A reflection is a flip over a line of symmetry, and a translation is a slide horizontally, vertically, or both. Each of these transformations produces a congruent image.

A rotation changes ordered pairs (x, y) in the coordinate plane. A 90° rotation counterclockwise about the point becomes $(-y, x)$, a 180° rotation counterclockwise about the point becomes $(-x, -y)$, and a 270° rotation the point becomes $(y, -x)$. Using the point $(6, -8)$,

- 90° rotation counterclockwise about the origin $(8, 6)$
- 180° rotation counterclockwise about the origin $(-6, 8)$
- 270° rotation counterclockwise about the origin $(-8, -6)$

A reflection also changes ordered pairs (x, y) in the coordinate plane. A reflection across the x-axis changes the sign of the y-coordinate, and a reflection across the y-axis changes the sign of the x-coordinate. A reflection over the line $y = x$ changes the points to (y, x), and a reflection over the line $y = -x$ changes the points to $(-y, -x)$. Using the point $(6, -8)$,

- A reflection across the x-axis $(6, 8)$
- A reflection across the y-axis $(-6, -8)$
- A reflection over the line $y = x$ $(-8, 6)$
- A reflection over the line $y = -x$ $(8, -6)$

A translation changes ordered pairs (x, y) left or right and/or up or down. Adding a positive value to an x-coordinate is a translation to the right, and adding a negative value to an x-coordinate is a translation to the left. Adding a positive value to a y-coordinate is a translation up, and adding a negative value to a y-coordinate is a translation down. Using the point $(6, -8)$,

> **KEEP IN MIND**
>
> A rotation is a turn, a reflection is a flip, and a translation is a slide.

- A translation of $(x + 3)$ is a translation right 3 units $(9, -8)$
- A translation of $(x - 3)$ is a translation left 3 units $(3, -8)$
- A translation of $(y + 3)$ is a translation up 3 units $(6, -5)$
- A translation of $(y - 3)$ is a translation down 3 units $(6, -11)$

Example

$\triangle ABC$ has points $A\ (3, -2)$, $B\ (2, -1)$, and $C\ (-1, 4)$, which after a transformation become $A'\ (2, 3)$, $B'\ (1, 2)$, and $C'\ (-4, -1)$. What is the transformation between the points?

A. Reflection across the x-axis

B. Reflection across the y-axis

C. Rotation of $90°$ counterclockwise

D. Rotation of $270°$ counterclockwise

The correct answer is **C**. The correct solution is a rotation of $90°$ counterclockwise because the points (x, y) become $(y, -x)$.

Let's Review!

- The terms *point*, *line*, and *plane* help define many terms in geometry.
- Symmetry allows a figure to carry its shape onto itself. This can be reflectional or rotational symmetry.
- Three transformations are rotation (turn), reflection (flip), and translation (slide).

SIMILARITY, RIGHT TRIANGLES, AND TRIGONOMETRY

This lesson defines and applies terminology associated with coordinate planes. It also demonstrates how to find the area of two-dimensional shapes and the surface area and volume of three-dimensional cubes and right prisms.

Coordinate Plane

The **coordinate plane** is a two-dimensional number line with the horizontal axis called the **x-axis** and the vertical axis called the **y-axis**. Each **ordered pair** or **coordinate** is listed as (x,y). The center point is the origin and has an ordered pair of (0, 0). A coordinate plane has four quadrants.

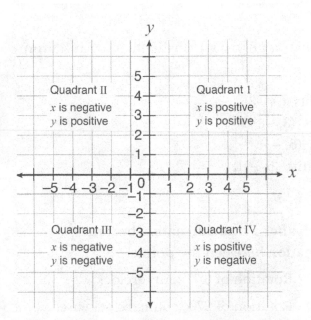

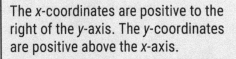

KEEP IN MIND

The x-coordinates are positive to the right of the y-axis. The y-coordinates are positive above the x-axis.

To graph a point in the coordinate plane, start with the x-coordinate. This point states the number of steps to the left (negative) or to the right (positive) from the origin. Then, the y-coordinate states the number of steps up (positive) or down (negative) from the x-coordinate.

Given a set of ordered pairs, points can be drawn in the coordinate plane to create polygons. The length of a segment can be found if the segment has the same first coordinate or the same second coordinate.

Examples

1. **Draw a triangle with the coordinates (–2, –1), (–3, 5), (–4, 2).**

A.

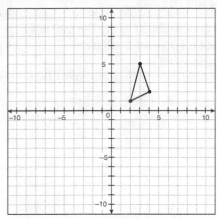

C.

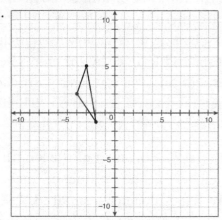

B.

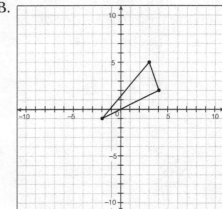

D.

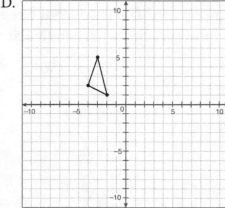

The correct answer is **C**. The first point is in the third quadrant because x is negative and y is negative, and the last two points are in the second quadrant because x is negative and y is positive.

2. **Given the coordinates for a rectangle (4, 8), (4, –2), (–1, –2), (–1, 8), find the length of each side of the rectangle.**

   A. 3 units and 6 units

   B. 3 units and 10 units

   C. 5 units and 6 units

   D. 5 units and 10 units

   The correct answer is **D**. The correct solution is 5 units and 10 units. The difference between the x-coordinates is 4–(–1) = 5 units, and the difference between the y-coordinates is 8–(–2) = 10 units.

3. **The dimensions for a soccer field are 45 meters by 90 meters. One corner of a soccer field on the coordinate plane is (–45, –30). What could a second coordinate be?**

   A. (–45, 30)   B. (–45, 45)   C. (–45, 60)   D. (–45, 75)

   The correct answer is **C**. The correct solution is (–45, 60) because 90 can be added to the y-coordinate, –30 + 90 = 60.

Area of Two-Dimensional Objects

The **area** is the number of unit squares that fit inside a two-dimensional object. A unit square is one unit long by one unit wide, which includes 1 foot by 1 foot and 1 meter by 1 meter. The unit of measurement for area is units squared (or feet

BE CAREFUL!

Make sure that you apply the correct formula for area of each two-dimensional object.

squared, meters squared, and so on). The following are formulas for calculating the area of various shapes.

- Rectangle: The product of the length and the width, $A = lw$.
- Parallelogram: The product of the base and the height, $A = bh$.
- Square: The side length squared, $A = s^2$.
- Triangle: The product of one-half the base and the height, $A = \frac{1}{2}bh$.
- Trapezoid: The product of one-half the height and the sum of the bases, $A = \frac{1}{2}h(b_1 + b_2)$.
- Regular polygon: The product of one-half the **apothem** (a line from the center of the regular polygon that is perpendicular to a side) and the sum of the perimeter, $A = \frac{1}{2}ap$.

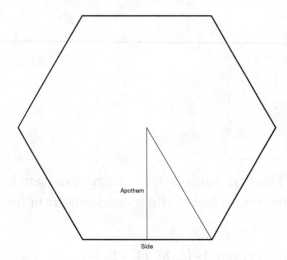

Examples

1. **A trapezoid has a height of 3 centimeters and bases of 8 centimeters and 10 centimeters. Find the area in square centimeters.**

   A. 18   B. 27   C. 52   D. 55

   The correct answer is **B**. The correct solution is 27. Substitute the values into the formula and simplify using the order of operations, $A = \frac{1}{2}h(b_1 + b_2) = \frac{1}{2}(3)(8 + 10) = \frac{1}{2}(3)(18) = 27$ square centimeters.

2. A regular decagon has a side length of 12 inches and an apothem of 6 inches. Find the area in square inches.

    A. 120   B. 360   C. 720   D. 960

    The correct answer is **B**. The correct solution is 360. Simplify using the order of operations, $A = \frac{1}{2}ap = \frac{1}{2}(6)(12(10)) = 360$ square inches.

3. Two rectangular rooms need to be carpeted. The dimensions of the first room are 18 feet by 19 feet, and the dimensions of the second room are 12 feet by 10 feet. What is the total area to be carpeted in square feet?

    A. 118   B. 236   C. 342   D. 462

    The correct answer is **D**. The correct solution is 462. Substitute the values into the formula and simplify using the order of operations, $A = lw + lw = 18(19) + 12(10) = 342 + 120 = 462$ square feet.

4. A picture frame is in the shape of a right triangle with legs 12 centimeters and 13 centimeters and hypotenuse of 17 centimeters. What is the area in square centimeters?

    A. 78   B. 108   C. 117   D. 156

    The correct answer is **A**. The correct solution is 78. Substitute the values into the formula and simplify using the order of operations, $A = \frac{1}{2}bh = \frac{1}{2}(12)(13) = 78$ square centimeters.

Surface Area and Volume of Cubes and Right Prisms

A three-dimensional object has length, width, and height. **Cubes** are made up of six congruent square faces. A **right prism** is made of three sets of congruent faces, with at least two sets of congruent rectangles.

BE CAREFUL!

Surface area is a two-dimensional calculation, and volume is a three-dimensional calculation.

The **surface area** of any three-dimensional object is the sum of the area of all faces. The formula for the surface area of a cube is $SA = 6s^2$ because there are six congruent faces. For a right rectangular prism, the surface area formula is $SA = 2lw + 2lh + 2hw$ because there are three sets of congruent rectangles. For a triangular prism, the surface area formula is twice the area of the base plus the area of the other three rectangles that make up the prism.

The **volume** of any three-dimensional object is the amount of space inside the object. The volume formula for a cube is $V = s^3$. The volume formula for a rectangular prism is the area of the base times the height, or $V = Bh$.

Examples

1. **A cube has a side length of 5 centimeters. What is the surface area in square centimeters?**

   A. 20   B. 25   C. 125   D. 150

   The correct answer is **D**. The correct solution is 150. Substitute the values into the formula and simplify using the order of operations, $SA = 6s^2 = 6(5^2) = 6(25) = 150$ square centimeters.

2. **A cube has a side length of 5 centimeters. What is the volume in cubic centimeters?**

   A. 20   B. 25   C. 125   D. 180

   The correct answer is **C**. The correct solution is 125. Substitute the values into the formula and simplify using the order of operations, $V = s^3 = 5^3 = 125$ cubic centimeters.

3. **A right rectangular prism has dimensions of 4 inches by 5 inches by 6 inches. What is the surface area in square inches?**

   A. 60   B. 74   C. 120   D. 148

   The correct answer is **D**. The correct solution is 148. Substitute the values into the formula and simplify using the order of operations, $SA = 2lw + 2lh + 2hw = 2(4)(5) + 2(4)(6) + 2(6)(5) = 40 + 48 + 60 = 148$ square inches.

4. **A right rectangular prism has dimensions of 4 inches by 5 inches by 6 inches. What is the volume in cubic inches?**

   A. 60   B. 62   C. 120   D. 124

   The correct answer is **C**. The correct solution is 120. Substitute the values into the formula and simplify using the order of operations, $V = lwh = 4(5)(6) = 120$ cubic inches.

Let's Review!

- The coordinate plane is a two-dimensional number line that is used to display ordered pairs. Two-dimensional shapes can be drawn on the plane, and the length of the objects can be determined based on the given coordinates.
- The area of a two-dimensional object is the amount of space inside the shape. There are area formulas to use to calculate the area of various shapes.
- For a three-dimensional object, the surface area is the sum of the area of the faces and the volume is the amount of space inside the object. Cubes and right rectangular prisms are common three-dimensional solids.

CIRCLES

This lesson introduces concepts of circles, including finding the circumference and the area of the circle.

Circle Terminology

A **circle** is a figure composed of points that are equidistant from a given point. The **center** is the point from which all points are equidistant. A **chord** is a segment whose endpoints are on the circle, and the **diameter** is a chord that goes through the center of the circle. The **radius** is a segment with one endpoint at the center of the circle and one endpoint on the circle. **Arcs** have two endpoints on the circle and all points on a circle between those endpoints.

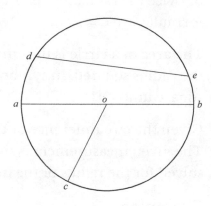

In the circle at the right, O is the center, $\overline{OC}$ is the radius, $\overline{AB}$ is the diameter, $\overline{DE}$ is a chord, and $\overparen{AD}$ is an arc.

Example

Identify a diameter of the circle.

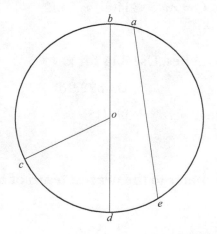

| | KEEP IN MIND | |

KEEP IN MIND

The radius is one-half the length of the diameter of the circle.

A. $\overline{BD}$ B. $\overline{OC}$ C. $\overline{DO}$ D. $\overline{AE}$

The correct answer is **A**. The correct solution is $\overline{BD}$ because points B and D are on the circle and the segment goes through the center O.

Circumference and Area of a Circle

The **circumference** of a circle is the perimeter, or the distance, around the circle. There are two ways to find the circumference. The formulas are the product of the diameter and pi or the product of twice the radius and pi. In symbol form, the formulas are $C = \pi d$ or $C = 2\pi r$.

The **area** of a circle is the amount of space inside a circle. The formula is the product of pi and the radius squared. In symbol form, the formula is $A = \pi r^2$. The area is always expressed in square units.

Given the circumference or the area of a circle, the radius and the diameter can be determined. The given measurement is substituted into the appropriate formula. Then, the equation is solved for the radius or the diameter.

Examples

1. **Find the circumference in centimeters of a circle with a diameter of 8 centimeters. Use 3.14 for π.**

    A. 12.56   B. 25.12   C. 50.24   D. 100.48

    The correct answer is **B**. The correct solution is 25.12 because $C = \pi d \approx 3.14(8) \approx 25.12$ centimeters.

2. **Find the area in square inches of a circle with a radius of 15 inches. Use 3.14 for π.**

    A. 94.2   B. 176.63   C. 706.5   D. 828.96

    The correct answer is **C**. The correct solution is 706.5 because $A = \pi r^2 \approx 3.14(15)^2 \approx$

    $3.14(225) \approx 706.5$ square inches.

3. **A circle has a circumference of 70 centimeters. Find the diameter to the nearest tenth of a centimeter. Use 3.14 for π.**

    A. 11.1   B. 22.3   C. 33.5   D. 44.7

    The correct answer is **B**. The correct solution is 22.3 because $C = \pi d; 70 = 3.14d; d \approx 22.3$ centimeters.

4. **A circle has an area of 95 square centimeters. Find the radius to the nearest tenth of a centimeter. Use 3.14 for π.**

    A. 2.7   B. 5.5   C. 8.2   D. 10.9

    The correct answer is **B**. The correct solution is 5.5 because
    $A = \pi r^2; 95 = 3.14r^2; 30.25 = r^2; r \approx 5.5$ centimeters.

Finding Circumference or Area Given the Other Value

Given the circumference of a circle, the area of the circle can be found. First, substitute the circumference into the formula and find the radius. Substitute the radius into the area formula and simplify.

Reverse the process to find the circumference given the area. First, substitute the area into the area formula and find the radius. Substitute the radius into the circumference formula and simplify.

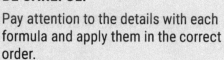

BE CAREFUL!

Pay attention to the details with each formula and apply them in the correct order.

Examples

1. The circumference of a circle is 45 inches. Find the area of the circle in square inches. Round to the nearest tenth. Use 3.14 for π.

    A. 51.8   B. 65.1   C. 162.8   D. 204.5

    The correct answer is **C**. The correct solution is 162.8.

    $C = 2\pi r; 45 = 2(3.14)r; 45 = 6.28r; r \approx 7.2$ inches. $A = \pi r^2 \approx 3.14\,(7.2)^2 \approx 3.14(51.84) \approx 162.8$ square inches.

2. The area of a circle is 60 square centimeters. Find the circumference of the circle in centimeters. Round to the nearest tenth. Use 3.14 for π.

    A. 4.4   B. 13.8   C. 19.1   D. 27.6

    The correct answer is **D**. The correct solution is 27.6.

    $A = \pi r^2; 60 = 3.14\,r^2; 19.11 = r^2; r \approx 4.4$ centimeters. $C = 2\pi r; C = 2(3.14)4.4 \approx 27.6$ centimeters.

Let's Review!

- Key terms related to circles are *radius, diameter, chord,* and *arc*. Note that the diameter is twice the radius.
- The circumference or the perimeter of a circle is the product of pi and the diameter or twice the radius and pi.
- The area of the circle is the product of pi and the radius squared.

MEASUREMENT AND DIMENSION

This lesson applies the formulas of volume for cylinders, pyramids, cones, and spheres to solve problems.

Volume of a Cylinder

A **cylinder** is a three-dimensional figure with two identical circular bases and a rectangular lateral face.

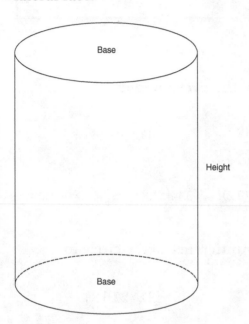

KEEP IN MIND

The volume of a cylinder can be expressed in terms of π, and the volume is measured in cubic units.

The volume of a cylinder equals the product of the area of the base and the height of the cylinder. This is the same formula used to calculate the volume of a right prism. In this case, the area of a base is a circle, so the formula is $V = Bh = \pi r^2 h$. The height is the perpendicular distance between the two circular bases.

Example

Find the volume of a cylinder in cubic centimeters with a radius of 13 centimeters and a height of 12 centimeters.

   A. 156π B. 312π C. $1{,}872\pi$ D. $2{,}028\pi$

The correct answer is **D**. The correct solution is $2{,}028\pi$. Substitute the values into the formula and simplify using the order of operations, $V = \pi r^2 h = \pi 13^2 (12) = \pi(169)(12) = 2{,}028\pi$ cubic centimeters.

Volume of a Pyramid and a Cone

A **pyramid** is a three-dimensional solid with
one base and all edges from the base meeting
at the top, or apex. Pyramids can have any two-
dimensional shape as the base. A **cone** is similar to
a pyramid, but it has a circle instead of a polygon
for the base.

BE CAREFUL!

Make sure that you apply the correct
formula for area of the base for a
pyramid.

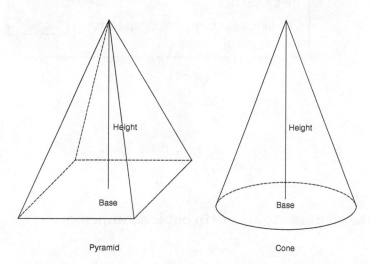

The formula for the volume of a pyramid is similar to a prism, $V = \frac{1}{3}Bh$ where B is the area of
the base. The base is a circle for a cone, and the formula for the volume is $V = \frac{1}{3}Bh = \frac{1}{3}\pi r^2 h$.

Examples

1. **A regular hexagonal pyramid has base with side lengths of 5 centimeters and an apothem
    of 3 centimeters. If the height is 6 centimeters, find the volume in cubic centimeters.**

    A. 90　　　　　　B. 180　　　　　　C. 270　　　　　　D. 360

    The correct answer is **A**. The correct solution is 90. Substitute the values into the formula
    and simplify using the order of operations, $V = \frac{1}{3}Bh = \frac{1}{3}(\frac{1}{2}ap)h = \frac{1}{3}(\frac{1}{2}(3)(30))6 = 90$ cubic
    centimeters.

2. **A cone has a radius of 10 centimeters and a height of 9 centimeters. Find the volume in
    cubic centimeters.**

    A. 270π　　　　　B. 300π　　　　　C. 810π　　　　　D. 900π

    The correct answer is **B**. The correct solution is 300π. Substitute the values into the formula
    and simplify using the order of operations, $V = \frac{1}{3}\pi r^2 h = \frac{1}{3}\pi 10^2(9) = \frac{1}{3}\pi(100)(9) = 300\pi$ cubic
    centimeters.

Volume of a Sphere

A **sphere** is a round, three-dimensional solid, with every point on its surface equidistant to the center. The formula for the volume of a sphere is represented by just the radius of the sphere. The volume of a sphere is $V = \frac{4}{3}\pi r^3$. The volume of a hemi (half) of a sphere is $V = \left(\frac{1}{2}\right)\frac{4}{3}\pi r^3 = \frac{2}{3}\pi r^3$.

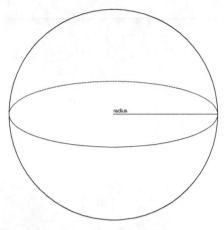

BE CAREFUL!

The radius is cubed, not squared, for the volume of a sphere.

Example

A sphere has a radius of 3 centimeters. Find the volume of a sphere in cubic centimeters.

A. 18π B. 27π C. 36π D. 45π

The correct answer is **C**. The correct solution is 36π. Substitute the values into the formula and simplify using the order of operations, $V = \frac{4}{3}\pi r^3 = \frac{4}{3}\pi 3^3 = \frac{4}{3}\pi(27) = 36\pi$ cubic centimeters.

Let's Review!

- The volume is the capacity of a three-dimensional object and is expressed in cubic units.
- The volume formula for a cylinder is the product of the area of the base (which is a circle) and the height of the cylinder.
- The volume formula for a pyramid or cone is one-third of the product of the area of the base (a circle in the case of the cone) and the height of the pyramid or cone.
- The volume formula for a sphere is $V = \frac{4}{3}\pi r^3$.

CHAPTER 11 GEOMETRY PRACTICE QUIZ 1

1. The bottom of a plastic pool has an area of 64 square feet. What is the radius to the nearest tenth of a foot? Use 3.14 for π.

   A. 2.3
   C. 6.9

   B. 4.5
   D. 10.2

2. The area of a circular hand mirror is 200 square centimeters. Find the circumference of the mirror to the nearest tenth of a centimeter. Use 3.14 for π.

   A. 25.1
   C. 75.3

   B. 50.2
   D. 100.4

3. The circumference of a pie is 300 centimeters. Find the area of one-fourth of the pie to the nearest tenth of a square centimeter. Use 3.14 for π.

   A. 1,793.6
   C. 7,174.4

   B. 2,284.8
   D. 14,348.8

4. A regular hexagon has a rotational order of 6. What is the smallest number of degrees for the figure to be rotated onto itself?

   A. 30°
   C. 90°

   B. 60°
   D. 120°

5. A right triangle has a base of 6 inches and a hypotenuse of 10 inches. Find the height in inches of the triangle if the area is 24 square inches.

   A. 4
   C. 8

   B. 6
   D. 10

6. $\triangle GHI$ has points $G(2, 7)$, $H(-3, -8)$, and $I(-6, 0)$. After a transformation, the points are $G'(7, 2)$, $H'(-8, -3)$, and $I'(0, -6)$. What is the transformation between the points?

   A. Reflection across the x-axis

   B. Reflection across the y-axis

   C. Reflection across the line of $y = x$

   D. Reflection across the line of $y = -x$

7. Name the right angle in the diagram.

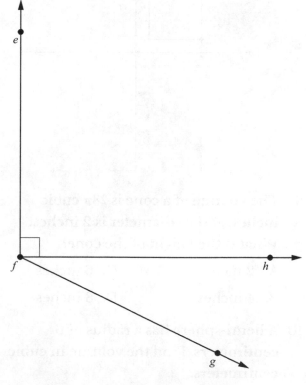

   A. $\angle EHF$
   C. $\angle EFH$

   B. $\angle EFG$
   D. $\angle EGF$

8. Draw a rectangle with the coordinates $(5,7), (5,1), (1,1), (1,7)$.

A.

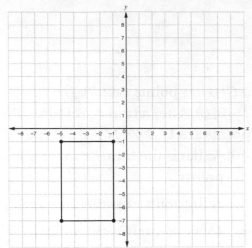

C.

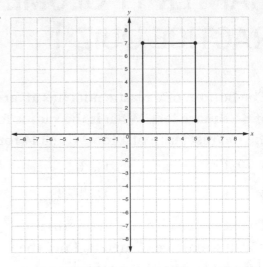

B.

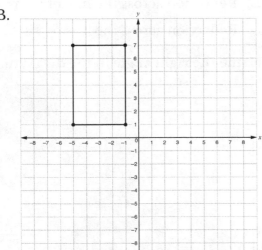

D.

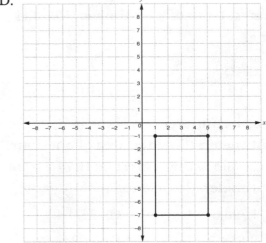

9. The volume of a cone is 28π cubic inches, and its diameter is 2 inches. What is the height of the cone?

   A. 2 inches   C. 6 inches

   B. 4 inches   D. 8 inches

10. A hemi-sphere has a radius of 6 centimeters. Find the volume in cubic centimeters.

   A. 72π C. 288π

   B. 144π D. 576π

11. A rectangular pyramid has a height of 7 meters and a volume of 112 cubic meters. Find the area of the base in square meters.

   A. 16   C. 42

   B. 28   D. 48

12. A right rectangular prism has dimensions of 3 inches by 6 inches by 9 inches. What is the surface area in square inches?

   A. 162   C. 232

   B. 198   D. 286

CHAPTER 11 GEOMETRY
PRACTICE QUIZ 1 – ANSWER KEY

1. B. The correct solution is 4.5 because $A = \pi r^2; 64 = 3.14 r^2; 20.38 = r^2$; $r \approx 4.5$ feet. **See Lesson: Circles.**

2. B. The correct solution is 50.2. $A = \pi r^2; 200 = 3.14 r^2; 63.69 = r^2; r \approx 8.0$ centimeters. $C = 2\pi r; C = 2$ (3.14)8.0 $\approx$ 50.2 centimeters. **See Lesson: Circles.**

3. A. The correct solution is 1,793.6. $C = 2\pi r; 300 = 2(3.14)r; 300 = 6.28r; r \approx 47.8$ centimeters. $A = \frac{1}{4}\pi r^2 \approx \frac{1}{4}(3.14)(47.8)^2 \approx \frac{1}{4}3.14(2,284.84) \approx 1793.6$ square centimeters. **See Lesson: Circles.**

4. B. The correct solution is 60°. For a regular hexagon, divide 360° by the six sides to obtain 60°. **See Lesson: Congruence.**

5. C. The correct solution is 8. Substitute the values into the formula, $24 = \frac{1}{2}(6)h$ and simplify the right side of the equation, $24 = 3h$. Divide both sides of the equation by 3, $h = 8$ inches. **See Lesson: Similarity, Right Triangles, and Trigonometry.**

6. C. The correct solution is a reflection across the line of $y = x$ because the points (x, y) become (y, x). **See Lesson: Congruence.**

7. C. The correct solution is $\angle EFH$ because the vertex of the right angle is F and the other two points are E and H. **See Lesson: Congruence.**

8. C. All points are in the first quadrant. **See Lesson: Similarity, Right Triangles, and Trigonometry.**

9. C. The correct solution is 6 inches. Substitute the values into the formula, $2\pi = \frac{1}{3}\pi(1)^2 h$ and simplify using the right side of the equation by applying the exponent and multiplying, $2\pi = \frac{1}{3}\pi$ $(1)h, 2\pi = \frac{1}{3}\pi h$. Multiply both sides of the equation by 3 to get a solution of 6 inches. **See Lesson: Measurement and Dimension.**

10. B. The correct solution is 144π. Substitute the values into the formula and simplify using the order of operations, $V = \frac{2}{3}\pi r^3 = \frac{2}{3}\pi(6^3) = \frac{2}{3}\pi(216) = 144\pi$ cubic centimeters. **See Lesson: Measurement and Dimension.**

11. D. The correct solution is 48. Substitute the values into the formula, $112 = \frac{1}{3}B(7)$ and simplify the right side of the equation, $112 = \frac{7}{3}B$. Multiply both sides of the equation by the reciprocal, B = 48 square meters. **See Lesson: Measurement and Dimension.**

12. B. The correct solution is 198. Substitute the values into the formula and simplify using the order of operations, $SA = 2lw + 2lh + 2hw = 2(3)(6) + 2(6)(9) + 2(9)(3) = 36 + 108 + 54 = 198$ square inches. **See Lesson: Similarity, Right Triangles, and Trigonometry.**

CHAPTER 11 GEOMETRY PRACTICE QUIZ 2

1. **What is the intersection of two walls in a room?**

   A. A ray   C. A point

   B. A line   D. A plane

2. **What is the rotational symmetry for a rectangle?**

   A. 0°   C. 180°

   B. 90°   D. 270°

3. **Select the square with the correct lines of symmetry.**

   A.

   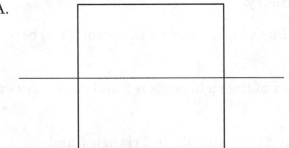

   B.

   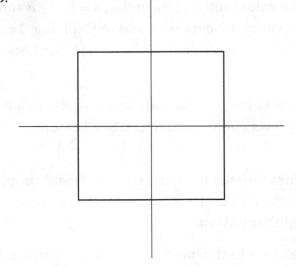

C.

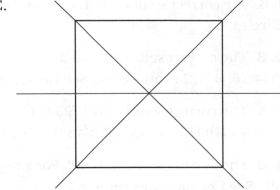

D.

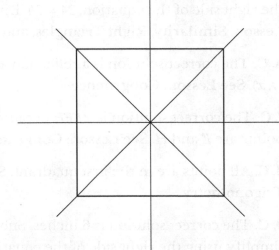

4. **Three vertices of a rectangle are (−6,5), (−6,0), (12, 5). What is the fourth coordinate?**

   A. (12, 0)   C. (−12, 0)

   B. (0, 12)   D. (0, −12)

5. **A cube has a surface area of 54 square feet. What is the side length in feet?**

   A. 2   C. 4

   B. 3   D. 5

6. A trapezoid has bases of 8 inches and 12 inches and a height of 6 inches. Find the area in square inches.

   A. 18   C. 60

   B. 20   D. 72

7. A dime has a radius of 8.5 millimeters. Find the circumference in millimeters of the dime. Use 3.14 for ϖ.

   A. 11.64   C. 53.38

   B. 26.69   D. 106.76

8. Half of a circular garden with a radius of 11.5 feet needs weeding. Find the area in square feet that needs weeding. Round to the nearest hundredth. Use 3.14 for ϖ.

   A. 207.64   C. 519.08

   B. 415.27   D. 726.73

9. A circle has an area of 12 square feet. Find the diameter to the nearest tenth of a foot. Use 3.14 for ϖ.

   A. 1.0   C. 3.0

   B. 2.0   D. 4.0

10. A square pyramid has a volume of 189 cubic feet and a height of 7 feet. Find the length in feet of a side of the base.

    A. 3   C. 12

    B. 9   D. 18

11. A rectangular pyramid has a length of 10 centimeters, a width of 11 inches, and a height of 12 inches. Find the volume in cubic inches.

    A. 220   C. 660

    B. 440   D. 880

12. A sphere has a volume of 972π cubic millimeters. Find the radius in millimeters.

    A. 3   C. 27

    B. 9   D. 81

229

CHAPTER 11 GEOMETRY
PRACTICE QUIZ 2 – ANSWER KEY

1. B. The correct solution is a line. The walls are two planes, and two planes intersect at a line. **See Lesson: Congruence.**

2. C. The correct solution is 180°. For a rectangle, there is rotational symmetry every 180°. **See Lesson: Congruence.**

3. D. The correct solution is the square with four lines of symmetry. There is a horizontal line, a vertical line, and two diagonals of symmetry that map the rectangle onto itself. **See Lesson: Congruence.**

4. A. The correct solution is (12, 0) because this point shows a rectangle with sides lengths of 5 units and 18 units. **See Lesson: Similarity, Right Triangles, and Trigonometry.**

5. B. The correct solution is 3. Substitute the values into the formula $54 = 6s^2$. Solve the equation by dividing both sides of the equation by 6 and applying the square root, $9 = s^2; s = 3$ feet. **See Lesson: Similarity, Right Triangles, and Trigonometry.**

6. C. The correct solution is 60. Substitute the values into the formula and simplify using the order of operations, $A = \frac{1}{2}h(b_1 + b_2) = \frac{1}{2}(6)(8 + 12) = \frac{1}{2}(6)(20) = 60$ square inches. **See Lesson: Similarity, Right Triangles, and Trigonometry.**

7. C. The correct solution is 53.38 because $C = 2\pi r \approx (2)3.14(8.5) \approx 53.38$ millimeters. **See Lesson: Circles.**

8. A. The correct solution is 207.64 because $A = \frac{1}{2}\pi r^2 \approx \frac{1}{2}(3.14)(11.5)^2 \approx \frac{1}{2}(3.14)(132.25) \approx 207.64$ square feet. **See Lesson: Circles.**

9. D. The correct solution is 4.0 because $A = \pi r^2; 12 = 3.14 r^2; 3.82 = r^2 ; r \approx 2.0$. The diameter is twice the radius, or about 4.0 feet. **See Lesson: Circles.**

10. B. The correct solution is 9. Substitute the values into the formula, $189 = \frac{1}{3}s^2(7)$ and simplify the right side of the equation, $189 = \frac{7}{3}s^2$. Multiply both sides by the reciprocal and apply the square root, $81 = s^2, s = 9$ feet. **See Lesson: Measurement and Dimension.**

11. B. The correct solution is 440. Substitute the values into the formula and simplify using the order of operations, $V = \frac{1}{3}Bh = \frac{1}{3}lwh = \frac{1}{3}(10)(11)12 = 440$ cubic inches. **See Lesson: Measurement and Dimension.**

12. B. The correct solution is 9 millimeters. Substitute the values into the formula, $972\pi = \frac{4}{3}\pi r^3$, then multiply by the reciprocal, $729 = r^3$, and apply the cube root, $r = 9$ millimeters. **See Lesson: Measurement and Dimension.**

CHAPTER 12 STATISTICS AND PROBABILITY

INTERPRETING GRAPHICS

This lesson discusses how to create a bar, line, and circle graph and how to interpret data from these graphs. It also explores how to calculate and interpret the measures of central tendency.

Creating a Line, Bar, and Circle Graph

A line graph is a graph with points connected by segments that examines changes over time. The horizontal axis contains the independent variable (the input value), which is usually time. The vertical axis contains the dependent variable (the output value), which is an item that measures a quantity. A line graph will have a title and an appropriate scale to display the data. The graph can include more than one line.

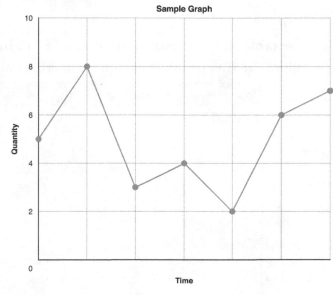

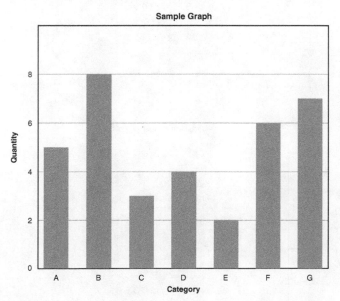

A bar graph uses rectangular horizontal or vertical bars to display information. A bar graph has categories on the horizontal axis and the quantity on the vertical axis. Bar graphs need a title and an appropriate scale for the frequency. The graph can include more than one bar.

BE CAREFUL

Make sure to use the appropriate scale for each type of graph.

231

A circle graph is a circular chart that is divided into parts, and each part shows the relative size of the value. To create a circle graph, find the total number and divide each part by the total to find the percentage. Then, to find the part of the circle, multiply each percent by 360°. Draw each part of the circle and create a title.

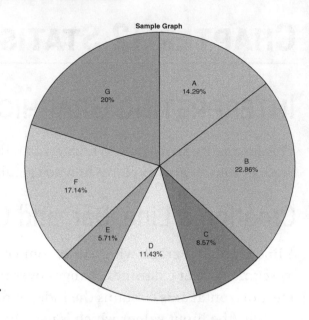

Sample Graph

Examples

1. The table shows the amount of rainfall in inches. Select the line graph that represents this data.

Day	1	2	3	4	5	6	7	8	9	10	11	12
Rainfall Amount	0.5	0.2	0.4	1.1	1.6	0.9	0.7	1.3	1.5	0.8	0.5	0.1

A.

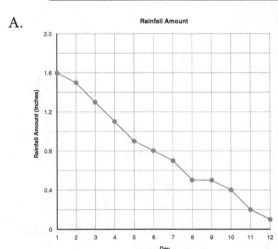

C.

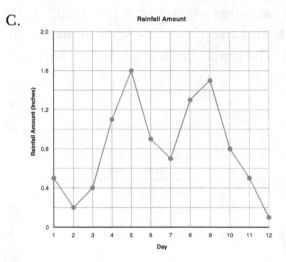

B.

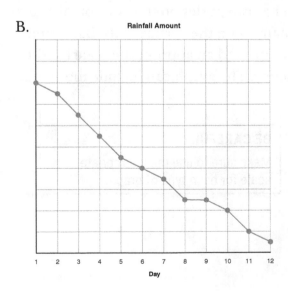

D.

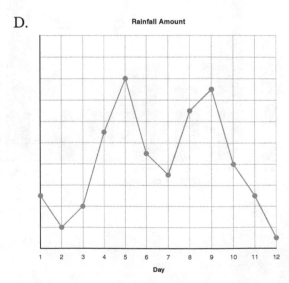

The correct answer is **C**. The graph is displayed correctly for the days with the appropriate labels.

2. **Students were surveyed about their favorite pet, and the table shows the results. Select the bar graph that represents this data.**

Pet	Quantity
Dog	14
Cat	16
Fish	4
Bird	8
Gerbil	7
Pig	3

A.
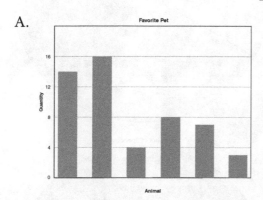

C.
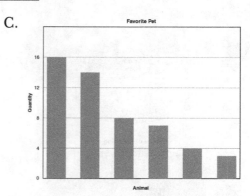

B.
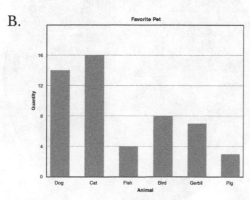

D.
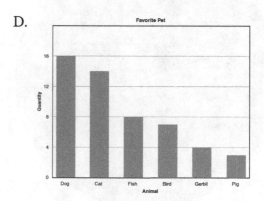

The correct answer is **B**. The bar graph represents each pet correctly and is labeled correctly.

3. The table shows the amount a family spends each month. Select the circle graph that represents the data.

Item	Food/Household Items	Bills	Mortgage	Savings	Miscellaneous
Amount	$700	$600	$400	$200	$100

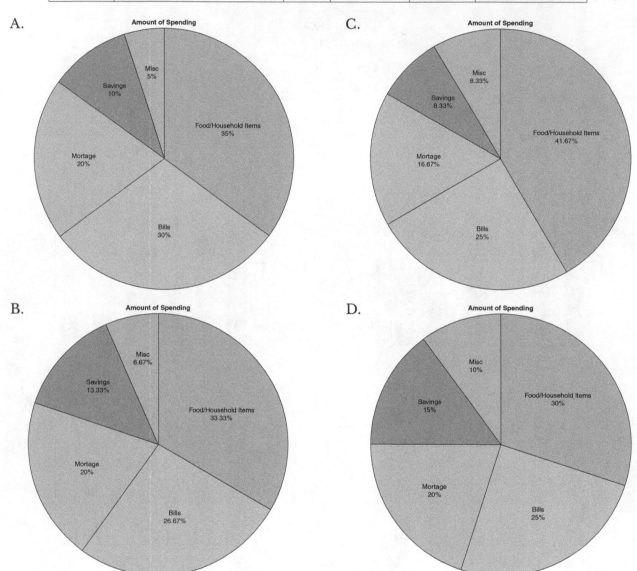

A.

C.

B.

D.

The correct answer is **A**. The total amount spent each month is $2,000. The section of the circle for food and household items is $\frac{700}{2,000} = 0.35 = 35\%$. The section of the circle for bills is $\frac{600}{2,000} = 0.30 = 30\%$. The section of the circle for mortgage is $\frac{400}{2,000} = 0.20 = 20\%$. The section of the circle for savings is $\frac{200}{2,000} = 0.10 = 10\%$. The section of the circle for miscellaneous is $\frac{100}{2,000} = 0.05 = 5\%$.

Interpreting and Evaluating Line, Bar, and Circle Graphs

Graph and charts are used to create visual examples of information, and it is important to be able to interpret them. The examples from Section 1 can show a variety of conclusions.

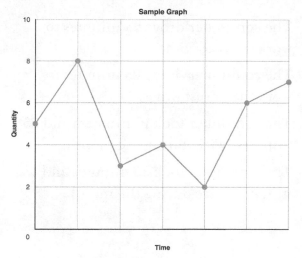

- The minimum value is 2, and the maximum value is 8.
- The largest decrease is between the second and third points.
- The largest increase is between the fifth and sixth points.

KEEP IN MIND

Read and determine the parts of the graph before answering questions related to the graph.

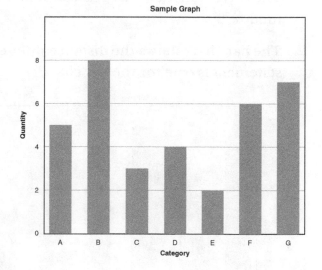

- Category B is the highest with 8.
- Category E is the lowest with 2.
- There are no categories that are the same.

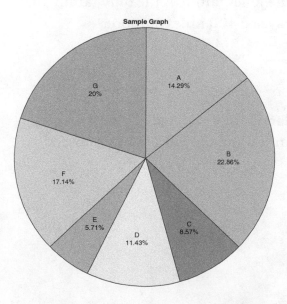

- Category B is the largest with 22.86%.
- Category E is the smallest with 5.71%.
- All of the categories are less than one-fourth of the graph.

235

Examples

1. The line chart shows the number of minutes a commuter drove to work during a month. Which statement is true for the line chart?

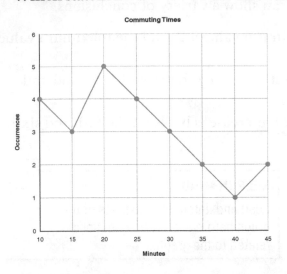

A. The commuter drove 25 minutes to work the most times

B. The commuter drove 25 minutes to work the fewest times.

C. The commuter took 10 minutes and 25 minutes twice during the month.

D. The commuter took 35 minutes and 45 minutes twice during the month.

The correct answer is **D.** The commuter took 35 minutes and 45 minutes twice during the month.

2. The bar chart shows the distance different families traveled for summer vacation. Which statement is true for the bar chart?

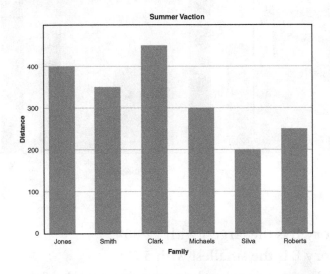

A. All families drove more than 200 miles.

B. The Clark family traveled 250 miles more than the Silva family.

C. The Roberts family traveled more miles than the Michaels family.

D. The Jones family is the only family that traveled 400 miles or more.

The correct answer is **B.** The correct solution is the Clark family traveled 250 miles more than the Silva family. The Clark family traveled 450 miles, and the Silva family traveled 200 miles, making the difference 250 miles.

3. Students were interviewed about their favorite subject in school. The circle graph shows the results. Which statement is true for the circle graph?

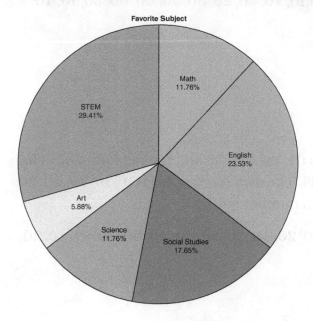

Favorite Subject

A. Math is the smallest percent for favorite subject.

B. The same number of students favor science and social studies.

C. English and STEM together are more than half of the respondents.

D. English and social students together are more than half of the respondents.

The correct answer is **C**. The correct solution is English and STEM together are more than half of the respondents because these values are more than 50% combined.

Mean, Median, Mode, and Range

The mean, median, mode, and range are common values related to data sets. These values can be calculated using the data set 2, 4, 7, 6, 8, 5, 6, and 3.

The mean is the sum of all numbers in a data set divided by the number of elements in the set. The sum of items in the data set is 41. Divide the value of 41 by the 8 items in the set. The mean is 5.125.

The median is the middle number of a data set when written in order. If there are an odd number of items, the median is the middle number. If there are an even number of items, the median is the mean of the middle two numbers. The

KEEP IN MIND

The mean, median, mode, and range can have the same values, depending on the data set.

numbers in order are 2, 3, 4, 5, 6, 6, 7, 8. The middle two numbers are 5 and 6. The mean of the two middle numbers is 5.5, which is the median.

The mode is the number or numbers that occur most often. There can be no modes, one mode, or many modes. In the data set, the number 6 appears twice, making 6 the mode.

The range is the difference between the highest and lowest values in a data set. The highest value is 8 and the lowest value is 2, for a range of 6.

Examples

1. **Find the mean and the median for the data set 10, 20, 40, 20, 30, 50, 40, 60, 30, 10, 40, 20, 50, 70, and 80.**

    A. The mean is 40, and the median is 38.

    B. The mean is 38, and the median is 40.

    C. The mean is 36, and the median is 50.

    D. The mean is 50, and the median is 36.

    The correct answer is **B**. The correct solution is the mean is 38 and the median is 40. The sum of all items is 570 divided by 15, which is 38. The data set in order is 10, 10, 20, 20, 20, 30, 30, 40, 40, 40, 50, 50, 60, 70, 80. The median number is 40.

2. **Find the mode and the range for the data set 10, 20, 40, 20, 30, 50, 40, 60, 30, 10, 40, 20, 50, 70, and 80.**

    A. The mode is 20, and the range is 70.

    B. The mode is 40, and the range is 70.

    C. The modes are 20 and 40, and the range is 70.

    D. The modes are 20, 40, and 70, and the range is 70.

    The correct answer is **C**. The correct solution is the modes are 20 and 40 and the range is 70. The modes are 20 and 40 because each of these numbers appears three times. The range is the difference between 80 and 10, which is 70.

Let's Review!

- A bar graph, line graph, and circle graph are different ways to summarize and represent data.
- The mean, median, mode, and range are values that can be used to interpret the meaning of a set of numbers.

STATISTICAL MEASURES

This lesson explores the different sampling techniques using random and non-random sampling. The lesson also distinguishes among different study techniques. In addition, it provides simulations that compare results with expected outcomes.

Probability and Non-Probability Sampling

A population includes all items within a set of data, while a sample consists of one or more observations from a population.

The collection of data samples from a population is an important part of research and helps researcher draw conclusions related to populations. Probability sampling creates a sample from a population by using random sampling techniques. Every person within a population has an equal chance of being selected for a sample. Non-probability sampling creates a sample from a population without using random sampling techniques.

KEEP IN MIND

Probability sampling is random, and non-probability sampling is not random.

There are four types of probability sampling. Simple random sampling is assigning a number to each member of a population and randomly selecting numbers. Stratified sampling uses simple random sampling after the population is split into equal groups. Systematic sampling chooses every n^{th} member from a list or a group. Cluster random sampling uses natural groups in a population: the population is divided into groups, and random samples are collected from groups.

Each type of probability sampling has an advantage and a disadvantage when finding an appropriate sample.

Probability Sampling	Advantage	Disadvantage
Simple random sampling	Most cases have a sample representative of a population	Not efficient for large samples
Stratified random sampling	Creates layers of random samples from different groups representative of a population	Not efficient for large samples
Systematic sampling	Creates a sample representative of population without a random number selection	Not as random as simple random sampling
Cluster random sampling	Relatively easy and convenient to implement	Might not work if clusters are different from one another

There are four types of non-probability sampling. Convenience sampling produces samples that are easy to access. Volunteer sampling asks for volunteers or recommendations for a sample. Purposive sampling bases samples on specific characteristics by selecting samples from a group that meets the qualifications of the study. Quota sampling is choosing samples of groups of the subpopulation.

Examples

1. **A factory is studying the quality of beverage samples. There are 50 bottles randomly chosen from one shipment every 60 minutes. What type of sampling is used?**

    A. Systematic sampling

    B. Simple random sampling

    C. Cluster random sampling

    D. Stratified random sampling

    The correct answer is **C**. The correct solution is cluster random sampling because bottles of beverage are selected within specific boundaries.

2. **A group conducting a survey asks a person for his or her opinion. Then, the group asks the person being surveyed for the names of 10 friends to obtain additional options. What type of sampling is used?**

    A. Quota sampling

    B. Volunteer sampling

    C. Purposive sampling

    D. Convenience sampling

    The correct answer is **B**. The correct solution is volunteer sampling because the group is looking for recommendations.

Census, Surveys, Experiments, Observational Studies

Various sampling techniques are used to collect data from a population. These are in the form of a census, a survey, observational studies, or experiments.

A census collects data by asking everyone in a population the same question. Asking everyone at school or everyone at work are examples of a

> **KEEP IN MIND**
>
> A census includes everyone within a population, and a survey includes every subject of a sample. An observational study involves watching groups randomly, and an experiment involves assigning groups.

census. A survey collects data on every subject within a sample. The subjects can be determined by convenience sampling or by simple random sampling. Examples of surveys are asking sophomores at school or first shift workers at work.

In an observational study, data collection occurs by watching or observing an event. Watching children who play outside and observing if they drink water or sports drinks is an example. An experiment is way of finding information by assigning people to groups and collecting data on observations. Assigning one group of children to drink water and another group to drink sports drinks after playing and making comparisons is an example of an experiment.

Examples

1. **A school wants to create a census to identify students' favorite subject in school. Which group should the school ask?**

    A. All staff

    B. All students

    C. All sophomores

    D. All male students

    The correct answer is **B**. The correct solution is all students because this gathers information on the entire population.

2. **A researcher records the arrival time of employees at a job based on their actual start time. What type of study is this?**

    A. Census

    B. Survey

    C. Experiment

    D. Observational study

    The correct answer is **D**. The correct solution is observational study because the researcher is observing the time the employees arrive at work.

3. **The local county wants to test the water quality of a stream by collecting samples. What should the county collect?**

    A. The water quality at one spot

    B. The water quality under trees

    C. The water quality under bridges

    D. The water quality at different spots

    The correct answer is **D**. The correct solution is the water quality at different spots because this survey allows for the collection of different samples.

Simulations

A simulation enables researchers to study real-world events by modeling events. Advantages of simulations are that they are quick, easy, and inexpensive; the disadvantage is that the results are approximations. The steps to complete a simulation are as follows:

KEEP IN MIND

A simulation is only useful if the results closely mirror real-world outcomes.

- Describe the outcomes.
- Assign a random value to the outcomes.
- Choose a source to generate the outcomes.
- Generate values for the outcomes until a consistent pattern emerges.
- Analyze the results.

Examples

1. A family has two children and wants to simulate the gender of the children. Which object would be beneficial to use for the simulation?

   A. Coin

   C. Six-sided number cube

   B. Four-section spinner

   D. Random number generator

   The correct answer is **B**. The correct solution is a four-section spinner because there are four possible outcomes of the event (boy/boy, boy/girl, girl/boy, and girl/girl).

2. There are six options from which to choose a meal at a festival. A model using a six-sided number cube is used to represent the simulation.

Hamburger	Chicken	Hot Dog	Bratwurst	Pork Chop	Fish	Total
1	2	3	4	5	6	
83	82	85	89	86	75	500

   Choose the statement that correctly answers whether the simulation of using a six-sided number cube is consistent with the actual number of dinners sold and then explains why or why not.

   A. The simulation is consistent because it has six equally likely outcomes.

   B. The simulation is consistent because it has two equally likely outcomes.

   C. The simulation is not consistent because of the limited number of outcomes.

   D. The simulation is not consistent because of the unlimited number of outcomes.

   The correct answer is **A**. The correct solution is the simulation is consistent because it has six equally likely outcomes. The six-sided number cube provides consistent outcomes because there is an equal opportunity to select any dinner.

Let's Review!

- Probability (random) sampling and non-probability (not random) sampling are ways to collect data.
- Censuses, surveys, experiments, and observational studies are ways to collect data from a population.
- A simulation is way to model random events and compare the results to real-world outcomes.

STATISTICS & PROBABILITY: THE RULES OF PROBABILITY

This lesson explores a sample space and its outcomes and provides an introduction to probability, including how to calculate expected values and analyze decisions based on probability.

Sample Space

A **sample space** is the set of all possible outcomes. Using a deck of cards labeled 1–10, the sample space is 1, 2, 3, 4, 5, 6, 7, 8, 9, and 10. An **event** is a subset of the sample space. For example, if a card is drawn and the outcome of the event is an even number, possible results are 2, 4, 6, 8, 10.

The **union** of two events is everything in both events, and the notation is $A \cup B$. The union of events is associated with the word *or*. For example, a card is drawn that is either a multiple of 3 or a multiple of 4. The set containing the multiples of 3 is 3, 6, and 9. The set containing the multiples of 4 is 4 and 8. The union of the set is 3, 4, 6, 8, and 9.

The **intersection** of two events is all of the events in both sets, and the notation is $A \cap B$. The intersection of events is associated with the word *and*. For example, a card is drawn that is even and a multiple of 4. The set containing even numbers is 2, 4, 6, 8, and 10. The set containing the multiples of 4 is 4 and 8. The intersection is 4 and 8 because these numbers are in both sets.

The **complement** of an event is an outcome that is not part of the set. The complement of an event is associated with the word *not*. A card is drawn and is not a multiple of 5. The set not containing multiples of 5 is 1, 2, 3, 4, 6, 7, 8, and 9. The complement of not a multiple of 5 is 1, 2, 3, 4, 6, 7, 8, and 9.

Examples

Use the following table of the results when rolling two six-sided number cubes.

1, 1	1, 2	1, 3	1, 4	1, 5	1, 6
2, 1	2, 2	2, 3	2, 4	2, 5	2, 6
3, 1	3, 2	3, 3	3, 4	3, 5	3, 6
4, 1	4, 2	4, 3	4, 4	4, 5	4, 6
5, 1	5, 2	5, 3	5, 4	5, 5	5, 6
6, 1	6, 2	6, 3	6, 4	6, 5	6, 6

1. **How many possible outcomes are there for the union of rolling a sum of 3 or a sum of 5?**

    A. 2   B. 4   C. 6   D. 8

    The correct answer is **C**. The correct solution is 6 possible outcomes. There are two options for the first event (2, 1) and (1, 2). There are 4 options for the second event (4, 1), (3, 2), (2, 3), and (1, 4). The union of two events is six possible outcomes.

2. **How many possible outcomes are there for the intersection of rolling a double and a multiple of 3?**

    A. 0   B. 2   C. 4   D. 6

    The correct answer is **B**. The correct solution is 2 possible outcomes. There are six options for the first event (1, 1), (2, 2), (3, 3), (4, 4), (5, 5), and (6, 6). There are 12 options for the second event of the multiple of three. The intersection is (3, 3) and (6, 6) because these numbers meet both requirements.

3. **How many possible outcomes are there for the complement of rolling a 3 and a 5?**

    A. 16   B. 18   C. 27   D. 36

    The correct answer is **A**. The correct solution is 16 possible outcomes. There are 16 options of not rolling a 3 or a 5.

Probability

The **probability** of an event is the number of favorable outcomes divided by the total number of possible outcomes.

BE CAREFUL!

Make sure that you apply the correct formula for the probability of an event.

$$Probability = \frac{number\ of\ favorable\ outcomes}{number\ of\ possible\ outcomes}$$

Probability is a value between 0 (event does not happen) and 1 (event will happen). For example, the probability of getting heads when a coin is flipped is $\frac{1}{2}$ because heads is 1 option out of 2 possibilities. The probability of rolling an odd number on a six-sided number cube is $\frac{3}{6} = \frac{1}{2}$ because there are three odd numbers, 1, 3, and 5, out of 6 possible numbers.

The probability of an "or" event happening is the sum of the events happening. For example, the probability of rolling an odd number or a 4 on a six-sided number cube is $\frac{4}{6}$. The probability of rolling an odd number is $\frac{3}{6}$, and the probability of rolling a 4 is $\frac{1}{6}$. Therefore, the probability is $\frac{3}{6} + \frac{1}{6} = \frac{4}{6} = \frac{2}{3}$.

The probability of an "and" event happening is the product of the probability of two or more events. The probability of rolling 6 three times in a row is $\frac{1}{216}$. The probability of a single event is $\frac{1}{6}$, and this fraction is multiplied three times to find the probability, $\frac{1}{6} \times \frac{1}{6} \times \frac{1}{6}$. There are cases of "with replacement" when the item is returned to the pile and "without replacement" when the item is not returned to the pile.

The probability of a "not" event happening is 1 minus the probability of the event occurring. For example, the probability of not rolling 6 three times in a row is $1 - \frac{1}{216} = \frac{215}{216}$.

Examples

1. A deck of cards contains 40 cards divided into 4 colors: red, blue, green, and yellow. Each group has cards numbered 0–9. What is the probability of selecting an 8?

   A. $\frac{1}{10}$ B. $\frac{1}{8}$ C. $\frac{1}{4}$ D. $\frac{1}{2}$

   The correct answer is **A**. The correct solution is $\frac{1}{10}$. There are 4 cards out of 40 that contain the number 8, making the probability $\frac{4}{40} = \frac{1}{10}$.

2. A deck of cards contains 40 cards divided into 4 colors: red, blue, green, and yellow. Each group has cards numbered 0–9. What is the probability of selecting an even or a red card?

   A. $\frac{1}{4}$ B. $\frac{3}{8}$ C. $\frac{5}{8}$ D. $\frac{3}{4}$

   The correct answer is **C**. The correct solution is $\frac{5}{8}$. There are 20 even cards and 10 red cards. The overlap of 5 red even cards is subtracted from the probability, $\frac{20}{40} + \frac{10}{40} - \frac{5}{40} = \frac{25}{40} = \frac{5}{8}$.

3. A deck of cards contains 40 cards divided into 4 colors: red, blue, green, and yellow. Each group has cards numbered 0–9. What is the probability of selecting a blue card first, replacing the card, and selecting a 9?

   A. $\frac{1}{100}$ B. $\frac{1}{80}$ C. $\frac{1}{40}$ D. $\frac{1}{20}$

   The correct answer is **C**. The correct solution is $\frac{1}{40}$. There are 10 blue cards and 4 cards that contain the number 9. The probability of the event is $\frac{10}{40} \times \frac{4}{40} = \frac{40}{1600} = \frac{1}{40}$.

4. A deck of cards contains 40 cards divided into 4 colors: red, blue, green, and yellow. Each group has cards numbered 0–9. What is the probability of NOT selecting a green card?

   A. $\frac{1}{4}$ B. $\frac{3}{8}$ C. $\frac{1}{2}$ D. $\frac{3}{4}$

   The correct answer is **D**. The correct solution is $\frac{3}{4}$. There are 10 cards that are green, making the probability of NOT selecting a green card $1 - \frac{10}{40} = \frac{30}{40} = \frac{3}{4}$.

Calculating Expected Values and Analyzing Decisions Based on Probability

The **expected value** of an event is the sum of the products of the probability of an event times the payoff of an event. A good example is calculating the expected value for buying a lottery ticket. There is a one in a hundred million chance that a person would win $50 million. Each ticket costs $2. The expected value is

$$\frac{1}{100,000,000}(50,000,000-2) + \frac{99,999,999}{100,000,000}(-2) = \frac{49,999,998}{100,000,000} - \frac{199,999,998}{100,000,000} = -\frac{150,000,000}{100,000,000} = -\$1.50$$

On average, one should expect to lose $1.50 each time the game is played. Analyzing the information, the meaning of the data shows that playing the lottery would result in losing money every time.

BE CAREFUL!

The expected value will not be the same as the actual value unless the probability of winning is 100%.

Examples

1. What is the expected value of an investment if the probability is $\frac{1}{5}$ of losing \$1,000, $\frac{1}{4}$ of no gain, $\frac{2}{5}$ of making \$1,000, and $\frac{3}{20}$ of making \$2,000?

    A. \$0 B. \$200 C. \$500 D. \$700

    The correct answer is **C**. The correct solution is \$500. The expected value is $\frac{1}{5}(-1,000) + \frac{1}{4}(0) + \frac{2}{5}(1,000) + \frac{3}{20}(2,000) = -200 + 0 + 400 + 300 = \$500$.

2. The table below shows the value of the prizes and the probability of winning a prize in a contest.

Prize	\$10	\$100	\$5,000	\$50,000
Probability	1 in 50	1 in 1,000	1 in 50,000	1 in 250,000

    Calculate the expected value.

    A. \$0.10 B. \$0.20 C. \$0.50 D. \$0.60

    The correct answer is **D**. The correct solution is \$0.60. The probability for each event is

Prize	\$10	\$100	\$5,000	\$50,000	Not Winning
Probability	1 in 50 = 0.02	1 in 1,000 = 0.001	1 in 50,000 = 0.00002	1 in 250,000 = 0.000004	0.978976

    The expected value is $0.02(10) + 0.001(100) + 0.00002(5,000) + 0.000004(50,000) + 0.978976(0) =$

    $0.2 + 0.1 + 0.1 + 0.2 + 0 = \$0.60$.

3. Which option results in the largest loss on a product?

    A. 40% of gaining \$100,000 and 60% of losing \$100,000

    B. 60% of gaining \$250,000 and 40% of losing \$500,000

    C. 30% of gaining \$400,000 and 70% of losing \$250,000

    D. 60% of gaining \$250,000 and 40% of losing \$450,000

    The correct answer is **C**. The correct solution is 30% of gaining \$400,000 and 70% of losing \$250,000. The expected value is $0.30(400,000) + 0.7(-250,000) = 120,000 + (-175,000) = -55,000$.

Let's Review!

- The sample space is the number of outcomes of an event. The union, the intersection, and the complement are related to the sample space.
- The probability of an event is the number of possible events divided by the total number of outcomes. There can be "and," "or," and "not" probabilities.
- The expected value of an event is based on the payout and probability of an event occurring.

INTERPRETING CATEGORICAL AND QUANTITATIVE DATA

This lesson discusses how to represent and interpret data for a dot plot, a histogram, and a box plot. It compares multiple sets of data by using the measures of center and spread and examines the impact of outliers.

Representing Data on a Number Line

There are two types of data: quantitative and categorical. Quantitative variables are numerical, such as number of people in a household, bank account balance, and number of cars sold. Categorical variables are not numerical, and there is no inherent way to order them. Example are classes in college, types of pets, and party affiliations. The information for these data sets can be arranged on a number line using dot plots, histograms, and box plots.

A dot plot is a display of data using dots. The dots represent the number of times an item appears. Below is a sample of a dot plot.

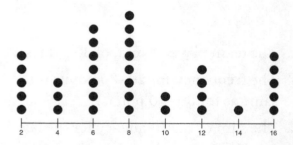

The mean and median can be determined by looking at a dot plot. The mean is the sum of all items divided by the number of dots. The median is the middle dot or the average of the middle two dots.

A histogram is a graphical display that has bars of various heights. It is similar to a bar chart, but the numbers are grouped into ranges. The bins, or ranges of values, of a histogram have equal lengths, such as 10 or 50 units. Continuous data such as weight, height, and amount of time are examples of data shown in a histogram. In the histogram to the right, the bin length is 8 units.

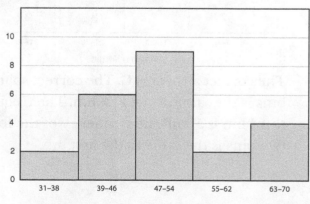

It is not possible to calculate the mean and median by looking at a histogram because there is a bin size rather than a single value on the horizontal axis. Histograms are beneficial when working with a large set of data.

BE CAREFUL!
Make sure to carefully interpret the data for any graphical display.

A box plot (or box-and-whisker plot) is a graphical display of the minimum, first quartile, median, third quartile, and maximum of a set of data. Recall the minimum is the smallest value and the maximum is the largest value in a set of data. The median is the middle number when the data set is written in order. The first quartile is the middle number between the minimum and the median. The third quartile is the middle number between the median and the maximum.

In the data display below, the minimum is 45, the first quartile is 50, the median is 57, the third quartile is 63, and the maximum is 75. With most box-and-whisker plots, the data is not symmetrical.

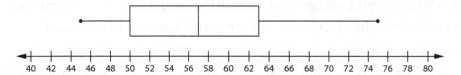

Example

The histogram below shows a basketball team's winning margin during the season. Which statement is true for the histogram?

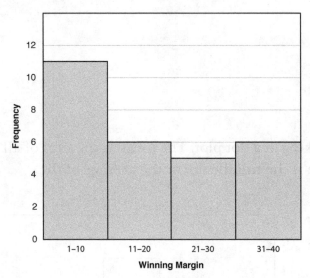

A. The team played a total of 30 games.

B. The frequency for 20–30 points is the same as for 30–40 points.

C. The sum of the frequency for the last two bins is the same as the first bin.

D. The frequency for 0–10 is twice the frequency for any other winning margin.

The correct answer is **C**. The correct solution is the sum of the frequency for the last two bins is the same as the first bin. The frequency of the first bin is 11, the frequency of the third bin is 5, and the frequency of the fourth bin is 6. The sum of the frequency of the last two bins is the same as the first bin.

Comparing Center and Spread of Multiple Data Sets

The measures of center are the mean (average) and median (middle number when written in order). These values describe the expected value of a data set. Very large or very small numbers affect the mean, but they do not affect the median.

The measures of spread are standard deviation (how far the numbers of a data set are from the mean) and interquartile range (the difference between the third and first quartile values).

To find the standard deviation:

- Find the mean.
- Find the difference between the mean and each member of the date set and square that result.
- Find the mean of the squared differences from the previous step.
- Apply the square root.

The larger the value for the standard deviation, the greater the spread of values from the mean. The larger the value for the interquartile range, the greater the spread of the middle 50% of values from the median.

Symmetric data has values that are close together, and the mean, median, and mode occur near the same value. The mean and standard deviation are used to explain multiple data sets and are evident in dot plots.

For example, consider this data set.

10, 10, 11, 11, 11, 12, 12, 12, 12, 12, 13, 13, 13, 14, 14

The mean is found by finding the sum of the numbers in the data set and dividing it by the number of items in the set, as follows:

$10 + 10 + 11 + 11 + 11 + 12 + 12 + 12 + 12 + 12 + 13 + 13 + 13 + 14 + 14 = 180 \div 15 = 12$.

The standard deviation calculation is shown in the table below.

Data	Data – Mean	(Data – Mean)^2
10	–2	4
10	–2	4
11	–1	1
11	–1	1
11	–1	1
12	0	0
12	0	0
12	0	0
12	0	0

Data	Data – Mean	(Data – Mean)²
12	0	0
13	1	1
13	1	1
13	1	1
14	2	4
14	2	4

The sum of the last column is 22. The standard deviation is $\sqrt{\frac{22}{15}} \approx 1.211$.

Next, consider this data set.

8, 8, 9, 10, 11, 12, 12, 12, 12, 12, 13, 14, 15, 16, 16

The mean is $8 + 8 + 9 + 10 + 11 + 12 + 12 + 12 + 12 + 12 + 13 + 14 + 15 + 16 + 16 = 180 \div 15 = 12$.

The standard deviation calculation is shown in the table below.

Data	Data – Mean	(Data – Mean)²
8	−4	16
8	−4	16
9	−3	9
10	−2	4
11	−1	1
12	0	0
12	0	0
12	0	0
12	0	0
12	0	0
13	1	1
14	2	4
15	3	9
16	4	16
16	4	16

The sum of the last column is 92. The standard deviation is $\sqrt{\frac{92}{15}} \approx 2.476$.

Therefore, the second set of data has values that are farther from the mean than the first data set.

When data is skewed, a group of its values are close and the remaining values are evenly spread. The median and interquartile range are used to explain multiple data sets and are evident in dot plots and box plots.

KEEP IN MIND

Compare the same measure of center or variation to draw accurate conclusions when comparing data sets.

The data set 10, 10, 11, 11, 11, 11, 11, 11, 12, 12, 12, 13, 13, 14, 15 has a median of 11 and an interquartile range of 2. The data set 10, 11, 12, 12, 13, 13, 14, 14, 14, 14, 14, 14, 14, 15, 15 has a median of 14 and an interquartile range of 2. The median is greater in the second data set, but the spread of data is the same for both sets of data.

Example

The box plots below show the heights of students in inches for two classes. Choose the statement that is true for the median and the interquartile range.

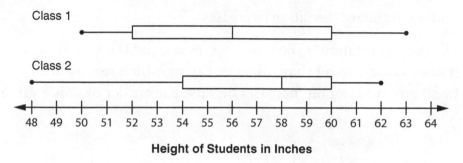

Height of Students in Inches

A. The median and interquartile range are greater for class 1.

B. The median and interquartile range are greater for class 2.

C. The median is greater for class 1, and the interquartile range is greater for class 2.

D. The median is greater for class 2, and the interquartile range is greater for class 1.

The correct answer is **D**. The correct solution is the median is greater for class 2, and the interquartile range is greater for class 1. The median is 58 inches for class 2 and 56 inches for class 1. The interquartile range is 8 inches for class 1 and 6 inches for class 2.

Determining the Effect of Extreme Data Points

An outlier is a value that is much smaller or much larger than rest of the values in a data set. This value has an impact on the mean and standard deviation values and occasionally has an impact on the median and interquartile range values.

The data set of 10, 10, 11, 11, 11, 12, 12, 12, 12, 12, 13, 13, 13, 14, 14 has a mean of 12 and a standard deviation of 1.211. If an outlier of 50 is added, the data set has a mean of has a mean of 14.38 and a standard deviation of 9.273. The outlier has

BE CAREFUL!
There may be a high outlier and a low outlier that may not have an impact on data.

increased the mean by more than 2, and the spread of the data has increased significantly.

The data set 10, 10, 11, 11, 11, 11, 11, 11, 12, 12, 12, 13, 13, 14, 15 has a median of 11 and an interquartile range of 2. If an outlier of 50 is added, the median slightly increases to 11.5 and the interquartile range remains 2.

Example

A little league basketball team scores 35, 38, 40, 36, 41, 42, 39, 35, 29, 32, 37, 33 in its first 12 games. In its next game, the team scores 12 points. Which statement describes the mean and standard deviation?

   A. The mean increases, and the standard deviation increases.

   B. The mean decreases, and the standard deviation increases.

   C. The mean increases, and the standard deviation decreases.

   D. The mean decreases, and the standard deviation decreases.

The correct answer is **B**. The correct solution is the mean decreases, and the standard deviation increases. The outlier value is lower than all other values, which results in a decrease for the mean. The standard deviation increases because the outlier of 12 is a value far away from the mean.

Let's Review!

- Dot plots, histograms, and box plots summarize and represent data on a number line.
- The mean and standard deviation are used to compare symmetric data sets.
- The median and interquartile range are used to compare skewed data sets.
- Outliers can impact measures of center and spread, particularly mean and standard deviation.

CHAPTER 12 STATISTICS AND PROBABILITY PRACTICE QUIZ 1

1. Two companies have made a chart of paid time off. Which statement describes the mean and standard deviation?

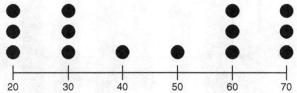

Paid Time off for Employees at Company A

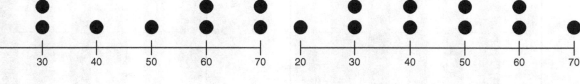

Paid Time off for Employees at Company B

A. The means are the same, but the standard deviation is smaller for Company B.

B. The means are the same, but the standard deviation is smaller for Company A.

C. The mean is greater for Company A, and the standard deviation is smaller for Company A.

D. The mean is greater for Company B, and the standard deviation is smaller for Company B.

2. A basketball player scores 18, 17, 20, 23, 15, 24, 22, 28, 5. What is the effect of removing the outlier on the mean and standard deviation?

A. The mean and the standard deviation increase.

B. The mean and the standard deviation decrease.

C. The standard deviation increases, but the mean decreases.

D. The standard deviation decreases, but the mean increases.

3. Find the median from the dot plot.

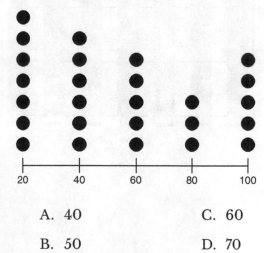

A. 40   C. 60

B. 50   D. 70

4. The table shows the number of students in grades kindergarten through sixth grade. Select the correct bar graph for this data.

Grade	Kindergarten	1st	2nd	3rd	4th	5th	6th
Number of Students	135	150	140	155	145	165	170

A.

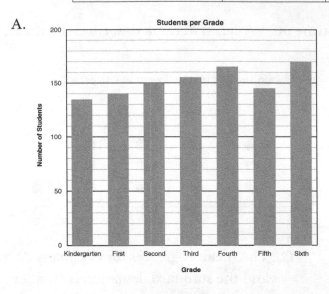

C.

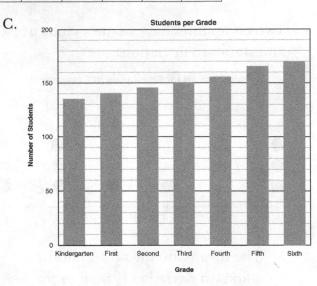

B.

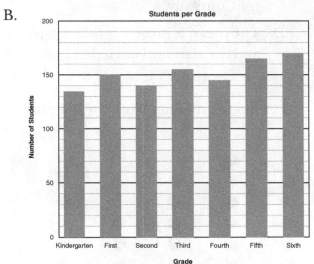

D.

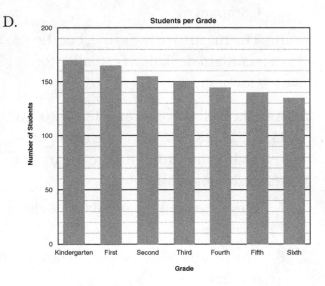

5. The bar chart shows the number of items collected for a charity drive. Which statement is true for the bar chart?

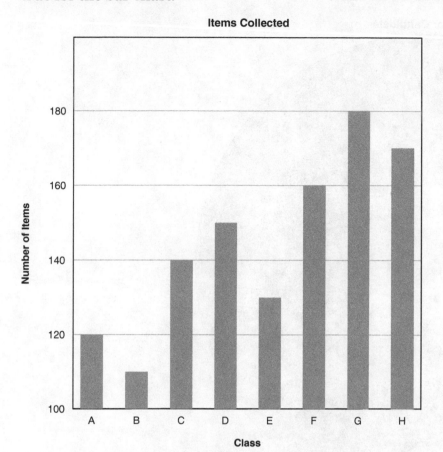

A. Classes F, G, and H each collected more than 150 items.

B. Classes D, F, and G each collected more than 150 items.

C. Classes C, D, and E each collected more than 140 items.

D. Classes A, B, and C each collected more than 140 items.

6. The circle graph shows the number of votes for each candidate. How many votes were cast for candidate D if there were 25,000 voters?

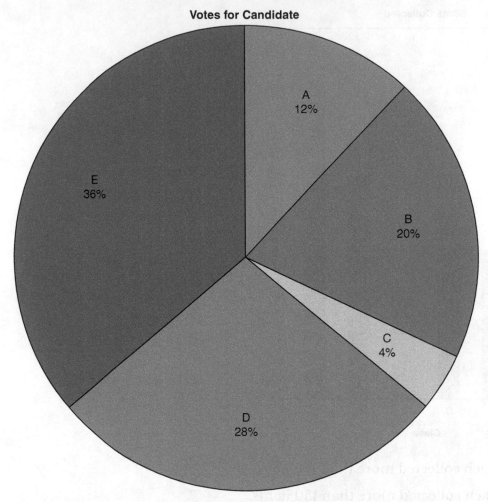

Votes for Candidate

A. 3,000 votes
B. 5,000 votes
C. 7,000 votes
D. 9,000 votes

7. A factory is investigating defects in screwdrivers that have been placed in containers to be shipped to stores. Random containers are selected for the team leader to review. What type of sampling is used?

A. Systematic sampling
B. Simple random sampling
C. Cluster random sampling
D. Stratified random sampling

8. A study looked at a random sample of people and watched their use of social media on mobile devices. The researcher looked at which group of users were happier. What type of study is this?

A. Census
B. Survey
C. Experiment
D. Observational study

9. There are four available pen colors to choose. A simulation is used to represent the number of times each pen is used.

Red	Blue	Black	Green	Total
1,248	1,260	1,247	1,245	5,000

Choose the statement that correctly explains why or why not seeing these results questions the probability of one out of four for each color.

A. Yes, because of the limited number of outcomes

B. Yes, because not enough simulations were completed

C. No, because the probability of each color is not exactly one out of four

D. No, because the probability of each color is very close to one out of four

10. A bag contains 10 red marbles, 8 black marbles, and 7 white marbles. What is the probability of selecting a black marble first and a red marble second with no replacement?

A. $\frac{8}{25}$

B. $\frac{16}{125}$

C. $\frac{2}{15}$

D. $\frac{7}{75}$

11. Which option results in the greatest gain on an investment?

A. 100% of gaining $1,000

B. 60% of gaining $2,500 and 40% of gaining $0

C. 75% of gaining $1,000 and 25% of gaining $1,500

D. 70% of gaining $1,500 and 30% of gaining $1,000

12. There are 60 students attending classes in town. There are 40 students in dance class and 30 students in art class. Find the number of students in either dance or art class.

A. 30

B. 40

C. 50

D. 60

CHAPTER 12 STATISTICS AND PROBABILITY PRACTICE QUIZ 1 – ANSWER KEY

1. **A.** The correct solution is the means are the same, but the standard deviation is smaller for Company B. The standard deviation is smaller for Company B because more values are closer to the mean. **See Lesson: Interpreting Categorical and Quantitative Data.**

2. **D.** The correct solution is the standard deviation decreases, but the mean increases. The standard deviation from 6.226 and 3.951 when the low outlier is removed. The mean increases from 19.11 to 20.88 because the outlier, 5, is the lowest value. **See Lesson: Interpreting Categorical and Quantitative Data.**

3. **B.** The correct solution is 50. The middle two values are 40 and 60, and the average of these values is 50. **See Lesson: Interpreting Categorical and Quantitative Data.**

4. **B.** The correct solution is B because the number of students for each grade is correct. **See Lesson: Interpreting Graphics.**

5. **A.** The correct solution is classes F, G, and H collected more than 150 items. Class F collected 160 items, class G collected 180 items, and class H collected 170 items. **See Lesson: Interpreting Graphics.**

6. **C.** The correct solution is 7,000 votes because 28% of 25,000 is 7,000 voters. **See Lesson: Interpreting Graphics.**

7. **D.** The correct solution is stratified random sampling because the screwdrivers are placed into containers and the containers are randomly selected. **See Lesson: Statistical Measures.**

8. **D.** The correct solution is observational study because people were not randomly assigned to group and their behaviors were observed. **See Lesson: Statistical Measures.**

9. **D.** The correct solution is no, because the probability of each color is very close to one out of four. The more simulations, the closer the results will be to the actual probability of one out of four for each color. **See Lesson: Statistical Measures.**

10. **C.** The correct solution is $\frac{2}{15}$. There are 8 marbles out of 25 for the first event and 10 marbles out of 24 for the second event. The probability of the event is $\frac{8}{25} \times \frac{10}{24} = \frac{80}{600} = \frac{2}{15}$. **See Lesson: Statistics & Probability: The Rules of Probability.**

11. **B.** The correct solution is 60% of gaining \$2,500 and 40% of gaining \$0. The expected value is $0.60(2,500) + 0.40(0) = \$1,500$. **See Lesson: Statistics & Probability: The Rules of Probability.**

12. **C.** The correct solution 50 because there are 70 students in both classes less the total students is 10 students. Then, subtract 10 students from the total, which is 50 students. **See Lesson: Statistics & Probability: The Rules of Probability.**

CHAPTER 12 STATISTICS AND PROBABILITY PRACTICE QUIZ 2

1. The bar chart shows the number of items collected for a charity drive. What is the total number of items collected for the three highest classes?

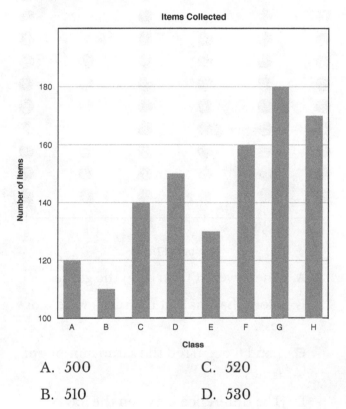

A. 500

B. 510

C. 520

D. 530

2. The bar chart shows the number of boys and girls who participate in sports. What year had the most participants?

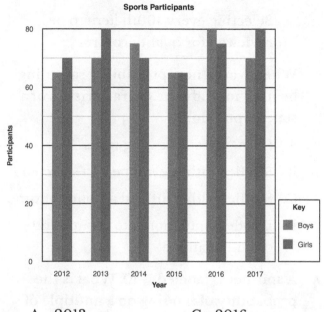

A. 2013

B. 2014

C. 2016

D. 2017

3. Find the range for the data set 34, 45, 27, 29, 36, 60, 52, 48, 41, 65, 44, 50, 64, 58, 47, and 31.

A. 3

B. 5

C. 36

D. 38

4. Identify the study that is a survey.

A. A researcher interviews all nurses at all hospitals.

B. A researcher interviews all nurses at all hospitals in the state.

C. A researcher interviews all nurses at 10 hospitals that are near her.

D. A researcher interviews all nurses at 10 hospitals in different regions.

5. Which of the following examples uses probability sampling?

   A. Surveying every resident of a town of 10,000 people

   B. Selecting 1,000 social media friends to answer a survey

   C. Surveying the first 1,000 fans who enter a basketball arena

   D. Selecting every 100th item to be reviewed for quality control

6. When would non-probability sampling be used to study the characteristics of a state population?

   A. Demonstrate existing traits

   B. Studies with the nth person selected

   C. Studies with a limited amount of time

   D. Divide population into groups and obtain a sample

7. A spinner is labeled 1–10. What is the probability of landing on a multiple of 3?

   A. $\frac{1}{10}$ C. $\frac{3}{10}$

   B. $\frac{1}{5}$ D. $\frac{2}{5}$

8. If a letter is chosen at random from the word SUBSTITUTE, what is the probability that the letter chosen is "S" or "T"?

   A. $\frac{1}{5}$ C. $\frac{2}{5}$

   B. $\frac{3}{10}$ D. $\frac{1}{2}$

9. There is a group of 100 people, 68 of whom like hot drinks and 72 of whom like cold drinks. How many people like cold and hot drinks?

   A. 4   D. 140

   B. 40

   C. 100

10. The dot plot shows the results of rolling a dice for a game. Which statement is true for the dot plot?

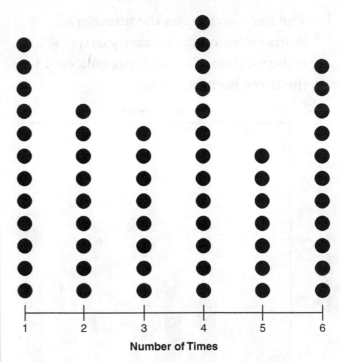

Results of Rolling a Dice

Number of Times

   A. There were 60 turns in the game.

   B. More than half of the turns were 3 or less.

   C. 1 and 6 occurred the same number of times.

   D. The difference between the lowest and highest frequency is 3.

11. The temperatures of two cities are shown for the first 10 days in February in degrees Fahrenheit.

City 1: 11, 12, 14, 15, 15, 16, 16, 17, 19, 20

City 2: 15, 15, 16, 17, 18, 18, 19, 20, 21, 21

Which statement describes the mean and standard deviation?

A. City 1 had the greater mean, but City 2 had a higher standard deviation.

B. City 2 had the greater mean, but City 1 had a higher standard deviation.

C. City 1 had the greater mean, and City 1 had a higher standard deviation.

D. City 2 had the greater mean, and City 2 had a higher standard deviation.

12. The histogram below shows the amount a family spent on groceries during the year. Which statement is true for the histogram?

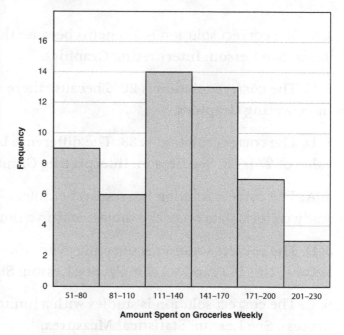

A. The lowest frequency is between $80 and $110.

B. The highest frequency is between $140 and $170.

C. More than half of the amount spent is greater than $140.

D. More than half of the amount spent is between $110 and $170.

CHAPTER 12 STATISTICS AND PROBABILITY PRACTICE QUIZ 2 — ANSWER KEY

1. B. The correct solution is 510 items because the three largest classes collected 180, 170, and 160 items. **See Lesson: Interpreting Graphics.**

2. C. The correct solution is 2016 because there were 155 total participants. **See Lesson: Interpreting Graphics.**

3. D. The correct solution is 38. The difference between the highest value of 65 and the lowest value of 27 is 38. **See Lesson: Interpreting Graphics.**

4. A. The correct solution is a researcher interviewing all nurses at all hospitals because this study collects data on every subject within a sample. **See Lesson: Statistical Measures.**

5. D. The correct solution is selecting every 100th item to be reviewed for quality control because this is a random sample. **See Lesson: Statistical Measures.**

6. C. The correct solution is studies with a limited amount of time because this is a non-random process. **See Lesson: Statistical Measures.**

7. C. The correct solution is $\frac{3}{10}$. There are three options, 3, 6, and 9, out of 10, making the probability $\frac{3}{10}$. **See Lesson: Statistics & Probability: The Rules of Probability.**

8. D. The correct solution is $\frac{1}{2}$. There are 2 S's and 3 T's in the word SUBSTITUTE out of 10 letters. The probability is $\frac{3}{10} + \frac{2}{10} = \frac{5}{10} = \frac{1}{2}$. **See Lesson: Statistics & Probability: The Rules of Probability.**

9. B. The correct solution is 40 because the sum of the drinks is 140 and less the people in the group is 40. **See Lesson: Statistics & Probability: The Rules of Probability.**

10. A. The correct solution is there were 60 turns in the game. The sum of the results is 12 + 9 + 8 + 13 + 7 + 11, which is 60 turns. **See Lesson: Interpreting Categorical and Quantitative Data.**

11. B. The correct solution is City 2 had the greater mean, but City 1 had a higher standard deviation. City 2 has the higher mean because the mean is 18 for City 2 and 15.5 for City 1. The standard deviation is greater for City 1 because the standard deviation is 2.655 for City 1 and 2.145 for City 2. **See Lesson: Interpreting Categorical and Quantitative Data.**

12. D. The correct solution is more than half of the amount spent is between $110 and $170. There are 14 weeks where the amount spent is between $110 and $140 and 13 weeks where the amount spent is between $140 and $170. This is 27 weeks, which is more than half the data set. **See Lesson: Interpreting Categorical and Quantitative Data.**

SECTION IV. ESSAY WRITING

Chapter 13 Essay Writing

The Writing Process

Effective writers break the writing task down into steps to tackle one at a time. They allow a certain amount of room for messiness and mistakes in the early stages of writing but attempt to create a polished finished product in the end.

KEEP IN MIND . . .

If your writing process varies from the steps outlined below, that's okay—as long as you can produce a polished, organized text in the end. Some writers like to write part or all of the first draft before they go back to outline and organize. Others make a plan in the prewriting phase, only to change the plan when they're drafting. It is not uncommon for writers to compose the body of an essay before the introduction, or to change the thesis statement at the end to make it fit the essay they wrote rather than the one they intended to write.

The point of teaching the writing process is not to force you to follow all the steps in order every time. The point is to give you a sense of the mental tasks involved in creating a well-written text. If you are drafting and something is not working, you will know you can bounce back to the prewriting stage and change your plan. If you are outlining and you end up fleshing out one of your points in complete sentences, you will realize you still need to go back to finish the rest of the plan before you continue drafting.

In other words, it is fine to change the order of steps from the writing process,* or to jump around between them. Published writers do it all the time, and you can too.

*But almost everyone really does benefit from saving the editing until the end.

The Writing Process

A writer goes through several discrete steps to transform an idea into a polished text. This series of steps is called the **writing process**. Individual writers' processes may vary somewhat, but most writers roughly follow the steps below.

Prewriting is making a plan for writing. Prewriting may include brainstorming, free writing, outlining, or mind mapping. The prewriting process can be messy and include errors. Note that if a writing task requires research, the prewriting process is longer because you need to find, read, and organize source materials.

Drafting is getting the bulk of the text down on the page in complete sentences. Although most writers find drafting difficult, two things can make it easier: 1) prewriting to make a clear plan, and 2) avoiding perfectionism. Drafting is about moving ideas from the mind to the page, even if they do not sound right or the writer is not sure how to spell a word. For writing tasks that involve research, drafting also involves making notes about where the information came from.

Revising is making improvements to the content and structure of a draft. Revising may involve moving ideas around, adding information to flesh out a point, removing chunks of text that are redundant or off-topic, and strengthening the thesis statement. Revising may also mean improving readability by altering sentence structure, smoothing transitions, and improving word choice.

Editing is fixing errors in spelling, grammar, and punctuation. Many writers feel the urge to do this throughout the writing process, but it saves time to wait until the end. There is no point perfecting the grammar and spelling in a sentence that is going to get cut later.

For research projects, you also need to craft **citations,** or notes that tell readers where you got your information. If you noted this information while working on your prewriting and first draft, all you need to do now is format it correctly. (If you did not make notes as you worked, you will have to search laboriously through all your research materials again.) If you are using MLA or APA styles, citations are included in parentheses at the ends of sentences. If you are using Chicago style, citations appear in footnotes or endnotes.

Prewriting Techniques

Prewriting encompasses a wide variety of tasks that happen before you start writing. Many new writers skip or skimp on this step, perhaps because a writer's prewriting efforts are not clearly visible in the final product. But writers who spend time gathering and organizing information tend to produce more polished work.

Thinking silently is a valid form of prewriting. So is telling someone about what you are planning to write. For very short pieces based on your prior knowledge, it may be enough to use these—but most long writing tasks go better if you also use some or all of the strategies below.

Gathering Information

- **Conducting research** involves looking for information in books, articles, websites, and other sources. Internet research is almost always necessary, but do not overlook the benefits of a trip to a library, where you can find in-depth printed sources and also get help from research librarians.
- **Brainstorming** is making a list of short phrases or sentences related to the topic. Brainstorming works best if you literally write down every idea that comes to mind, whether or not you think you can use it. This frees up your mind to find unconscious associations and insights.
- **Free writing** is writing whatever comes to mind about your topic in sentences and paragraphs. Free writing goes fast and works best if you avoid judging your ideas as you go.

Organizing information

- **Mind mapping** arranges ideas into an associative structure. Write your topic, main idea, or argument in a circle in the middle of the page. Then draw lines and make additional circles for supporting points and details. You can combine this step with brainstorming to make a big mess of ideas, some of which you later cross out if you decide not to use them. Or you can do this after brainstorming, using the ideas from your brainstormed list to fill in the bubbles.

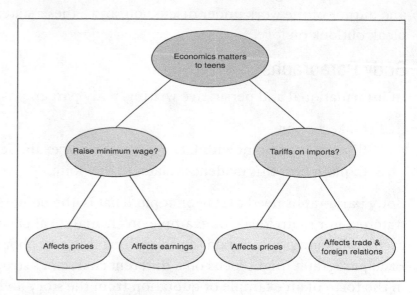

- **Outlining** arranges ideas into a linear structure. It starts with an introduction, includes supporting points and details to back them up, and ends with a conclusion. Traditionally, an outline uses Roman numerals for main ideas and letters for minor ideas.

Example:

I. Introduction - Economics should be a required subject in high school because it affects political and social issues that matter to students.

II. Domestic Issues - Minimum wage
   a. How do people decide if the minimum wage should be raised?
   b. They need to know how changes to the minimum wage affect workers, businesses, and prices.

III. Foreign Issues - Tariffs
   a. How do people decide if they favor taxes on imports?
   b. They need to know how tariffs affect prices and trade.

IV. Conclusion – These issues affect how much money high school graduates can earn and what they can afford to buy.

Paragraph Organization

Paragraphs need to have a clear, coherent organization. Whether you are providing information, arguing a point, or entertaining the reader, the ultimate goal is to make it easy for people to follow your thoughts.

Introductions

The opening of a text must hook the reader's interest, provide necessary background information on the topic, and state the main point. In an academic essay, all of this typically happens in a single paragraph. For instance, an analytical paper on the theme of unrequited love in a novel might start with a stark statement about love, a few sentences identifying the title and author of the work under discussion, and a thesis statement about the author's apparently bleak outlook on love.

Body Paragraphs

In informational and persuasive writing, body paragraphs should typically do three things:

1. Make a point.
2. Illustrate the point with facts, quotations, or examples.
3. Explain how this evidence relates to the point.

Body paragraphs need to stay on topic. That is, the point needs to relate clearly to the thesis statement or main idea. For example, in an analytical paper about unrequited love in a novel, each body paragraph should say something different about the author's bleak outlook on love. Each paragraph might focus on a different character's struggles with love, presenting evidence in the form of an example or quotation from the story and explaining what it suggests about the author's outlook. When you present evidence like this, you must introduce it clearly, stating where it came from in the book. Don't assume readers understand exactly what it has to do with your main point; spell it out for them with a clear explanation.

The structure above is useful in most academic writing situations, but sometimes you need to use other structures:

Chronological – Describe how events happen in order.
Sequential – Present a series of steps.
Descriptive – Describe a topic in a coherent spatial order, e.g. from top to bottom.
Cause/Effect – Present an action and its results.
Compare/Contrast – Describe the similarities and differences between two or more topics.

Conclusions

Like introductions, conclusions have a unique structure. A conclusion restates the thesis and main points in different words and, ideally, adds a bit more. For instance, it may take a broader outlook on the topic, giving readers a sense of why it matters or how the main point affects the world. A text should end with a sentence or two that brings the ideas together and makes the piece feel finished. This can be a question, a quotation, a philosophical statement, an intense image, or a request that readers take action.

Let's Review!

- The writing process includes prewriting, drafting, revision, and editing.
- For projects that involve research, writers must include the creation of citations within the writing process.
- Effective writers spend time gathering and organizing information during the prewriting stage.
- Writers must organize paragraphs coherently so that readers can follow their thoughts.

ESSAY REVISIONS AND TRANSITIONS

A well-written essay should be easy to follow and convincing. The words should be well-chosen, and the transitions should be smooth.

Content, Organization, and Coherence

To revise an essay effectively, you must read through your own work with a critical eye. As you read, consider the content, organization, and flow of ideas.

Content

Every time you write, you are setting out to communicate something. Check to make sure you have clearly and succinctly stated an argument or main point, usually in a one-sentence thesis statement at the end of the first paragraph. Does your essay follow through on this point? By the end, you should have defended or developed it completely without leaving any holes or veering off onto other subjects. If you have not done this, add or delete information.

Organization

The ideas in your essay need to appear in an order that makes sense and avoids repetition. As you revise, check to make sure your ideas flow in a logical order, and move sentences around if they do not. Some topics lend themselves naturally to a particular type of organization. For instance, sometimes you will use chronological order, or you will outline causes first and effects second.

However, many analytical and persuasive papers do not fall into one natural organization. In this case, just choose an order that makes sense to you. In an argumentative paper, for instance, you could place your strongest arguments first and last, with the less impactful ones in the middle. No matter what, be sure each paragraph makes a point that is clearly distinguishable from the points in the other paragraphs. Do not just repeat the same idea in different words.

Coherence

When the ideas in an essay flow in a logical and consistent way that readers can easily follow, we say the writing has **coherence**. A well-written essay makes it possible for readers to follow the writer's thoughts. Make sure you have clear topic sentences in each paragraph to link back to the main idea. Do not bounce off onto new subtopics without explaining how they relate. Within paragraphs, explain your points and evidence explicitly. Do not leave gaps or make readers guess how one point relates to another.

Rhetorical Effectiveness and Use of Evidence

When you revise a persuasive essay, you must evaluate your work for **rhetorical effectiveness**. In other words, you need to make sure it is convincing. The cornerstones of rhetorically effective writing are reason, trust, and emotions.

Every good argument is grounded in logic and reasoning. When you offer opinions, you should present facts and logic to back them up. For example, if you are arguing that young children should not be required to do hours of homework every night, you could cite a study showing that kids under twelve did not learn more when they spent additional time doing homework outside of class.

Good arguments must also inspire trust. One of the primary ways to do this is to use credible sources and identify them clearly. The evidence above would generally be considered trustworthy if the study was conducted by a Harvard professor with a doctorate in education. It is a good idea to share information like this in an essay. It is not a good idea to use evidence if it comes from a source that is not credible.

It is also appropriate to engage the emotions in persuasive writing. In an essay opposing homework, you could call on readers' nostalgia and sense of fun by briefly describing the enjoyable activities kids could do instead of homework. But be careful. Good writing never uses personal attacks or scare tactics. In other words, it would be inappropriate to call people who believe in homework "fun killers" or to make an exaggerated suggestion that kids forced to do too much homework will suffer deep psychological damage.

Using Evidence

There are several rules of thumb for using evidence to back up your ideas.

- It must genuinely back up your thesis. Imagine you are arguing that kids under 12 should not do homework at all, and you find a study that says elementary school kids who did three hours of homework per night did not learn any more than kids who did only one hour. The study supports limited homework; it does not clearly support your thesis.
- If evidence comes from an outside source, it must be introduced and cited correctly. In general, you should name and share the credentials of your source the first time you introduce it. Afterward, you may refer to the same source by last name only.
- You need to explain how the evidence fits the argument. Readers may not understand what you are thinking about the evidence you present unless you spell it out for them.
- You need the right amount of evidence—not too much, not too little. Back up every opinion. One to three pieces of evidence per point should suffice. Do not continue piling on additional evidence to support a point you have already defended.

Word Choice

After you have revised for major issues like content, organization, and evidence, it is time to consider your word choice. This means you should attempt to use the right word at the right time. Below are several thoughts to consider as you hone your word choice.

Simplicity

The first goal of writing is to be understood. Many students try to use the biggest words they can, but it is usually a better style choice to choose an ordinary word. Do not use fancy vocabulary unless you have a good reason.

Precision

Sometimes the need for precision is a good reason for choosing a fancier word. There are times when it is best to say you hurt your knee, and there are times when it is best to say you injured your anterior cruciate ligament. Consider what your readers need to know and why. An audience of doctors might need or appreciate the medical terminology, whereas a general audience would likely be better served by the simpler language.

Tone

You can establish a clear tone by considering and manipulating the connotations of the words you use. Many words have a positive or negative connotation, whereas others are more neutral. *Cheap* has a negative tone, whereas *economical* is positive and *inexpensive* is neutral. If you are writing about making a purchase, choosing one or another of these words can subtly convey your attitude about what you bought.

Formality

Our language contains many levels of formality. Academic writing usually calls for slightly more formal language than daily speech. In academic writing, you should avoid slang, contractions, and abbreviations like *idk* or *tfw* that are commonly used in text messages and on the Internet. Depending on the writing task, you may also choose more formal words like *purchase* rather than less formal words like *buy*.

Inclusivity

Aim to use language that includes everyone, not language that plays into stereotypes and gender biases. Avoid referring to the entire human race as *man* or *mankind*. Use gender-neutral words like *firefighter* over gender-specific words like *fireman*. Do not assume people are male or female just because they belong to a certain profession. For example, do not automatically refer to a doctor as *he* or a preschool teacher as *she*. Note that using plurals can make it possible to write around gendered pronouns entirely. That is, if you refer to doctors or preschool teachers in the plural, you can refer back to them neutrally as *they*.

Transitions

At the very end of your revision process, read your work and make sure that your ideas flow smoothly from one to the next. Use connecting words and phrases, or **transitions**, to link ideas and help readers follow the flow of your thoughts. The number of possible ways to transition between ideas is almost limitless. Below are a few common transition words, categorized by the way they link ideas.

Type of Transition	Example
Time and sequence transitions help show when events happened in time.	first, second, next, now, then, at this point, after, afterward, before this, previously, formerly, thereafter, finally, in conclusion
Addition or emphasis transitions let readers know when you are building on an established line of thought or stressing an important idea.	moreover, also, likewise, furthermore, above all, indeed, in fact
Example transitions introduce ideas that illustrate a point.	for example, for instance, to illustrate, to demonstrate
Causation transitions indicate a cause-and-effect relationship.	as a result, consequently, thus, therefore
Contrast transitions indicate a difference between ideas.	nevertheless, despite, in contrast, however

Different types of transitions are necessary in different parts of an essay. Within a paragraph, you should use short transitions of one or two words to show how the information in one sentence is linked to the information preceding it. But when you are starting a new paragraph or making another major shift in thought, you may take time to explain relationships more thoroughly.

> **Between Sentences:** Clara was in a minor car accident last week. *Afterward*, she experienced headaches and dizziness that worsened over time.

> **Between Paragraphs:** *Because of her worsening headaches and dizziness,* Clara has found it increasingly difficult to work at her computer.

Note that longer transitions are long because they have content to explain how ideas relate. Some long transitions, such as the very wordy "due to the fact that" take up space without adding more meaning than simpler words like "because." Very long-winded transitions are considered poor style.

Let's Review!

- When you revise an essay, consider content, organization, and coherence first.
- Rhetorically effective writing appeals to the reader's reason and inspires trust and emotions appropriately.
- Use clear evidence to back up every opinion in your writing.
- Aim to use exactly the right words for the writing task at hand.
- Use appropriate transitions to create a smooth flow of ideas.

ACTIVE AND PASSIVE VOICE

Active and passive voice are two different styles of writing that are used to create a certain effect. This lesson will cover how to recognize, form, and use (1) active voice and (2) passive voice in writing.

Active Voice

Active voice is most often used in non-scientific academic writing. In active voice, the subject of the sentence performs the action of the verb.

Active voice sentences are more concise. Using the active voice prevents wordy and convoluted sentences and makes the meaning clear. The subject is acting on something and not being acted on.

- The dog bit the boy.
- Half of the class failed the exam.
- The actress joined the cast of the play.
- He turned on the window fan.

Passive Voice

Passive voice is used in scientific writing. In passive voice, the subject is being acted upon as the subject receives the action of the verb.

The words "by the" indicate the subject in a passive voice sentence. Passive voice will always include a form of the verb "to be."

Passive voice in academic writing can make the essay seem uninteresting, but sometimes passive voice can be a stylistic choice. Scientific writing uses passive voice to remain objective.

- The boy was bitten by the dog.
- The exam was failed by half of the class.
- The cast of the play was joined by the actress.
- The window fan was turned on by him.

Let's Review!

- In **active voice**, the subject performs the action of the verb. These sentences are clearer and more concise.
- In **passive voice**, the subject is acted upon. The subject receives the action of the verb. The use of the verb "to be" and the words "by the" indicate passive voice.

THE WRITING SECTION

The Writing Section of the TASC exam consists of a 45-minute "Extended Response" essay that assesses your writing skills. This test builds on the skills required in the English and reading tests by allowing you to demonstrate practical knowledge of the conventions of standard written English. You will be asked to read a pair of passages and write an argumentative essay that develops your perspective about the issue.

You will be assessed on your ability to clearly state a main idea, provide specific examples and details to back up your main idea, and follow the conventions of standard English. You will not be allowed to outside resources, such as a dictionary, but you may use plain scratch paper (provided at the testing center) to plan your essay and write your rough draft(s).

How to Write an Argumentative Essay

The purpose of the TASC extended response essay is to analyze the arguments that are presented in the stimulus text and explain why one of these arguments is better. It is not an opinion essay; therefore, your own opinion about the subject matter is not relevant.

A successful argumentative essay should:

- Clearly state the issue and your position on it in the introduction
- Use language appropriate to the audience you are addressing
- Support your position with facts, statistics, and reasons from the stimulus texts
- Show clear reasoning
- Conclude with a summary of your main points and state your claim

An argumentative essay follows the traditional paragraph structure that includes an introductory paragraph, body paragraphs, and a concluding paragraph. Your essay should be between 4 to 7 paragraphs long. Aim for 3 to 7 sentences in each paragraph, with 300-500 words in total.

The Introductory Paragraph:

The goal of your **introductory paragraph** is to introduce your topic. The introduction should contain a strong opening sentence that states your claim or thesis statement. In this exercise, you will be analyzing two stimulus texts that contain opposing viewpoints about a topic and determining which argument is stronger. Your position statement should be clear and direct so the reader understands what you are trying to accomplish with your essay.

The Body Paragraphs:

The **body paragraphs** are where you will develop your position about your subject. This is where you present reasoning and evidence to support your claim. You can state facts, examples, and explanations from the stimulus text to support your main ideas. Each body paragraph should contain one well-developed example.

Your goals for each body paragraph are to: introduce an example, describe the example, explain how the example fully supports your thesis. Use evidence from the stimulus prompt and NOT your own opinions to support your position. Be sure to use transition words at the beginning of each body paragraph to introduce your next example.

The Conclusion:

The ultimate goal of your conclusion is to summarize your main points and restate your claim. In your **concluding paragraph**, you might introduce the opposing side to your argument. Then refute their position by reinforcing the validity of your thesis. Use a strong ending sentence to emphasize the main point of your essay.

Sample Essay Prompts

Before you sit for your exam, practice writing a sample essay to become familiar with the process and comfortable with the format. Below is an essay prompt.

Try to follow the paragraph organization as outlined in this lesson. Then, once you have written your draft, review the rules of grammar and conventions of English (spelling, punctuation, capitalization) in the Reasoning Through Language Arts section of this study guide to help you fine-tune your writing. If the opportunity permits, ask a teacher, relative, or friend read your essay and offer feedback on your work.

Essay Prompt:
Is Curling a Sport?

Curling has been around for centuries. The first recorded curling match took place in 16th century Scotland, as evidenced by paintings of peasants playing the game. When people immigrated to North America, they brought curling with them. In 1807, the first Canadian curling club was established in Montreal, followed by the first American club in 1828, located in Michigan. Even with its lengthy history, the debate over whether or not curling is a sport wages on the Internet, in bars, amongst sportswriters, and even in ice arenas.

Proponents say that curling meets the definition of "sport" found in the dictionary. Curling requires physical exertion, coordination, and skill; it adheres to a specific set of rules, and is recognized as a sport by athletic associations, fans, the media, and more. They point to curling's inclusion in the Olympics, starting with the 1924 Winter Olympics in Chamonix, France, as further evidence of its qualification as a sport.

Opponents say that curling should be considered a "game" and not a "sport." They argue that curling does not require rigorous physical activity and can be played professionally by people who are generally non-athletic or overweight. They argue that curling is a game or leisure activity.

Pro Arguments

According to fitness tracking programs, participating in curling burns 272 calories. This is approximately the same amount of calories per hour as bowling or practicing yoga. While this is not as much as gymnasts, who burn 345 calories per hour, the standard curling competition includes eight 15-minute long matches that are completed in about two hours.

Curling matches adhere to a set of rules that is governed by the World Curling Federation. There are specific guidelines for equipment, such as the stones, brooms, and specialized footwear. Each of the four players on a curling team has a specific role to play. The "lead" player sets up the match by throwing the first two stones. The "second" playing throws the next two stones. The third player is called the "vice skip." This is the player who holds the broom. And lastly, the "skip" is the captain and chief strategist of the team.

Con Arguments

Unlike a sport, curling does not require rigorous physical activity. Burning 272 calories per hour while curling is much less than the number of calories burned per hour in competitive sports. Soccer players burn 900/hour while football, basketball players burn 727 calories/hour. Professional curlers are sometimes overweight, old, or out of shape. There is no running, jumping, or cardiovascular activity in curling.

Sports experts agree that curling lacks the athletic rigor needed to be a real sport. Curling was ranked 56 out of 60 activities by a panel of sports scientists, athletes, and journalists assembled by ESPN. They ranked the athletic difficulty of 60 activities based on ten categories such as endurance, agility, and strength.

Prompt

In your response, analyze both positions presented in the article to determine which one is best supported. Use relevant and specific evidence from the article to support your response.

You should expect to spend up to 45 minutes for planning, drafting, and editing your response.

SECTION V. FULL-LENGTH PRACTICE EXAMS

ISEE PRACTICE EXAM 1

SECTION I. VERBAL REASONING

You have 20 minutes to complete 40 questions.

This section is divided into two parts containing two types of questions. Answer the questions in Part One and then move on to complete Part Two.

Part One – Synonyms

Directions: Each synonym question consists of a word in capital letters followed by four answer choices. Select the one word that is most nearly the same in meaning as the word in capital letters.

1. **ACCENTUATE**
   - A. disappear
   - B. emphasize
   - C. express
   - D. mask

2. **INNATE**
   - A. acquired
   - B. extrinsic
   - C. inherent
   - D. learned

3. **HAPLESS**
   - A. blessed
   - B. favored
   - C. well-off
   - D. woeful

4. **DIVERGENT**
   - A. alike
   - B. contrary
   - C. equal
   - D. uniform

5. **SORDID**
   - A. clean
   - B. dirty
   - C. incorrupt
   - D. unacquisitive

6. **VIVACIOUS**
   - A. boring
   - B. dispirited
   - C. lively
   - D. unhappy

7. **FETTER**
   - A. allow
   - B. bind
   - C. help
   - D. smooth

8. **FLACCID**
   - A. firm
   - B. limp
   - C. stiff
   - D. taut

9. **INCLEMENT**
   - A. bitter
   - B. clear
   - C. fair
   - D. mild

10. **DUTIFUL**
    - A. betraying
    - B. faithless
    - C. irresponsible
    - D. obedient

11. **RANCID**
    - A. pure
    - B. rotten
    - C. sharp
    - D. sweet

12. **SAGACIOUS**
    - A. foolish
    - B. irrational
    - C. obtuse
    - D. wise

278

13. TIMOROUS

A. bold   C. **fearful**

B. brazen   D. forthcoming

14. ENVIOUS

A. content   C. **jealous**

B. generous   D. pleased

15. CONFOUND

A. clarify   C. **puzzle**

B. divide   D. separate

16. BILK

A. assist   C. lose

B. encourage   D. **swindle**

(D)

17. WANE

A. develop   C. **lessen**

B. enhance   D. reach

18. RETRACT

A. admit   C. sanction

B. reaffirm   D. **withdraw**

19. PLACATE

A. incite   C. stroke

B. **soothe**   D. trouble

20. JUBILANT

A. crestfallen   C. disconsolate

B. defeated   D. **joyful**

Part Two – Sentence Completion

Directions: Answer the following sample questions. Select the word or pair of words that most correctly completes the sentence.

Note: *To assist you in finding the right answer among the answer choices, one-word answers are listed alphabetically and two-word answers are listed alphabetically by the first word.*

21. The little girl has such a _____ nature that her mom never knows what adventures each day will hold.

     A. **capricious**   C. staid

     B. cautious   D. steadfast

22. While pet ownership can be an immensely enjoyable experience, animal experts discourage folks from adopting _____ animals as pets.

     A. cultivated   C. genteel

     B. **feral**   D. lofty

23. The clouds were so dark and _____ that we suspected a tornado might be approaching.

     A. auspicious   C. heartening

     B. **baleful**   D. propitious

24. The football coach hired an instructor to teach his team yoga poses to help them stay _____ and prevent injury throughout the season.

     A. inflexible   C. rigid

     B. **limber**   D. stiff

25. The teacher returned the student's first draft, citing that it needed to be more _____ and thoughtfully organized.

    A. cryptic   C. opaque

    B. obscure   D. pellucid

26. They stopped at a _____ country store for homemade maple syrup on their way home from Maine.

    A. chic   C. modernistic

    B. fresh   D. quaint

27. The villain planned to _____ the wealthy young lady and demand a large ransom from her family.

    A. abduct   C. redeem

    B. deliver   D. restore

28. The hikers, who had been trudging through a blinding snowstorm, were relieved to stumble upon the abandoned cabin. However, they were quickly disappointed by the _____ supplies that had been left in the pantry by the previous campers.

    A. ample   C. meager

    B. copious   D. surplus

29. The large oak tree had branches that were not _____; therefore, they broke during the fierce thunderstorm due to the strong winds.

    A. brittle   C. pliable

    B. immutable   D. uniform

30. Studies warn that excessively playing video games can have a _____ effect on a person's health.

    A. advantageous   C. deleterious

    B. benignant   D. propitious

31. The girl was _____ as she opened the letter from the college and learned that she had been accepted into their program.

    A. melancholy   C. stoic

    B. radiant   D. sullen

32. The _____ fumes from the failed chemistry experiment caused a school-wide evacuation; this delighted the students, who as a result, were dismissed early on a Friday!

    A. delectable   C. noxious

    B. innocuous   D. pleasing

33. As the ambulances began flooding the hospital with people injured in a massive car accident, the lead nurse ordered work to be done on the most _____ patients and directed other patients to the waiting room.

    A. exigent   C. minor

    B. incidental   D. stable

34. Having just obtained her driver's license that morning, Marcie agreed with _____ to drive to the store to get groceries for her mother.

    A. alacrity

    B. equivocation

    C. perfunctoriness

    D. reticence

35. After a heated discussion about their school presentation, the group realized it was easier to _____ to their demanding classmate's ideas in order to finish the project quickly.

    A. battle   C. repudiate

    B. concede   D. thwart

36. In the fairy tale we read at school, the handsome prince was so _____ that he ran around talking to mailboxes as if they were people!

    A. balanced   C. daft
    B. clear   D. judicious

37. The neighborhood children were afraid of "Old Mrs. Hubbard" as they could never predict her _____ temperament; sometimes she called out pleasant greetings to them while other times she screeched at them for being too loud as they walked past her house on their way home from school.

    A. abiding   C. persistent
    B. mercurial   D. unvarying

38. The officer's _____demeanor while questioning the suspicious looking man caused him to stutter as he tried to recount what happened during the alleged burglary.

    A. brusque   C. politic
    B. diplomatic   D. voluble

39. The musicians could hear the _____ in their performance and blamed it on their lack of practice in the previous week.

    A. accord   C. dissonance
    B. concordance   D. harmony

40. The waitress at our favorite restaurant is always a bit grumpy, so we were pleasantly surprised by her _____ greeting when we arrived for our weekly lunch date.

    A. hard headed   C. insipid
    B. flat   D. saccharine

Section II. Quantitative Reasoning

Part One Word Problems

4137

1. Peter has 397 baseball cards in his
collection and his brother Evan has 451.
Evaluate the expression to determine
how many cards they have together in
total.

   397 + 451

   A. 748   C. 857

   B. 848   D. 925

2. Which term correctly describes a prime
number?

   A. An integer   C. A natural
                          number
   B. A whole
      number   D. All of the
                          above

3. Convert 14 centimeters to inches.

   A. 5.51 inches   C. 16.54 inches

   B. 11.46 inches   D. 35.56 inches

4. Which decimal is the least?

   A. 0.786   C. 0.687

   B. 0.876   D. 0.768

5. At the grocery store, a researcher asks
random people about the number of text
messages they send daily. What type of
study is this?

   A. Census   C. Experiment

   B. Survey   D. Observational
                        study

6. Solve the inequality for the unknown.

   $\frac{2}{3}x-4 \leq \frac{4}{5}x + 2$

   A. $x \leq -45$ C. $x \leq 90$

   B. $x \geq -45$ D. $x \geq 90$

7. Solve the system of equations.

   $x + 2y = 10$
   $x + y = 5$

   A. $(5, 0)$ C. $(-5, 0)$

   B. $(0, 5)$ D. $(0, -5)$

8. In a word game, a player loses 8 points
when using an invalid word. If there
were 65 invalid words, how many points
were lost during the game?

   A. −520   C. −73

   B. −480   D. −57

9. A service group collects trash from area
roadways for four straight weeks. The
amount of trash they pick up is about 19
$\frac{1}{2}$, $15\frac{1}{3}$, $20\frac{7}{10}$, and $16\frac{3}{5}$ pounds. Estimate the
total number of pounds collected.

   A. 70   C. 72

   B. 71   D. 73

10. Perform the operation.

    $(-3x + 5xy-6y)-(4x + 2xy-5y)$

    A. $-7x + 7xy-y$ C. $-7x + 3xy-y$

    B. $-7x + 7xy-11y$ D. $-7x + 3xy-11y$

11. The error on one manufacturing
machine is 2×10^{-4}, and the error on a
second machine is 8×10^{-5}. How many
times larger is the error on the first
machine?

    A. 1   C. 3

    B. 2   D. 4

282

12. Elementary school students were surveyed about their favorite animals at a zoo. The circle graph shows the results. Which statement is true for the circle graph?

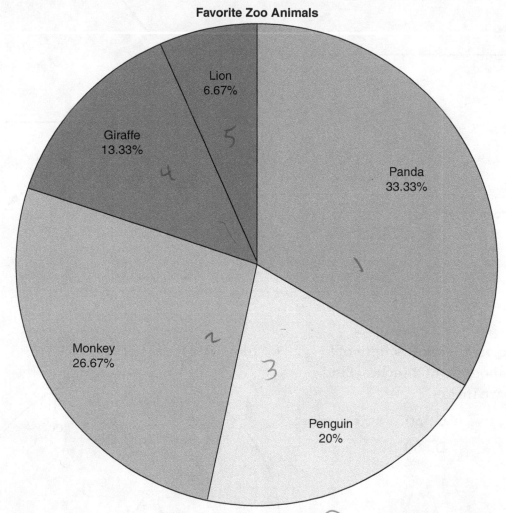

Favorite Zoo Animals

Lion
6.67%

Giraffe
13.33%

Panda
33.33%

Monkey
26.67%

Penguin
20%

A. The penguins were the second-favorite animals.

B. No group of animals makes up one-third of the graph.

C. Sixty percent of the students like pandas and monkeys.

D. Fifty percent of the students like giraffes, lions, and penguins.

13. **Select the drawing of $\overleftrightarrow{FH}$ and $\overrightarrow{AB}$ intersecting at point Z.**

A.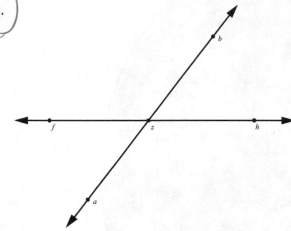

B.

C.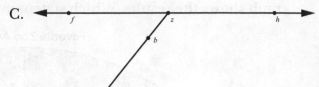

D.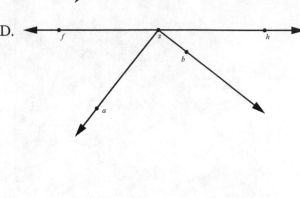

14. **A regular hexagon has a side length of 5 inches and an apothem of 2 inches. Find the area in square inches.**

A. 30   C. 50

B. 40   D. 60

15. **Identify a radius of the circle.**

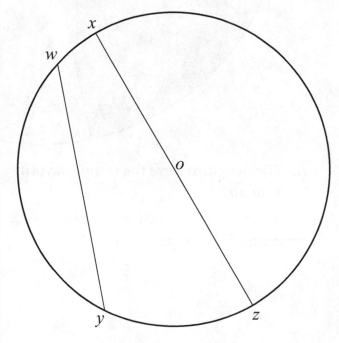

A. $\overline{WY}$ C. $\overline{XO}$

B. $\overline{XZ}$ D. $\overline{YZ}$

16. A circle has a circumference of 180 inches. Find the diameter to the nearest tenth of an inch. Use 3.14 for π.

    A. 28.7
    B. 57.3
    C. 86.0
    D. 114.6

17. A cylinder has a height of 14 centimeters and an outer radius of 8 centimeters. There is a hole cut out of the center with a radius of 4 centimeters. Find the volume of the solid part of the cylinder.

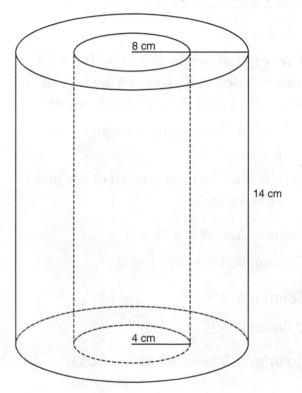

    A. 224π cubic centimeters
    B. 672π cubic centimeters
    C. 896π cubic centimeters
    D. 1,120π cubic centimeters

18. The data set represents the number of weekly pop-up ads for 12 families: 125, 145, 150, 130, 150, 120, 170, 165, 175, 145, 150, and 130. Find the median.

    A. 145
    B. 145.5
    C. 147
    D. 147.5

19. Students were surveyed on if they liked math, social studies, or science as a subject. Describe an intersection of the events.

    A. Students who like math or social studies
    B. Students who like math and social studies
    C. Students who do not like math, social studies, or science
    D. Students who like math

20. The histogram below shows the number of text messages between a group of friends in a week. Which statement is true for the histogram?

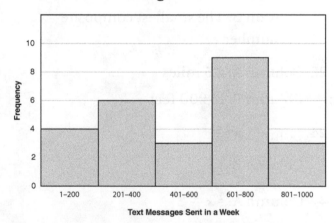

    A. There are 30 friends in the group.
    B. The highest frequency is 8 friends.
    C. The bin size is 1,000 text messages.
    D. Two bins have the same frequency.

285

Part Two: Quantitative Comparisons

Directions: In this section, the question will present two different values as either Column A or Column B. These quantities may be accompanied by additional information in many forms including charts or diagrams. All of the answer options for each question within this section will remain consistent and are outlined within the box below.

> A. The quantity in Column A is greater.
> B. The quantity in Column B is greater.
> C. The two quantities are equal.
> D. The relationship cannot be determined from the information given.

21. Column A: $(3 \times (4 + 9) \div 13 - 2) + 1$

    Column B: $(-2)^2$ *B*

22. Column A: The smallest prime number

    Column B: The smallest composite number   *B*

23. Column A: 2.5 miles

    Column B: 13,200 feet   *C*

24. Column A: $\frac{5}{12}$ *A*

    Column B: $\frac{1}{4}$

25. Column A: $\frac{2}{3} \times \frac{4}{15}$

    Column B: $\frac{1}{3} \div \frac{5}{8}$ *B*

26. $2(x-4) = 5(x + 2)$

    Column A: x *B*

    Column B: 2

27. $2y + x = -20$
    $y = -x-12$

    Column A: x *A*

    Column B: y

28. The original height of a plant is 3.5 inches. The plant grows an average of 0.75 inches every month for 6 months.

    Column A: The original height of the plant   *A*

    Column B: The total growth of the plant after 4 months

29. Column A: $(4y^2 + 3)(2y + 5)$ *A*

    Column B: $8y^3 + 20y^2 + 6y$

30. Column A: $5^6 \times 5^{-3}$

    Column B: $\frac{(-7)^2}{(-7)^{-1}}$ *A*

31. Column A: The order of rotational symmetry for a parallelogram   *B*

    Column B: The order of rotational symmetry for an equilateral triangle

32. A cubic storage bin has a volume of 216 cubic feet.

    Column A: The side length of the storage bin in feet   *A*

    Column B: 5 feet

33. Column A: The radius of a circle   *B*

    Column B: The diameter of a circle

A. The quantity in Column A is greater.

B. The quantity in Column B is greater.

C. The two quantities are equal.

D. The relationship cannot be determined from the information given.

34. A cone has a volume of $\frac{512}{3}\pi$ cubic meters and a height of 8 meters.

Column A: The radius of the cone in meters

B

Column B: 32 meters

35. Data Set: 34, 31, 37, 35, 38, 33, 39, 32, 36, 35, 37, 33

Column A: The median for the data set

Column B: 34

A

36. There are 12 boys' and 14 girls' names in a hat.

Column A: The probability of selecting a boys' name twice in a row without replacement

Column B: The probability of selecting a girls' name twice in a row without replacement

B

37. The dot plot shows the results of a favorite pet survey given to children. Each dot represents 5 respondents.

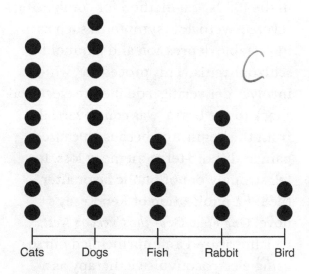

Favorite Pet

C

Column A: The number of students who favor dogs

Column B: The number of students who favor fish or rabbits

287

SECTION III. READING 7|42.

55 MINUTES, 42 QUESTIONS

Directions: Each passage (or pair of passages) below is followed by a number of questions. Read each passage (or pair), then choose the best answer to each question based on what is stated or implied in the passage (or passages), and in any graphics that may accompany the passage.

Read the passages below and answer questions 1-9.

Electroconvulsive therapy was pioneered in the 1930s as a method for combatting severe psychiatric symptoms such as intractable depression and paranoid
5   schizophrenia. This procedure, which involves delivering a deliberate electrical shock to the brain, was controversial from the beginning because it caused pain and short-term memory loss. It
10 fell strongly out of public favor after the 1962 publication of Ken Kesey's novel *One Flew Over the Cuckoo's Nest,* which featured an unprincipled nurse using electroconvulsive therapy as a
15 means of control over her patients. Paradoxically, medical advances at the time of the novel's publication made electroconvulsive therapy significantly safer and more humane.

20 Although the public is still generally opposed to electroconvulsive therapy, it remains a genuine option for psychiatric patients whose symptoms do not improve with medication. Medical professionals
25 who offer this option should be especially careful to make clear distinctions between myth and reality. On this topic,

unfortunately, many patients tend to rely on fiction rather than fact.

30 *

We were led into a stark exam room, where three doctors positioned themselves so Mama and I had no direct path to the door. The one in charge
35 cleared his throat and told me my mother needed electroshock. My brain buzzed—almost as if it was hooked up to some crackpot brainwashing machine— as Big Doctor droned on about his
40 sadistic intentions. I didn't hear any of it. All I could think was that these people wanted to tie my mother down and stick wires in her ears.

When Big Doctor was finished, he flipped
45 through the papers on his clipboard and asked if I had questions. I mumbled something noncommittal. Then, when he and his silent escort left, I grabbed Mama and beat it out of that wacko ward as fast
50 as I could make her go.

1. **What is the purpose of the first paragraph of Passage 1?**
    A. To inform
    B. To distract
    C. To persuade
    D. To entertain

2. What is the purpose of the second paragraph of Passage 1?

A. To inform
B. To distract
C. To persuade
D. To entertain

3. What is the primary purpose of Passage 2?

A. To inform
B. To distract
C. To persuade
D. To entertain

4. With which statement would the author of Passage 1 likely agree?

A. Patients who suffer from mental illness should sue Ken Kesey for libel.

B. Electroconvulsive therapy is a ready solution for every psychiatric complaint.

C. No twenty-first century patient should ever receive electroconvulsive therapy.

D. Medical patients should try options such as medication before electroconvulsive therapy.

5. Which detail from Passage 1 supports the conclusion that patients should try other options before electing to undergo electroconvulsive therapy?

A. This procedure...was controversial from the beginning because it caused pain and short-term memory loss.

B. Ken Kesey's novel *One Flew Over the Cuckoo's Nest*...featured an unprincipled nurse using electroconvulsive therapy as a means of control over her patients.

C. Electroconvulsive therapy...remains a genuine option for patients whose symptoms do not improve with medication.

D. Paradoxically, medical advances at the time of the novel's publication made electroconvulsive therapy significantly safer and more humane.

6. The author of Passage 1 would most likely criticize the author of Passage 2 for:

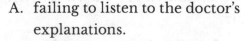

A. failing to listen to the doctor's explanations.

B. making no attempt to protect her ailing mother.

C. feeling threatened by her physical circumstances.

D. asking too many questions and wasting the doctor's time.

7. The author of Passage 1 would most likely criticize the doctor in Passage 2 for:

   A. revealing medical information to the patient's family members.

   B. denying the patient and her family the chance to ask questions.

   C. taking control of the meeting instead of letting underlings speak.

   D. neglecting to anticipate the feelings of his patient and her family.

8. Which details from Passage 2 suggest that the author has a negative outlook about medical professionals?

   A. She describes feeling trapped in a room by doctors, one of whom she calls "sadistic."

   B. She describes feeling outnumbered when she makes reasoned arguments to a doctor she calls "wacko."

   C. She describes feeling bored by the idea that the doctor wants to "tie [her] mother down and stick wires in her ears."

   D. She describes feeling excited by the prospect of seeing her mother hooked up to a pseudo-medical "brainwashing machine."

9. The author of Passage 1 supports her points primarily by:

   A. telling humanizing stories.

   B. relying on facts and logic.

   C. pointing to expert sources.

   D. using fear tactics and manipulation.

Read the paragraph below and answer questions 10-17.

Until about 1850, few people living in temperate climates had ever had the opportunity to taste a banana. Only after the invention of the steamship
5 could importers and exporters reliably transport this fruit to North America and Europe. Railways and refrigeration were two other vital components in the development of the banana trade. Today,
10 bananas are a major export in several Central and South American countries as well as the Philippines. Around the world, people in climates that cannot support banana production now have
15 access to plentiful inexpensive bananas.

10. Which sentence provides an effective summary of the text above?

    A. The author of this paragraph really likes bananas and researched them thoroughly.

    B. Shipping and refrigeration technology helped bananas become a major export crop.

    C. This paragraph should include more detail about the development of the banana trade.

    D. Before 1850, most Americans and Europeans had never had the opportunity to taste a banana.

11. **Read the following summary of the paragraph above.**

    According to John K. Miller, the invention of shipping and refrigeration technology helped bananas become a major export crop. The banana trade
    5 is an important source of income for many countries around the world, and consumers can buy bananas easily even in places where bananas do not grow.

    What makes this summary effective?

    A. It makes a judgment on the original text without being unfair.

    B. It restates the ideas of the original text in completely new words.

    C. It rearranges the ideas of the original text into a different sequence.

    D. It highlights ideas from the original text that were not stated explicitly.

12. **Which summary sentence retains language too close to the original text?**

    A. The author of this paragraph really likes bananas and researched them thoroughly.

    B. This paragraph should include more detail about the development of the banana trade.

    C. Before 1850, most Americans and Europeans had never had the opportunity to taste a banana.

    D. The technological developments of the Industrial Revolution helped create a global banana trade.

13. **Which summary sentence fails to be objective?**

    A. The author of this paragraph really likes bananas and researched them thoroughly.

B. This paragraph should include more detail about the development of the banana trade.

C. Before 1850, most Americans and Europeans had never had the opportunity to taste a banana.

D. The technological developments of the Industrial Revolution helped create a global banana trade.

14. **Read the following sentence.**

    Nobody would eat bananas today if modern shipping and refrigeration technology had never been invented.

    Why does this sentence NOT belong in a summary of the paragraph above?

    A. It concerns supporting details and not main ideas.

    B. It adheres too closely to the original author's language.

    C. It fails to make a clear judgment about the original text.

    D. It does not accurately state an idea from the original text.

15. **Reread the opening sentence from lines 1-3 ("Until about 1850, ... banana"). What type of sentence is this, and why?**

    A. Fact; the research of the passage explains why countries around the world did not have access to bananas.

    B. Fact; the writing suggests that the author is likely a primary source to discuss the topic of the passage.

    C. Opinion; the people from this time period cannot verify if banana trade could reach countries with temperate climates.

D. Opinion; the research and data the author used makes the sentence an educated assumption.

16. **Where would a reader likely have found this passage?**

A. A fantasy novel

B. A history textbook

C. A science magazine discussing fruit trade

D. A geography study about plantations

17. **What type of data would best help support the main idea of the passage?**

A. A survey of whether or not consumers like bananas in cold climate countries

B. A pie chart of where banana exports go from the Philippines

C. A line graph displaying the value of banana exports from Central America since 1800

D. A bar graph of banana export values from Central America, South America and the Philippines in 2018

Read the following passage and answer questions 18-25.

You know what I hate? Businesses that rely on contract workers and freelancers instead of regular employees.

Don't hit me with arguments about grater
5 freedom for workers. Freedom isn't free if your bleeding out in the street.

Sound the alarm, people! Workers are suffering! No benefits means you're out of luck if you get sick and can't do your job.
10 Plus, studies show freelancers don't make as much money as regular employees.

--From Rod's Job Blog at rodtalksaboutjobs.com

18. **Which of the following is NOT a sign that the reader should be skeptical of this source?**

A. The passage contains typos and spelling errors.

B. The author presents opinion information as if it is fact.

C. There is no clear information about the author's credentials.

D. The passage comes from a personal blog with a .com address.

19. **Why should a reader be skeptical of the point about freelancers not making as much money as regular employees?**

A. The argument is not based in logic.

B. Some freelancers make plenty of money.

C. The source of the information is not clear.

D. The sentence contains grammatical errors.

20. A reader should be skeptical of lines 5-6 ("Freedom isn't free … street") because it:

A. appears to use objective language but is actually hiding gender bias.

B. uses emotional language without responding to the opposing argument.

C. seems to present an expert point of view but does not name the source.

D. makes no attempt to defend regular workers in a discussion of the economy.

21. A student is writing a paper on employment trends and wants to quote an expert's opinion. What type of site would provide the most credible alternative to Rod's Job Blog?

A. A different post on Rod's Jobs Blog

B. A different blog with a .net address

C. An opinion article by a recognized expert in the field

D. A government website tracking employment statistics

22. In line 7, what does the author mean by "Sound the alarm, people!"?

A. The author is asking for help about changing the working conditions for contract workers.

B. The author is dramatizing how the "Workers are suffering!"

C. The author is trying to increase the urgency of the problem by yelling at the audience.

D. The author is calling attention to the idea that businesses are reaping benefits while contract workers are being taken advantage of.

23. What could the author of this blog do to make his argument stronger?

A. Edit the passage to get rid of the spelling errors and exclamatory sentences.

B. Elaborate on their own experience as a contract worker.

C. Select a business that relies on freelancers and expose the salary difference with their contracted work and a regular employee.

D. Explain more clearly that businesses save tons of money by not having to pay large salaries for contracted workers.

24. Reread the following sentence from lines 4-5 ("Don't hit … workers") Which of the following would be a more formal way to rewrite the sentence?

A. I disagree with the argument about contract workers having greater freedom.

B. Stop telling me that freelancers have more freedom!

C. Is there actually greater freedom for workers?

D. I've already heard arguments about greater freedom for workers.

25. What is the author's intended purpose of the blog post?

B

A. To expose how the author was personally taken advantage of as a contract worker.

B. To argue that freelancers are not enjoying the perks of contract work most businesses would argue they have.

C. To increase awareness that non-benefitted workers are suffering.

D. To make the argument that minimum wages for freelancers need to be increased.

Please read the text below and answer questions 26-34.

A global temperature change of a few degrees is more significant than it may seem at first glance. This is not merely a change in weather in any one location.
5   Rather, it is an average change in temperatures around the entire surface of the planet. It takes a vast amount of heat energy to warm every part of our world—including oceans, air, and
10 land—by even a tiny measurable amount. Moreover, relatively small changes in the earth's surface temperatures have historically caused enormous changes in climate. In the last ice age 20,000
15 years ago, when much of the northern hemisphere was buried under huge sheets of ice, mean global temperatures were only about five degrees Celsius lower than they are now. Scientists
20 predict a temperature rise of two to six degrees Celsius by 2100. What if this causes similarly drastic changes to the world we call home?

26. Which sentence is the topic sentence?

A. What if this causes similarly drastic changes to the world we call home?

B. A global temperature change of a few degrees is more significant than it may seem at first glance.

C. It takes a vast amount of heat energy to warm every part of our world—including oceans, air, and land—by even a tiny measurable amount.

D. In the last ice age 20,000 years ago, when much of the northern hemisphere was buried under huge sheets of ice, mean global temperatures were only about five degrees Celsius lower than they are now.

27. In the paragraph above, global temperature change is:

A. the topic.

B. the main idea.

C. a supporting detail.

D. the topic sentence.

28. Which sentence summarizes the main idea of the paragraph?

C

A. A small change in weather at any one location is a serious problem.

B. The author is manipulating facts to make global warming sound scary.

C. People should be concerned by even minor global temperature change.

D. It takes an enormous amount of energy to warm the earth even a little.

29. What function does the information about temperature differences in the last ice age play in the paragraph?

   A. Topic

   B. Opinion

   C. Main idea

   D. Supporting detail

30. Which sentence would best function as a supporting detail in this paragraph?

   A. Electricity and heat production create one quarter of all carbon emissions globally.

   B. The world was only about one degree cooler during the Little Ice Age from 1700 to 1850.

   C. China has surpassed the United States as the single largest producer of carbon emissions.

   D. Methane emissions are, in some ways, more concerning than carbon dioxide emissions.

31. The author wants to include a line graph demonstrating the mean global temperature changes between the last ice age to the present. Why should the author not do this?

   A. The mean global temperature changes are small and would not visually add emphasis to the argument.

   B. The mean global temperature changes are small, but the majority of the difference, and basis of the argument, comes from changes in cold weather locations.

   C. The temperature rise predicted for 2100 is between two and six degrees Celsius, but cannot go into the graph because it has not happened yet.

   D. The temperature rise predicted for 2100 is between two and six degrees Celsius, but the line graph would not show the temperature change between each element of ocean, air, and land.

32. What graphic(s) would best assist the passage to support the author's argument?

   A. Images related to the ice age and cold weather locations now.

   B. A pie chart to show where the polar bear populations live.

   C. A graph to demonstrate the global volume of ice sheets and glaciers over the past fifty years.

   D. A line graph of the volume of sun rays on the Earth through the protective ozone layer throughout the past fifty years.

33. Select a more formal rewrite for the sentence from lines 7-10 ("It takes ... measureable amount").

   A. It takes a lot of heat energy from the sun to move the temperature up for the entire globe.

   B. Every part of the world- including oceans, air, and land- requires a crazy amount of sunlight.

   C. A lot of heat energy is required to push the temperature scale upwards for our globe, which is defined by the oceans, air, and land.

   D. Between the oceans, air, and land, it takes a vast amount of heat energy to shift every part of our world to a warmer measurable temperature.

34. The author of the passage has written the argument in a formal manner. Why does it end with a question?

   A. The question cannot be answered by the author because the impact is unknown.

   B. The question is meant to leave a reader with an open-ended question to think critically about global temperature change affects for the future.

   C. The scientific prediction for a global temperature rise is meant to guide a reader to the answer that global temperature changes may be fatal to the earth's surface.

   D. It is a rhetorical question and is meant to show the author's frustration with scientists who do not support the argument.

Read the passage below and answer questions 35-42.

When my 13-year-old daughter entered the house, the door slammed open with a celebratory "bang!" I was instantly dismayed to see that my first-born
5 stomped right by me as I held my arms open for a warm hug.

"How was your day, honey?" I asked as she gave me her quintessential eye roll.

I sat across from her ready to hear how
10 marvelous her day was. However, I only got an earful of all the drama that had ensued at school: "So-and-so said this," "gym was a drag," "Mr. Fletcher doesn't like me because I am not a math genius."

15 My head ached from nodding so much, so I got up quickly to bring her something.

"Mom! How could you get up when I'm in the middle of telling you about my life?"
20 she barked.

Despite her protest, her eyes could not help but light up when I brought her a freshly baked chocolate chip cookie on a plate.

25 I guess life isn't all that bad, is it?

35. Which adjectives best describe the tone of the passage?

   A. Ironic, furious

   B. Honest, furious

   C. Ironic, amusing

   D. Honest, amusing

36. Which sentence from the passage is clearly ironic?

   A. "How was your day, honey?"

   B. I sat across from her ready to hear how marvelous her day was.

   C. My head ached from nodding so much, so I got up quickly to bring her something.

   D. "Mom! How could you get up when I'm in the middle of telling you about my life?"

37. The author of the passage first establishes the ironic tone by:

   A. describing the slamming of the door as "celebratory."

   B. quoting the daughter's words.

   C. explaining how the mother got up to get the daughter cookie.

   D. having the mother state that life "isn't all that bad."

38. Which adjective could describe an effective reader's mood when reading line 25 ("I guess life ..., is it?") in the passage?

   A. Entertained   C. Empathetic

   B. Frustrated   D. Dismissive

39. Which word or phrase does *not* function as a transition in the passage?

   A. Instantly   C. So

   B. However   D. Despite

40. The transitions "however" and "despite" link ideas in the passage by showing:

   A. when events happen in time.

   B. how certain ideas contrast.

   C. examples that illustrate ideas.

   D. cause-and-effect relationships.

41. Reread lines 7-8 ("How was ... roll").

   Which transition would you use if the next sentence describes the daughter *also* making a "tsk" sound to show her frustration?

   A. Finally   C. To illustrate

   B. Furthermore   D. Nevertheless

42. The author details how her daughter states, "Mr. Fletcher doesn't like me because I am not a math genius." Why does the author not take this statement seriously?

   A. The daughter is being rude to the author.

   B. The author knows what her daughter's math skills truly are.

   C. The author cannot verify how Mr. Fletcher feels about her daughter at the moment.

   D. It is her daughter's opinion stated as if it is a fact because her daughter is being dramatic.

SECTION IV. MATHEMATICS ACHIEVEMENT

1. If 17 widgets failed but the other 1,273 worked properly, what is the failure rate of that widget?

    A. 1.30%   C. 1.34%

    B. 1.32%   D. 1.36%

2. $462 \div 53$

    Evaluate the expression.

    A. 1R3   C. 8R38

    B. 8R0   D. 8R53

3. What points in the diagram are collinear?

    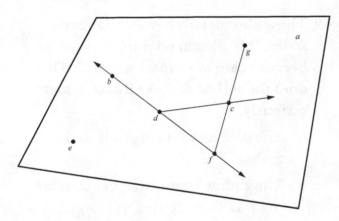

    A. Points D, C, and F

    B. Points B, D, and F

    C. Points B, C, and E

    D. Points B, C, and D

4. Convert 4 tons to pounds.

    A. 2,000 pounds

    B. 4,000 pounds

    C. 8,000 pounds

    D. 10,000 pounds

5. What shape is used to measure the distance between two cities on a map?

    A. A ray   C. A point

    B. A line   D. A line segement

6. A circular dinner plate has a diameter of 13 inches. A ring is placed along the edge of the plate. Find the circumference of the ring in inches. Use 3.14 for π.

    A. 31.4   C. 62.8

    B. 40.82   D. 81.64

7. $(3x^2-2)(x-3)$

    Multiply.

    A. $3x^3 + 9x^2 - 2x + 6$

    B. $3x^3 - 9x^2 - 2x + 6$

    C. $3x^3 + 9x^2 - 2x - 6$

    D. $3x^3 - 9x^2 - 2x - 6$

8. Select the drawing of $\overrightarrow{AB}$ and $\overrightarrow{CD}$ intersecting at D.

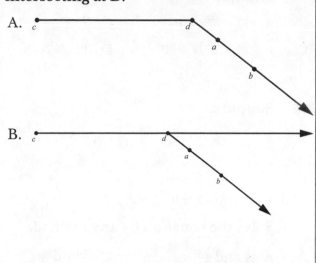

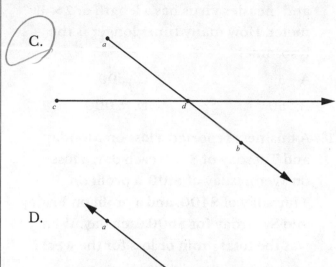

9. How many men does a company employ if it has 420 employees and 35% are women?

   A. 35

   B. 147

   C. 273

   D. 420

10. $1\frac{6}{7} \div \frac{3}{14}$

    Divide.

    A. $\frac{39}{91}$

    B. $1\frac{1}{2}$

    C. $7\frac{1}{14}$

    D. $8\frac{2}{3}$

11. The top 5 leading scorers on a basketball team average 21.3, 19.8, 15.5, 13.9, and 12.4 points per game. What is the estimated average of these players?

    A. 15

    B. 16

    C. 17

    D. 18

12. -3×5

    Evaluate the expression.

    A. -15

    B. -2

    C. 2

    D. 15

13. The volume of a hemi-sphere is $\frac{16}{3}\pi$ cubic feet. What is the diameter in feet?

    A. 1

    B. 2

    C. 3

    D. 4

14. $b + 5 = -15$

    Solve the equation for the unknown.

    A. -75

    B. -20

    C. -10

    D. -3

15. $\left(\frac{x^3 y^{-2}}{x^{-2} y^3}\right)^5$

    Simplify.

    A. $\frac{1}{x^{25} y^{25}}$

    B. $\frac{y^{25}}{x^{25}}$

    C. $\frac{x^{25}}{y^{25}}$

    D. $x^{25} y^{25}$

16. A cylinder has a radius of 5 centimeters and a height of 12 centimeters. Find the volume in cubic centimeters. State the answer in terms of π.

    A. 300π

    B. 360π

    C. 600π

    D. 720π

17. A lysosome has a length of 1×10^{-6} meter, and measles virus has a length of 2×10^{-9} meter. How many times longer is the lysosome?

    A. 5

    B. 50

    C. 500

    D. 5,000

18. A business reported a loss on Monday and Tuesday of $300 each day, a loss on Wednesday of $100, a profit on Thursday of $400, and a profit on Friday and Saturday for $600 each day. What was the total profit or loss for the week?

    A. $600

    B. $900

    C. $1,400

    D. $2,300

19. A shoebox in the shape of a right rectangular prism has a surface area of 400 square inches. What is the length in inches if the other two dimensions are 8 inches and 14 inches?

    A. 2

    B. 3

    C. 4

    D. 5

20. $6x^2y^2(3x^2y^3)$

    Multiply.

    A. $18x^2y^6$

    B. $18x^2y^5$

    C. $18x^4y^6$

    D. $18x^4y^5$

21. A 12-sided number cube is rolled in a game. What is the probability of rolling a 10 or greater on the first roll and a 1 on the second roll?

    A. $\frac{1}{144}$

    B. $\frac{1}{48}$

    C. $\frac{1}{12}$

    D. $\frac{1}{3}$

22. Which number is prime?

    A. 4

    B. 27

    C. 49

    D. 61

23. $(4x + 5)(3x-2)$

    Multiply.

    A. $12x^2-7x + 10$

    B. $12x^2 + 7x + 10$

    C. $12x^2 + 7x-10$

    D. $12x^2-7x-10$

24. $\left(\frac{x^0}{y^{-2}}\right)^2$

    Simplify.

    A. $\frac{1}{y^4}$

    B. $\frac{x}{y^4}$

    C. y^4

    D. x^4y^4

25. $12x^2 + 5x-3 = 0$

    Solve the equation by any method.

    A. $\frac{4}{3}$ and $\frac{1}{3}$

    B. $-\frac{4}{3}$ and $-\frac{1}{3}$

    C. $\frac{4}{3}$ and 3

    D. $-\frac{4}{3}$ and 3

26. A feeding trough is in the shape of a half-cylinder. Find the volume in cubic feet if the diameter is 4 feet and the length is 16 feet.

    A. 16π

    B. 32π

    C. 64π

    D. 128π

27. $(6x^2 + 3xy-5y^2)-(4x^2-2xy + 6y^2)$

    Perform the operation.

    A. $2x^2 + xy-11xy^2$

    B. $2x^2 + xy + xy^2$

    C. $2x^2 + 5xy-11y^2$

    D. $2x^2 + 5xy + xy^2$

28. The combined area of two identical rectangular tarps is 448 square feet. What is the length in feet of one tarp if the width is 14 feet?

    A. 8

    B. 16

    C. 24

    D. 32

29.
$$y = -3x$$
$$x^2 + y^2 = 20$$

Solve the system of equations.

A. (1.4, 4.2) and (-1.4, -4.2)

B. (-1.4, 4.2) and (1.4, -4.2)

C. (-2, 6) and (2, -6)

D. (2, 6) and (-2, -6)

30. A pair of six-sided number cubes is rolled. What is the probability of NOT rolling a sum greater than or equal to 10?

A. $\frac{1}{6}$

C. $\frac{2}{3}$

B. $\frac{1}{3}$

D. $\frac{5}{6}$

31. The list shows the commute time of workers on two different streets.

Street 1: 5, 5, 10, 10, 10, 15, 15, 15, 15, 15, 15, 20, 20, 20, 25, 25, 30, 30, 35, 40, 45

Street 2: 5, 10, 15, 15, 20, 20, 20, 20, 25, 25, 25, 30, 30, 30, 30, 30, 30, 35, 40, 45, 45

Which statement describes the median and interquartile range?

A. Street 1 had the greater median, but Street 2 had a higher interquartile range.

B. Street 2 had the greater median, but Street 1 had a higher interquartile range.

C. Street 1 had the greater median, and Street 1 had a higher interquartile range.

D. Street 2 had the greater median, and Street 2 had a higher interquartile range.

32. A half circle has an area of 50 square inches. Find the radius to the nearest tenth of an inch. Use 3.14 for π.

A. 1.4

C. 4.2

B. 2.8

D. 5.6

301

33. The data below show the number of cars that drove through an intersection on a Saturday.

1, 48, 60, 43, 41, 70, 75, 80, 101, 90, 121, 114, 99, 153, 205, 175, 222, 96, 201, 158, 141, 117, 74, 29

Select a histogram for the data.

A.

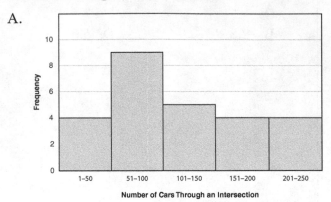

B.

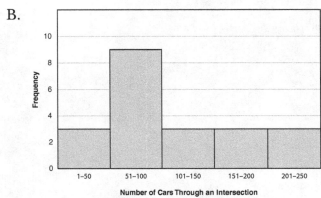

C.

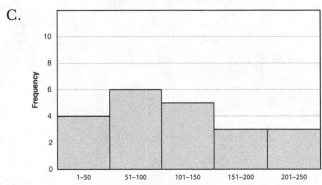

D.

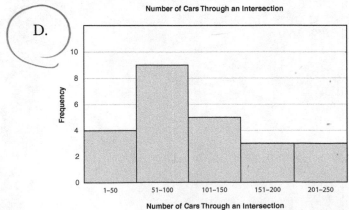

34. Draw a triangle with the coordinates $(-5,0),(-1,0),(5,3)$.

A.

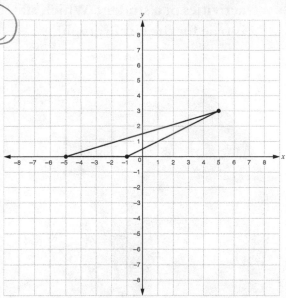

C.

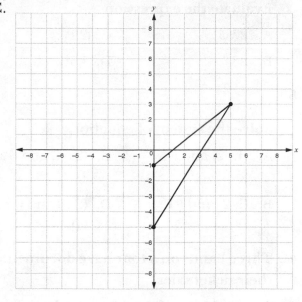

B.

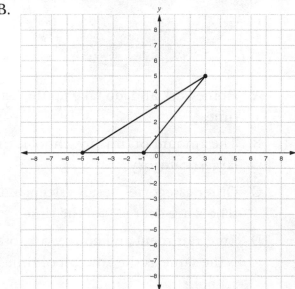

D.

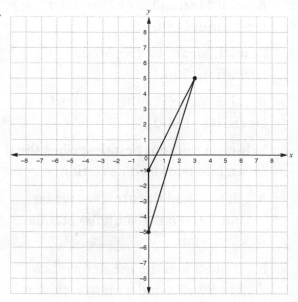

35. A student takes several 10-point math quizzes during the year. Find the mode score from the quizzes.

5, 7, 8, 6, 5, 6, 7, 8, 9, 7, 8, 10, 10, 9, 8, 7, 6, 8, 7, 9, 8, 10, 10, 9, 5, 7, 8, 9, 10, 7, 8, 9, 10

A. 7   C. 9

B. 8   D. 10

36. $x^2 + 10x - 10 = 0$

Solve the equation by completing the square.

A. $-5 \pm \sqrt{10}$ C. $-5 \pm \sqrt{35}$

B. $5 \pm \sqrt{10}$ D. $5 \pm \sqrt{35}$

37. Benjamin buys $3\frac{1}{3}, 2\frac{1}{2}$, and $1\frac{3}{4}$ of yards of fabric at a store. How many total yards did he purchase?

A. $6\frac{5}{12}$ C. $7\frac{7}{12}$

B. $6\frac{5}{9}$ D. $7\frac{7}{9}$

303

38. 1,566 ÷ 54

Evaluate the expression.

A. 2755   C. 29

B. 28   D. 1,512

39. $y = -2x$
$x^2 + y^2 = 5$

Solve the system of equations.

A. (1, -2) and (-1, 2)   C. (2, -1) and (-2, 1)

B. (1, 2) and (-1, -2)   D. (2, 1) and (-2, -1)

40. Three bands on a tour have documented their ticket sales.

Band 1: Mean: 13,500, Standard Deviation: 1,000

Band 2: Mean: 14,250, Standard Deviation: 500

Band 3: Mean 12,500, Standard Deviation: 1,500

Which statement best describes the mean and standard deviation?

A. Band 1 had the greater average, but Band 3 had a higher standard deviation.

B. Band 2 had the greater average, but Band 3 had a higher standard deviation.

C. Band 1 had the greater average, but Band 2 had a higher standard deviation.

D. Band 2 had the greater average, but Band 1 had a higher standard deviation.

41. The circle graph shows the daily activities of a student. Which statement is true for the circle graph?

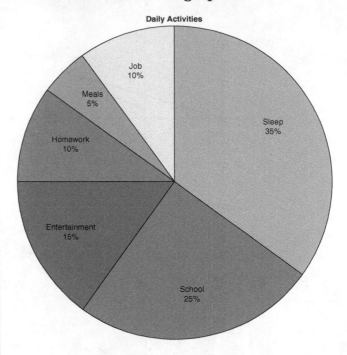

Daily Activities

A. Homework and job take up the least time.

B. The amount of time in school is the largest category.

C. Other categories besides sleep and school are over 50% of the time.

D. Entertainment and homework total is the same as the amount of time in school.

42. $\frac{3}{10} \times \frac{1}{7}$

Multiply.

A. $\frac{3}{70}$ C. $\frac{2}{7}$

B. $\frac{3}{17}$ D. $\frac{2}{3}$

43. A store wants to ask every twentieth customer about his or her shopping experience. What sampling technique is used?

   A. Systematic sampling

   B. Simple random sampling

   C. Cluster random sampling

   D. Stratified random sampling

44. $x^2 + 10x + 8 = 0$

   Solve the equation by the quadratic formula.

   A. –0.88 and 9.13

   B. 0.88 and –9.13

   C. –0.88 and –9.13

   D. 0.88 and 9.13

45. Convert 69 grams to ounces.

   A. 2.30 ounces

   B. 2.44 ounces

   C. 40.44 ounces

   D. 40.70 ounces

46. Which is different from the others?

   A. 6.4%

   B. $\frac{8}{125}$

   C. 128:2000

   D. All of the above are equal.

47. Write 62.42% as a fraction.

   A. $\frac{31}{50000}$ C. $\frac{3121}{50000}$

   B. $\frac{31}{5000}$ D. $\frac{3121}{5000}$

48. What cannot be a factor of a number?

   A. Zero

   B. A prime number

   C. A natural number

   D. A composite number

ISEE PRACTICE EXAM 1
ANSWER KEY WITH EXPLANATORY ANSWERS

Section I. Verbal Reasoning

1. **B.** Accentuate means to highlight or emphasize. **See Lesson: Synonyms, Antonyms, and Analogies.**

2. **C.** Innate means inborn, native, or inherent. **See Lesson: Synonyms, Antonyms, and Analogies.**

3. **D.** Hapless means unlucky or woeful. **See Lesson: Synonyms, Antonyms, and Analogies.**

4. **B.** Divergent means different or contrary. **See Lesson: Synonyms, Antonyms, and Analogies.**

5. **B.** Sordid means dirty. **See Lesson: Synonyms, Antonyms, and Analogies.**

6. **C.** Vivacious means spirited, full of life, or lively. **See Lesson: Synonyms, Antonyms, and Analogies.**

7. **B.** Fetter means to restrain, tie, or bind. **See Lesson: Synonyms, Antonyms, and Analogies.**

8. **B.** Flaccid means limp. **See Lesson: Synonyms, Antonyms, and Analogies.**

9. **A.** Inclement means stormy, severe, or bitter. **See Lesson: Synonyms, Antonyms, and Analogies.**

10. **D.** Dutiful means careful to fulfill obligations, or obedient. **See Lesson: Synonyms, Antonyms, and Analogies.**

11. **B.** Rancid means spoiled, disgusting to the smell or taste, or rotten. **See Lesson: Synonyms, Antonyms, and Analogies.**

12. **D.** Sagacious means shrewd or wise. **See Lesson: Synonyms, Antonyms, and Analogies.**

13. **C.** Timorous means timid or fearful. **See Lesson: Synonyms, Antonyms, and Analogies.**

14. **C.** Envious means jealous. **See Lesson: Synonyms, Antonyms, and Analogies.**

15. **C.** Confound means to frustrate or puzzle. **See Lesson: Synonyms, Antonyms, and Analogies.**

16. **D.** Bilk means to cheat or swindle. **See Lesson: Synonyms, Antonyms, and Analogies.**

17. **C.** Wane means to decrease gradually, or lessen. **See Lesson: Synonyms, Antonyms, and Analogies.**

18. **D.** Retract means to withdraw. **See Lesson: Synonyms, Antonyms, and Analogies.**

19. **B.** Placate means to appease or soothe. **See Lesson: Synonyms, Antonyms, and Analogies.**

20. **D.** Jubilant means happy or joyful. **See Lesson: Synonyms, Antonyms, and Analogies.**

21. **A.** Capricious means impulsive or unpredictable. **See Lesson: Synonyms, Antonyms, and Analogies.**

22. **B.** Feral means savage or untamed. **See Lesson: Synonyms, Antonyms, and Analogies.**

23. **B.** Baleful means harmful or threatening. **See Lesson: Synonyms, Antonyms, and Analogies.**

24. **B.** Limber means flexible or pliable. **See Lesson: Synonyms, Antonyms, and Analogies.**

25. **D.** Pellucid means clear. **See Lesson: Synonyms, Antonyms, and Analogies.**

26. **D.** Quaint means old-fashioned. **See Lesson: Synonyms, Antonyms, and Analogies.**

27. **A.** Abduct means to kidnap or take by force. **See Lesson: Synonyms, Antonyms, and Analogies.**

28. **C.** Meager means scant, insufficient, or sparse. **See Lesson: Synonyms, Antonyms, and Analogies.**

29. **C.** Pliable means **See Lesson: Synonyms, Antonyms, and Analogies.**

30. **C.** Deleterious means **See Lesson: Synonyms, Antonyms, and Analogies.**

31. **B.** Radiant means bright or beaming. **See Lesson: Synonyms, Antonyms, and Analogies.**

32. **C.** Noxious means harmful or toxic. **See Lesson: Synonyms, Antonyms, and Analogies.**

33. **A.** Exigent means critical or urgent. **See Lesson: Synonyms, Antonyms, and Analogies.**

34. **A.** Alacrity means with speed or readiness. **See Lesson: Synonyms, Antonyms, and Analogies.**

35. **B.** Concede means to give in or accept. **See Lesson: Synonyms, Antonyms, and Analogies.**

36. **C.** Daft means insane or foolish. **See Lesson: Synonyms, Antonyms, and Analogies.**

37. **B.** Mercurial means fluctuating or unpredictable. **See Lesson: Synonyms, Antonyms, and Analogies.**

38. **A.** Brusque means abrupt or dismissive. **See Lesson: Synonyms, Antonyms, and Analogies.**

39. **C.** Dissonance means a lack or harmony. **See Lesson: Synonyms, Antonyms, and Analogies.**

40. **D.** Saccharine means overly sweet. **See Lesson: Synonyms, Antonyms, and Analogies.**

Section II. Quantitative Reasoning

1. B. The correct solution is 848. Use the addition algorithm. Carrying will be necessary when adding the digits in the tens place. **See Lesson: Basic Addition and Subtraction.**

2. D. A prime number is a positive whole number greater than or equal to 2. All primes are therefore natural numbers and integers. **See Lesson: Factors and Multiples.**

3. A. The correct solution is 5.51 inches. $14\ cm \times \frac{1\ in}{2.54\ cm} = \frac{14}{2.54} = 5.51\ in$. **See Lesson: Standards of Measure.**

4. C. The correct solution is 0.687 because 0.687 contains the smallest value in the tenths place. **See Lesson: Decimals and Fractions.**

5. B. The correct solution is a survey because the sampling is convenient and only the results are recorded. **See Lesson: Statistical Measures.**

6. B. The correct solution is $x \geq -45$.

$10x-60 \leq 12x + 30$	Multiply all terms by the least common denominator of 15 to eliminate the fractions.
$-2x-60 \leq 30$	Subtract $12x$ from both sides of the inequality.
$-2x \leq 90$	Add 60 to both sides of the inequality.
$x \geq -45$	Divide both sides of the inequality by -2.

See Lesson: Equations with One Variable.

7. B. The correct solution is (0, 5).

$y = -x + 5$	Solve the second equation for y by subtracting x from both sides of the equation.
$x + 2(-x + 5) = 10$	Substitute $-x + 5$ in for y in the first equation.
$x-2x + 10 = 10$	Apply the distributive property.
$-x + 10 = 10$	Combine like terms on the left side of the equation.
$-x = 0$	Subtract 10 from both sides of the equation.
$x = 0$	Divide both sides of the equation by -1.
$0 + y = 5$	Substitute 0 in the second equation for x.
$y = 5$	Simplify using order of operations.

See Lesson: Equations with Two Variables.

8. A. The correct solution is -520 because $-8 \times 65 = -520$ points. **See Lesson: Solving Real World Mathematical Problems.**

9. D. The correct solution is 73. The estimated weights are 20, 15, 21, and 17 pounds, and the total weight is about 73 pounds. **See Lesson: Solving Real World Mathematical Problems.**

10. C. The correct solution is $-7x + 3xy - y$.

$(-3x + 5xy - 6y) - (4x + 2xy - 5y)$

$= (-3x + 5xy - 6y) + (-4x - 2xy + 5y)$

$= (-3x - 4x) + (5xy - 2xy) + (-6y + 5y)$

$= -7x + 3xy - y$

See Lesson: Polynomials.

11. C. The correct solution is 3 because 2×10^{-4} is 0.0002 and 8×10^{-5} is 0.00008. So, the error on the first machine is about 3 times larger. **See Lesson: Powers, Exponents, Roots, and Radicals.**

12. C. The correct solution is that 60 percent of the students like pandas and monkeys: 33.33% plus 26.67% equals 60%. **See Lesson: Interpreting Graphics.**

13. B. The two lines intersect at point Z. **See Lesson: Congruence.**

14. A. The correct solution is 30. Substitute the values into the formula and simplify using the order of operations, $A = \frac{1}{2}ap = \frac{1}{2}(2)(6(5)) = 30$ square inches. **See Lesson: Similarity, Right Triangles, and Trigonometry.**

15. C. The correct solution is $\overline{XO}$ because X is on the circle and O is the center of the circle. **See Lesson: Circles.**

16. B. The correct solution is 57.3 because $C = \pi d$; $180 = 3.14d$; $d \approx 57.3$ inches. **See Lesson: Circles.**

17. B. The correct solution is 672π cubic centimeters. Substitute the values into the formula and simplify using the order of operations, $V = \pi r_1^2 h - \pi r_2^2 h = \pi 8^2(14) - \pi 4^2(14) = \pi(64)(14) - \pi(16)(14) = 896\pi - 224\pi = 672\pi$ cubic centimeters. **See Lesson: Measurement and Dimension.**

18. D. The correct solution is 147.5. The data set written in order is 120, 125, 130, 130, 145, 145, 150, 150, 150, 165, 170, 175. The middle two numbers are 145 and 150, and the mean of the numbers is 147.5. **See Lesson: Interpreting Graphics.**

19. B. The correct solution is students who like math and social studies because it is the intersection of two events. **See Lesson: Statistics & Probability: The Rules of Probability.**

20. D. The correct solution is two bins have the same frequency. The bins 400–600 and 800–1,000 have three friends. **See Lesson: Interpreting Categorical and Quantitative Data.**

21. B. Follow the order of operations (the PEMDAS mnemonic). Begin with the innermost parentheses and work outward, multiplying and dividing from left to right before adding and subtracting from left to right. Column A equals 2.

$(3 \times (4 + 9) \div 13 - 2) + 1$

$(3 \times 13 \div 13 - 2) + 1$

$(39 \div 13 - 2) + 1$

$(3 - 2) + 1$

$1 + 1$

2

For Column B, use the rules of exponents and multiplication with signed numbers. A negative number multiplied by another negative number becomes positive. Column B equals 4.

See Lesson: Basic Multiplication and Division.

22. B. A prime number is defined as a number with only 1 and itself as factors. These cannot be the same number, so prime numbers begin at the numerical value 2. A composite number has factors other than 1 and itself. The smallest composite number is 4, so Column B is greater.

See Lesson: Factors and Multiples.

23. C. Convert 2.5 miles to feet to show that the two quantities are equal. $2.5 \, mi \times \frac{5280 \, ft}{1 \, mi} = 13{,}200 \, ft$.
See Lesson: Standards of Measure.

24. A. Column A has the largest numerator when Column B is changed to a fraction with the lowest common denominator. The lowest common denominator is 12. $\frac{1}{4} = \frac{3}{12}$ and this is smaller than $\frac{5}{12}$. **See Lesson: Decimals and Fractions.**

25. B. The correct solution for Column A is $\frac{2}{3} \times \frac{4}{15} = \frac{8}{45}$. The correct solution for Column B is $\frac{1}{3} \times \frac{8}{5} = \frac{8}{15}$. Use a common denominator of 45 to compare the fractions and convert, $\frac{8}{15} \times \frac{3}{3} = \frac{24}{45}$. The quantity in Column B greater. **See Lesson: Multiplication and Division of Fractions.**

26. B. The correct solution for Column A is −6.

$2x-8 = 5x + 10$	Apply the distributive property.
$-3x-8 = 10$	Subtract $5x$ from both sides of the equation.
$-3x = 18$	Add 8 to both sides of the equation.
$x = -6$	Divide both sides of the equation by −3.

See Lesson: Equations with One Variable.

27. A. The correct solution for the system of equations is (-4, -8). The quantity in Column A is greater.

	The second equation is already solved for y.
$2(-x-12) + x = -20$	Substitute $-x-12$ in for y in the first equation.
$-2x-24 + x = -20$	Apply the distributive property.
$-x-24 = -20$	Combine like terms on the left side of the equation.
$-x = 4$	Add 24 to both sides of the equation.
$x = -4$	Divide both sides of the equation by -1.
$y = -(-4)-12$	Substitute -4 in the second equation for x.
$y = 4-12 = -8$	Simplify using order of operations.

See Lesson: Equations with Two Variables.

28. A. The original height of the plant is 3.5 inches. After four months of growth, the plant will grow a total of 3 inches. The height of the plant is 0.5 inches taller than the growth seen after four months and the quantity in Column B is greater. **See Lesson: Solving Real World Mathematical Problems.**

29. A. The correct solution for Column A is $8y^3 + 20y^2 + 6y + 15$.

$$(4y^2 + 3)(2y + 5) = 4y^2(2y + 5) + 3(2y + 5) = 8y^3 + 20y^2 + 6y + 15$$

Column B has already been solved into simplest terms. When comparing the two quantities, although y is not defined, the solution to A will always be a value of 15 more than Column B. **See Lesson: Polynomials.**

30. A. The correct solution for Column A is 125 because $5^6 \times 5^{-3} = 5^{6+(-3)} = 5^3 = 125$. The correct solution for Column B is –343 because $\frac{(-7)^2}{(-7)^{-1}} = (-7)^{2-(-1)} = (-7)^3 = -343$. **See Lesson: Powers, Exponents, Roots, and Radicals.**

31. B. For a parallelogram, there is rotational symmetry every 180° and Column A has a correct solution of 2. The correct solution for Column B is 3 because an equilateral triangle can be rotated 120°, 240°, and 360° to map onto itself. The quantity in Column B is greater. **See Lesson: Congruence.**

32. A. The correct solution for Column A is 6. Substitute the values into the formula, $216 = s^3$ Apply the cube root to both sides of the equation, $s = 6$ feet. The quantity in Column A is greater. **See Lesson: Similarity, Right Triangles, and Trigonometry.**

33. B. The radius of a circle is $\frac{1}{2}$ the diameter. The quantity in Column B is greater. **See Lesson: Circles.**

34. B. The correct solution for Column A is 8 meters. Substitute the values into the formula, $\frac{512}{3}\pi = \frac{1}{3}\pi r^2(8)$ and simplify the right side of the equation, $\frac{512}{3}\pi = \frac{8}{3}\pi r^2$. Multiply by the reciprocal of $\frac{3}{8\pi}$ with a result of $64 = r^2$, and apply the square root, $r = 8$ meters. The quantity in Column B is greater. **See Lesson: Measurement and Dimension.**

35. A. The correct solution for Column A is 35. The data set in order is 31, 32, 33, 33, 34, 35, 35, 36, 37, 37, 38, 39, and the middle numbers are both 35. Therefore, the median is 35. **See Lesson: Interpreting Graphics.**

36. B. By estimation, there are more girls' names than boys' names. The correct solution for Column A by solving is $\frac{66}{325}$. There are 12 out of 26 boys' name on the first draw and 11 out of 25 boys' name on the second draw. The probability of the event is $\frac{12}{26} \times \frac{11}{25} = \frac{132}{650} = \frac{66}{325}$. The correct solution for Column B by solving is $\frac{91}{325}$. There are 14 out of 26 girls' name on the first draw and 13 out of 25 girls' name on the second draw. The probability of the event is $\frac{14}{26} \times \frac{13}{25} = \frac{182}{650} = \frac{91}{325}$. **See Lesson: Statistics & Probability: The Rules of Probability.**

37. C. The two quantities are equal because the dot plot shows 9 dots for dog lovers and 9 total dots for fish and rabbit lovers. There 45 children like dogs as their favorite pet. There are 20 students that favor fish and 25 students that favor rabbits for a total of 45 children, making the two quantities equal. **See Lesson: Interpreting Categorical and Quantitative Data.**

Section III. Reading

1. A. Passage 1 is intended to inform readers about electroconvulsive therapy. **See Lesson: Understanding the Author's Purpose, Point of View, and Rhetorical Strategies.**

2. C. The second paragraph of passage 1 makes opinion statements about what doctors should do. This is a sign of persuasive writing. **See Lesson: Understanding the Author's Purpose, Point of View, and Rhetorical Strategies.**

3. D. Passage 2 tells a story, which is meant to entertain. **See Lesson: Understanding the Author's Purpose, Point of View, and Rhetorical Strategies.**

4. D. Passage 1 says that electroconvulsive therapy is "a genuine option for patients whose symptoms do not improve with medication." This suggests that medication should be tried first. **See Lesson: Understanding the Author's Purpose, Point of View, and Rhetorical Strategies.**

5. C. The detail about electroconvulsive therapy as "a genuine option for patients whose symptoms do not improve with medication" suggests that patients should try an option like medication first, before contemplating electroconvulsive therapy. **See Lesson: Understanding the Author's Purpose, Point of View, and Rhetorical Strategies.**

6. A. The author of Passage 1 is aware that many people have negative preconceived ideas about electroconvulsive therapy. This is true of the author of Passage 2, who does not inform herself about the facts of the situation. **See Lesson: Understanding the Author's Purpose, Point of View, and Rhetorical Strategies.**

7. D. The author of Passage 1 specifically recommends extra care in communication about electroconvulsive therapy. The doctor in Passage 2 does not seem to make any extra effort to differentiate between myth and reality. **See Lesson: Understanding the Author's Purpose, Point of View, and Rhetorical Strategies.**

8. A. The author of Passage 2 describes doctors blocking her "direct path to the door," which suggests that she feels trapped in the room. This suggests a negative, fearful outlook which is further reinforced by the comment about Big Doctor being "sadistic." **See Lesson: Understanding the Author's Purpose, Point of View, and Rhetorical Strategies.**

9. B. The author of Passage 1 uses primarily facts and logic, although she could strengthen her points by clearly identifying sources or establishing her credentials. **See Lesson: Understanding the Author's Purpose, Point of View, and Rhetorical Strategies.**

10. B. A summary must restate the ideas of the original text, not comment on them with judgments or speculation, and without adhering too closely to the wording of the original. This paragraph explains how shipping and refrigeration technology helped bananas become a major export crop. **See Lesson: Summarizing Text and Using Text Features.**

11. B. These sentences, like all effective summaries, restate the ideas of the original text in different words. Although a summary can sometimes state an implicit idea from the original text, this one does not need to do so. **See Lesson: Summarizing Text and Using Text Features.**

12. C. The structure and word choice of this sentence are so close to the original that it qualifies as plagiarism. **See Lesson: Summarizing Text and Using Text Features.**

13. B. This sentence comments on the original text rather than summarizing it. Some types of writing allow this, but it is not a summary. **See Lesson: Summarizing Text and Using Text Features.**

14. D. It would be inaccurate to say that nobody would eat bananas if modern shipping and refrigeration technology had never been invented. This is not in the original text, and logically speaking, bananas would still be eaten in the tropics regardless of changes in technology. **See Lesson: Summarizing Text and Using Text Features.**

15. A. The opening sentence of the passage makes a general claim to be read as fact since it is supported by the details of the passage. **See Lesson: Facts, Opinions, and Evaluating an Argument.**

16. C. Although this passage relates to history, a general history textbook is not highly specific to assert that the passage came from it. It likely came from a science magazine discussing fruit trade. **See Lesson: Types of Passages, Text Structure, Genre and Theme.**

17. C. The line graph would display how banana exports from Central America have risen since a time period before steamships, railways, and refrigeration to support the passage. **See Lesson: Evaluating and Integrating Data.**

18. B. This author is not very trustworthy, but he does not make any attempt to conceal the fact that he is sharing his personal opinions rather than facts. The fact that he begins with the sentence "You know what I hate?" is a clear cue that this is argumentative writing. **See Lesson: Understanding Primary Sources, Making Inferences and Drawing Conclusions.**

19. C. The sentence about freelancers not making as much money is one of the few logical points this blog post makes, but the writer does not share his sources. This makes it difficult for the reader to verify the information. **See Lesson: Understanding Primary Sources, Making Inferences and Drawing Conclusions.**

20. B. The passage raises the opposing argument that freelancing provides greater freedom for workers, but the writer does not respond to this argument. Instead, he makes a manipulatively emotional argument. **See Lesson: Understanding Primary Sources, Making Inferences and Drawing Conclusions.**

21. C. A government website tracking statistics might be a good source, but it would provide facts rather than opinions. An opinion article by an expert in the field would more likely offer what the student is looking for. **See Lesson: Understanding Primary Sources, Making Inferences and Drawing Conclusions.**

22. D. The author demonstrates a frustration with business relying on contract workers because they supposedly do not have to support employees with health benefits and still pay a smaller wage. **See Lesson: Facts, Opinions, and Evaluating an Argument.**

23. C. Using a specific example to support the author's claim would help make the argument stronger, despite making a manipulatively emotional argument. **See Lesson: Facts, Opinions, and Evaluating an Argument.**

24. A. Throughout the passage, the author is sharing personal opinions without many facts to show their reasoning. Stating "I disagree" is a more formal way to share that concluded opinion. **See Lesson: Formal and Informal Language.**

25. B. While the author of the passage is misguided in creating a compelling argument, the purpose of the writing is meant to discuss how freelancers cannot enjoy workplace freedom due to their unbenefited health and lower wages. **See Lesson: Types of Passages, Text Structure, Genre and Theme.**

26. B. The first sentence of this paragraph expresses the main idea that people should be concerned by even a small amount of climate change. This makes it the topic sentence. **See Lesson: Main Ideas, Topic Sentences, and Supporting Details.**

27. A. The topic of a sentence is a word or phrase that describes what the text is about. **See Lesson: Main Ideas, Topic Sentences, and Supporting Details.**

28. C. This paragraph argues that a small change in global temperatures could have a major result. This idea is expressed in a topic sentence at the beginning of the paragraph. **See Lesson: Main Ideas, Topic Sentences, and Supporting Details.**

29. D. The information about temperature differences in the last ice age supports the main idea that people should be concerned by global climate change. This makes it a supporting detail. **See Lesson: Main Ideas, Topic Sentences, and Supporting Details.**

30. B. All of the above sentences relate to the topic of global climate change, but only the sentence about the Little Ice Age relates directly to the main idea that a small amount of climate fluctuation is cause for concern. **See Lesson: Main Ideas, Topic Sentences, and Supporting Details.**

31. A. The author's argument discusses how small temperature changes have a large impact on the planet. A line graph to show the small change in mean global temperatures. **See Lesson: Evaluating and Integrating Data.**

32. C. A graph with the change in volume of ice on Earth's surface would show the most change to add visual emphasis to the passage. While all options have an element related to global temperature change, the graphic(s) would not provide dramatic evidence for a reader. **See Lesson: Evaluating and Integrating Data.**

33. D. To make the sentence more formal, the rewrite should avoid choppy sentence structure and unnecessary definitions or jargon. **See Lesson: Formal and Informal Language.**

34. B. The author describes how the ice age occurred with a global temperature that is five degrees less than today. With the scientific prediction that the same level of temperature change is possible, the ending question harmonizes the details and adds emphasis to the argument. **See Lesson: Formal and Informal Language.**

35. C. This passage ironically is an amusing description of an adolescent written by an adult who has enough experience to know that her daughter's huge emotions will pass and the little girl inside her will poke out. **See Lesson: Tone, Mood, and Transition Words.**

36. B. Authors use irony when their words do not literally mean what they say. The daughter is clearly having an awful day based on her words and actions, and the use of the word "marvelous" adds an ironic tone to the passage. **See Lesson: Tone, Mood, and Transition Words.**

37. A. This passage establishes irony in the opening sentence by applying a positive adjective, "celebratory" to an ordinary occurrence that is usually negative, such as the banging of a door. **See Lesson: Tone, Mood, and Transition Words.**

38. A. Effective readers would likely know this is just the life of an adolescent since we have all been through this time in our lives. Entertained would be a more likely reaction. **See Lesson: Tone, Mood, and Transition Words.**

39. A. The word "instantly" explains how quickly the mother felt "dismayed" but does not transition between ideas. **See Lesson: Tone, Mood, and Transition Words.**

40. B. "However" and "despite" both indicate a difference between ideas. **See Lesson: Tone, Mood, and Transition Words.**

41. B. "Furthermore" would be the transition to use as in: *Furthermore, she made a "tsk" sound.* This would show how the author is building on an established line of thought. **See Lesson: Tone, Mood, and Transition Words.**

42. D. The author wrote this passage to show how her daughter is being dramatic with descriptions of being "stomped right by" and being given a "quintessential eye roll". The author is not concerned about the statement because her daughter is making an assumption about her teacher because she had a bad day. **See Lesson: Facts, Opinions, and Evaluating an Argument**

Section IV. Mathematics Achievement

1. B. The failure rate is 1.32%. The failure rate is the fraction of all widgets that failed. In this case, the total number of widgets is $17 + 1{,}273 = 1{,}290$. The failure rate is therefore $\frac{17}{1290}$, which is about 1.32%. **See Lesson: Ratios, Proportions, and Percentages.**

2. C. Because 462 is not evenly divisible by 53, remainder division is necessary. Use the division algorithm to obtain 8R38. **See Lesson: Basic Multiplication and Division.**

3. B. The correct solution is points B, D, and F because these points are line $\overleftrightarrow{BF}$. **See Lesson: Congruence.**

4. C. The correct solution is 8,000 pounds. $4\,T \times \frac{2{,}000\,lb}{1\,T} = 8{,}000\,lb$. **See Lesson: Standards of Measure.**

5. D. The correct solution is line segment because the cities represent the endpoints and the segment is the distance between the two points. **See Lesson: Congruence.**

6. B. The correct solution is 40.82 because $C = \pi d \approx 3.14(13) \approx 40.82$ inches. **See Lesson: Circles.**

7. B. The correct solution is $3x^3 - 9x^2 - 2x + 6$.

$(3x^2 - 2)(x-3) = 3x^2(x-3) - 2(x-3) = 3x^3 - 9x^2 - 2x + 6$

See Lesson: Polynomials.

8. C. The two rays intersect at point D. **See Lesson: Congruence.**

9. C. The company employs 273 men. If 35% of the company's employees are women, 65% are men. Set up a proportion using 65%, which is equal to $\frac{65}{100}$ or $\frac{13}{20}$:

$$\frac{13}{20} = \frac{?}{420}$$

The unknown number is the product of 13 and $420 \div 20 = 21$, which is 273. **See Lesson: Ratios, Proportions, and Percentages.**

10. D. The correct answer is $8\frac{2}{3}$ because $\frac{13}{7} \div \frac{3}{14} = \frac{13}{7} \times \frac{14}{3} = \frac{182}{21} = 8\frac{14}{21} = 8\frac{2}{3}$. **See Lesson: Multiplication and Division of Fractions.**

11. C. The correct solution is 17. The rounded scores are 21, 20, 16, 14, and 12 points. The average $21 + 20 + 16 + 14 + 12 = 83$; $83 \div 5 \approx 17$ points for each player. **See Lesson: Solving Real World Mathematical Problems.**

12. A. When multiplying signed numbers, remember that the product of a negative and a positive is negative. Other than the sign, the process is the same as multiplying whole numbers. **See Lesson: Basic Multiplication and Division.**

13. D. The correct solution is 4 feet. Substitute the values into the formula $\frac{16}{3}\pi = \frac{2}{3}\pi r^3$, multiply both sides by the reciprocal, $8 = r^3$. Apply the cube root, $r = 2$ feet, and double the radius to find the diameter of 4 feet. **See Lesson: Measurement and Dimension.**

14. B. The correct solution is −20 because 5 is subtracted from both sides of the equation. **See Lesson: Equations with One Variable.**

15. C. The correct solution is $\frac{x^{25}}{y^{25}}$ because $\left(\frac{x^3 y^{-2}}{x^{-2} y^3}\right)^5 = \left(x^{3-(-2)} y^{-2-3}\right)^5 = \left(x^5 y^{-5}\right)^5 = x^{5 \times 5} y^{-5 \times 5} = x^{25} y^{-25} = \frac{x^{25}}{y^{25}}$. **See Lesson: Powers, Exponents, Roots, and Radicals.**

16. A. The correct solution is 300π. Substitute the values into the formula and simplify using the order of operations, $V = \pi r^2 h = \pi(5^2)(12) = \pi(25)(12) = 300\pi$ cubic centimeters. **See Lesson: Measurement and Dimension.**

17. C. The correct solution is 500 because 1×10^{-6} is 0.000001 and 2×10^{-9} is about 0.000000002. So, the lysosome is 500 times longer. **See Lesson: Powers, Exponents, Roots, and Radicals.**

18. B. The correct solution is $900 because $-300 + (-300) + (-100) + 400 + 600 + 600 = \$900$. **See Lesson: Solving Real World Mathematical Problems.**

19. C. The correct solution is 4. Substitute the values into the formula, $400 = 2l(8) + 2l(14) + 2(8)(14)$, and simplify using order of operations, $400 = 16l + 28l + 224; 400 = 44l + 224$. Then, subtract 224 from both sides of the equation and divide both sides of the equation by 44, $176 = 44l$; $l = 4$ inches. **See Lesson: Similarity, Right Triangles, and Trigonometry.**

20. D. The correct solution is $18x^4 y^5$. $6x^2 y^2(3x^2 y^3) = 18x^4 y^5$. **See Lesson: Polynomials.**

21. B. The correct solution is $\frac{1}{48}$. There are 12 total events, and there are 3 options for the first roll and 1 option for the second roll. The probability of the event is $\frac{3}{12} \times \frac{1}{12} = \frac{3}{144} = \frac{1}{48}$. **See Lesson: Statistics & Probability: The Rules of Probability.**

22. D. A prime number has only 1 and itself as factors. One approach is to start at 2 and test each successive whole number to determine whether it is a factor by dividing. If the quotient is a whole number, it is a factor. Alternatively, recall the multiplication table: 4, 27, and 49 are all products of various whole numbers (2×2, 3×9, and 7×7, respectively). Therefore they are all composite, leaving 61 by elimination. **See Lesson: Factors and Multiples.**

23. C. The correct solution is $12x^2 + 7x{-}10$.

$$(4x + 5)(3x{-}2) = 4x(3x{-}2) + 5(3x{-}2) = 12x^2{-}8x + 15x{-}10 = 12x^2 + 7x{-}10$$

See Lesson: Polynomials.

24. C. The correct solution is y^4 because $\left(\frac{x^0}{y^{-2}}\right)^2 = \frac{x^{0\times2}}{y^{-2\times2}} = \frac{x^0}{y^{-4}} = \frac{1}{y^{-4}} = y^4$. **See Lesson: Powers, Exponents, Roots, and Radicals.**

25. D. The correct solutions are $-\frac{4}{3}$ and 3. The equation can be solved by factoring.

$(3x + 4)(x{-}3) = 0$	Factor the equation.
$(3x + 4) = 0$ *and* $(x{-}3) = 0$	Set each factor equal to 0.
$3x + 4 = 0$	Subtract 4 from both sides of the equation and divide both sides of the equation by 3 to solve.
$3x = -4$	
$x = -\frac{4}{3}$	
$x{-}3 = 0$	Add 3 to both sides of the equation.
$x = 3$	

See Lesson: Solving Quadratic Equations.

26. B. The correct solution is 32π. The radius is one-half of the diameter, or 2 feet. Substitute the values into the formula and simplify using the order of operations, $V = \frac{1}{2}\pi r^2 h = \frac{1}{2}\pi(2^2)(16) = \frac{1}{2}\pi(4)(16) = 32\pi$ cubic feet. **See Lesson: Measurement and Dimension.**

27. C. The correct solution is $2x^2 + 5xy{-}11y^2$.

$$(6x^2 + 3xy{-}5y^2){-}(4x^2{-}2xy + 6y^2) = (6x^2 + 3xy{-}5y^2) + (-4x^2 + 2xy{-}6y^2) = (6x^2{-}4x^2) + (3xy + 2xy) + (-5y^2{-}6y^2) = 2x^2 + 5xy{-}11y^2$$

See Lesson: Polynomials.

28. B. The correct solution is 16. Substitute the values into the formula $448 = 2l(14)$ and simplify the right side of the equation, $448 = 28l$. Divide both sides of the equation by 28, $l = 16$ feet. **See Lesson: Similarity, Right Triangles, and Trigonometry.**

29. B. The correct solutions are (-1.4, 4.2) and (1.4, -4.2).

$x^2 + (-3x)^2 = 20$	Substitute $-3x$ in for y in the second equation.
$x^2 + 9x^2 = 20$	Apply the exponent.
$10x^2 = 20$	Combine like terms on the left side of the equation.
$x^2 = 2$	Divide both sides of the equation by 10.
$x = \pm 1.4$	Apply the square root to both sides of the equation.
$y = -3(1.4) = -4.2$	Substitute 1.4 in the first equation and multiply.
$y = -3(-1.4) = 4.2$	Substitute -1.4 in the first equation and multiply.

See Lesson: Equations with Two Variables.

30. D. The correct solution is $\frac{5}{6}$. There are 6 results that have a sum of 10 or greater. The probability of not rolling a 10 or greater is $1 - \frac{6}{36} = \frac{30}{36} = \frac{5}{6}$. **See Lesson: Statistics & Probability: The Rules of Probability.**

31. D. The correct solution is Street 2 had the greater median, and Street 2 had a higher interquartile range. The larger median is Street 2. The higher interquartile range is Street 2, which means the data is more spread out from the median. **See Lesson: Interpreting Categorical and Quantitative Data.**

32. D. The correct solution is 5.6 because $A = \frac{1}{2}\pi r^2; 50 = (\frac{1}{2})3.14 r^2; 50 = 1.57 r^2; 31.85 = r^2$; $r \approx 5.6$ inches. **See Lesson: Circles.**

33. D. The correct solution is D. Each bin contains 50 cars, and the frequencies are 4, 9, 5, 3, and 3. **See Lesson: Interpreting Categorical and Quantitative Data.**

34. A. The first two points are on the negative x-axis, and the third point is in the first quadrant. **See Lesson: Similarity, Right Triangles, and Trigonometry.**

35. B. The correct solution is 8. The quiz score of 8 occurred 8 times, which is the mode. **See Lesson: Interpreting Graphics.**

36. C. The correct solutions are $-5 \pm \sqrt{35}$. **See Lesson: Solving Quadratic Equations.**

$x^2 + 10x = 10$	Add 10 to both sides of the equation.
$x^2 + 10x + 25 = 10 + 25$	Complete the square, $(\frac{10}{2})^2 = 5^2 = 25$.
	Add 25 to both sides of the equation.
$x^2 + 10x + 25 = 35$	Simplify the right side of the equation.
$(x + 5)^2 = 35$	Factor the left side of the equation.
$x + 5 = \pm \sqrt{35}$	Apply the square root to both sides of the equation.
$x = -5 \pm \sqrt{35}$	Subtract 5 from both sides of the equation.

37. C. The correct solution is $7\frac{7}{12}$ because $3\frac{1}{3} + 2\frac{1}{2} + 1\frac{3}{4} = 3\frac{4}{12} + 2\frac{6}{12} + 1\frac{9}{12} = 6\frac{19}{12} = 7\frac{7}{12}$ yards of fabric. **See Lesson: Solving Real World Mathematical Problems.**

38. C. Use the division algorithm. Determining the first digit of the quotient requires using the first three digits in the dividend. **See Lesson: Basic Multiplication and Division.**

39. A. The correct solutions are (1, -2) and (-1, 2).

$x^2 + (-2x)^2 = 5$	Substitute $-2x$ in for y in the second equation.
$x^2 + 4x^2 = 5$	Apply the exponent.
$5x^2 = 5$	Combine like terms on the left side of the equation.
$x^2 = 1$	Divide both sides of the equation by 5.
$x = \pm 1$	Apply the square root to both sides of the equation.
$y = -2(1) = -2$	Substitute 1 in the first equation and multiply.
$y = -2(-1) = 2$	Substitute -1 in the first equation and multiply.

See Lesson: Equations with Two Variables.

40. B. The correct solution is Band 2 had the greater average, but Band 3 had a higher standard deviation. The largest mean is Band 2. Although Band 1 had a higher deviation than Band 2, option B is the best answer because Band 3 had the largest standard deviation, which means the data are more spread out from the mean. **See Lesson: Interpreting Categorical and Quantitative Data.**

41. D. The correct solution is entertainment and homework total is the same as the amount of time in school because the sum of entertainment and homework is 25%. **See Lesson: Interpreting Graphics.**

42. A. The correct solution is $\frac{3}{70}$ because $\frac{3}{10} \times \frac{1}{7} = \frac{3}{70}$. **See Lesson: Multiplication and Division of Fractions.**

43. A. The correct solution is systematic sampling because a specific number of customers from a group of customers are selected. **See Lesson: Statistical Measures.**

44. C. The correct solutions are –0.88 and –9.13. **See Lesson: Solving Quadratic Equations.**

$x = \frac{-10 \pm \sqrt{10^2 - 4(1)(8)}}{2(1)}$	Substitute 1 for a, 10 for b, and 8 for c.
$x = \frac{-10 \pm \sqrt{100 - 32}}{2}$	Apply the exponent and perform the multiplication.
$x = \frac{-10 \pm \sqrt{68}}{2}$	Perform the subtraction.
$x = \frac{-10 \pm 8.25}{2}$	Apply the square root.
$x = \frac{-10 + 8.25}{2}, x = \frac{-10 - 8.25}{2}$	Separate the problem into two expressions.
$x = \frac{-1.75}{2} = -0.88, x = \frac{-18.25}{2} = -9.13$	Simplify the numerator and divide.

45. B. The correct solution is 2.44 ounces. $69\ g \times \frac{1\ oz}{28.3\ g} = \frac{69}{28.3} = 2.44\ oz$. **See Lesson: Standards of Measure.**

46. D. All of the answer choices are equal. Although answer C is not in lowest terms, it is equal to $\frac{8}{125}$, which is equal to 0.064 or 6.4%. **See Lesson: Ratios, Proportions, and Percentages.**

47. D. The correct answer is $\frac{3121}{5000}$ because 62.42% as a fraction is $\frac{6242}{10000} = \frac{3121}{5000}$. **See Lesson: Decimals and Fractions.**

48. A. A number is divisible by its factors. Because division by 0 is undefined, 0 cannot be a factor. **See Lesson: Factors and Multiples.**

ISEE PRACTICE EXAM 2

SECTION I. VERBAL REASONING

You have 20 minutes to complete 40 questions.

This section is divided into two parts containing two types of questions. Answer the questions in Part One and then move on to complete Part Two.

Part One – Synonyms

Directions: Each synonym question consists of a word in capital letters followed by four answer choices. Select the one word that is most nearly the same in meaning as the word in capital letters.

1. **DESOLATE**
   A. bleak
   B. bright
   C. inhabited
   D. protected

2. **IMMUTABLE**
   A. alterable
   B. fluctuating
   C. unstable
   D. unchangeable

3. **BOISTEROUS**
   A. aloof
   B. calm
   C. loud
   D. solemn

4. **ODIOUS**
   A. delightful
   B. disgusting
   C. pleasant
   D. unpleasant

5. **RECALCITRANT**
   A. amenable
   B. compliant
   C. defiant
   D. yielding

6. **ACCOST**
   A. confront
   B. dodge
   C. evade
   D. slight

7. **SACROSANCT**
   A. mundane
   B. profane
   C. revered
   D. secular

8. **FORESAKE**
   A. abandon
   B. continue
   C. maintain
   D. return

9. **PRUDENT**
   A. careful
   B. hasty
   C. leery
   D. wasteful

10. **UMBRAGE**
    A. comfort
    B. delight
    C. favor
    D. offense

11. **SCURRILOUS**
    A. clean
    B. moral
    C. upright
    D. vulgar

12. **ELUCIDATE**
    A. clarify
    B. conceal
    C. distract
    D. mystify

13. PACIFY

    A. appease   C. provoke

    B. irritate   D. soften

14. TRANQUIL

    A. chaotic   C. serene

    B. excited   D. turbulent

15. CIRCUMSPECT

    A. cautious   C. indiscreet

    B. foolish   D. negligent

16. EXACERBATE

    A. aggravate   C. improve

    B. alleviate   D. pacify

17. WINSOME

    A. charming   C. gloomy

    B. dour   D. melancholy

18. VIGOR

    A. dullness   C. inertia

    B. energy   D. repose

19. DILIGENT

    A. careful   C. lethargic

    B. ignorant   D. negligent

20. PITTANCE

    A. generosity   C. smidgen

    B. plenty   D. whole

Part Two – Sentence Completion.

Directions: Answer the following sample questions. Select the word or pair of words that most correctly completes the sentence.

Note: *To assist you in finding the right answer among the answer choices, one-word answers are listed alphabetically and two-word answers are listed alphabetically by the first word.*

21. When James noticed the dish towel had caught fire near the stove, he _____ it with water to extinguish the flames.

    A. desiccated   C. scorched

    B. doused   D. seared

22. Jacqueline, a seasoned traveler, has learned to never leave home without her favorite coat because it is _____ to even the most driving rain and brutal windstorms.

    A. absorbent   C. negotiable

    B. impervious   D. porous

23. As we biked through the Danish countryside, we admired the _____ tulips in gardens along the route.

    A. burgeoning   C. perishing

    B. expiring   D. withering

24. The boy could not explain how the vase came to be broken, but he denied any _____ intent.

    A. amiable   C. genial

    B. benevolent   D. malicious

25. Eliza has a gift for _____ the most delightful stories of adventure whenever she is caught coming home past curfew by her grandmother.

    A. authenticating   C. fabricating

    B. confirming   D. substantiating

26. The computer store technician suggested he _____ the manual before attempting to use his futuristic, high-tech computer.

    A. evade   C. overlook

    B. neglect   D. peruse

27. The indignant student angrily _____ the accusation that he had cheated on the test.

    A. avowed   C. repudiated

    B. conceded   D. validated

28. The _____veterinarian provided free services and vaccines to the pets of low-income families at her clinic once a month.

    A. benevolent   C. truculent

    B. malevolent   D. virulent

29. The shady salesperson _____ the unsuspecting young man into thinking that the old jalopy had an engine that would not break down.

    A. debunked   C. disclosed

    B. deluded   D. divulged

30. We had to _____our vacation in Hawaii due to weather reports of a possible volcanic eruption.

    A. abbreviate   C. amplify

    B. aggrandize   D. augment

31. In a celebration befitting a hero, the admiral awarded the returning soldiers for their _____ military service during the long campaign.

    A. contemptible   C. ignominious

    B. detestable   D. meritorious

32. The teacher used a soft voice to _____ the small child down the slide at recess.

    A. browbeat   C. oblige

    B. cajole   D. pester

33. The ants were attracted by the _____ aroma of the cheese that was left on the picnic blanket after we finished lunch.

    A. bland   C. mellow

    B. insipid   D. pungent

34. The teacher read a story about rich children who _____ a little girl because she came from a poor family to support her lesson about being kind to others, no matter what their circumstances.

    A. commended   C. ostracized

    B. endorsed   D. sanctioned

35. While ice fishing with her dad, Carley was careful not to get too close to the _____water as she peered into the fishing hole on the pond.

    A. algid   C. sultry

    B. fervent   D. torrid

36. The _____ man was unhappy with his appearance, so he joined a gym and began a weight loss program.

    A. angular   C. lanky

    B. gaunt   D. portly

37. The mountain path looked
_____ as it wound its way
through the dark forest lined with steep
cliffs to the ominous fog covered peak.

A. assuring   C. fortifying

B. daunting   D. heartening

38. The man could not stop the
_____ rush of water coming
from the broken pipe so he hastily called
the plumber.

A. meager   C. scant

B. profuse   D. trickling

39. The children knew that their
stern nanny would be arriving
to _____ them for breaking a
dish while clearing the supper table.

A. acquit   C. pardon

B. chastise   D. spare

40. Principal Flynn hoped this year's Senior
Prank would not be as _____ as
last year as it had taken him weeks to get
the chalk-paint designs off his new car!

A. honest   C. nefarious

B. just   D. sublime

SECTION II. QUANTITATIVE REASONING

Part One: Word Problems

1. Given an expression with no parentheses, which should be evaluated first?

   A. Division

   B. Addition

   C. Subtraction

   D. Any of the above

2. If a number has 3 and 5 as factors, which statement best describes that number?

   A. The number is 15.

   B. The number is prime.

   C. The number has 15 as a factor.

   D. The number has only two prime factors.

3. Identify 1435 in 12-hour clock time.

   A. 12:35 a.m.

   B. 2:35 a.m.

   C. 12:35 p.m.

   D. 2:35 p.m.

4. Write 290% as a fraction.

   A. $2\frac{9}{200}$

   B. $2\frac{9}{100}$

   C. $2\frac{9}{20}$

   D. $2\frac{9}{10}$

5. Multiply the following numbers.

   $\frac{2}{5} \times 3$

   A. $\frac{2}{15}$

   B. $1\frac{1}{5}$

   C. $2\frac{3}{5}$

   D. $3\frac{2}{5}$

6. Solve the equation for the unknown.

   $\frac{1}{2}x + 3 = \frac{1}{4}x - 2$

   A. −20

   B. −10

   C. 10

   D. 20

7. Solve the system of equations.

   $-4x + 5y = 32$
   $4x - y = 0$

   A. (2, 2)

   B. (8, 8)

   C. (2, 8)

   D. (8, 2)

8. Four walls in a room need to be painted. The dimensions of two walls are $12\frac{1}{2}$ feet by $11\frac{3}{4}$ feet, and the other two walls are $11\frac{3}{4}$ feet by $10\frac{1}{8}$ feet. What is the estimated area in square feet to be painted?

   A. 242

   B. 276

   C. 484

   D. 552

9. In a state, the highest elevation is 1,450 feet and the lowest elevation is −80 feet. What is the difference in the elevations in feet?

   A. 1,370

   B. 1,430

   C. 1,530

   D. 1,570

10. Apply the polynomial identity to rewrite $x^2 - 100$.

    A. $(x-10)^2$

    B. $(x-10)(x + 10)$

    C. $(x + 10)^2$

    D. $x^2 - 10^2$

11. The land area of Colorado about 1×10^5 square miles, and the land area of Ohio is about 4×10^4 square miles. How many times larger is the land area of Colorado?

    A. 2

    B. 3

    C. 4

    D. 5

12. Select the statement that is true for the angles.

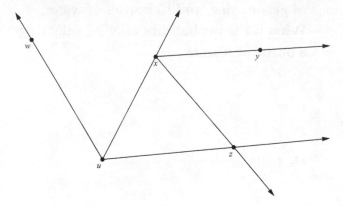

A. Points *X* and *Y* are vertices of angles.

B. Points *X* and *U* are vertices of angles.

C. Points *W* and *Y* are vertices of angles.

D. Points *W* and *U* are vertices of angles.

13. $\triangle DEF$ has points $D(-3, 6)$, $E(-2, -4)$, and $F(5, 0)$. After a transformation, the points are $D'(6, 3)$, $E'(-4, 2)$, and $F'(0, -5)$. What is the transformation between the points?

A. Reflection across the *x*-axis

B. Reflection across the *y*-axis

C. Rotation of 90° counterclockwise

D. Rotation of 270° counterclockwise

14. Given the coordinates for a square $(-3,-5),(-3,4),\,(6,4)\,(6,-5)$, find the length of each side of the square.

A. 3 units   C. 9 units

B. 6 units   D. 12 units

15. A box in the shape of a right rectangular prism has dimensions of 6 centimeters by 7 centimeters by 8 centimeters. What is the volume in cubic centimeters?

A. 280   C. 560

B. 336   D. 672

16. A circular manhole cover has a circumference of 183 inches. Find the area to the nearest tenth of a square inch. Use 3.14 for π.

A. 574.6   C. 2,298.5

B. 846.8   D. 2,658.9

17. Identify an arc of the circle.

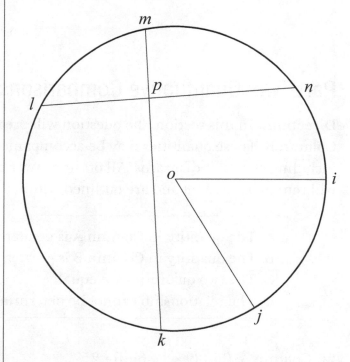

A. $\widehat{LM}$ C. $\widehat{OJ}$

B. $\widehat{PN}$ D. $\widehat{LP}$

18. A house has an attic in the shape of a square pyramid. The height of the attic is 6 feet, and perimeter of the base of the room is 200 feet. What is the volume in cubic feet of air in the empty attic?

A. 5,000   C. 15,000

B. 10,000   D. 20,000

19. A set of 8 numbers has 50 as the smallest number, and the median is 55. Which of the following sets could be the numbers?

   A. 50, 51, 53, 53, 55, 57, 59, 60

   B. 50, 52, 54, 54, 56, 58, 59, 60

   C. 50, 51, 53, 55, 56, 57, 58, 59

   D. 50, 52, 54, 54, 55, 58, 58, 59

20. A bucket contains 4 bottles of apple juice, 6 bottles of orange juice, 5 bottles of grape juice, and 10 bottles of water. What is the probability of NOT selecting a bottle of water?

   A. $\frac{1}{5}$

   B. $\frac{2}{5}$

   C. $\frac{3}{5}$

   D. $\frac{4}{5}$

Part Two: Quantitative Comparisons

Directions: In this section, the question will present two different values as either Column A or Column B. These quantities may be accompanied by additional information in many forms including charts or diagrams. All of the answer options for each question within this section will remain consistent and are outlined within the box below.

> A. The quantity in Column A is greater.
> B. The quantity in Column B is greater.
> C. The two quantities are equal.
> D. The relationship cannot be determined from the information given

21. Column A: $(15 \div (9 \times 2 \div 6) -1) \times 2$

   Column B: 2^3

22. Column A: The highest factor of 1,000

   Column B: A multiple of ten

23. Column A: 10 quarts

   Column B: 300 fluid ounces

24. Column A: 15%

   Column B: 0.15

25. Column A: $2 \times \frac{3}{4}$

   Column B: $\frac{5}{7} \div \frac{4}{7}$

26. $-x-15 = -17$

   Column A: x

   Column B: -2

27. $x + 3y = 34$
    $-3x + y = -12$

   Column A: x

   Column B: y

28. John has a $50 bill in his wallet. He goes to the movies and buys a ticket for $8.00 along with a popcorn, pretzel, chocolate bar and drink, each costing $4.25.

   Column A: The amount of money John spent

   Column B: The amount of change John received

A. The quantity in Column A is greater.
B. The quantity in Column B is greater.
C. The two quantities are equal.
D. The relationship cannot be determined from the information given

29. Column A: $27x^3 - 8$

    Column B: $(3x-2)(9x^2 + 6x + 4)$

30. $x^3 = -216$

    Column A: x

    Column B: -6

31. Column A: The number of symmetry lines for an isosceles trapezoid

    Column B: 1

32. **A cube has a side length of 15 millimeters.**

    Column A: The volume of the cube in cubic millimeters

    Column B: 4,000 millimeters³

33. **A circle has a diameter of 16 centimeters.**

    Column A: The area of the circle in ϖ square centimeters

    Column B: 16ϖ centimeters²

34. **A cylinder has a volume of 800π cubic centimeters and a radius of 10 centimeters.**

    Column A: The height of the cylinder in centimeters

    Column B: 40 centimeters

35. **A toy bin contains 12 yellow balls, 3 orange balls, and 5 white balls.**

    Column A: The probability of selecting a yellow ball

    Column B: The probability of selecting an orange or a white ball

329

A. The quantity in Column A is greater.

B. The quantity in Column B is greater.

C. The two quantities are equal.

D. The relationship cannot be determined from the information given

36. The bar chart shows the number of boys and girls who participate in sports.

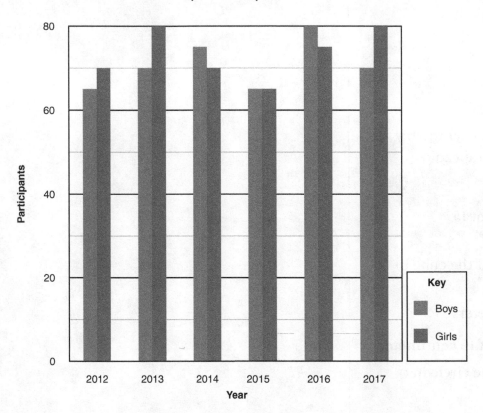

Column A: The difference between the number of girls and boys in 2013

Column B: The difference between the number of girls and boys in 2017

37. The box plot below shows the winning margin of two basketball teams during the season.

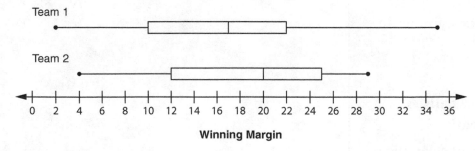

Column A: The interquartile range for Team 1

Column B: The interquartile range for Team 2

SECTION I. READING

55 MINUTES, 42 QUESTIONS

Directions: Each passage (or pair of passages) below is followed by a number of questions. Read each passage (or pair), then choose the best answer to each question based on what is stated or implied in the passage (or passages), and in any graphics that may accompany the passage.

Read the following text and answer questions 1-9.

WiseWear gear provides you with cutting-edge technology to enhance your performance and optimize your training. WiseWear products include
5   sensors to track your heart rate, activity level, and calorie burn during workouts. Information is automatically uploaded to your phone and organized so you can track your improvement over time with
10 just a tap of the screen.

Concerned about comfort? We've got you covered. WiseWear clothing is made with high-tech synthetic compression fabrics to promote circulation and wick away
15 sweat while you work out.

Top-level pro athletes, like ultra-marathoner Uri Schmidt, rely on WiseWear for training and competition. Shouldn't you do the same?

1. **The purpose of this passage is to:**

    A. decide.   C. persuade.

    B. inform.   D. entertain.

2. **With which statement would the author of this passage most likely agree?**

    A. Americans who work out put too much emphasis on performance and not enough on enjoyment.

    B. People who do not buy high-end exercise gear do not deserve to get a good workout and stay healthy.

    C. The best way to achieve a healthy body is to follow a simple exercise plan and avoid hyped-up gadgets.

    D. Consumers want help pushing their bodies to the limit and gathering information about their exercise performance.

3. **Which detail from the passage, if true, is factual?**

    A. WiseWear transforms the user into a better and more informed athlete.

    B. WiseWear gear is the most comfortable exercise clothing on the market.

    C. WiseWear products contain sensors that track the user's body signals.

    D. WiseWear users are bound to improve at the sport of their choice over time.

4. The author of the passage includes details about WiseWear's comfort and ease of use in order to appeal to the reader's:

   A. reason.   C. feelings.

   B. trust.   D. knowledge.

5. The author most likely includes the detail about a famous ultra-marathoner in order to make readers:

   A. understand that WiseWear gear is factually the best on the market.

   B. take a weak position when they attempt to argue against the point.

   C. trust that scientists have really studied WiseWear gear and proven it worthy.

   D. feel an association between WiseWear products and a person they admire.

6. Where would the author best place this passage to serve its purpose?

   A. In a fashion blog

   B. In a scientific journal

   C. In the sports section of a magazine

   D. As part of a research study on runners

7. What graphic(s) should the author use to best assist the passage's argument?

   A. A picture of the products offered

   B. A picture of Uri Schmidt wearing WiseWear gear in an ultra-marathon

   C. A phone screenshot for some of the tracked performance provided by the sensors of the products

   D. A graphic showing performance without WiseWear gear and with WiseWear gear

8. Reread lines 11-12 ("Concerned about ... covered"). Who is the "We" referring to?

   A. The author and any co-authors

   B. Ultra-marathoner Uri Schmidt and other top-level pro athletes

   C. The makers of WiseWear clothing

   D. The synthetic compression fabrics that help make the clothing comfortable

9. The author poses an informal question at the end of the passage. Why?

   A. It is meant to be a simply ironic question that entices a reader to buy the product.

   B. The entire passage is informal and it would be out of the text structure to make the question formalized.

   C. The author is switching the passage voice to be one of a pro athlete.

   D. The author proposed a question earlier within the passage and wants to keep the passage consistent with more informal questions.

Read the following text and summary. Then answer questions 10-17.

Original Text:

Nobody groaned when Candace arrived at the door. Several people's smiles did look a bit plastic for a moment, but they
5 could hardly be blamed for that.

Poor Gladys, who had to sit right next to Candace on the couch, accepted her fate with good grace. Afterward she developed a hilarious and highly popular
10 impression of Candace's donkey bray laugh, but in the moment Gladys was the picture of welcome and friendliness.

All of the *invited* guests took their cue from Gladys and showed Candace a good
15 time. By the time Candace went home, she looked pink with pleasure at how well she'd been treated. It was quite inspiring. After all, well-bred kids should never be unkind.

20 **Summary:**

When a widely disliked girl named Candace arrives uninvited to a party, all the invited guests pretend to welcome her. Because they resist the urge to be
25 cruel to her face, they congratulate themselves on their so-called kindness.

10. Which detail in the summary is implicitly but not explicitly included in the original text?

A. A girl named Candace arrives at a party.

B. The invited guests feel the urge to be cruel.

C. The invited guests pretend to welcome Candace.

D. Candace is pink with pleasure when she goes home.

11. Which detail from the original text most clearly implies that the invited guests dislike Candace?

A. It describes Candace looking "pink with pleasure."

B. It states that "well-bred kids should never be unkind."

C. It says the invited guests "showed Candace a good time."

D. It mentions "poor Gladys" who "had to" be near Candace.

12. Why wouldn't an effective summary comment on Candace's personality?

A. Only the invited guests really know who Candace is.

B. Her personality is irrelevant to the events of the story.

C. That would express a judgment about the original text.

D. The original text does not describe Candace's personality.

13. Which sequence shows in what order the events occurred?

A. Candace looks pink with pleasure, people's smiles look plastic, Candace leaves.

B. Candace arrives, Candace leaves, Gladys mocks Candace's "donkey bray laugh."

C. Candace arrives, Gladys accepts her fate with good grace, people's smiles look plastic.

D. Gladys pretends to welcome Candace, Gladys mocks Candace's "donkey bray laugh," Candace leaves.

14. What does the expression "Poor Gladys" from line 6 mean in the passage?

   A. Gladys does not have any wealth

   B. The author is ironically making fun of Gladys

   C. Gladys is pitied for sitting next to Candace

   D. Gladys is disliked by Candace because Candace purposefully sat next to her on the couch

15. What is the author implying in the summary by describing the actions of the invited guests as "so-called kindness" in line 26?

   A. *So* is acting as adjective. The guests were excessively kind which is highlighted by Candace being "pink with pleasure" in the original text.

   B. The guests are only considered kind because they resisted the urge to be cruel to Candace's face.

   C. The summary can explicitly describe the guests being kind, while the original text must only imply their kindness with the guests' actions.

   D. The expression shows that the guests believed that they were kind to Candace when they actually weren't because they made fun of her behind her back.

16. Based on the original text, which of the following is a fact?

   A. The party-goers dislike Candace

   B. Candace knew she was not invited to the party

   C. Everyone at the party is a well-bred kid

   D. Candace was treated cruelly at the party

17. The author uses several expressions that demonstrate that the invited guests hid their displeasure for Candace's presence at the party well. Which of the following phrases does not support this?

   A. she looked pink with pleasure

   B. she developed a hilarious and highly popular impression of Candace's donkey bray laugh

   C. smiles did look a bit plastic for a moment

   D. well-bred kids should never be unkind

Read the following passage and answer questions 18-25.

Adelia stood on the porch in her bathrobe.

"Mr. Snuggles?" she called. "Mr. Snuggles! Come on in, you little vermin."

5 She peered up and down the street. Sighing, she went back inside and, a moment later, emerged with a metal bowl and a spoon. She rapped on the bowl several times.

10 "Mr. Snuggles? Breakfast!"

When Mr. Snuggles did not appear, Adelia reached inside and grabbed some keys off a low table. Cinching her bathrobe tightly around her waist, she

15 climbed into the car.

"It's not like I have anything better to do than look for you again," she said.

18. **From the text above, you can infer that Adelia is:**

   A. looking for a pet.

   B. calling her son home.

   C. a kindhearted person.

   D. unconcerned for Mr. Snuggles.

19. **Which detail does not provide evidence to back up the conclusion that Adelia is feeling frustrated?**

   A. She calls Mr. Snuggles "you little vermin."

   B. She has not yet gotten dressed for the day.

   C. She complains about having to search for Mr. Snuggles.

   D. She sighs when Mr. Snuggles does not immediately appear.

20. **Which detail from the text supports the inference that Adelia cares what happens to Mr. Snuggles, even if she is angry at him?**

   A. She goes out to look for him.

   B. She keeps her car keys near the door.

   C. She is joking when she calls him "vermin."

   D. She says she wants to be doing something else.

21. **Which sentence of dialogue, if added to the passage, would support the conclusion that Mr. Snuggles actually belongs to someone else?**

   A. "What ever possessed me to adopt a cat?"

   B. "You shed on my sheets, you pee on my couch, and now *this*."

   C. "Next time Raul goes out of town, I'm going to babysit his plants instead."

   D. "If you make me late again, I'm going to lose my job. Then how will we eat?"

22. **Which detail provides evidence that Adelia is an adult?**

   A. Adelia uses advanced vocabulary such as the word "vermin".

   B. She called out to Mr. Snuggles and rapped on the metal bowl.

   C. She grabbed keys and climbed into the car.

   D. She went to look for Mr. Snuggles in her bathrobe.

23. Which clue from the text serves as evidence that Mr. Snuggles has done this before?

   A. She calls out, "Mr. Snuggles! Come on in, you little vermin."

   B. Adelia rapped on the bowl several times.

   C. She knew where the keys were without looking.

   D. She says, "It's not like I have anything better to do than look for you again."

24. In line 10, Adelia yells out "Breakfast!" Why is this acceptable?

   A. Adelia must yell out louder than she raps on the metal bowl with a spoon.

   B. She is calling out to Mr. Snuggles and trying to grab his attention wherever he is.

   C. Since Adelia is wearing a bathrobe, it is acceptable to speak informally.

   D. It is not acceptable. A reader can infer this because the name she calls out includes the title "Mr."

25. How would this passage best be described and why?

   A. Serious, the passage shows that Mr. Snuggles is gone and is in danger

   B. Comedic, the passage displays relatable details about how Adelia handles not knowing where Mr. Snuggles is

   C. Formal, the passage includes direct quotes from what Adelia is yelling and her actions in between

   D. Emotional, Adelia's yelling shows how uncontrollably angry she is

Please read the text below and answer questions 26-35.

It is perhaps unsurprising that fad diets are so common given the level of obesity in American society. But over the long term, most fad diets are harmful both 5 to the health and to the waistline. Many such diets advocate cutting out one major nutrient, such as fats or carbohydrates. Others suggest fasting over long periods or eating from fixed menu options that 10 may not meet the body's needs. Most of these diets are highly impractical, and many lead directly or indirectly to binge eating and other unhealthy behaviors.

26. The topic of this paragraph is:

   A. fasting.   C. fad diets.

   B. obesity.   D. binge eating.

27. The topic sentence of this paragraph is:

   A. But over the long term, most fad diets are harmful both to the health and to the waistline.

   B. Many such diets advocate cutting out one major nutrient, such as fats or carbohydrates.

   C. It is perhaps unsurprising that fad diets are so common given the level of obesity in American society.

   D. Most of these diets are highly impractical, and many lead directly or indirectly to binge eating and other unhealthy behaviors.

28. If the author added a description of a man who attempted several fad diets and ended up heavier than ever, what type of information would this be?

    A. A main idea

    B. A topic sentence

    C. A supporting detail

    D. An off-topic sentence

29. Read the following description of the paragraph:

The author argues unfairly against fad diets without taking their good qualities into account.

Why is this *not* a valid description of the main idea?

    A. It is not accurate; the author of the paragraph is stating facts, not opinions.

    B. It is not objective; the person summarizing the main idea is adding a judgment.

    C. It is not accurate; the author of the paragraph does not argue against fad diets.

    D. It is not objective; the person summarizing the main idea ignores a sentence about the benefits of dieting.

30. Why doesn't a statistic about early childhood obesity rates belong in this paragraph?

    A. It does not directly support the main idea that fad diets are harmful.

    B. Readers might feel hopeless to solve the problem the author identifies.

    C. Statistics should never be used as supporting details in persuasive writing.

    D. It would act as a second topic sentence and confuse readers about the main idea.

31. The author finds a scientific survey that reveals over 75% of adults quit a fad diet before they've reached four weeks of following one. Why would this be useful?

    A. It is not useful because it is a survey.

    B. Any statistic above 50% that supports a claim is beneficial information for the argument.

    C. The author has yet to incorporate any data from scientific studies.

    D. The survey shows a popular opinion that fad diets are impractical.

32. Reread lines 10-13 ("Most of these diets ... behaviors.") Why does the author need to elaborate further on this?

   A. The sentence is only an opinion until the author provides factual evidence to support the claim.

   B. The author has only explained why fad diets are impractical, but not given evidence that they lead to unhealthy behaviors.

   C. The sentence is unrelated and the author needs to relate the idea back to the passage for it to make sense.

   D. The author has not given any specific examples of a fad diet.

33. The author states that eating from a narrow selection of menu options may not meet the body's needs. Based on the passage, should this statement be considered an opinion or a fact?

   A. Opinion because the author does not give a direct example of a fad diet that does not meet the body's needs.

   B. Opinion because the author does not mention that a fad diet could meet the body's needs but still have a negative affect by oversupplying certain nutrition values.

   C. Fact because the passage is meant to be informative about negative health effects of fad dieting.

   D. Fact because the passage clearly only makes verifiable claims in support of their argument.

34. The author finds the following information in a related article:

"Many fat adults fail their diets because cutting out nutrients during the day leads them to eat a crazy amount of gross food before bed."

How could the author rewrite the quote to formalize it for the passage and properly support their argument?

   A. Related articles suggest that binge eating before bed is directly related to impractical fad diets.

   B. Fad diets lead adults who are fat to eat uncontrollably since they don't eat nutrients like fats or carbohydrates.

   C. Further information concludes that overweight adults will likely to binge eat late at night when they cut out nutrients from their diet.

   D. One study shows that eating gross foods late at night will continue a cycle of failed fad diets for adults.

35. The author decides to incorporate information about three different adults: two who tried a fad diet and one who followed a diet plan from a dietician. How might the author use this to shift the text structure to best support the argument?

A. The author can compare and contrast all of the results to reveal, if the evidence concludes, that all fad diets lead to unhealthy behaviors.

B. The information could be used, if the evidence concludes, as proof that fad diets are not the solution for overweight adults trying to lose weight.

C. The adults who tried a fad diet, if evidence concludes, did not succeed in their dieting goals could be depicted by each adult's physical description before and after their diet regime.

D. The author can create a cause and effect piece to prove, if evidence concludes, that fad diets are harmful to a person's health.

Read the passage and answer questions 36-42.

Dear Mr. O'Hara,

I am writing to let you know how much of a positive impact you have made on our daughter. Before being in your
5 algebra class, Violet was math phobic. She would shut down when new concepts would not come to her easily. As a result, she did not pass many tests. Despite this past struggle, she has blossomed in your
10 class! Your patience and dedication have made all the difference in the world. Above all, your one-on-one sessions with her have truly helped her in ways you cannot imagine. She is a more confident
15 and capable math student, thanks to you. We cannot thank you enough.

Fondly,

Bridgette Foster

36. Which adjective best describes the tone of this passage?

A. Arrogant   C. Friendly

B. Hopeless   D. Appreciative

37. Which phrase from the passage has an openly appreciative and warm tone?

A. I am writing to let you now

B. you have made on our daughter

C. made all the difference

D. We cannot thank you enough

38. What mood would this passage most likely evoke in the math teacher, Mr. O'Hara?

A. Calm

B. Grateful

C. Sympathetic

D. Embarrassment

39. **Which transition word or phrase from the passage adds emphasis to the writer's point?**

    A. Being

    B. As a result

    C. Despite

    D. Above all

40. **This passage is best described as:**

    A. a formal letter because it is properly addressed and signed.

    B. a formal letter because it is about a parent's daughter to the math teacher.

    C. an informal letter because it expresses an appreciative tone.

    D. an informal letter because it is signed with "Fondly".

41. **Based on the passage, a reader could assume that:**

    A. Mr. O'Hara enjoyed teaching Violet.

    B. Bridgette Foster could not help her daughter in math.

    C. Violet passed her math class with Mr. O'Hara.

    D. Mr. O'Hara taught Violet to love math.

42. **If Bridgette Foster wanted to submit another copy of her letter to the school, which of the following would help show the principal how good a teacher Mr. O'Hara is?**

    A. A description of Violet's test scores before and after Mr. O'Hara taught her

    B. A letter from Violet saying thank-you to Mr. O'Hara

    C. Additional signatures from Violet's family members on the letter

    D. A record of the lessons Mr. O'Hara tutored Violet in

SECTION IV. MATHEMATICS ACHIEVEMENT

1. A half circle has an area of 45 square centimeters. Find the diameter to the nearest tenth of a centimeter. Use 3.14 for π.

    A. 2.7
    B. 5.4
    C. 10.8
    D. 16.2

2. Solve the equation for the unknown.

    $3x-8+5+2x = 4x-x+6$

    A. $-\frac{9}{2}$
    B. $-\frac{2}{9}$
    C. $\frac{2}{9}$
    D. $\frac{9}{2}$

3. Which is different from the others?

    A. 0.5
    B. 1:2
    C. $\frac{1}{2}$
    D. 1:2 odds

4. Solve the equation by any method.

    $6x^2 + 19x + 10 = 0$

    A. $\frac{5}{2}$ and $\frac{2}{3}$
    B. $\frac{5}{2}$ and $-\frac{2}{3}$
    C. $-\frac{5}{2}$ and $\frac{2}{3}$
    D. $-\frac{5}{2}$ and $-\frac{2}{3}$

5. A surveyor asked students if they are attending school after high school. The students who responded "No" were excluded. What type of sampling is used?

    A. Quota sampling
    B. Volunteer sampling
    C. Purposive sampling
    D. Convenience sampling

6. The area of a half circle is 48 square centimeters. Find the circumference of the curved portion of the half circle to the nearest tenth of a centimeter. Use 3.14 for π.

    A. 17.3
    B. 24.5
    C. 34.5
    D. 49.0

7. How many dogs are necessary to make a cat-to-dog ratio of 3:2 in an area with 1,425 cats?

    A. 285
    B. 950
    C. 2,138
    D. 2,375

8. An even roll of a number cube results in +2 points, and an odd roll of a number cube is –3 points. If there are 14 even numbers and 11 odd numbers, then how many points are scored?

    A. –61
    B. –5
    C. 5
    D. 61

9. A research study aims to find the average age of all retail workers. A group asks all retail workers in Ohio their birth years. What is a name for this study?

    A. Census
    B. Survey
    C. Experiment
    D. Observational study

10. In a backyard, $\frac{1}{6}$ of the yard is a garden, $\frac{2}{5}$ is landscaped, and $\frac{1}{3}$ is for play. How much of the yard is available for other use?

    A. $\frac{1}{10}$
    B. $\frac{2}{15}$
    C. $\frac{13}{15}$
    D. $\frac{9}{10}$

11. Find the height in centimeters of a cylinder with a volume of 800π cubic centimeters and a radius of 10 centimeters.

    A. 8
    B. 10
    C. 40
    D. 80

**12. Select the figure that is rotated 270°
counterclockwise about the origin.**

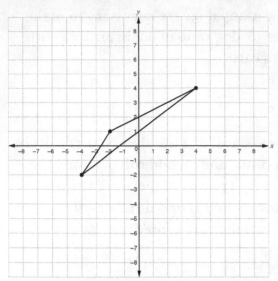

C.

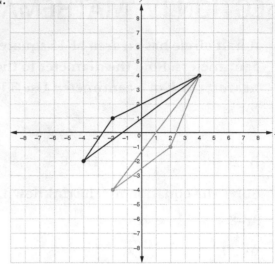

A.

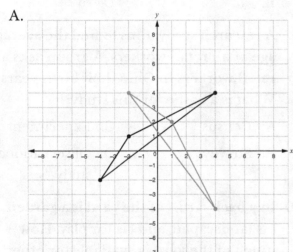

D.

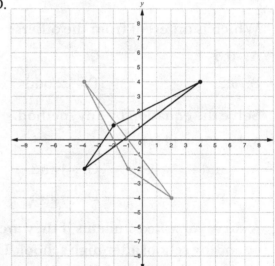

B.

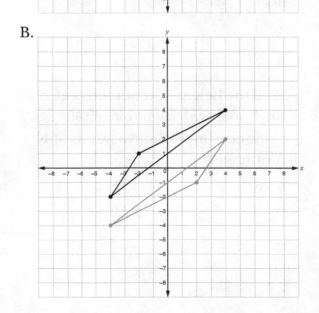

13. Solve the equation for the unknown.

$$\frac{3}{4}(x + 3) - 2 = 3 - \frac{2}{3}(x + 1)$$

A. $\frac{6}{5}$ C. $\frac{8}{5}$

B. $\frac{25}{17}$ D. $\frac{28}{17}$

14. Simplify.

$$\left((2^{-2})^{-1}\right)^{-2}$$

A. $\frac{1}{16}$ C. 8

B. $\frac{1}{8}$ D. 16

15. Write $\frac{1}{5}$ as a percent.

    A. 15%   C. 25%

    B. 20%   D. 30%

16. A right triangular prism has a triangular base with legs of 5 centimeters and 12 centimeters and a hypotenuse of 13 centimeters. What is the surface area in square centimeters if the height is 2 centimeters?

    A. 60   C. 180

    B. 120   D. 240

17. Simplify.

$(9x^{-2}y^3)^2$

    A. $\frac{1}{81x^4y^6}$ C. $\frac{81x^4}{y^6}$

    B. $\frac{81y^6}{x^4}$ D. $81x^4y^6$

18. A grain silo is made up of a cylinder with a hemisphere on top. The diameter of the silo is 40 feet, and the height of the cylinder is 50 feet. What is the volume to the nearest cubic foot? Use 3.14 for π.

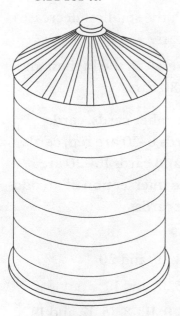

    A. 79,547   C. 385,173

    B. 96,293   D. 519,146

19. Solve the equation by the quadratic formula.

$12x^2 + x - 3 = 0$

    A. -0.46 and -0.54

    B. 0.46 and -0.54

    C. -0.46 and 0.54

    D. 0.46 and 0.54

20. The line chart shows the number of cars sold each month. Which statement is true?

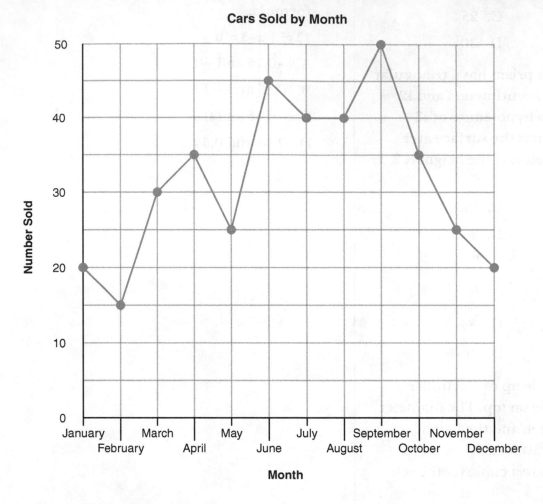

Cars Sold by Month

A. June had the most cars sold.

B. There were two months where 30 cars were sold.

C. The months with the smallest decreases all sold 5 fewer cars.

D. The difference between the highest and lowest month is 30 cars.

21. The original height of a plant is 1.75 inches. The plant grows an average of 1.08 inches each month for 6 months. What is the new height of the plant in inches?

A. 7.13

B. 7.23

C. 8.13

D. 8.23

22. In a deck of 20 number cards, cards 1–5 are green, cards 6–10 are red, cards 11–15 are yellow, and cards 16–20 are blue. Describe the intersection of an odd number and blue cards.

A. Cards 17 and 19

B. Cards 16, 17, 18, 19, and 20

C. Cards 11, 13, 15, 17, and 19

D. Cards 1, 3, 5, 7, 9, 11, 13, 15, 17, and 19

23. A family has three children. What is the probability that the family has three boys?

A. $\frac{1}{8}$ C. $\frac{1}{4}$

B. $\frac{1}{6}$ D. $\frac{1}{2}$

24. Solve the system of equations.

$$y = 4x$$
$$x^2 + y^2 = 17$$

A. (4, 1) and (-4, -1)

B. (-4, 1) and (4, -1)

C. (-1, 4) and (1, -4)

D. (1, 4) and (-1, -4)

25. Write $83.\overline{3}\%$ as a decimal.

A. $8.\overline{3}$ C. $0.08\overline{3}$

B. $0.8\overline{3}$ D. 0.0083

26. A college class had one group use a traditional textbook and another group use an online textbook. The attendance for the class was compared. Determine the independent variable.

A. Class attendance

B. Type of textbook

C. Grade for the class

D. Online version of the textbook

27. Multiply.

$$3\frac{1}{4} \times 2\frac{2}{3}$$

A. $6\frac{1}{2}$ C. $8\frac{1}{2}$

B. $6\frac{2}{3}$ D. $8\frac{2}{3}$

28. Multiply.

$$(5x + 2)(6x + 7)$$

A. $30x^2 + 47x + 14$ C. $30x^2 + 35x + 14$

B. $30x^2 + 12x + 14$ D. $30x^2 + 14$

29. A wedge of cheese is in the shape of a right triangular prism. The area of the base is 30 square inches. What is the height in inches of the cheese if the volume is 150 cubic inches?

A. 2.5   C. 7.5

B. 5   D. 10

30. The wait times in minutes for the last 15 customers at a restaurant are 20, 17, 18, 15, 19, 45, 22, 18, 25, 28, 16, 19, 23, 20, 25. What is the effect of removing the outlier on the mean and median?

A. The mean and median decrease.

B. There is no change to the mean or median.

C. The mean decreases, but there is no change to the median.

D. The median decreases, but there is no change to the mean.

31. Multiply.

$$(2x + 3)(x^2 - 3x - 4)$$

A. $2x^3 + 3x^2 - x - 12$

B. $2x^3 - 3x^2 - x - 12$

C. $2x^3 + 3x^2 - 17x - 12$

D. $2x^3 - 3x^2 - 17x - 12$

32. Perform the operation.

$$(8x + 2xy - 4y) + (-7x - 3xy + 2y)$$

A. $x + xy - 2y$ C. $x - xy + 2y$

B. $x - xy - 2y$ D. $x + xy + 2y$

33. A cell phone company projects $\frac{1}{2}$ of making \$3 million, $\frac{3}{10}$ of making \$1 million, and $\frac{1}{5}$ of losing \$2 million. What is the expected value?

A. \$1.4 million   C. \$1.8 million

B. \$1.5 million   D. \$2.0 million

34. Solve the equation by the square root method.

    $16x^2 = 49$

    A. $\pm \frac{7}{16}$
    C. $\pm \frac{49}{16}$

    B. $\pm \frac{7}{4}$
    D. $\pm \frac{49}{4}$

35. What is the minimum number of unique prime factors for a composite number?

    A. 0
    C. 2

    B. 1
    D. Not enough information

36. Given the coordinates for a square $(-6,6), (6,6), (6,-6)(-6,-6)$, find the length of each side of the square.

    A. 0 units
    C. 12 units

    B. 6 units
    D. 18 units

37. Solve the equation for the unknown x.

    $y = mx + b$

    A. $y - bm = x$
    C. $\frac{y-b}{m} = x$

    B. $y + bm = x$
    D. $\frac{y+b}{m} = x$

38. The area of a circle is 18 square inches. Find the circumference of the circle to the nearest tenth of an inch. Use 3.14 for π.

    A. 2.4
    C. 15.1

    B. 7.5
    D. 30.1

39. Which percent is closest to the ratio 7:3?

    A. 23%
    C. 73%

    B. 43%
    D. 233%

40. Solve the system of equations.

    $y = -4x - 4$
    $y = -5x - 4$

    A. (0, -4)
    C. (0, 4)

    B. (-4, 0)
    D. (4, 0)

41. Solve.

    $x^2 = 169$

    A. –10, 10
    C. –12, 12

    B. –11, 11
    D. –13, 13

42. Each section of a science class has 36 slots, and each section must be full to be assigned a professor. If 203 students try to sign up, how many will not receive a slot?

    A. 1
    C. 23

    B. 3
    D. 36

43. What are the rays that intersect at point Y?

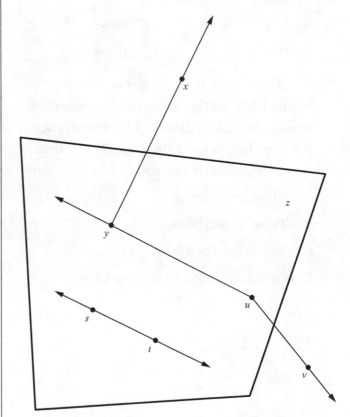

    A. $\overrightarrow{YX}$ and $\overrightarrow{UY}$
    C. $\overrightarrow{XY}$ and $\overrightarrow{UY}$

    B. $\overrightarrow{YX}$ and $\overrightarrow{YU}$
    D. $\overrightarrow{XY}$ and $\overrightarrow{YU}$

44. The box plot shows the number of weekly sales by a business during the year. Which statement is true for the box plot?

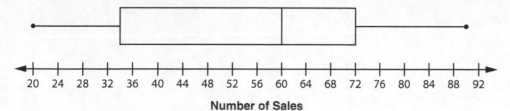

Number of Sales

A. The median is 34 sales.

B. The median is 72 sales.

C. The difference between the maximum and minimum is 40 sales.

D. The difference between the maximum and minimum is 70 sales.

45. Divide the following expression.

$\frac{8}{9} \div \frac{5}{7}$

A. $\frac{11}{45}$

B. $\frac{40}{63}$

C. $1\frac{11}{45}$

D. $1\frac{40}{63}$

46. Evaluate the expression.

$7,946 \div 58$

A. 79

B. 136

C. 137

D. 238

47. Convert 4,388 decimeters to meters.

A. 438.8 meters

B. 43.88 meters

C. 4.388 meters

D. 0.4388 meters

48. Elementary school teachers were told that children's parents were high school graduates, did not complete college, or were college graduates. Then, the children's grades were compared. Determine the dependent variable.

A. College graduate

B. Children's grades

C. High school graduate

D. Did not complete college

ISEE Practice Exam 2
Answer Key with Explanatory Answers

Section I. Verbal Reasoning

1. **A.** Desolate means deserted, lifeless, or bleak. **See Lesson: Synonyms, Antonyms, and Analogies.**

2. **D.** Immutable means not susceptible to change, unchangeable. **See Lesson: Synonyms, Antonyms, and Analogies.**

3. **C.** Boisterous means loud or energetic. **See Lesson: Synonyms, Antonyms, and Analogies.**

4. **B.** Odious means strongly displeasing or disgusting. **See Lesson: Synonyms, Antonyms, and Analogies.**

5. **C.** Recalcitrant means defiant. **See Lesson: Synonyms, Antonyms, and Analogies.**

6. **A.** Accost means to approach or confront aggressively. **See Lesson: Synonyms, Antonyms, and Analogies.**

7. **C.** Sacrosanct means holy, sacred, or revered. **See Lesson: Synonyms, Antonyms, and Analogies.**

8. **A.** Foresake means to forget or abandon. **See Lesson: Synonyms, Antonyms, and Analogies.**

9. **A.** Prudent means cautious or careful. **See Lesson: Synonyms, Antonyms, and Analogies.**

10. **D.** Umbrage means to have anger, resentment, or offense. **See Lesson: Synonyms, Antonyms, and Analogies.**

11. **D.** Scurrilous means crude or vulgar. **See Lesson: Synonyms, Antonyms, and Analogies.**

12. **A.** Elucidate means to clarify. **See Lesson: Synonyms, Antonyms, and Analogies.**

13. **A.** Pacify means to soothe, ease, or appease. **See Lesson: Synonyms, Antonyms, and Analogies.**

14. **C.** Tranquil means calm, peaceful, or serene. **See Lesson: Synonyms, Antonyms, and Analogies.**

15. **A.** Circumspect means cautious. **See Lesson: Synonyms, Antonyms, and Analogies.**

16. **A.** Exacerbate means to make more violent or to aggravate. **See Lesson: Synonyms, Antonyms, and Analogies.**

17. **A.** Winsome means attractive or charming. **See Lesson: Synonyms, Antonyms, and Analogies.**

18. **B.** Vigor means vitality or energy. **See Lesson: Synonyms, Antonyms, and Analogies.**

19. **A.** Diligent means showing care or careful. **See Lesson: Synonyms, Antonyms, and Analogies.**

20. **C.** Pittance means a very small amount or smidgen. **See Lesson: Synonyms, Antonyms, and Analogies.**

21. **B.** Doused means to drench or saturate. **See Lesson: Synonyms, Antonyms, and Analogies.**

22. **B.** Impervious means waterproof. **See Lesson: Synonyms, Antonyms, and Analogies.**

23. **A.** Burgeoning means to blossom. **See Lesson: Synonyms, Antonyms, and Analogies.**

24. **D.** Malicious means harmful. **See Lesson: Synonyms, Antonyms, and Analogies.**

25. **C.** Fabricating means to inventing or making something up. **See Lesson: Synonyms, Antonyms, and Analogies.**

26. **D.** Peruse means to examine carefully. **See Lesson: Synonyms, Antonyms, and Analogies.**

27. **C.** Repudiated means to reject. **See Lesson: Synonyms, Antonyms, and Analogies.**

28. **A.** Benevolent means kind or caring. **See Lesson: Synonyms, Antonyms, and Analogies.**

29. **B.** Deluded means to deceive or mislead. **See Lesson: Synonyms, Antonyms, and Analogies.**

30. **A.** Abbreviate means to shorten. **See Lesson: Synonyms, Antonyms, and Analogies.**

31. **D.** Meritorious means deserving praise. **See Lesson: Synonyms, Antonyms, and Analogies.**

32. **B.** Cajole means to urge or coax. **See Lesson: Synonyms, Antonyms, and Analogies.**

33. **D.** Pungent means having a sharp or strong smell. **See Lesson: Synonyms, Antonyms, and Analogies.**

34. **C.** Ostracized means to exclude from a community. **See Lesson: Synonyms, Antonyms, and Analogies.**

35. **A.** Algid means frigid or cold. **See Lesson: Synonyms, Antonyms, and Analogies.**

36. **D.** Portly means fat, chubby, or round. **See Lesson: Synonyms, Antonyms, and Analogies.**

37. **B.** Daunting means intimidating. **See Lesson: Synonyms, Antonyms, and Analogies.**

38. **B.** Profuse means abundant or lavish. **See Lesson: Synonyms, Antonyms, and Analogies.**

39. **B.** Chastise means to criticize or scold. **See Lesson: Synonyms, Antonyms, and Analogies.**

40. **C.** Nefarious means wicked or villainous. **See Lesson: Synonyms, Antonyms, and Analogies.**

Section II. Quantitative Reasoning

1. A. The order of operations (recall the mnemonic PEMDAS) requires multiplication and division before addition and subtraction. **See Lesson: Basic Multiplication and Division.**

2. C. Because 3 and 5 are prime factors of the number, its prime factorization includes them. Furthermore, because a number is the product of all its prime factors, the number in this question must either be 15 or have 15 as a factor. It may or may not be 15, so it may have more than two prime factors. See **Lesson: Factors and Multiples.**

3. D. The correct solution is 2:35 p.m. Subtract 1200 from the time, 1435 − 1200 = 2:35 p.m. See **Lesson: Standards of Measure.**

4. D. The correct answer is $2\frac{9}{10}$ because 290% as a fraction is $2\frac{90}{100} = 2\frac{9}{10}$. **See Lesson: Decimals and Fractions.**

5. B. The correct solution is $1\frac{1}{5}$ because $\frac{2}{5} \times \frac{3}{1} = \frac{6}{5} = 1\frac{1}{5}$. **See Lesson: Multiplication and Division of Fractions.**

6. A. The correct solution is −20.

$2x + 12 = x-8$	Multiply all terms by the least common denominator of 4 to eliminate the fractions.
$x + 12 = -8$	Subtract x from both sides of the equation.
$x = -20$	Subtract 12 from both sides of the equation.

See **Lesson: Equations with One Variable.**

7. C. The correct solution is (2, 8).

$4y = 32$	Add the equations.
$y = 8$	Divide both sides of the equation by 4.
$4x-8 = 0$	Substitute 8 in the second equation for y.
$4x = 8$	Add 8 to both sides of the equation.
$x = 2$	Divide both sides of the equation by 4.

See **Lesson: Equations with Two Variables.**

8. D. The correct solution is 552 because the dimensions of the walls are approximately 13 feet by 12 feet and 12 feet by 10 feet. The area is $2(13)(12) + 2(12)(10) = 312 + 240 = 552$ square feet. **See Lesson: Solving Real World Mathematical Problems.**

9. C. The correct solution is 1,530 because $1,450-(-80) = 1,450 + 80 = 1,530$ feet. **See Lesson: Solving Real World Mathematical Problems.**

10. B. The correct solution is $(x-10)(x + 10)$. The expression x^2-100 is rewritten as $(x-10)(x + 10)$ because the value of a is x and the value of b is 10. **See Lesson: Polynomials.**

11. B. The correct solution is 3 because the land area of Colorado is about 100,000 square miles and the land area of Ohio is about 40,000 square miles. So, the land area is about 3 times larger. **See Lesson: Powers, Exponents, Roots, and Radicals.**

12. B. The correct solution is points X and U are vertices of angles because these points are the intersection of two rays. **See Lesson: Congruence.**

13. D. The correct solution is a rotation of 270° counterclockwise because the points (x, y) become $(y, -x)$. **See Lesson: Congruence.**

14. C. The correct solution 9 units. The difference between the x-coordinates is $6-(-3) = 9$ units, and the difference between the y-coordinates is $4-(-5) = 9$ units. **See Lesson: Similarity, Right Triangles, and Trigonometry.**

15. B. The correct solution is 336. Substitute the values into the formula and simplify using the order of operations, $V = lwh = 6(7)(8)$ cubic centimeters. **See Lesson: Similarity, Right Triangles, and Trigonometry.**

16. D. The correct solution is 2,659.0. $C = 2\pi r$; $183 = 2(3.14)r$; $183 = 6.28r$; $r \approx 29.1$ centimeters. $A = \pi r^2 \approx 3.14(29.1)^2 \approx 3.14(846.81) \approx 2,658.9$ square inches. **See Lesson: Circles.**

17. A. The correct solution is $\widehat{LM}$ because L and M are on the circle. **See Lesson: Circles.**

18. A. The correct solution is 5,000. The side length of the square is 200 divided by 4, or 50 feet. Substitute the values into the formula and simplify using the order of operations, $V = \frac{1}{3}Bh = \frac{1}{3}(s^2)$ $h = \frac{1}{3}(50^2)6 = \frac{1}{3}(2500)(6) = 5,000$ cubic feet. **See Lesson: Measurement and Dimension.**

19. B. The correct solution is 50, 52, 54, 54, 56, 58, 59, 60. The middle two numbers are 54 and 56, which give an average of 55 for the median value. **See Lesson: Interpreting Graphics.**

20. C. The correct solution is $\frac{3}{5}$. There are 10 bottles of water, making the probability of not selecting a bottle of water $1-\frac{10}{25} = \frac{15}{25} = \frac{3}{5}$. **See Lesson: Statistics & Probability: The Rules of Probability.**

21. C. Follow the order of operations (the PEMDAS mnemonic). Begin with the innermost parentheses and work outward, multiplying and dividing from left to right before adding and subtracting from left to right.

(15 ÷ (9 x 2 ÷ 6) -1) x 2

(15 ÷ (18 ÷ 6) − 1) x 2

(15 ÷ 3 − 1) x 2

(5 − 1) x 2

4 x 2

8

See Lesson: Basic Multiplication and Division.

22. D. The highest factor of 1,000 is 1,000. 1,000 is a multiple of ten, but Column B has not given numerical boundaries to determine if the multiple of ten is less than, equal to, or greater than 1,000. The relationship cannot be determined from the information given.

See Lesson: Factors and Multiples.

23. A. Convert 10 quarts to fluid ounces to determine that Column A is equivalent to 320 fluid ounces. $10 \, qt \times \frac{2 \, pt}{1 \, qt} \times \frac{16 \, fl \, oz}{1 \, pt} = 320 \, fl. \, oz.$ **See Lesson: Standards of Measure.**

24. C. A percent is a ratio value with 100 as the denominator. 15% is equivalent to $\frac{15}{100}$ and 0.15.

See Lesson: Decimals and Fractions.

25. A. The correct solution for Column A is $\frac{2}{1} \times \frac{3}{4} = \frac{6}{4} = 1\frac{2}{4} = 1\frac{1}{2}$. The correct solution for Column B is $\frac{5}{7} \times \frac{7}{4} = \frac{35}{28} = 1\frac{7}{28} = 1\frac{1}{4}$. The quantity in Column A is greater. **See Lesson: Multiplication and Division of Fractions.**

26. A. The correct solution for Column A is 2.

$-x = -2$	Add 15 to both sides of the equation.
$x = 2$	Divide both sides of the equation by -1.

See Lesson: Equations with One Variable.

27. B. The correct solution for the system of equations is (7, 9). The quantity in Column B is greater.

$x = -3y + 34$	Solve the first equation for x by subtracting $3y$ from both sides of the equation.
$-3(-3y + 34) + y = -12$	Substitute $-3y + 34$ in for x in the second equation.
$9y - 102 + y = -12$	Apply the distributive property.
$10y - 102 = -12$	Combine like terms on the left side of the equation.
$10y = 90$	Add 102 both sides of the equation.
$y = 9$	Divide both sides of the equation by 10.
$x + 3(9) = 34$	Substitute 9 in the first equation for y.
$x + 27 = 34$	Simplify using order of operations.
$x = 7$	Subtract 27 from both sides of the equation.

See Lesson: Equations with Two Variables.

28. C. John spent a total of $25 because $8.00 + $4.25 + $4.25 + $4.25 + $4.25 = $25. Since he had a $50 bill, John would have received $25 back in change. **See Lesson: Solving Real World Mathematical Problems.**

29. C. When the polynomial identity is applied to Column A the correct solution is $(3x-2)(9x^2 + 6x + 4)$. The expression $27x^3 - 8$ is rewritten as $(3x-2)(9x^2 + 6x + 4)$ because the value of a is $3x$ and the value of b is 2. The two quantities are equal. **See Lesson: Polynomials.**

30. C. The correct solution is –6 because the cube root of –216 is –6. **See Lesson: Powers, Exponents, Roots, and Radicals.**

31. C. The correct solution for Column A is one line of symmetry. There is a vertical line of symmetry that maps the isosceles trapezoid onto itself. **See Lesson: Congruence.**

32. B. The correct solution for Column A is 3,375. Substitute the values into the formula and simplify using the order of operations, $V = s^3 = 15^3 = 3,375$ cubic millimeters. The quantity in Column B is greater. **See Lesson: Similarity, Right Triangles, and Trigonometry.**

33. A. The correct solution for Column A is 64ϖ. The radius is 8 centimeters and $A = \pi r^2 = \pi(8)^2 = 64\pi$ centimeters^2. **See Lesson: Circles.**

34. B. The correct solution for Column A is 8. Substitute the values into the formula, $800\pi = \pi$ $10^2 h$, and apply the exponent, $800\pi = \pi(100)h$. Then, divide both sides of the equation by 100π, $h = 8$ centimeters. The quantity in Column B is greater. **See Lesson: Measurement and Dimension.**

35. A. By estimation, there are more yellow balls than orange and white balls combined. The correct solution for Column A by solving is $\frac{3}{5}$ because there are 12 yellow balls out of 20 total balls. $\frac{12}{20} = \frac{3}{5}$. The correct solution for Column B is $\frac{2}{5}$. There are 3 orange balls and 5 white balls out of 20 total balls. The probability is $\frac{3}{20} + \frac{5}{20} = \frac{8}{20} = \frac{2}{5}$. **See Lesson: Statistics & Probability: The Rules of Probability.**

36. C. The correct solution for both Column A and Column B is 10 because the difference between boys and girls is 10 participants. **See Lesson: Interpreting Graphics.**

37. B. The interquartile range is 12 points for Team 1 and 13 points for Team 2. **See Lesson: Interpreting Categorical and Quantitative Data.**

Section III. Reading

1. C. This is an advertisement. Although it includes some information its primary purpose is to convince you to buy something. This makes it a persuasive text. **See Lesson: Understanding the Author's Purpose, Point of View, and Rhetorical Strategies.**

2. D. It is difficult to know much about the true feelings of advertising writers because it's their job to sell products, not say what they believe. However, it is a fair bet that advertising writers believe people will pay money for products presented the way they describe. **See Lesson: Understanding the Author's Purpose, Point of View, and Rhetorical Strategies.**

3. C. Much of the information in this advertisement is not verifiable, but the fact that the clothing tracks the body's signals with sensors is a fact. **See Lesson: Understanding the Author's Purpose, Point of View, and Rhetorical Strategies.**

4. C. The advertisement highlights several aspects of WiseWear gear, such as the comfort and ease of use, that suggest the potential customer will feel good using the products. These details appeal to the emotions. **See Lesson: Understanding the Author's Purpose, Point of View, and Rhetorical Strategies.**

5. D. Celebrity endorsements in advertisements appeal to the emotions by associating a product for sale with a person who is widely admired. **See Lesson: Understanding the Author's Purpose, Point of View, and Rhetorical Strategies.**

6. C. The passage is an advertisement for sports clothing. The audience it would appeal to would be interested in sports. **See Lesson: Types of Passages, Text Structure, Genre and Theme.**

7. D. Although a screenshot of what the gear can provide, it would only be a portion for the data the gear is said to provide and would not be the most compelling graphic for the advertisement. A sensor tracked performance graphic would be better utilized because the author is arguing that WiseWear gear enhances training and sport performance. Of the options given, the author should use a graphic showing the difference of athletic performance with and without the product. **See Lesson: Evaluating and Integrating Data.**

8. **C. The passage is an advertisement meant to appeal to an audience on behalf of the brand name. See Lesson: Understanding the Author's Purpose, Point of View, and Rhetorical Strategies.**

9. A. The passage is structured around appealing to a reader that would buy the WiseWear products. **See Lesson: Formal and Informal Language.**

10. B. The original text says explicitly that the invited guests welcome Candace, but it only implies that they want to be cruel to her. The original text shows this partly by saying that Gladys and the other guests mock Candace when she is gone. **See Lesson: Summarizing Text and Using Text Features.**

11. D. The original text shows the guests' dislike for Candace partly by expressing sympathy for the girl who has to sit next to her. **See Lesson: Summarizing Text and Using Text Features.**

12. D. The original text clearly implies that the invited guests at the party are being cruel, but it does not clearly show how Candace thinks or feels. **See Lesson: Summarizing Text and Using Text Features.**

13. B. The word "afterward" and the phrase "in the moment" indicate Gladys mocks Candace's laugh only after Candace is out of earshot. **See Lesson: Summarizing Text and Using Text Features.**

14. C. Gladys is pitied because she had to sit next to the uninvited guest. **See Lesson: Summarizing Text and Using Text Features.**

15. D. The author is emphasizing that the guests believed they were kind because the led Candace to believe she was welcomed at the party while everyone else knew that she wasn't. **See Lesson: Summarizing Text and Using Text Features.**

16. A. The original text describes how the party-goers hid how they felt about Candace to her face. However, it details that they took cues from Gladys to treat her well contrary to their feelings and made fun of her after she left. **See Lesson: Facts, Opinions, and Evaluating an Argument.**

17. C. Although Gladys made fun of Candace's laugh, Candace never saw that behavior because it happened *after* the party. Even if Candace did not see, the detail about several people's smiles looking plastic shows the instance that the guests did not hide their feelings. **See Lesson: Facts, Opinions, and Evaluating an Argument.**

18. A. Adelia is attempting to call a pet, not a child. You can infer this because she calls Mr. Snuggles "vermin" and bangs on a bowl with a spoon to get his attention. **See Lesson: Understanding Primary Sources, Making Inferences and Drawing Conclusions.**

19. B. Adelia's bathrobe is not evidence that she is frustrated at Mr. Snuggles. **See Lesson: Understanding Primary Sources, Making Inferences and Drawing Conclusions.**

20. A. Adelia tries repeatedly to call Mr. Snuggles, and when he does not come, she goes out to look for him. This implies that she does care about him, even if she is angry at him. **See Lesson: Understanding Primary Sources, Making Inferences and Drawing Conclusions.**

21. C. The line about Raul and his plants does not explicitly say Adelia is babysitting Mr. Snuggles, but it suggests that she is caring for the pet for someone else. **See Lesson: Understanding Primary Sources, Making Inferences and Drawing Conclusions.**

22. C. A reader can infer the Adelia is looking for a pet. A reader can also conclude that she is an adult looking for a pet because she goes to look for him in a car. **See Lesson: Understanding Primary Sources, Making Inferences and Drawing Conclusions.**

23. D. Adelia's statement using the word "again" provides evidence that she has had to go out and look for him in the past. **See Lesson: Understanding Primary Sources, Making Inferences and Drawing Conclusions.**

24. B. The reader can infer that Adelia is trying to get Mr. Snuggles to come home by offering breakfast and making sounds associated with being fed. **See Lesson: Formal and Informal Language.**

25. B. While a reader can infer that Mr. Snuggles is missing, Adelia's reaction shows that she is not overly concerned because he has gone missing before. Her actions display an annoyance, but the idea that she prioritizes finding him despite not being dressed provides clues that the passage is meant to entertain the reader. **See Lesson: Types of Passages, Text Structure, Genre and Theme.**

26. C. The topic of this paragraph is related to obesity, but it is more narrowly focused on the fad diets people use as they try to control their weight. **See Lesson: Main Ideas, Topic Sentences, and Supporting Details.**

27. A. The first sentence of this paragraph leads the reader toward the main idea, which is expressed next in a topic sentence about the harmfulness of fad diets. **See Lesson: Main Ideas, Topic Sentences, and Supporting Details.**

28. C. A description of a failed experience with fad diets would function as a supporting detail in this paragraph about the negative consequences of fad diets. **See Lesson: Main Ideas, Topic Sentences, and Supporting Details.**

29. B. Although this description of the paragraph would be valid in an opinion response, it is not merely a statement of the main idea because it adds the reader's judgment about the paragraph. **See Lesson: Main Ideas, Topic Sentences, and Supporting Details.**

30. A. Although a statistic about early childhood obesity might belong in a passage focusing on obesity rates, it would be off-topic information in this paragraph on the harm of fad dieting. **See Lesson: Main Ideas, Topic Sentences, and Supporting Details.**

31. D. Even though the author has not yet provided specific examples, it is not a requirement to use scientific data studies to strengthen an argument. If adults dislike following fad diets, the survey proves that fad diets are impractical in support of the author's claims. **See Lesson: Evaluating and Integrating Data.**

32. B. The author has not provided evidence to support the claim that fad diets may go beyond a failed diet, but actually lead to unhealthy behaviors. **See Lesson: Facts, Opinions, and Evaluating an Argument.**

33. C. The author describes that a fixed menu option *may* not meet a body's needs, to make it a more general statement, rather than an opinion. The passage has not provided any details to make a reader skeptic of their argument, but still lacks supporting evidence and details. **See Lesson: Facts, Opinions, and Evaluating an Argument.**

34. C. The author should be careful in utilizing the quote because of its highly informal language in respect to a more formal passage. However, if the author wanted to rewrite it, C is the only option that gets rid of all informal descriptions such as "fat adults" and "gross food" while not falsifying the quote. **See Lesson: Formal and Informal Language.**

35. D. The new found information could be utilized in many ways to shift the text structure, but only the last option describes how the author can use it to support their argument that fad diets are harmful. **See Lesson: Types of Passages, Text Structure, Genre and Theme.**

36. D. The tone of this letter is appreciative as the author openly thanks the teacher for all he has done for her daughter. **See Lesson: Tone, Mood, and Transition Words**

37. D. The author of the letter uses a lot of respectful and admiring language, but the line "We cannot thank you enough" has an especially appreciative and warm tone. **See Lesson: Tone, Mood, and Transition Words**

38. B. A teacher receiving a note like this would likely feel grateful. **See Lesson: Tone, Mood, and Transition Words**

39. D. The phrase "above all" adds emphasis to the writer's point that the teacher has made a significant impact on the daughter. **See Lesson: Tone, Mood, and Transition Words**

40. B. The relationship between the letter writer and who it is addressed to reveals that the letter would be considered formal, even if it did or did not follow formal writing patterns. **See Lesson: Formal and Informal Language.**

41. C. The letter describes how Mr. O'Hara was very patient and helped Violet into being a capable math student, but does not give direct insight to how either of them feel. It can be assumed that Violet passed her class because she "blossomed" and Bridgette Foster feels extreme gratitude. **See Lesson: Facts, Opinions, and Evaluating an Argument.**

42. A. Showing the principal how Mr. O'Hara's instruction improved Violet's test scores would be the best argument for demonstrating his teaching skills. **See Lesson: Facts, Opinions, and Evaluating an Argument.**

Section IV. Mathematics Achievement

1. C. The correct solution is 10.8 because $A = \frac{1}{2}\pi r^2$; $45 = (\frac{1}{2})3.14 \, r^2$; $45 = 1.57 \, r^2 = 28.66 = r^2$; $r \approx 5.4$. The diameter is twice the radius, or about 10.8 centimeters. **See Lesson: Circles.**

2. D. The correct solution is $\frac{9}{2}$.

$5x-3 = 3x + 6$	Combine like terms on the left and right sides of the equation.
$2x-3 = 6$	Subtract $3x$ from both sides of the equation.
$2x = 9$	Add 3 to both sides of the equation.
$x = \frac{9}{2}$	Divide both sides of the equation by 2.

See Lesson: Equations with One Variable.

3. D. The decimal 0.5 is equal to $\frac{1}{2}$, which is also equal to the ratio 1:2. But 1:2 odds are different because odds use colon notation in a different manner. **See Lesson: Ratios, Proportions, and Percentages.**

4. D. The correct solutions are $-\frac{5}{2}$ and $-\frac{2}{3}$. The equation can be solved by factoring.

$(2x + 5)(3x + 2) = 0$	Factor the equation.
$(2x + 5) = 0 \; (3x + 2) = 0$	Set each factor equal to 0.
$2x + 5 = 0$	Subtract 5 from both sides of the equation and divide both sides of the equation by 2 to solve.
$2x = -5$	

$x = -\frac{5}{2}$

$3x + 2 = 0$ Subtract 2 from both sides of the equation and divide both sides of the equation by 3 to solve.

$3x = -2$

$x = -\frac{2}{3}$

See Lesson: Solving Quadratic Equations.

5. C. The correct solution is purposive sampling because the surveyor chose the sample based on "Yes" responses. **See Lesson: Statistical Measures.**

6. A. The correct solution is 17.3. $A = \frac{1}{2}\pi r^2$; $48 = \frac{1}{2}(3.14)\,r^2$; $48 = 1.57\,r^2$; $30.57 = r^2$; $r \approx 5.5$ centimeters. $C = \frac{1}{2}(2\pi r)$; $C = \frac{1}{2}(2)(3.14)(5.5) \approx 17.3$ centimeters. **See Lesson: Circles.**

7. B. The correct answer is B. Set up the proportion of dogs to cats (or vice versa):

$\frac{2}{3} = \frac{?}{1,425}$

Since $1,425 \div 3 = 475$, the number of dogs is the product of 2 and 475, or 950. **See Lesson: Ratios, Proportions, and Percentages.**

8. B. The correct solution is –5 because $14(2) + 11(-3) = 28 + (-33) = -5$ points. **See Lesson: Solving Real World Mathematical Problems.**

9. B. The correct solution is survey because the group is focused on people in Ohio. **See Lesson: Statistical Measures.**

10. A. The correct solution is $\frac{1}{10}$ because $1 - \left(\frac{1}{6} + \frac{2}{5} + \frac{1}{3}\right) = 1 - \left(\frac{5}{30} + \frac{12}{30} + \frac{10}{30}\right) = 1 - \frac{27}{30} = 1 - \frac{9}{10} = \frac{1}{10}$ of the yard remaining. **See Lesson: Solving Real World Mathematical Problems.**

11. A. The correct solution is 8. Substitute the values into the formula, $800\pi = \pi\,10^2 h$, and apply the exponent, $800\pi = \pi(100)h$. Then, divide both sides of the equation by 100π, $h = 8$ centimeters. **See Lesson: Measurement and Dimension.**

12. A. The correct solution is A. This is a rotation of $270°$ counterclockwise because the point (x, y) becomes $(y, -x)$. **See Lesson: Congruence.**

13. B. The correct solution is $\frac{25}{17}$. **See Lesson: Equations with One Variable.**

$9(x + 3) - 24 = 36 - 8(x + 1)$	Apply the distributive property.
$9x + 27 - 24 = 36 - 8x - 8$	Multiply all terms by the least common denominator of 12 to eliminate the fractions.
$9x + 3 = 28 - 8x$	Combine like terms on both sides of the equation.
$17x + 3 = 28$	Add $8x$ to both sides of the equation.
$17x = 25$	Subtract 3 from both sides of the equation.
$x = \frac{25}{17}$	Divide both sides of the equation by 17.

14. A. The correct solution is $\frac{1}{16}$ because $\left((2^{-2})^{-1}\right)^{-2} = 2^{-2\times(-1)\times(-2)} = 2^{-4} = \frac{1}{2^4} = \frac{1}{16}$. **See Lesson: Powers, Exponents, Roots, and Radicals.**

15. B. The correct answer is 20% because $\frac{1}{5}$ as a percent is $0.2 \times 100 = 20\%$. **See Lesson: Decimals and Fractions.**

16. B. The correct solution is 120. Substitute the values into the formula and simplify using the order of operations, $SA = (2)\left(\frac{1}{2}\right)(5)(12) + (2)(5) + 2(12) + 2(13) = 60 + 10 + 26 + 24 = 120$ square centimeters. **See Lesson: Similarity, Right Triangles, and Trigonometry.**

17. B. The correct solution is $\frac{81y^6}{x^4}$ because $(9x^{-2}y^3)^2 = 9^2 x^{-2\times2} y^{3\times2} = 9^2 x^{-4} y^6 = 81 x^{-4} y^6 = \frac{81y^6}{x^4}$. **See Lesson: Powers, Exponents, Roots, and Radicals.**

18. A. The correct solution is 79,547. The radius is 20 feet. Substitute the values into both formulas and simplify using the order of operations, $V = \frac{2}{3}\pi r^3 + \pi r^2 h = \frac{2}{3}\pi 20^3 + \pi 20^2(50) = \frac{2}{3}(3.14)(8,000) + (3.14)(4,000)(50) = 16,747 + 62,800 = 79,547$ cubic feet. **See Lesson: Measurement and Dimension.**

19. B. The correct solutions are 0.46 and –0.54.

$x = \dfrac{-1 \pm \sqrt{1^2 - 4(12)(-3)}}{2(12)}$	Substitute 12 for a, 1 for b, and –3 for c.
$x = \dfrac{-1 \pm \sqrt{1 - (-144)}}{24}$	Apply the exponent and perform the multiplication.
$x = \dfrac{-1 \pm \sqrt{145}}{24}$	Perform the subtraction.
$x = \dfrac{-1 \pm 12.04}{24}$	Apply the square root.
$x = \dfrac{-1 + 12.04}{24}, x = \dfrac{-1 - 12.04}{24}$	Separate the problem into two expressions.
$x = \dfrac{11.04}{24} = 0.46, x = \dfrac{-13.04}{24} = -0.54$	Simplify the numerator and divide.

See Lesson: Solving Quadratic Equations.

20. C. The correct solution is the months with the smallest decreases all sold 5 fewer cars. There was a decline of 5 cars from January to February, June to July, and from November to December. **See Lesson: Interpreting Graphics.**

21. D. The correct solution is 8.23 because $1.75 + 1.08(6) = 1.75 + 6.48 = 8.23$ inches. **See Lesson: Solving Real World Mathematical Problems.**

22. A. The correct solution is cards 17 and 19. Odd number cards are 1, 3, 5, 7, 9, 11, 13, 15, 17, and 19. Blue cards are 16, 17, 18, 19, and 20. Cards 17 and 19 are the only two cards that are blue and odd numbers. **See Lesson: Statistics & Probability: The Rules of Probability.**

23. A. The correct solution is $\frac{1}{8}$. There are eight possibilities in the sample space, and only one of these options is three boys, $\frac{1}{2} \times \frac{1}{2} \times \frac{1}{2} = \frac{1}{8}$. The probability is $\frac{1}{8}$. **See Lesson: Statistics & Probability: The Rules of Probability.**

24. D. The correct solutions are (1, 4) and (-1, -4).

$x^2 + (4x)^2 = 17$	Substitute $4x$ in for y in the second equation.
$x^2 + 16x^2 = 17$	Apply the exponent.
$17x^2 = 17$	Combine like terms on the left side of the equation.
$x^2 = 1$	Divide both sides of the equation by 17.
$x = \pm 1$	Apply the square root to both sides of the equation.
$y = 4(1) = 4$	Substitute 1 in the first equation and multiply.
$y = 4(-1) = -4$	Substitute -1 in the first equation and multiply.

See Lesson: Equations with Two Variables.

25. B. The correct answer is $0.8\overline{3}$ because $83.\overline{3}\%$ as a decimal is $0.8\overline{3}$. **See Lesson: Decimals and Fractions.**

26. B. The correct solution is the type of textbook because the other variables do not change the type of textbook. **See Lesson: Interpreting Graphics.**

27. D. The correct solution is $8\frac{2}{3}$ because $\frac{13}{4} \times \frac{8}{3} = \frac{104}{12} = 8\frac{8}{12} = 8\frac{2}{3}$. **See Lesson: Multiplication and Division of Fractions.**

28. A. The correct solution is $30x^2 + 47x + 14$.

$(5x + 2)(6x + 7) = 5x(6x + 7) + 2(6x + 7)$

$= 30x^2 + 35x + 12x + 14 = 30x^2 + 47x + 14$

See Lesson: Polynomials.

29. B. The correct solution is 5. Substitute the values into the formula, $150 = 30h$. Divide both sides of the equation by 30, $h = 5$ inches **See Lesson: Similarity, Right Triangles, and Trigonometry.**

30. A. The correct solution is mean and median decrease. The mean time decreases from 22 to 20.36 minutes, and the median time decreases from 20 minutes to 19.5 minutes. **See Lesson: Interpreting Categorical and Quantitative Data.**

31. D. The correct solution is $2x^3 - 3x^2 - 17x - 12$.

$(2x + 3)(x^2 - 3x - 4)$

$= (2x + 3)(x^2) + (2x + 3)(-3x) + (2x + 3)(-4)$

$= 2x^3 + 3x^2 - 6x^2 - 9x - 8x - 12 = 2x^3 - 3x^2 - 17x - 12$

See Lesson: Polynomials.

32. B. The correct solution is $x{-}xy{-}2y$.

$$(8x + 2xy{-}4y) + ({-}7x{-}3xy + 2y) = (8x{-}7x) + (2xy{-}3xy) + ({-}4y + 2y) = x{-}xy{-}2y$$

See Lesson: Polynomials.

33. A. The correct solution is \$1.4 million. The expected value is $\frac{1}{2}(3) + \frac{3}{10}(1) + \frac{1}{5}({-}2) = 1.5 + 0.3{-}0.4 = $ \$1.4 million. **See Lesson: Statistics & Probability: The Rules of Probability.**

34. B. The correct solution is $\pm\frac{7}{4}$.

$x^2 = \frac{49}{16}$	Divide both sides of the equation by 16.
$x = \pm\frac{7}{4}$	Apply the square root to both sides of the equation.

See Lesson: Solving Quadratic Equations.

35. B. A prime number has only 1 and itself as factors; therefore, a composite number must have at least one other factor. If that factor is composite, the number has more factors. If that factor is prime, then it is the only prime factor of the number. For example, 9 has 3 as a prime factor; its only other factors are 1 and 9. But 1 is not a prime number. Neither is 9, which is composite. A composite number therefore has at least one unique prime factor. **See Lesson: Factors and Multiples.**

36. C. The correct solution 12 units. The difference between the x-coordinates is $6{-}({-}6) = 12$ units and the difference between the y-coordinates is $6{-}({-}6) = 12$ units. **See Lesson: Similarity, Right Triangles, and Trigonometry.**

37. C. The correct solution is $\frac{y-b}{m} = x$.

$y{-}b = mx$	Subtract b from both sides of the equation.
$\frac{y-b}{m} = x$	Divide both sides of the equation by m.

See Lesson: Equations with One Variable.

38. C. The correct solution is 15.1.

$A = \pi r^2$; $18 = 3.14 r^2$; $5.73 = r^2$; $r \approx 2.4$ centimeters. $C = 2\pi r$; $C = 2(3.14)2.4 \approx 15.1$ centimeters. **See Lesson: Circles.**

39. D. To convert a ratio to a percent, divide the numbers in the ratio (noting that its equivalent fraction is $\frac{7}{3}$) to get approximately 2.33. Then, multiply by 100%. **See Lesson: Ratios, Proportions, and Percentages.**

40. A. The correct solution is (0, -4).

	The first equation is already solved for y.
$-4x-4 = -5x-4$	Substitute $-4x-4$ in for y in the second equation.
$x-4 = -4$	Add $5x$ to both sides of the equation.
$x = 0$	Add 4 to both sides of the equation.
$y = -4(0)-4$	Substitute 0 in the first equation for x.
$y = 0-4 = -4$	Simplify using order of operations.

See Lesson: Equations with Two Variables.

41. D. The correct solution is $-13, 13$ because the square root of 169 is 13. The values of -13 and 13 make the equation true. **See Lesson: Powers, Exponents, Roots, and Radicals.**

42. C. This question is asking for the remainder of division. The quotient of $203 \div 36$ is the number of class sections that are assigned a professor, and the remainder is the number of students left over. The remainder in this case is 23. Because 23 is not enough to fill a section, 23 students will not receive a slot. **See Lesson: Basic Multiplication and Division.**

43. A. The correct solution is $\overrightarrow{YX}$ and $\overrightarrow{UY}$ because these rays intersect at point Y. **See Lesson: Congruence.**

44. D. The correct solution is the difference between the maximum and minimum is 70 sales. The maximum value is 90, and the minimum value is 20. The difference between these values is 70 sales. **See Lesson: Interpreting Categorical and Quantitative Data.**

45. C. The correct solution is $1\frac{11}{45}$ because $\frac{8}{9} \times \frac{7}{5} = \frac{56}{45} = 1\frac{11}{45}$. **See Lesson: Multiplication and Division of Fractions.**

46°. C. Use the division algorithm. Although it is a longer problem than some, the mechanics are simple. **See Lesson: Basic Multiplication and Division.**

47. A. The correct solution is 438.8 meters. $4{,}388 \ dm \times \frac{1 \, m}{10 \, dm} = \frac{4{,}388}{10} = 438.8 \ m$. **See Lesson: Standards of Measure.**

48. B. The correct solution is children's grades because it is dependent on the factors of the parent's education. **See Lesson: Interpreting Graphics.**

CPSIA information can be obtained
at www.ICGtesting.com
Printed in the USA
BVHW072108300819
557276BV00002B/3/P